CLAIM YOUR FREE BONUS GIFT!

As our way of saying thank you for your purchase, we want to give you a **very special gift** to help you in your scrapbooking.

To get your FREE gift from us, just visit this special page on our website:

www.scrapbookingcoach.com/gift

© Scrapbooking Coach 2023

All Rights Reserved

No part of this website or any of its contents may be reproduced, copied, modified or adapted, without prior written consent of the author, unless otherwise indicated for standalone materials.

Legal Notice

The author retains the right to change this guide at any time. This guide is for information purposes only and the author doesn't accept any responsibilities for any liabilities resulting from the use of this information. The reader assumes all responsibility for the use of the information herein.

Table of Contents

A Note from Anna	4
How To Get The Most Out Of This Book	5
Anniversary	6
Beach	18
Birthday	30
Boy Birthday	42
Boy	53
Christmas	65
Easter	76
Family	88
Girl Birthday	101
Friend	113
Girl	125
Pet	136
Romantic	148
Vacation	160
Wedding	172

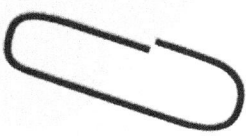

Welcome to 525 New and Exciting Double Page Scrapbook Sketches

After releasing Volume 2 of our best selling 525 New and Advanced Scrapbooking Sketches book, the response was positively overwhelming! *It motivated us to work on a new book full of inspiring scrapbooking ideas!*

Sifting through the positive feedback from scrappers all over the world, we decided to work on a new book totally devoted to double-page layouts!

So here it is: **525 New and Exciting Double Page Scrapbook Sketches**

525 totally new and exciting double-page sketches made especially for this book! Each sketch is guaranteed to help you create a gorgeous looking double-page layout that you'll be proud to share with everyone!

As you explore our 525 beautiful double-page sketches, *my wish for you is nothing but endless fun and more excitement in your scrapbooking journey!*

Also, if you have any feedback or perhaps a testimonial about how **525 New and Exciting Double Page Scrapbook Sketches** has inspired you, I'd love to hear from you. Please send me an email at: helpdesk@scrapbookingcoach.com

Thank you for your continued trust and support to me, and my Scrapbooking Coach team. I hope that you'll love this special edition double-page layouts as much as we loved creating them for you.

Be inspired to creatively preserve your most precious memories, now and always!

Anna Lyons

How To Get The Most Out Of This Book

Each chapter inside the **525 New And Exciting Double-Page Sketches - Special Edition!** showcases sketches by the number of photos you can arrange.

For example, if you have three photos to work with, browse the chapter that has sketches with three photos until you find a sketch that you like.

Once you've decided on a sketch, prepare your craft stash so you have all the necessary page elements to start scrapbooking!

You can follow each element according to the sketch, build the layers up, and watch your page come to life! *But don't limit yourself!* You can tweak and adjust each sketch as you please and create a scrapbook page masterpiece.

Anniversary

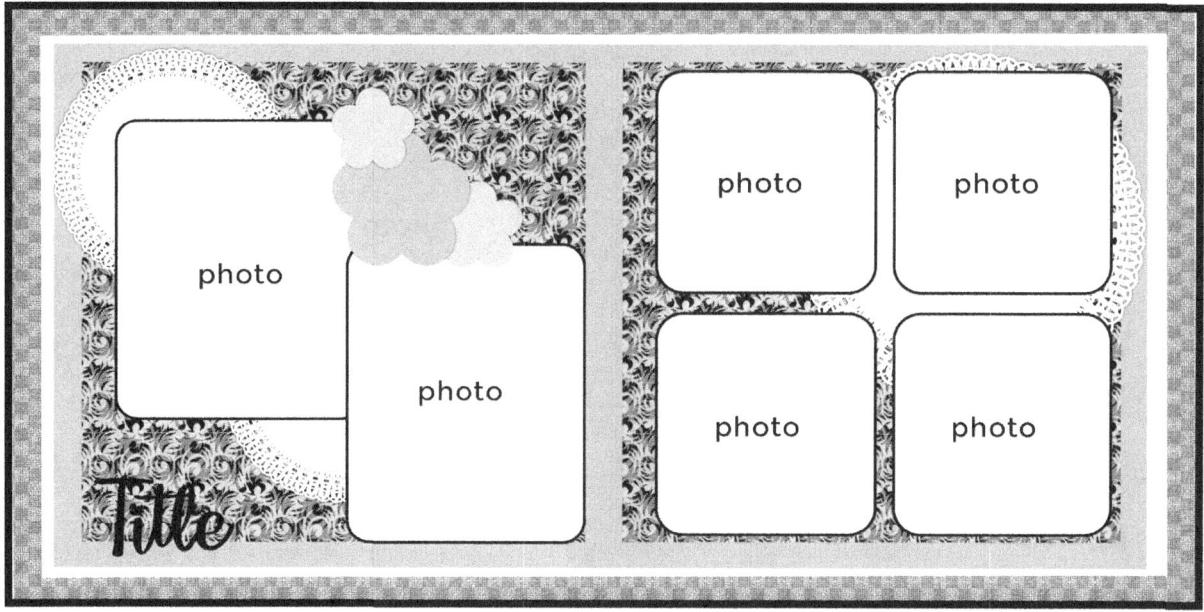
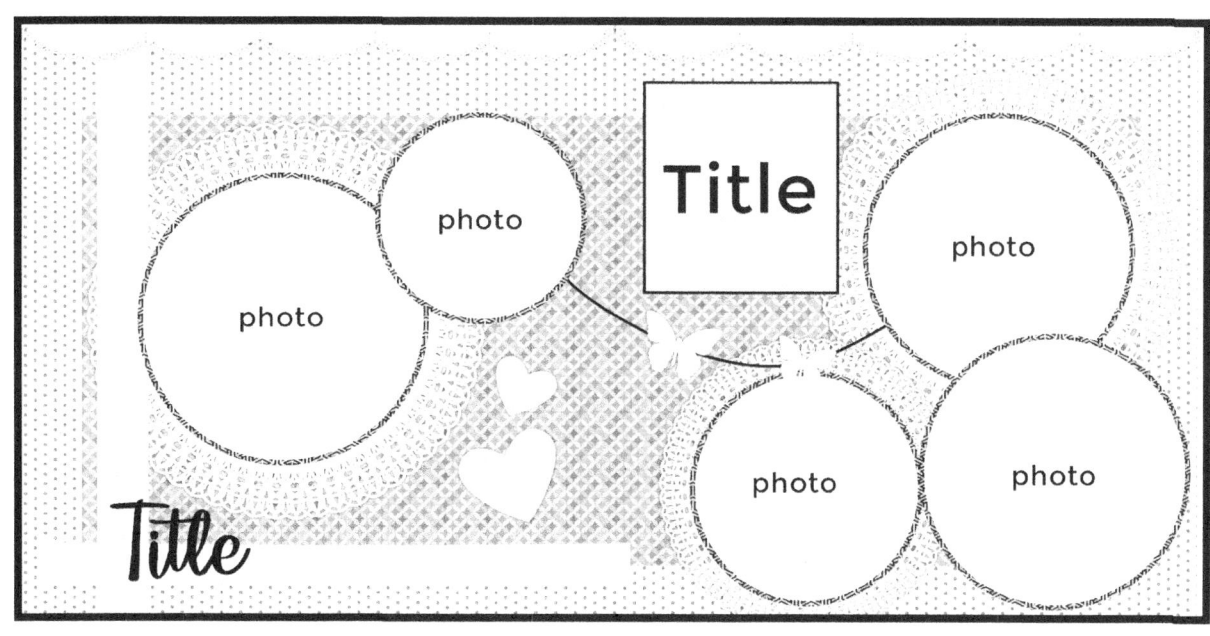

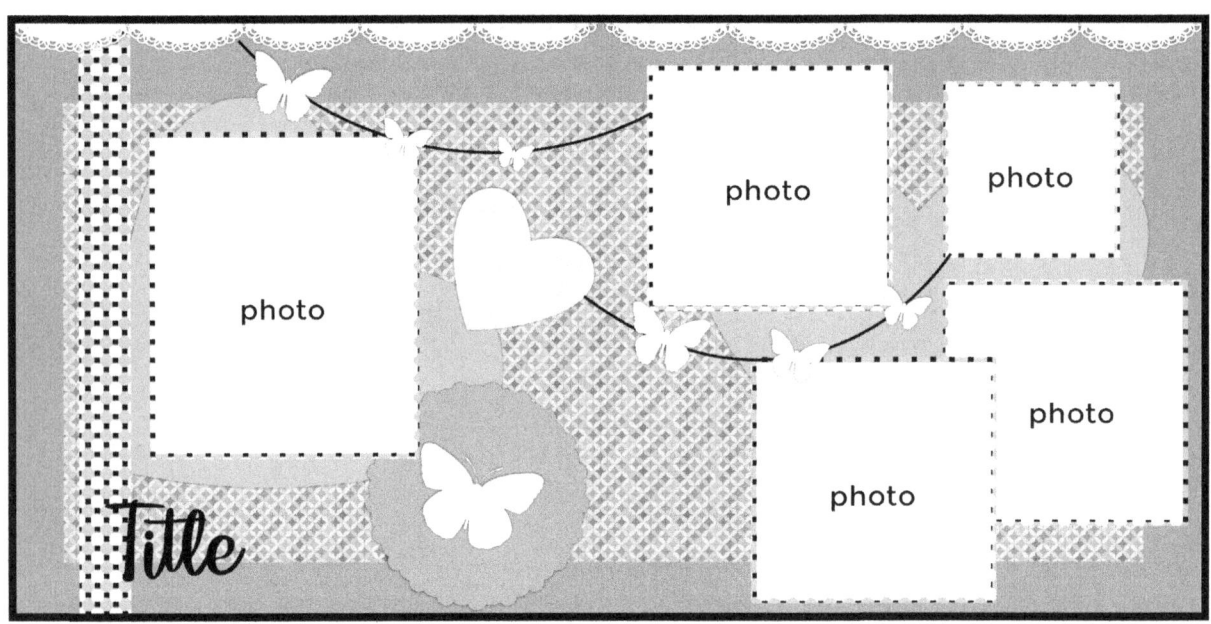

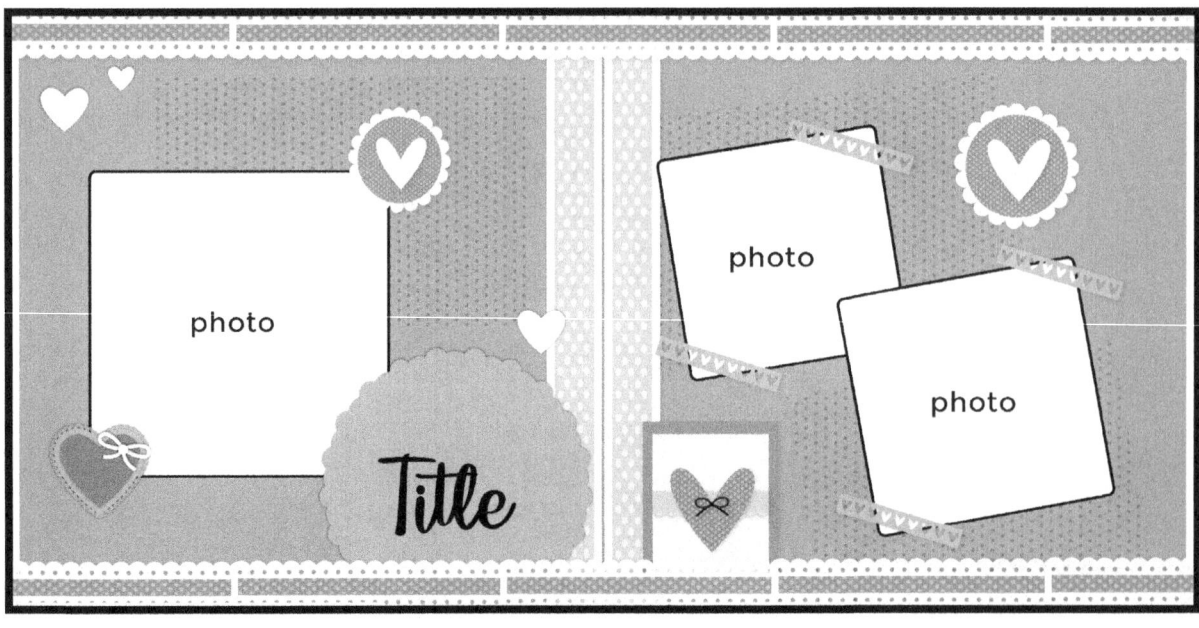

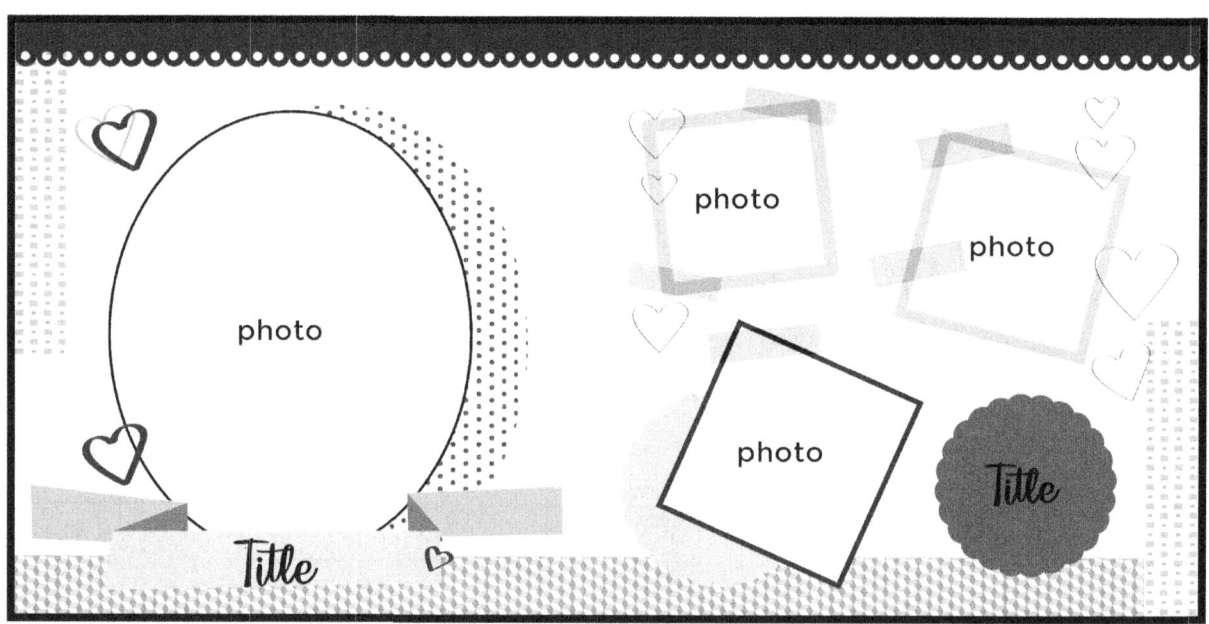
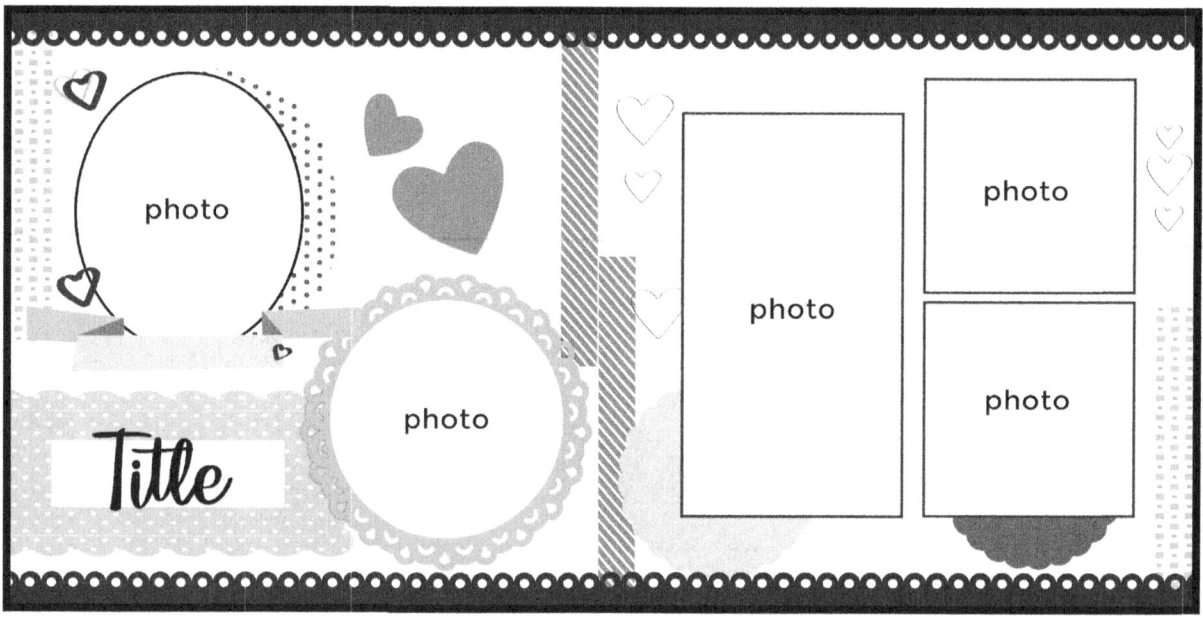

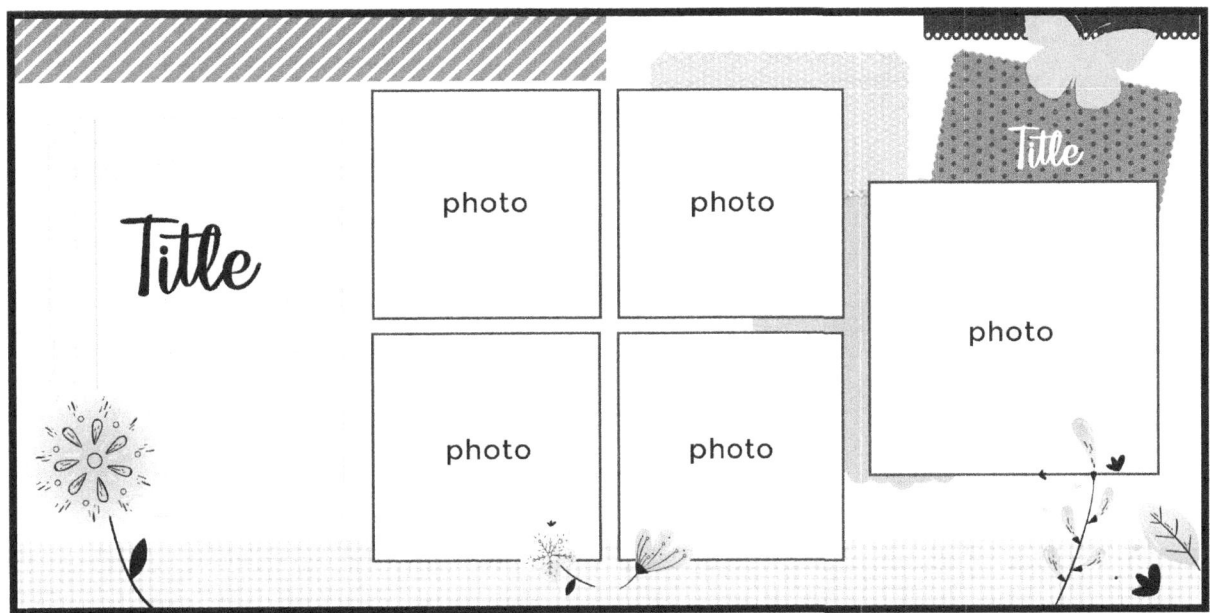
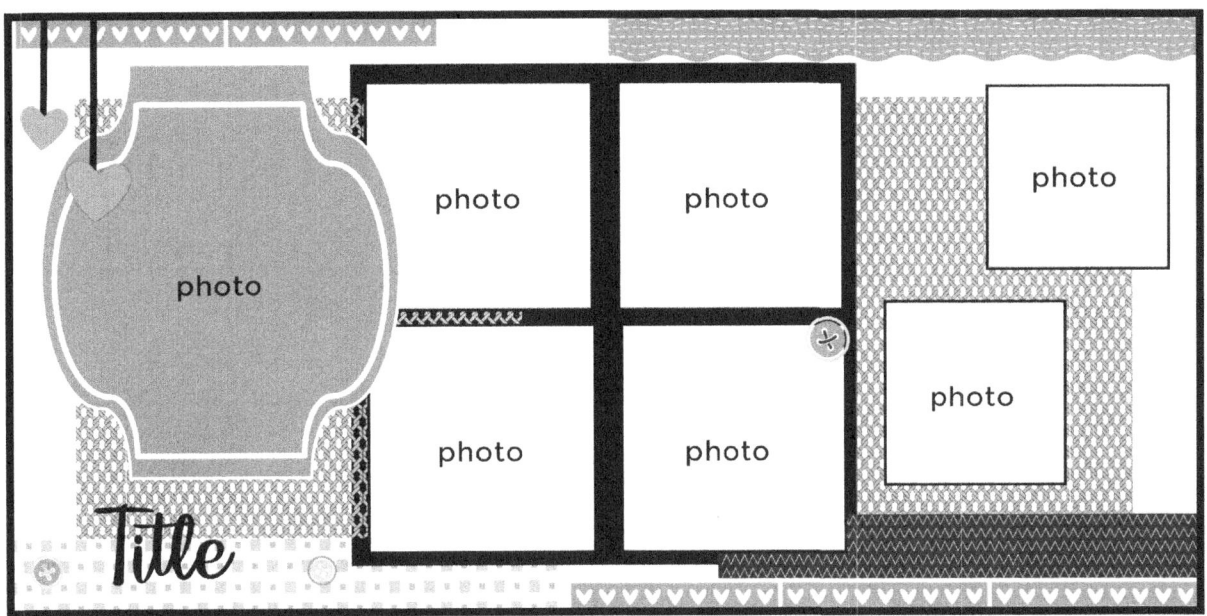
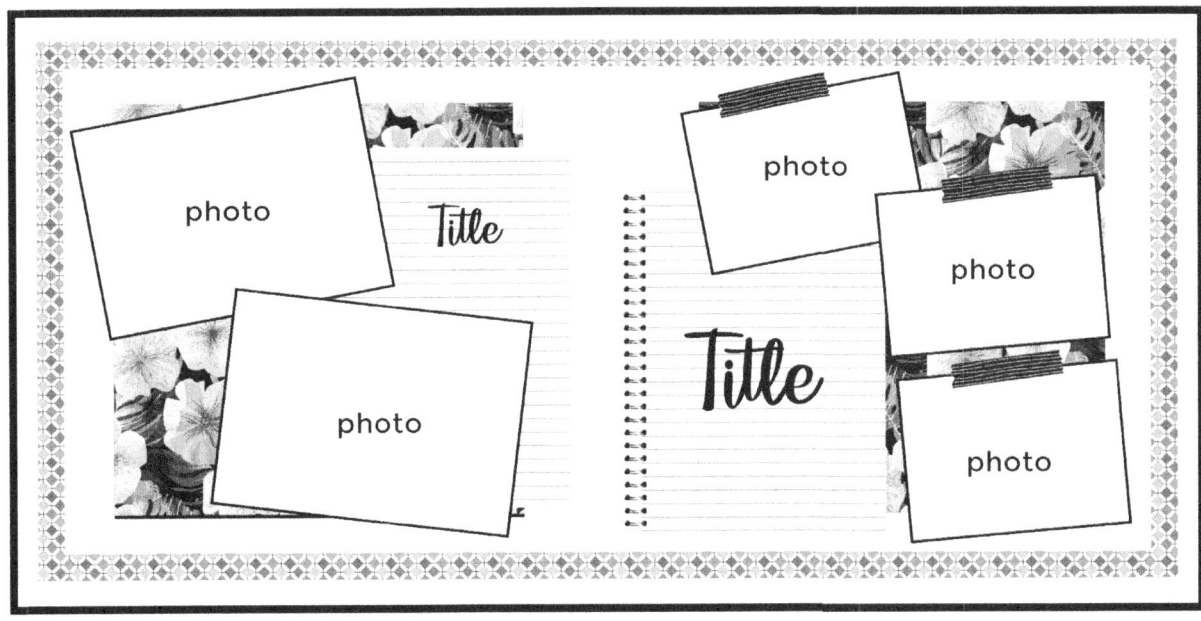

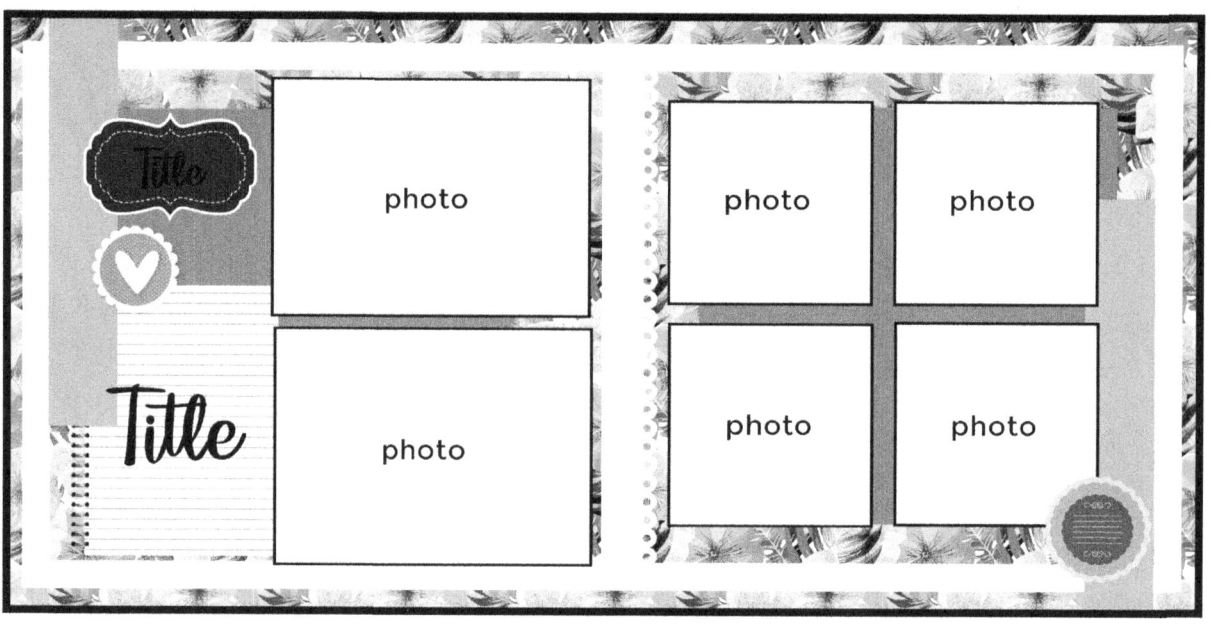

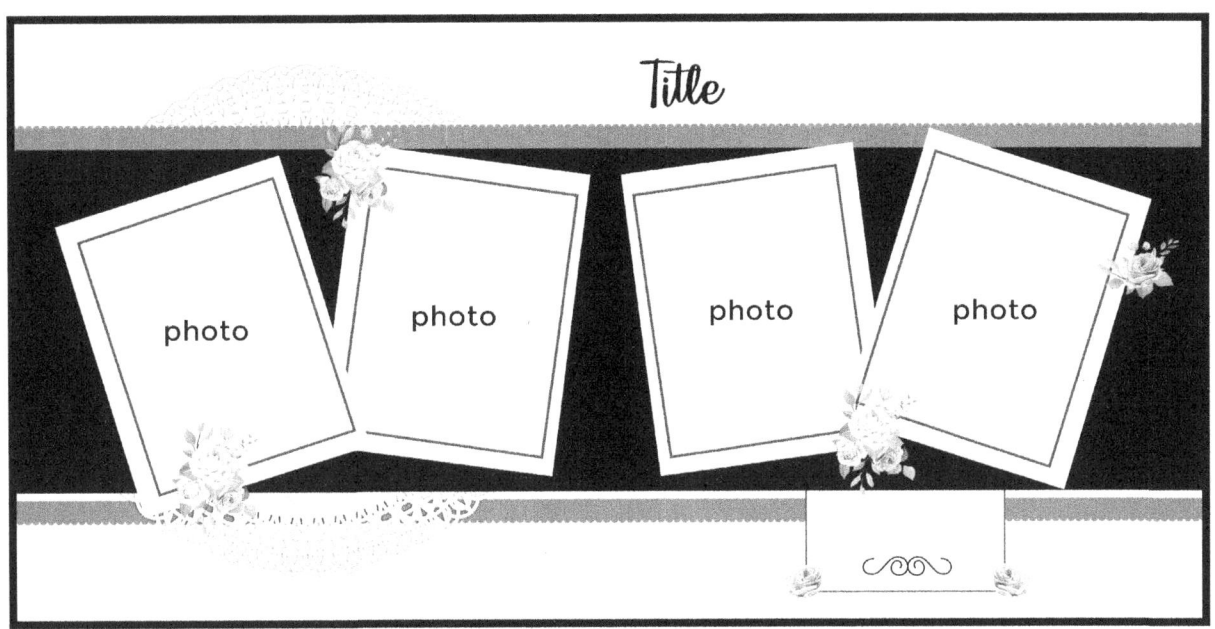
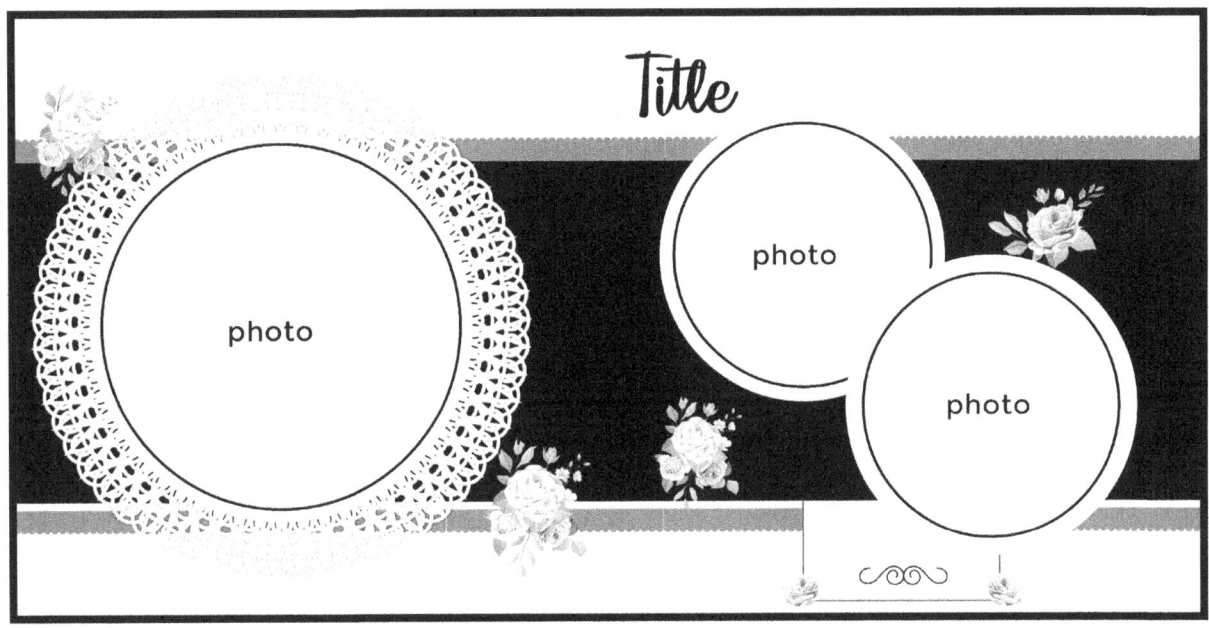

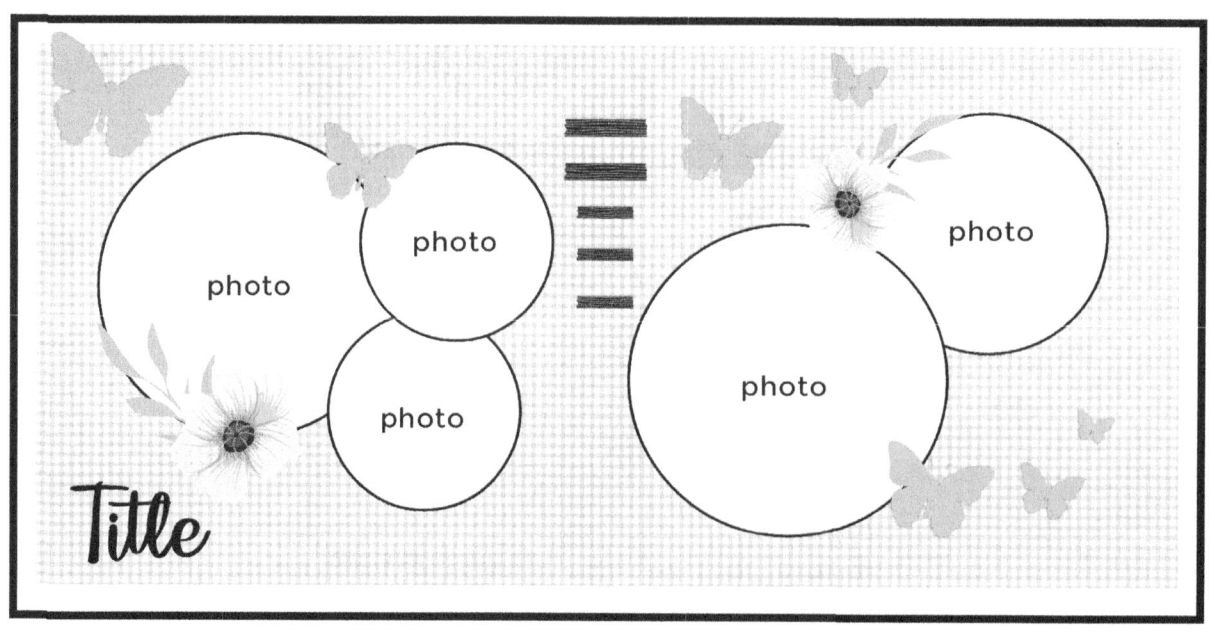

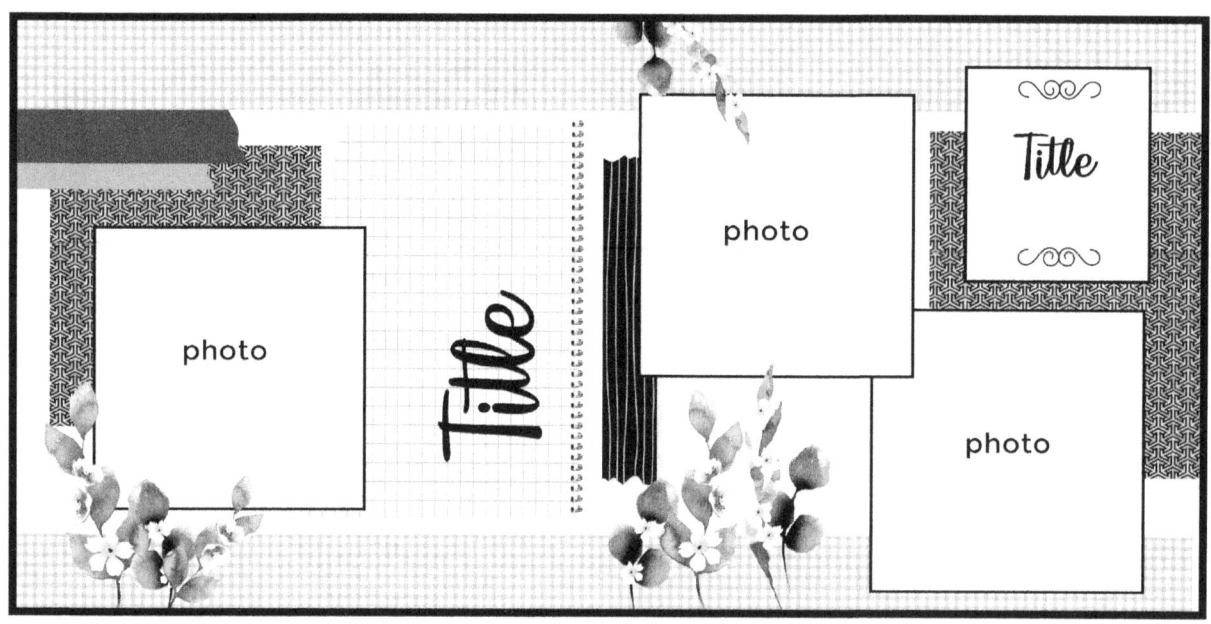

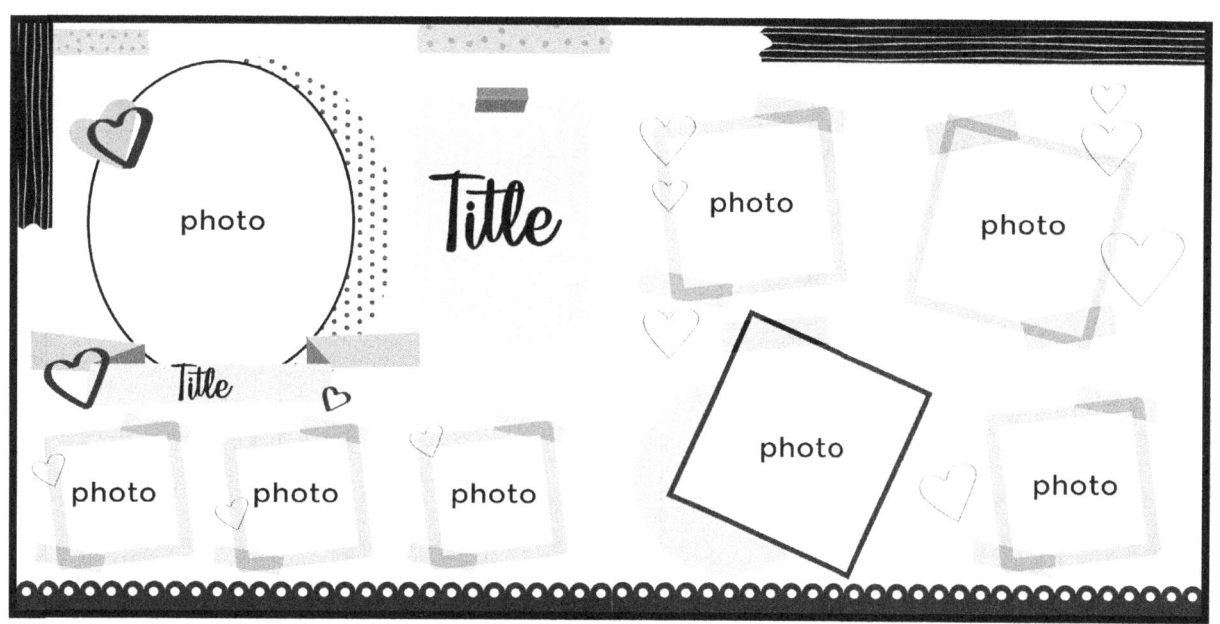

Beach

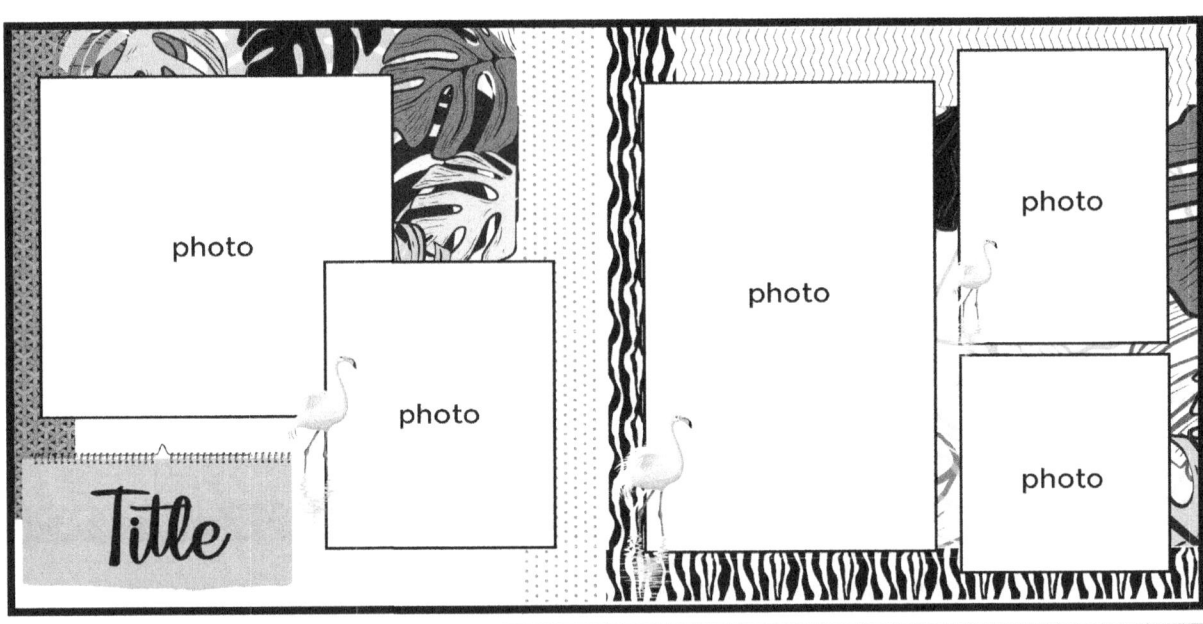

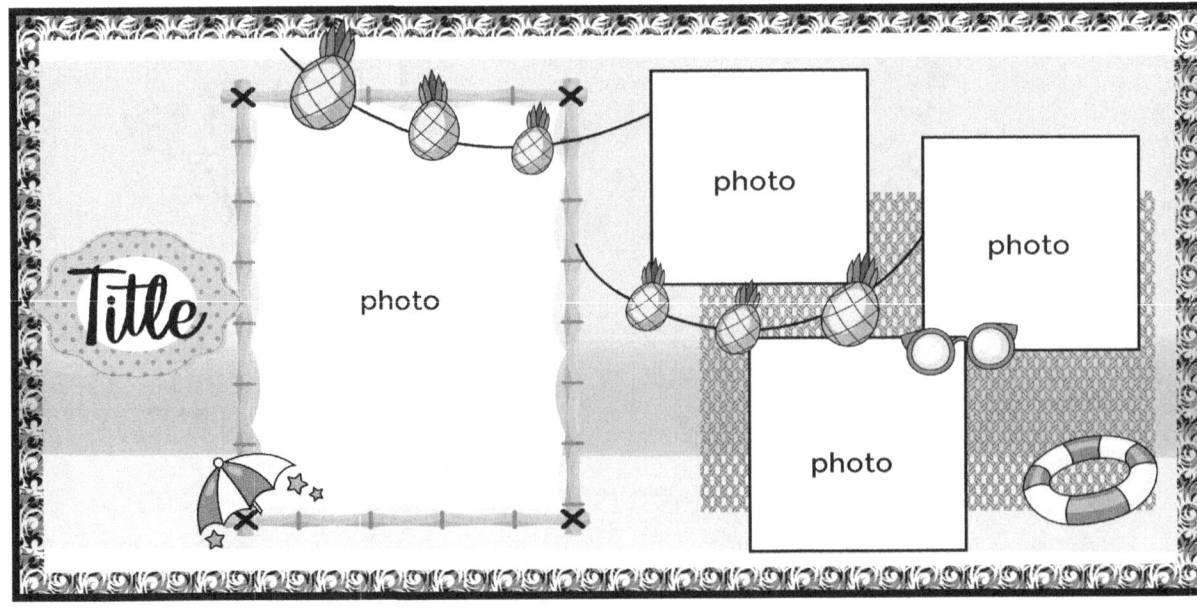

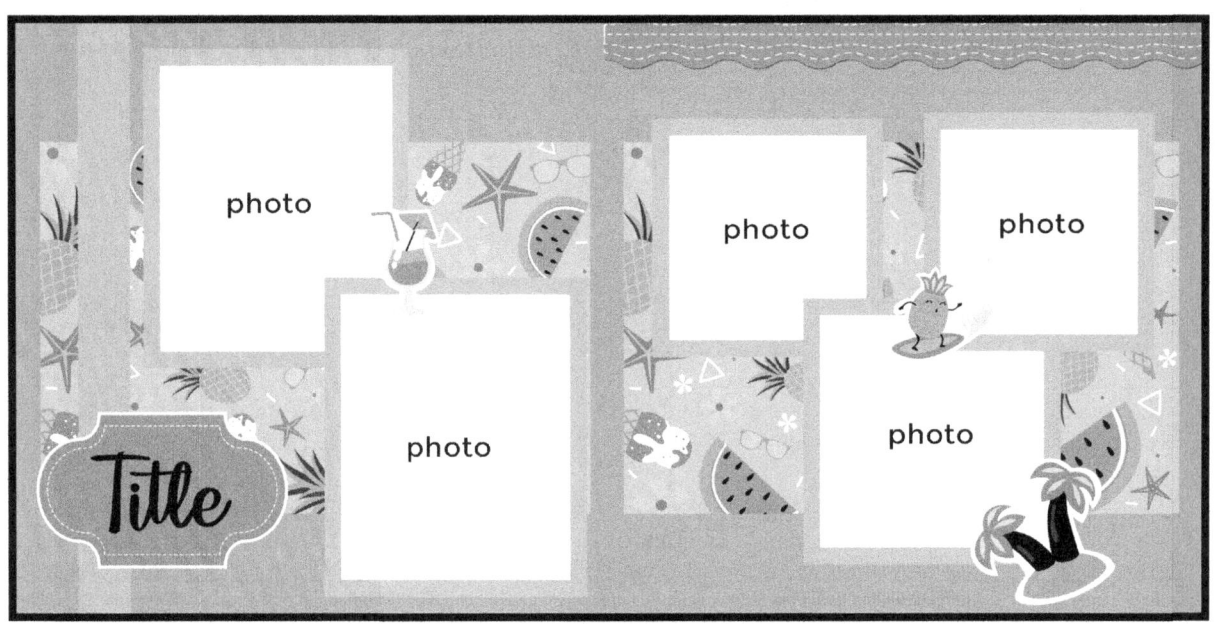

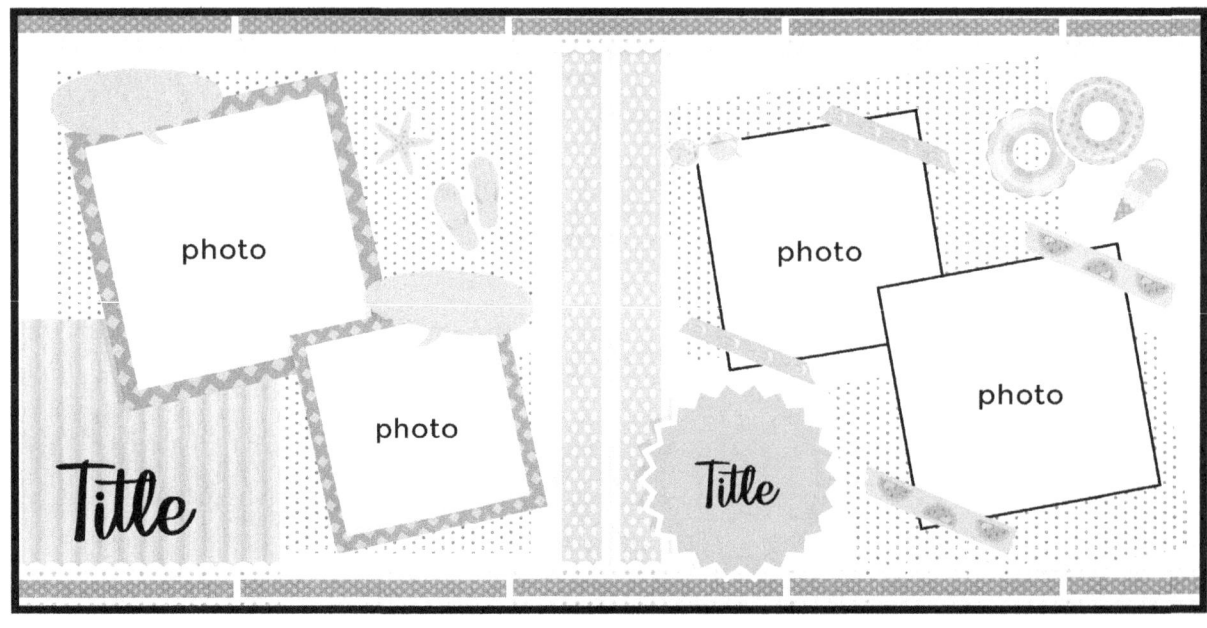

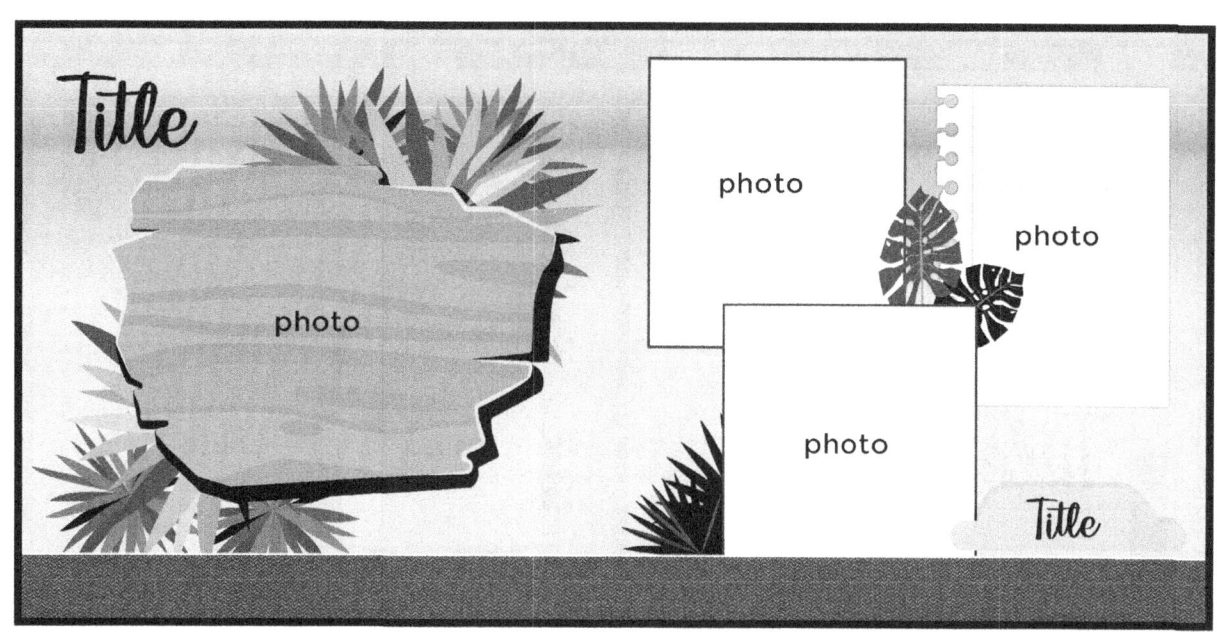
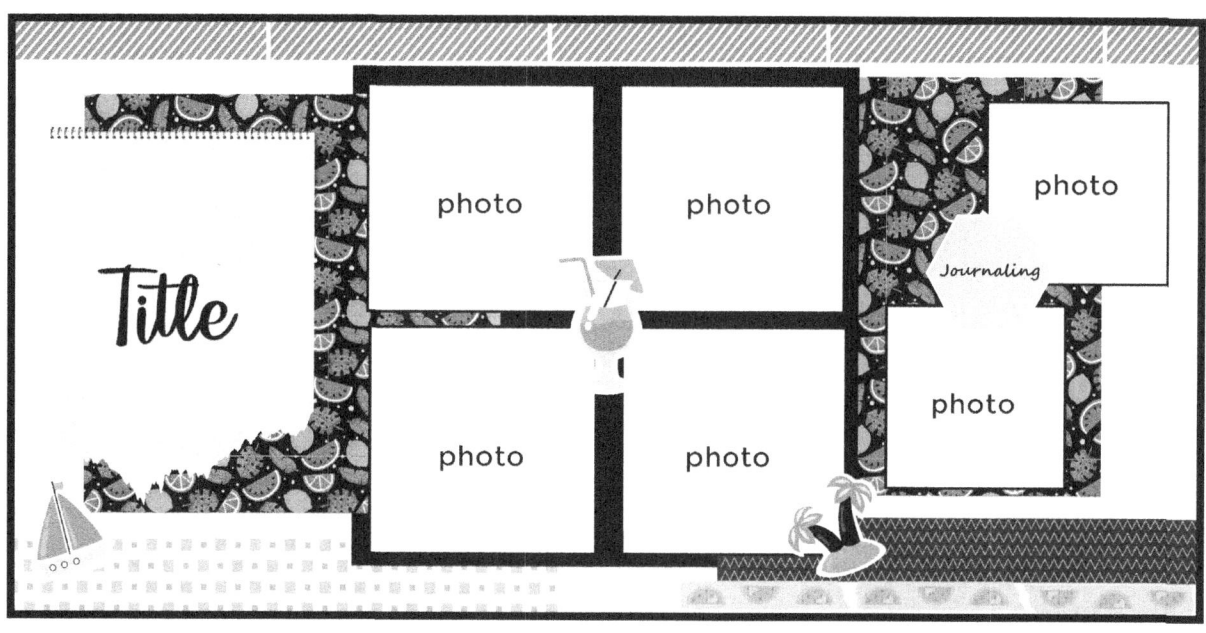

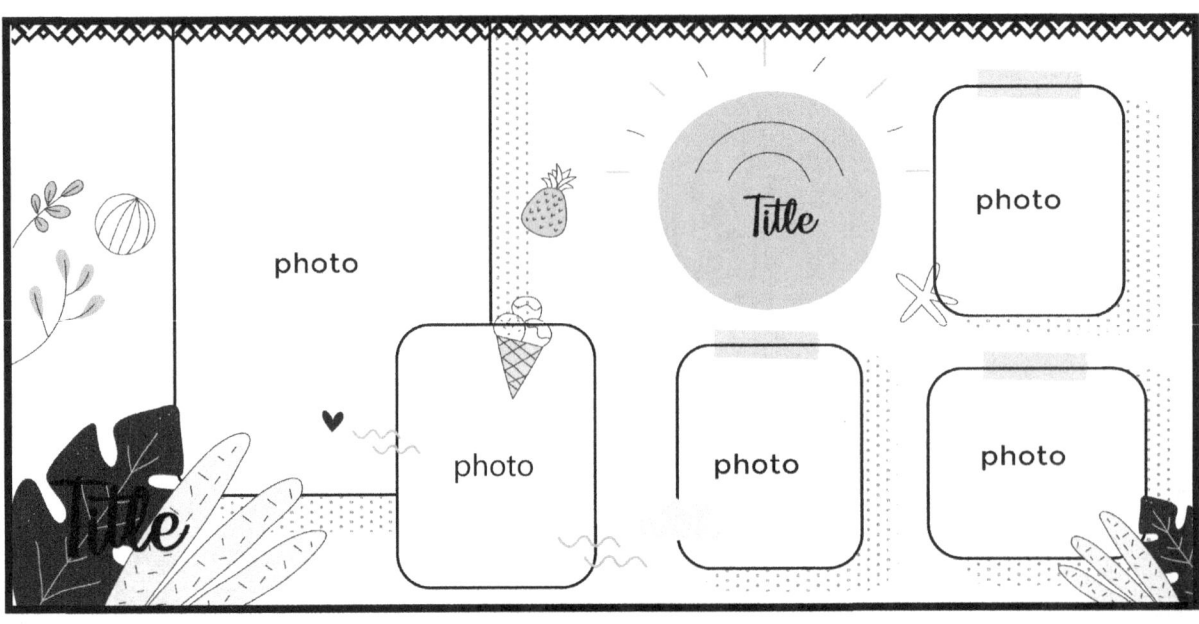

24

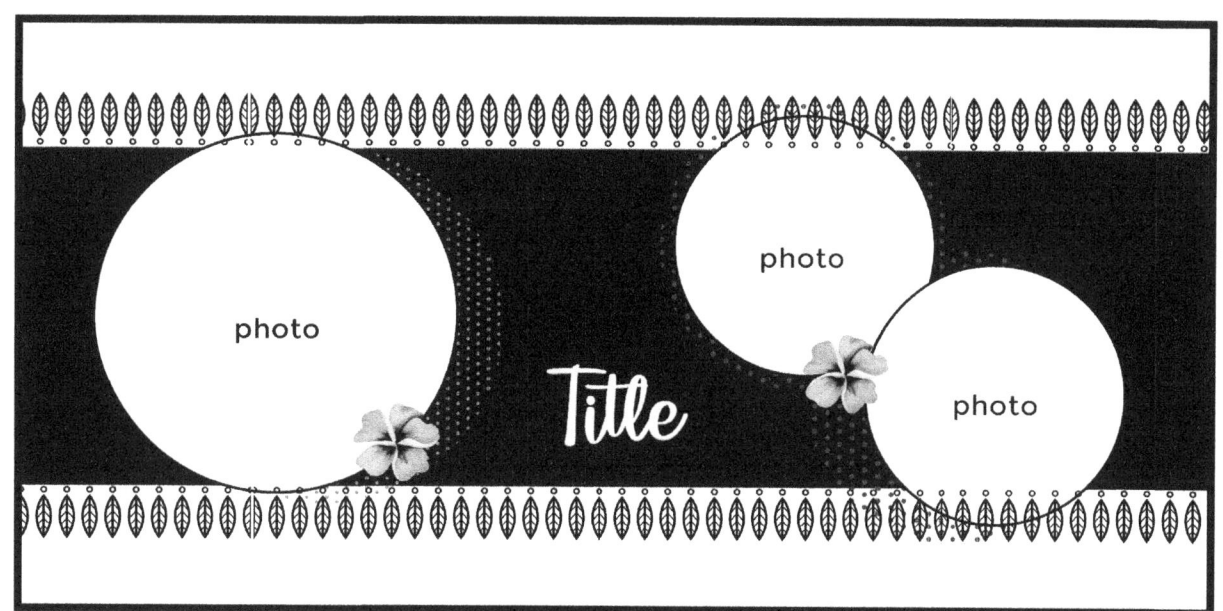

25

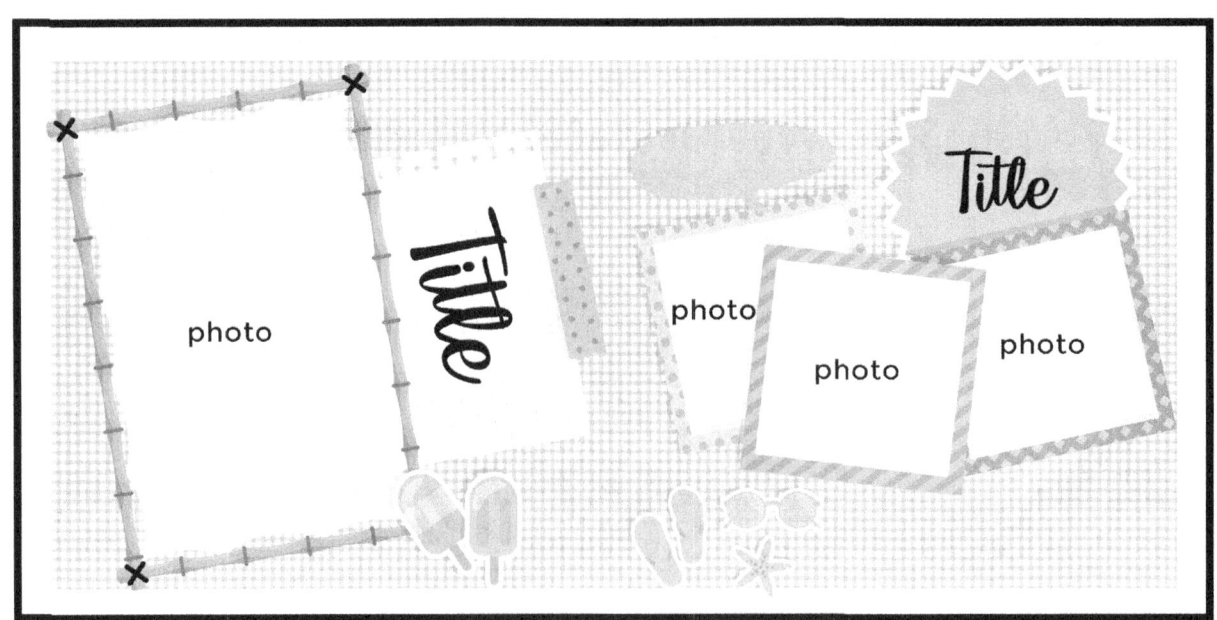

28

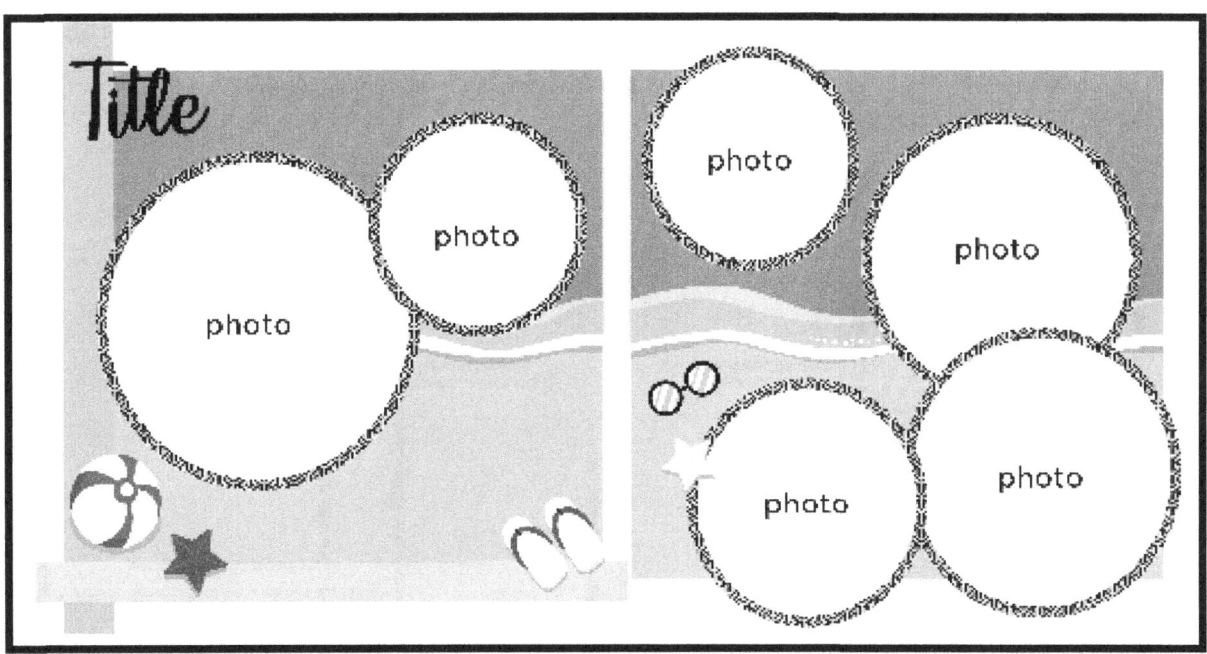

Birthday

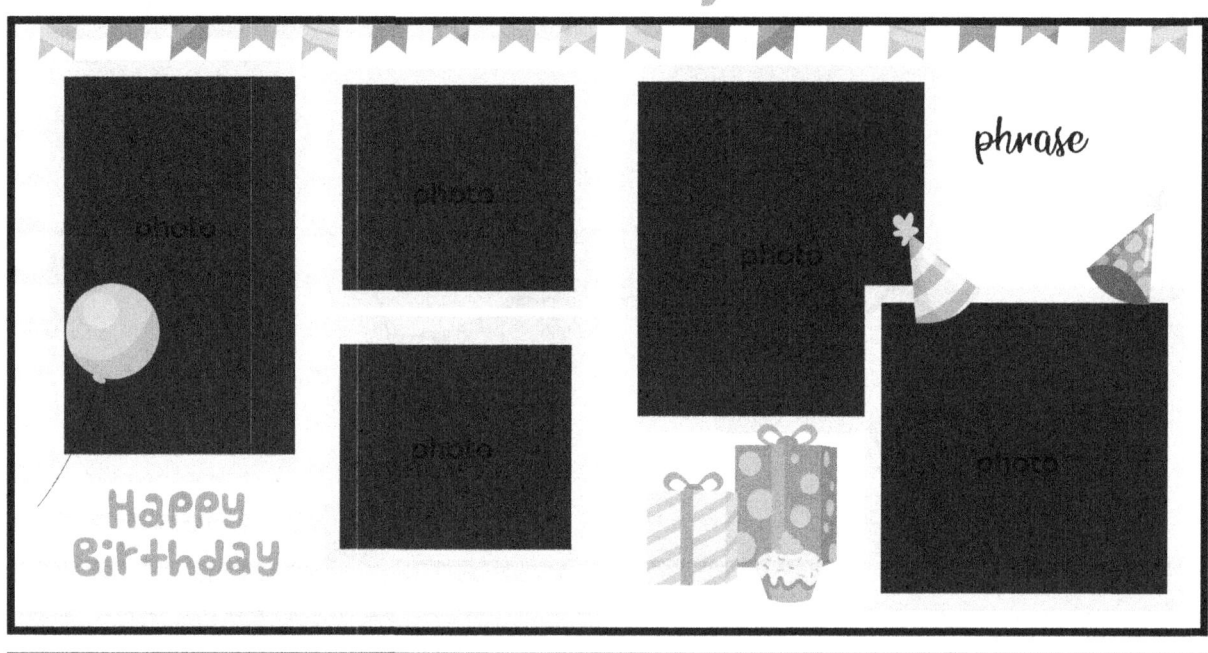
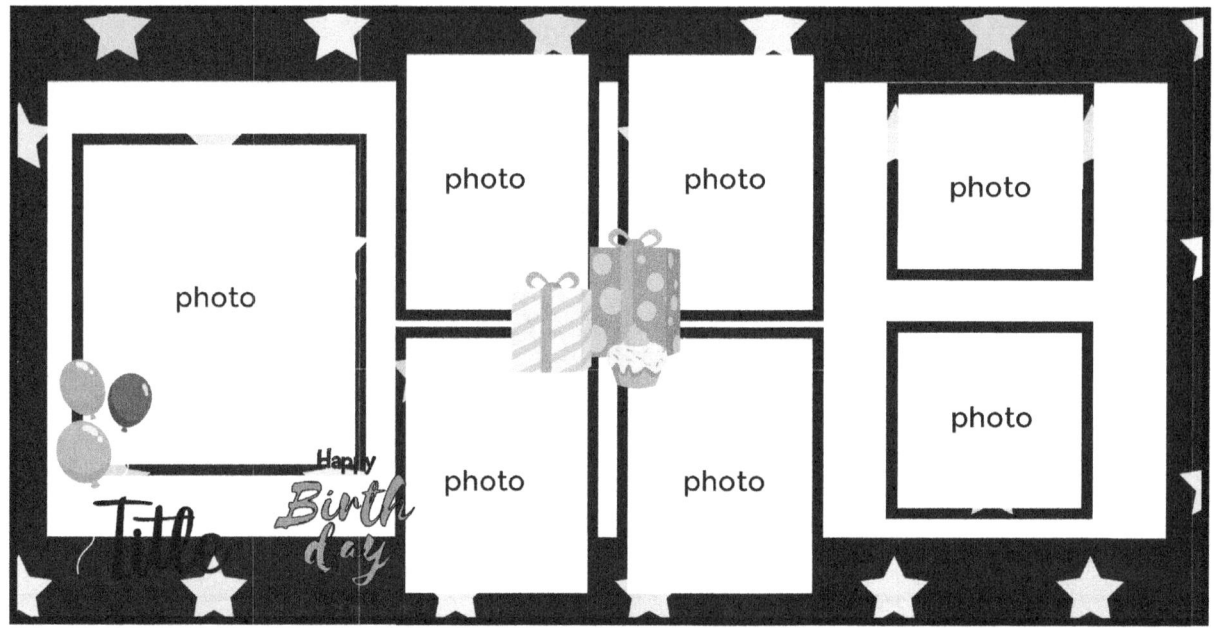

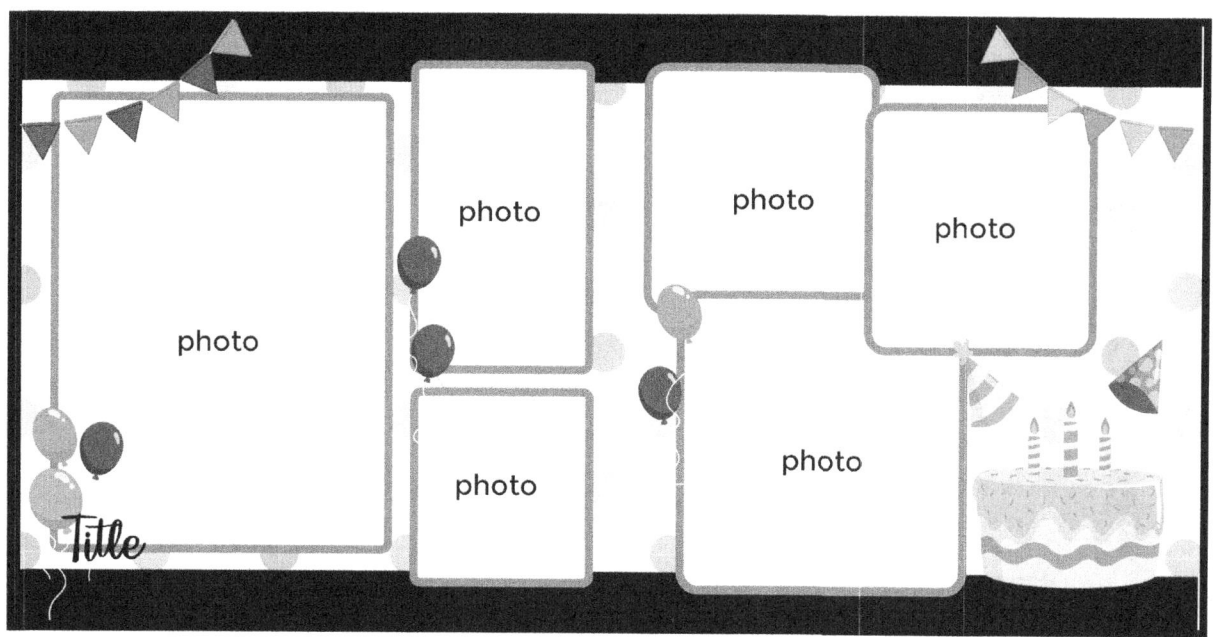
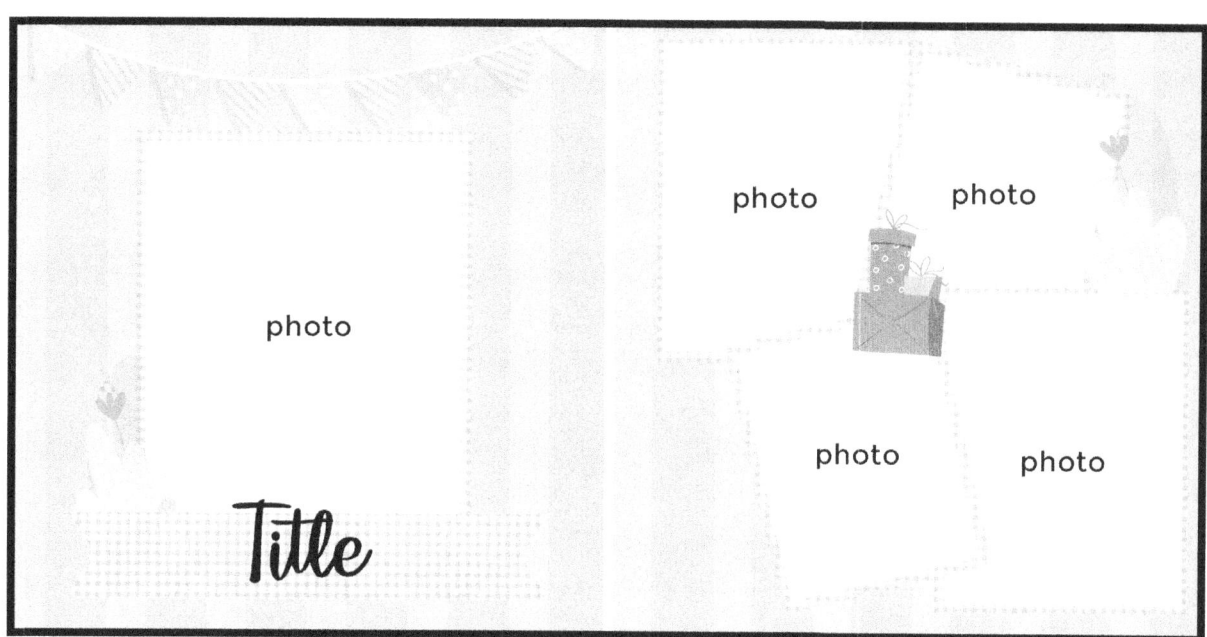

31

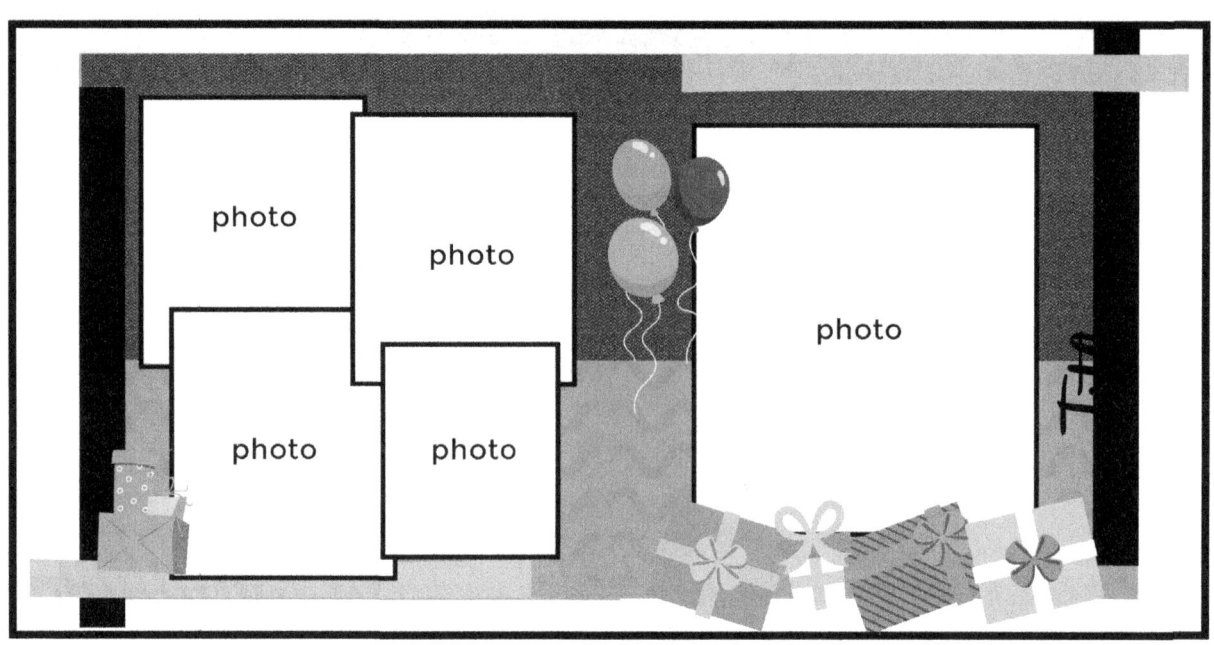
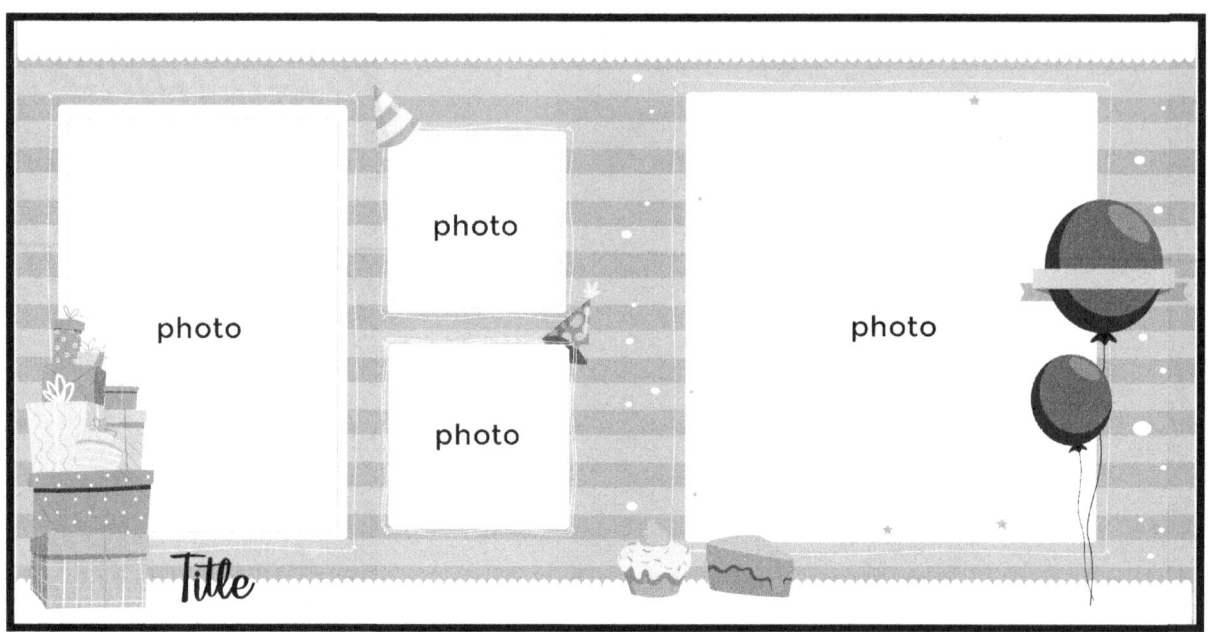
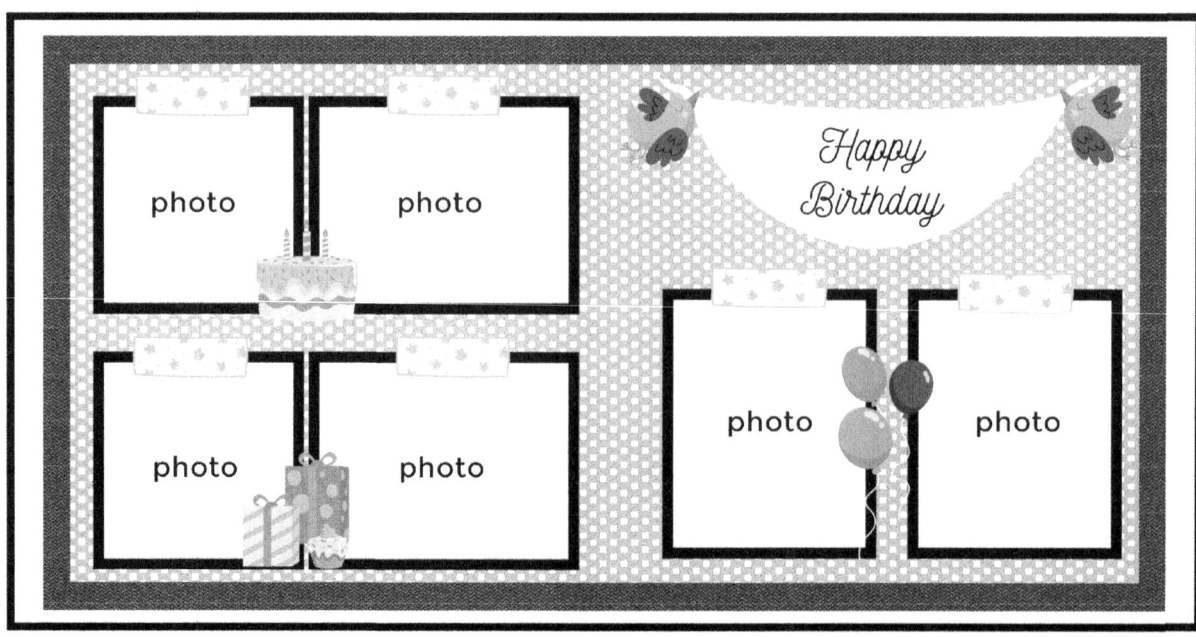

32

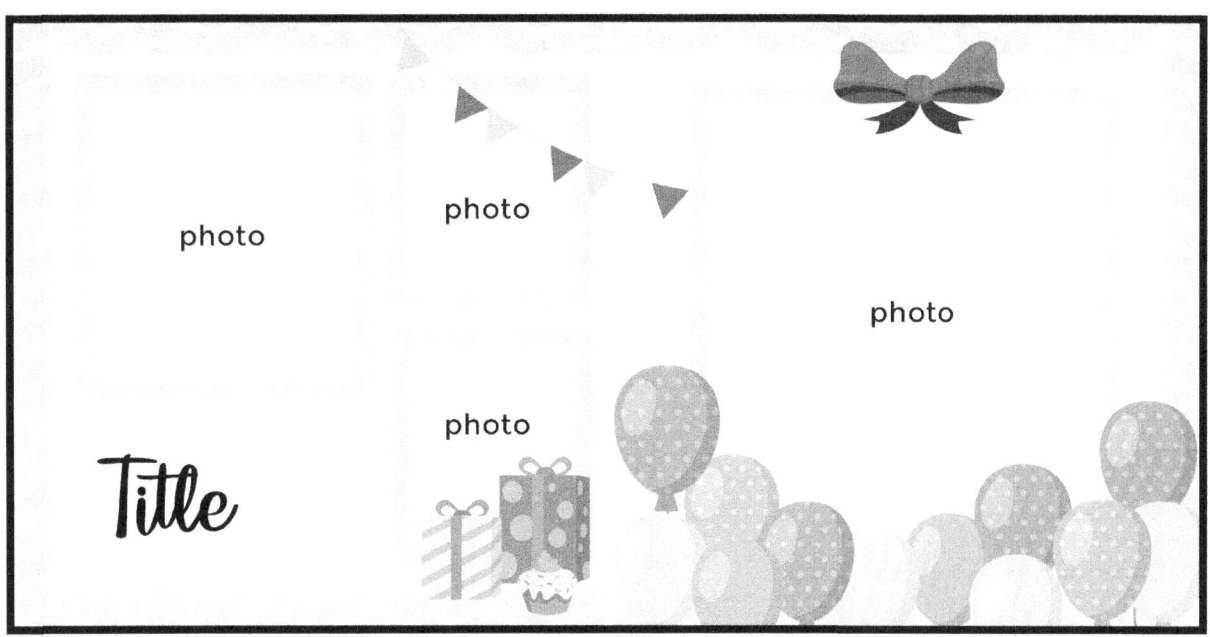

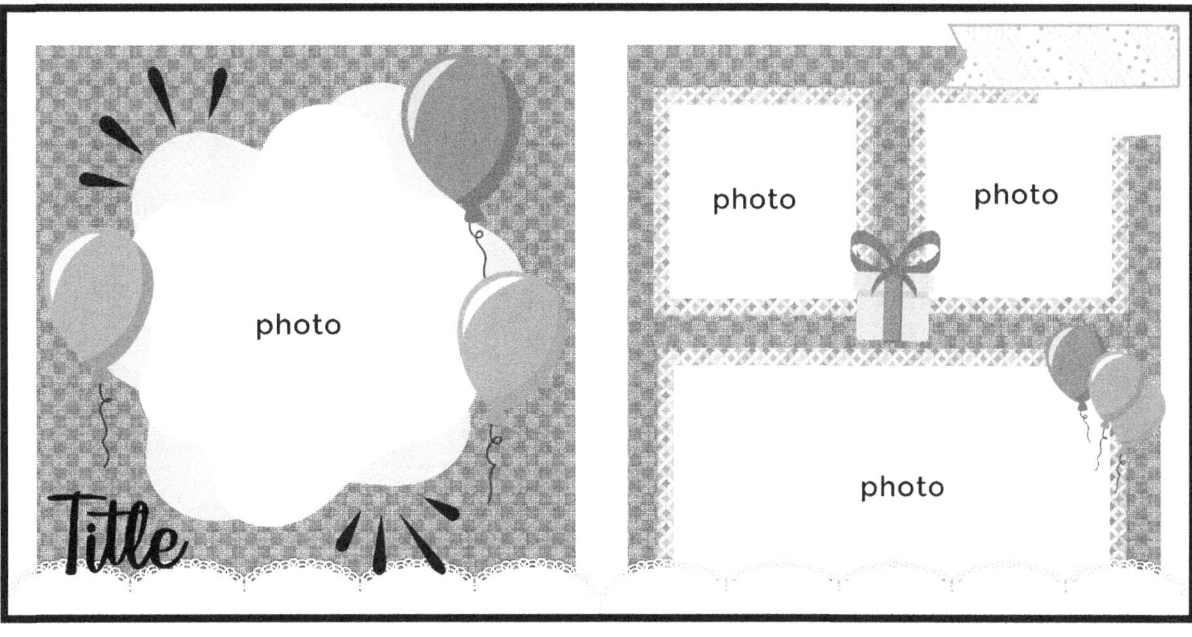

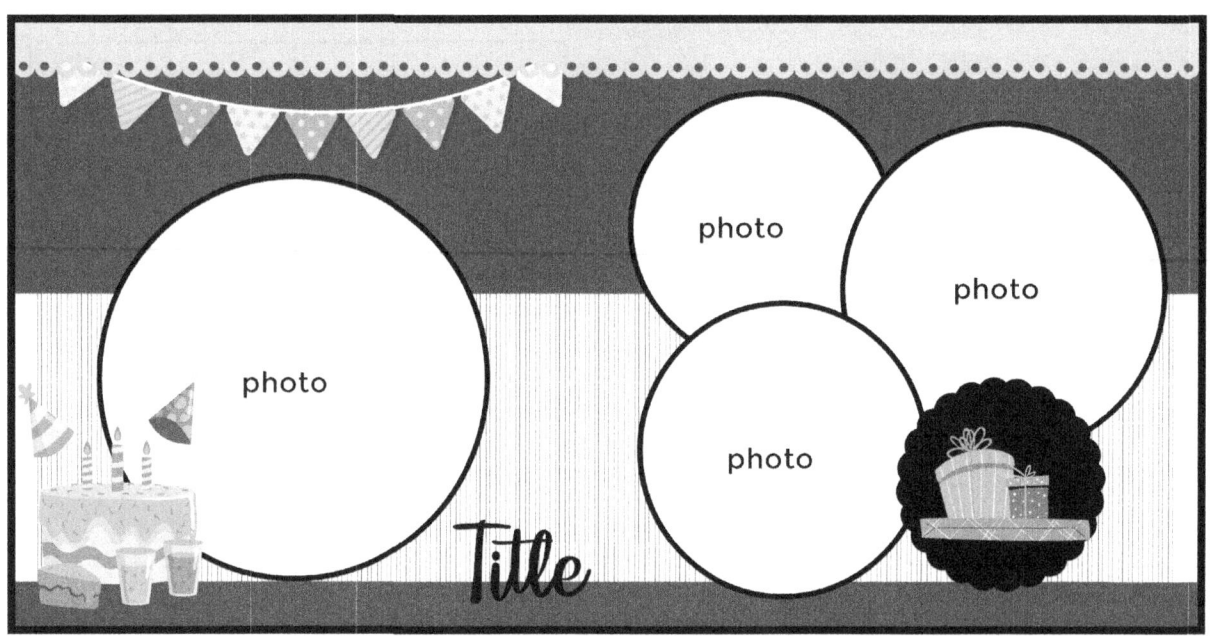

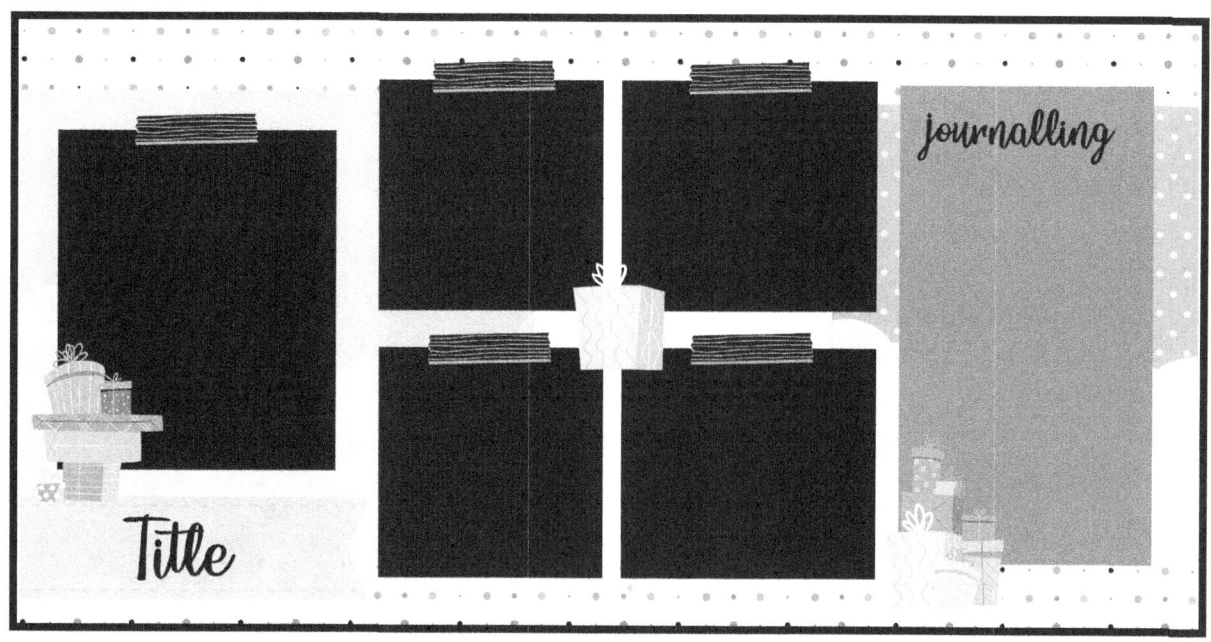

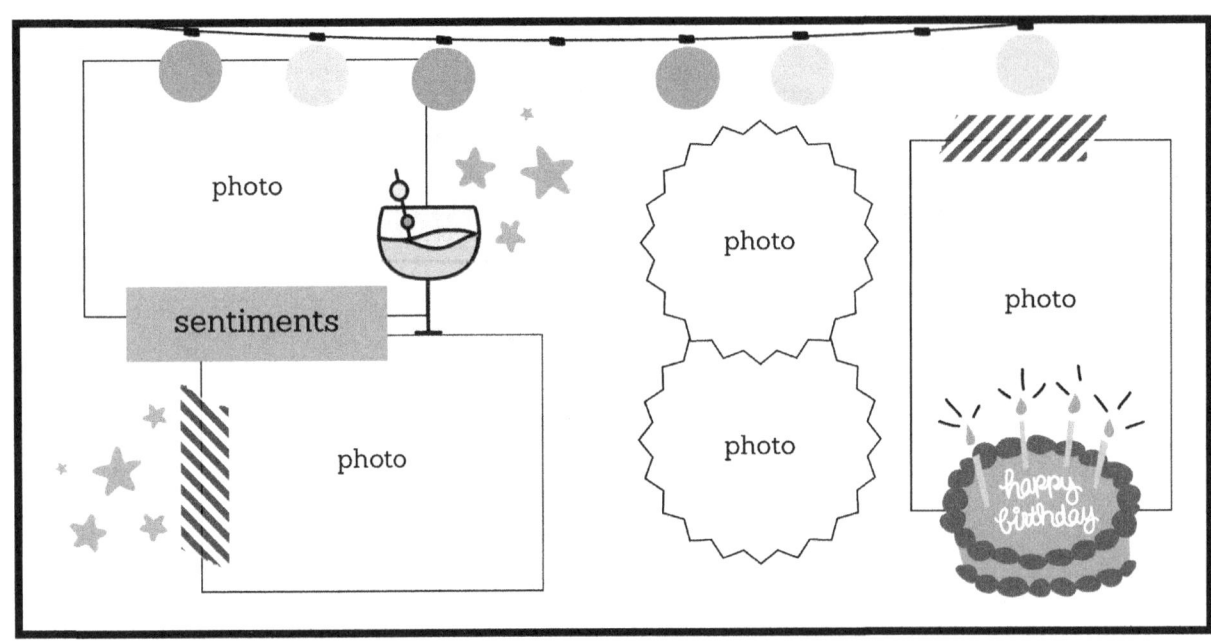
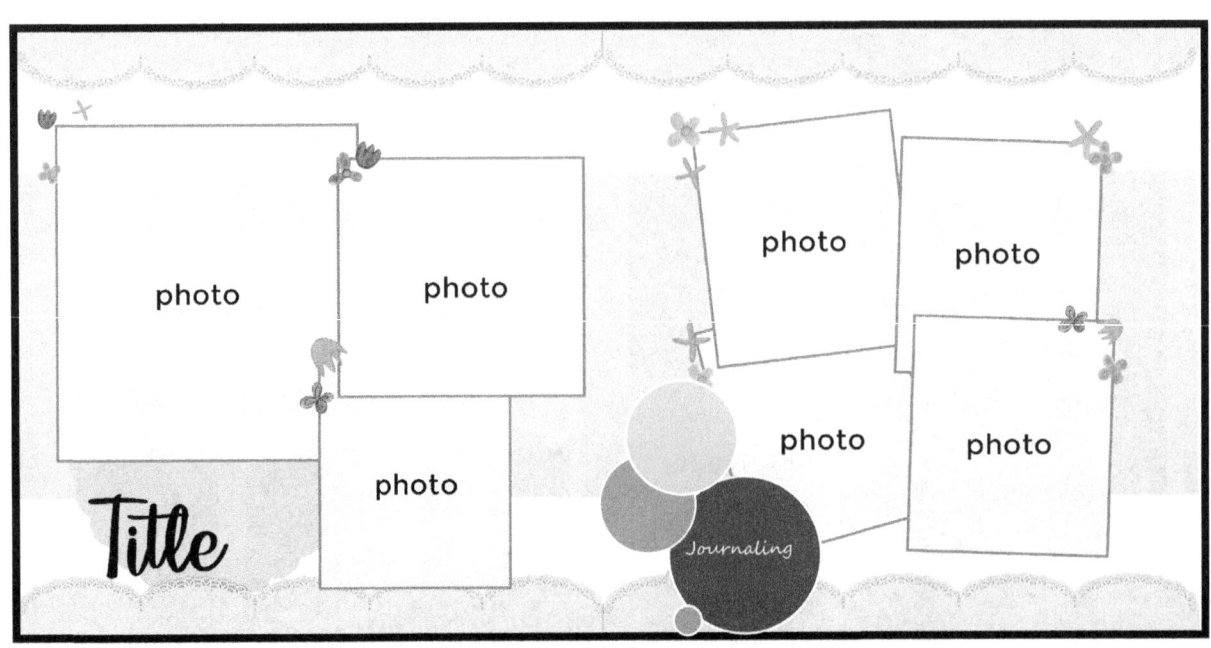

37

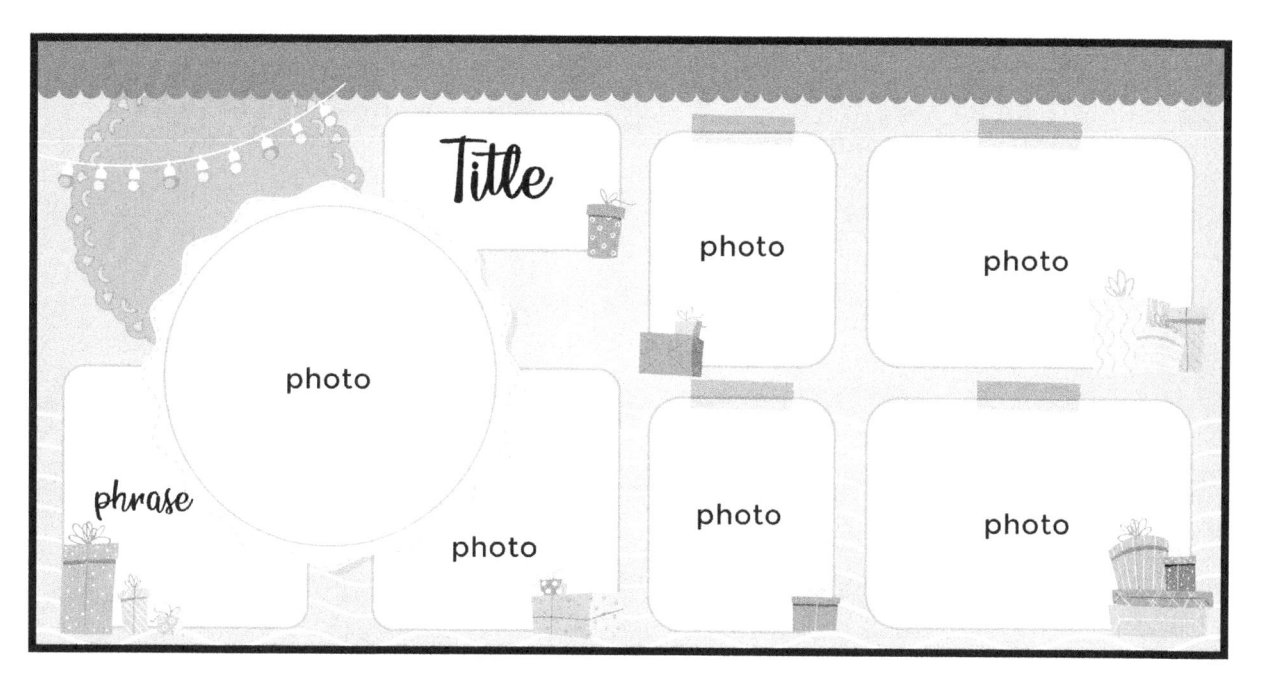

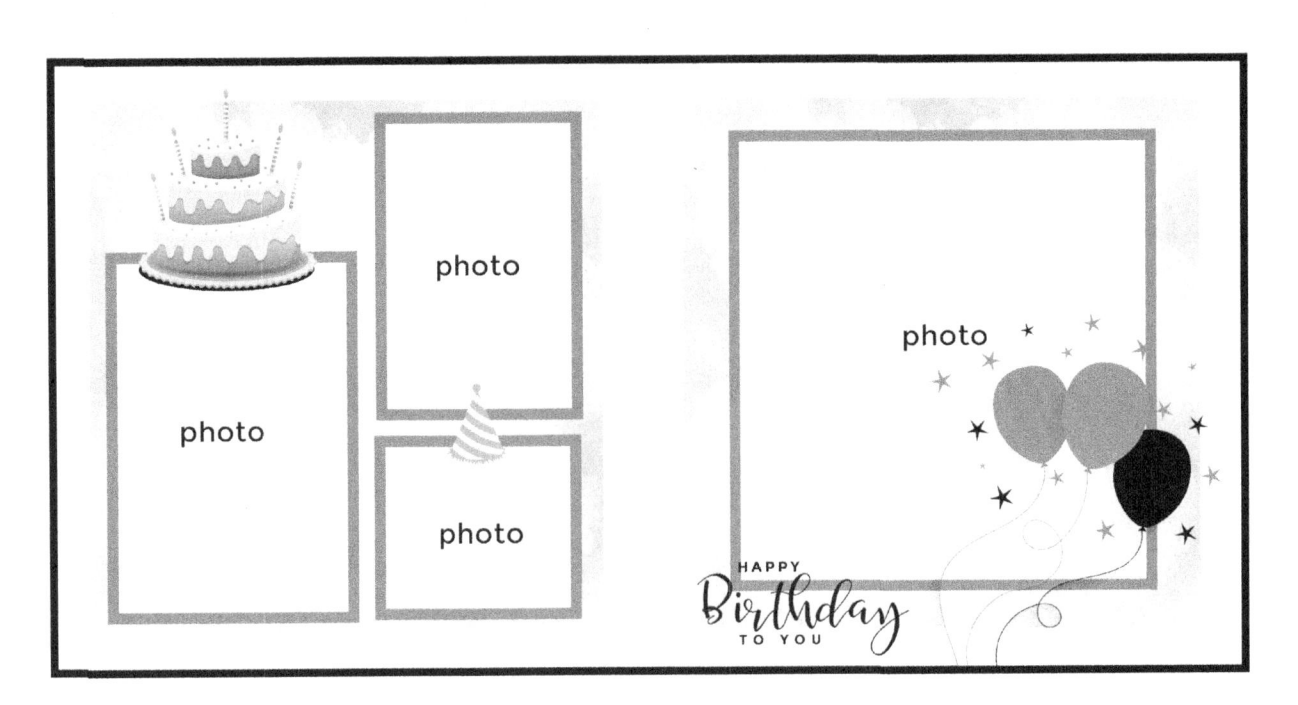

photo
photo
photo
photo

HAPPY
Birthday
TO YOU

phrase

photo
photo
photo
photo
photo

BEST
wishes

Magical
DAY

HAPPY
BIRTH
DAY
TO YOU!

Title
photo
photo
photo
photo
photo

HAPPY
BIRTH
DAY

38

39

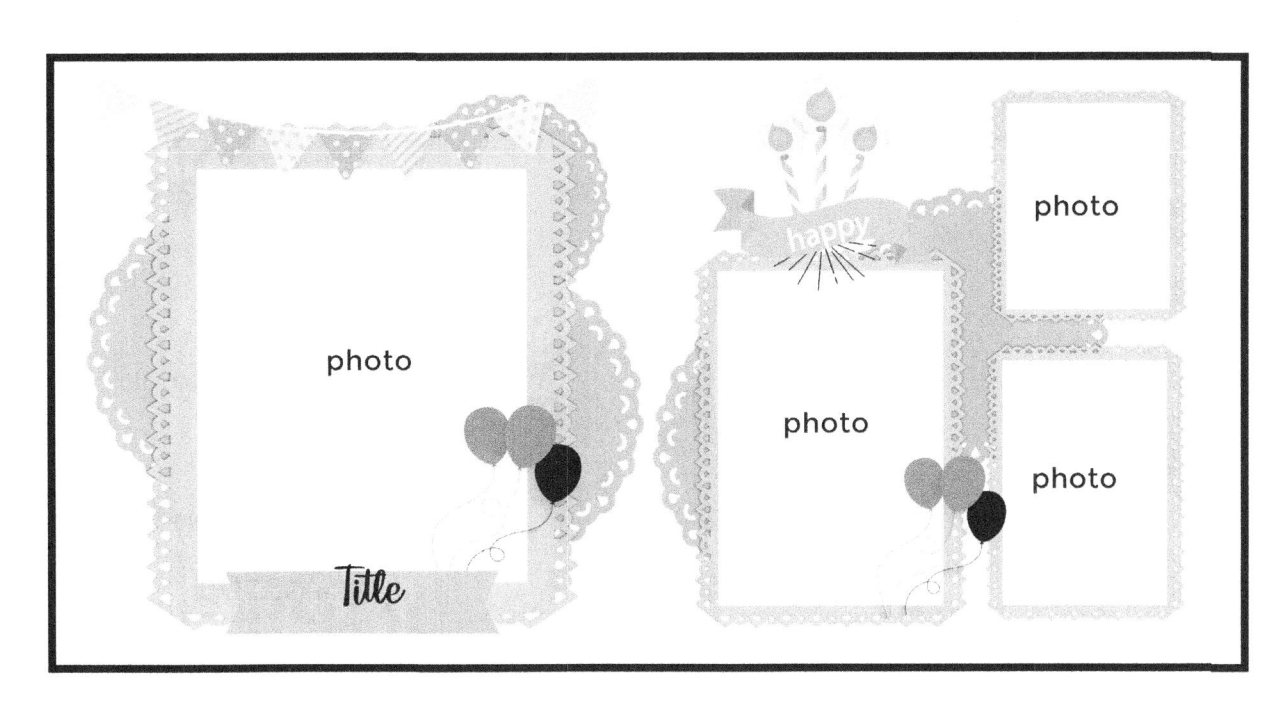

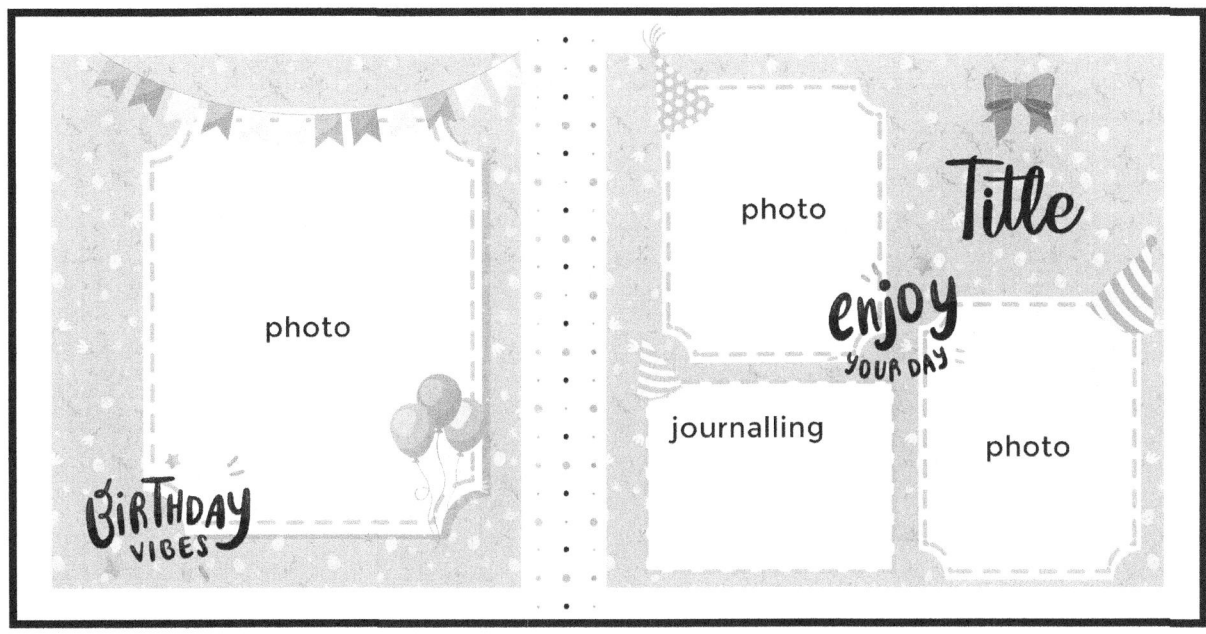

40

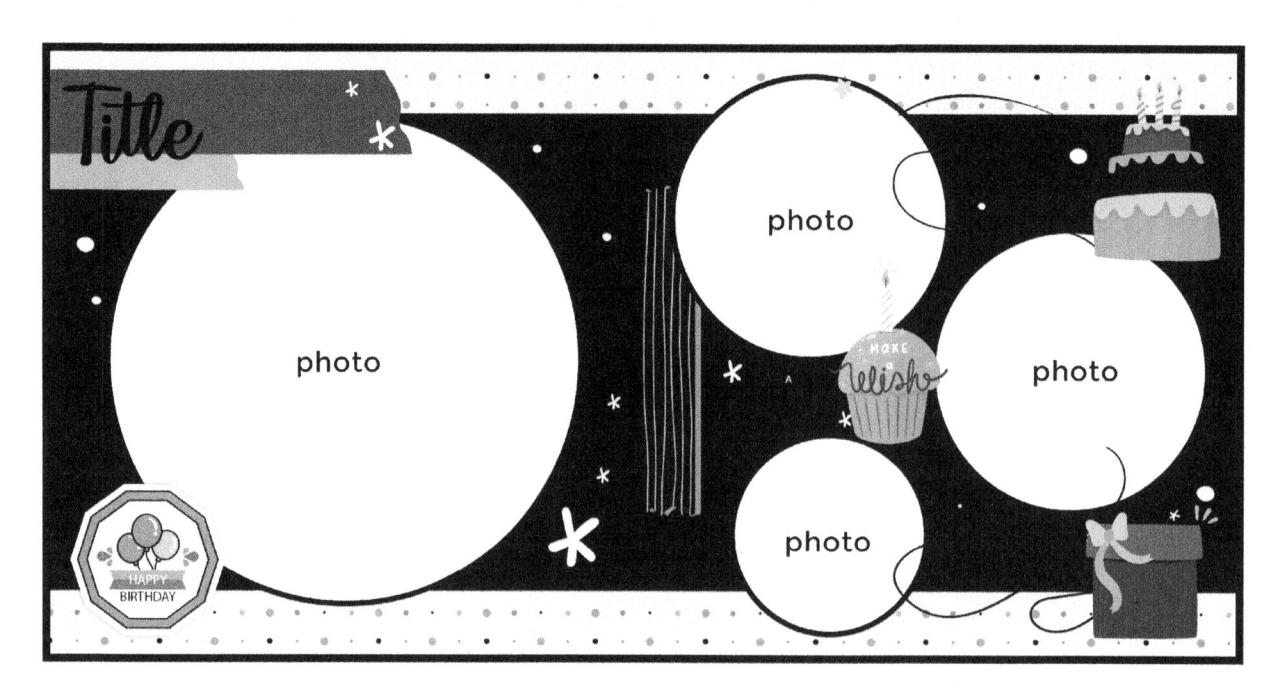

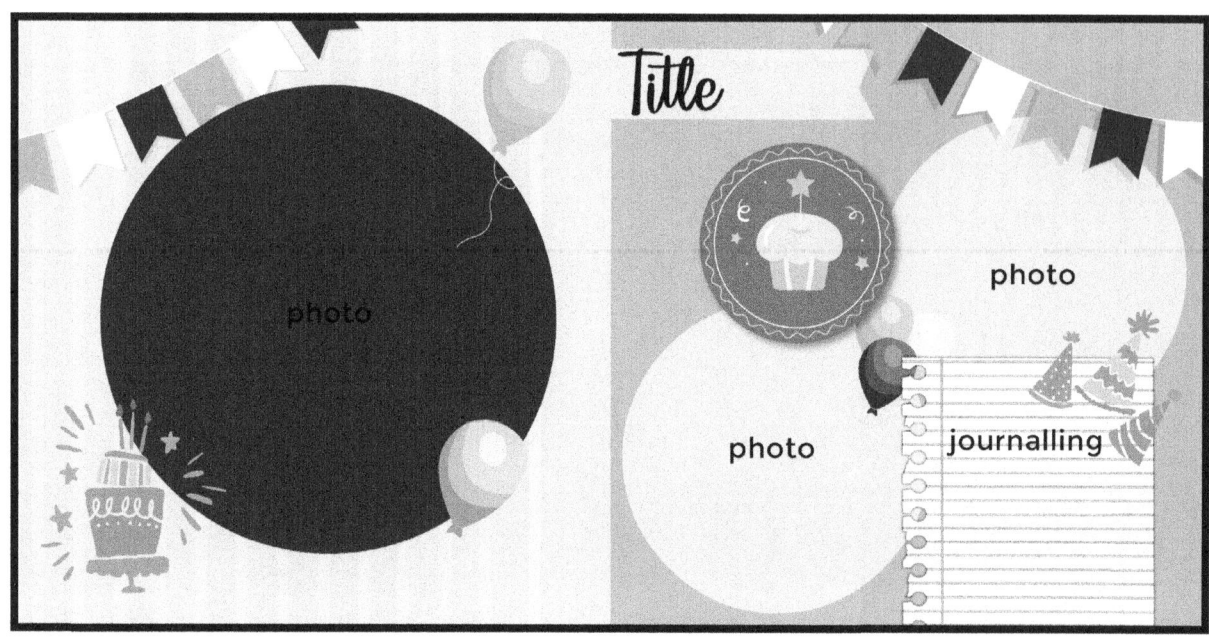

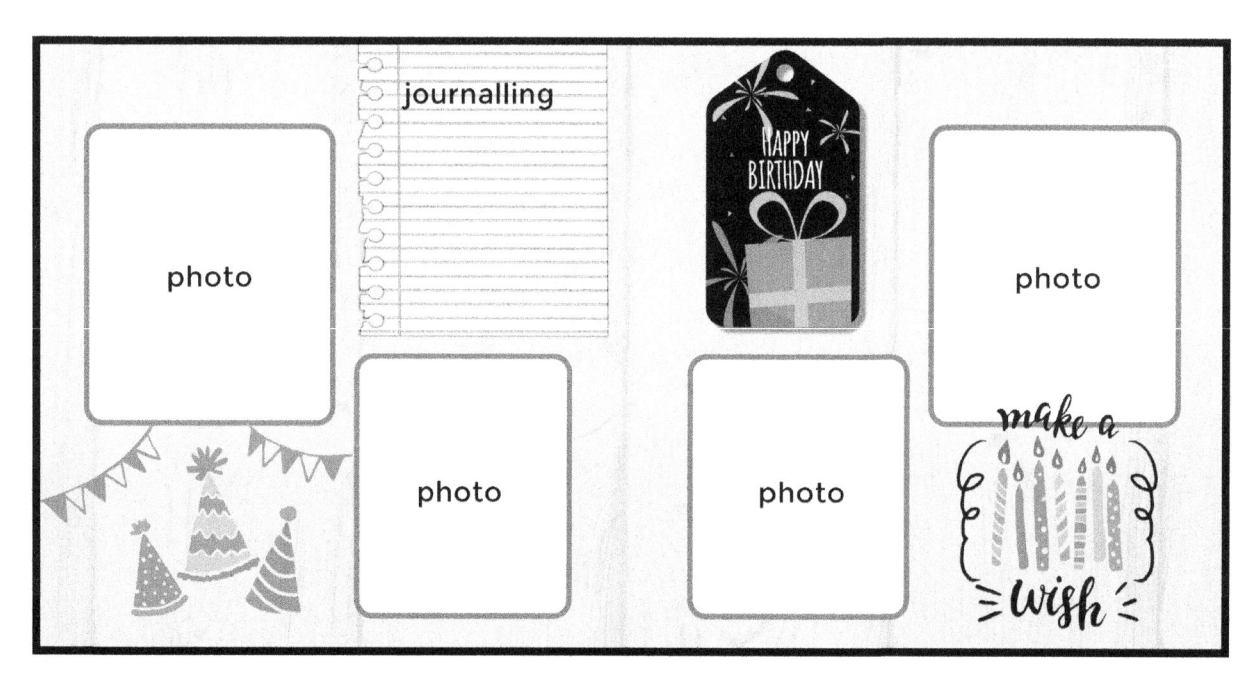

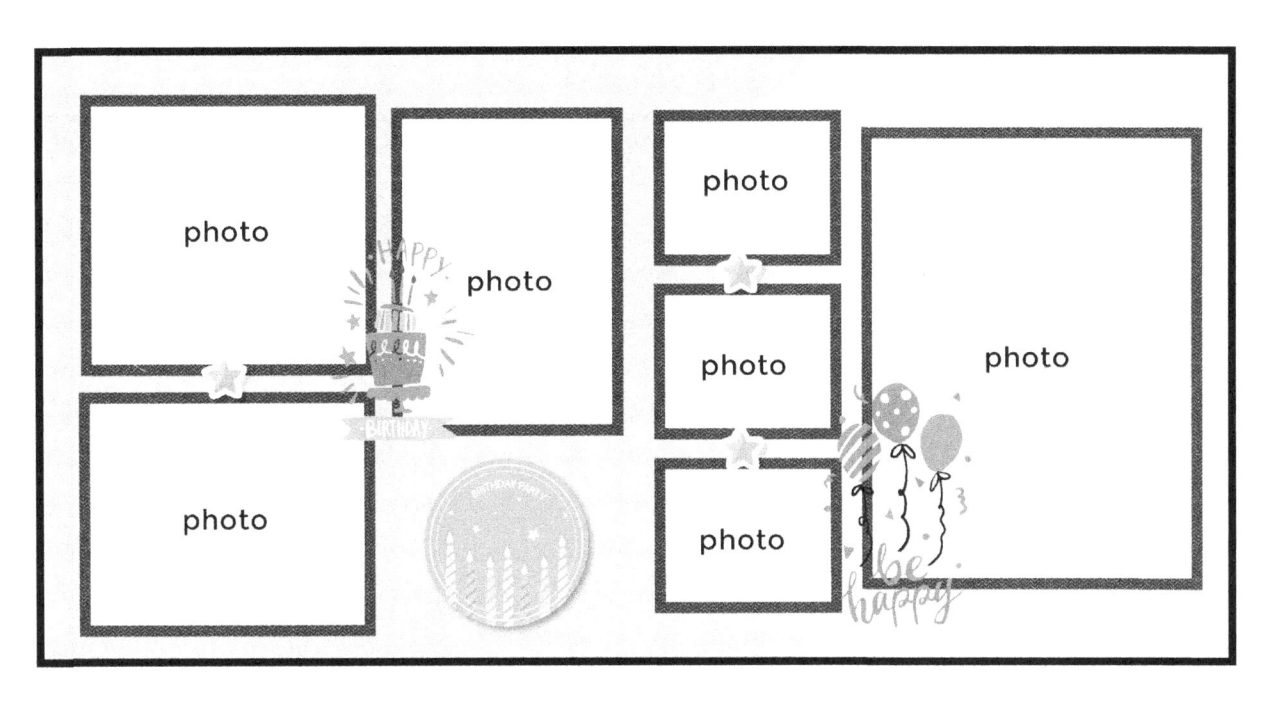

photo photo photo photo

photo photo photo photo

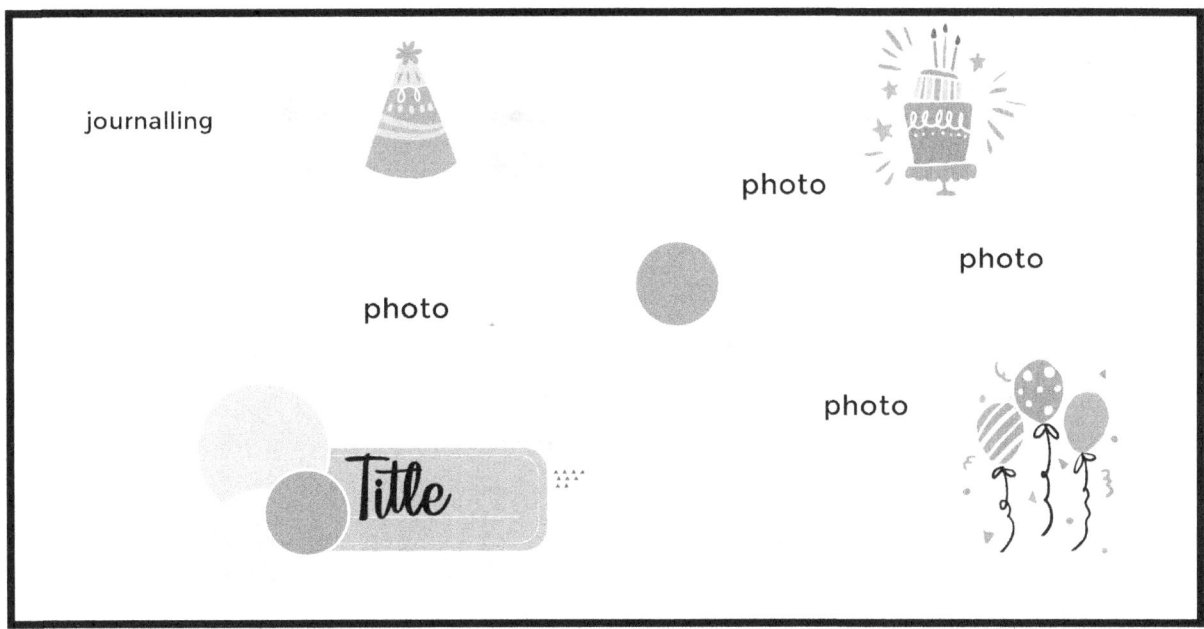

journalling

photo photo photo

Title

HAPPY BiRTHDAY

photo

sentiments

photo photo photo

Boy Birthday

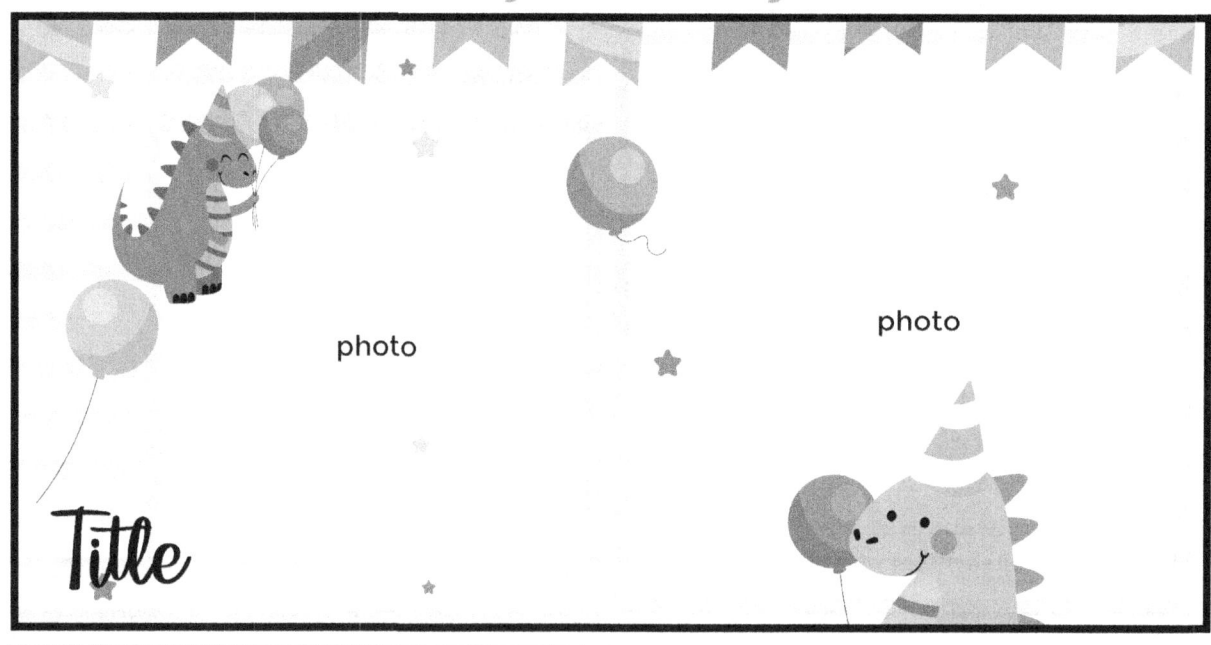

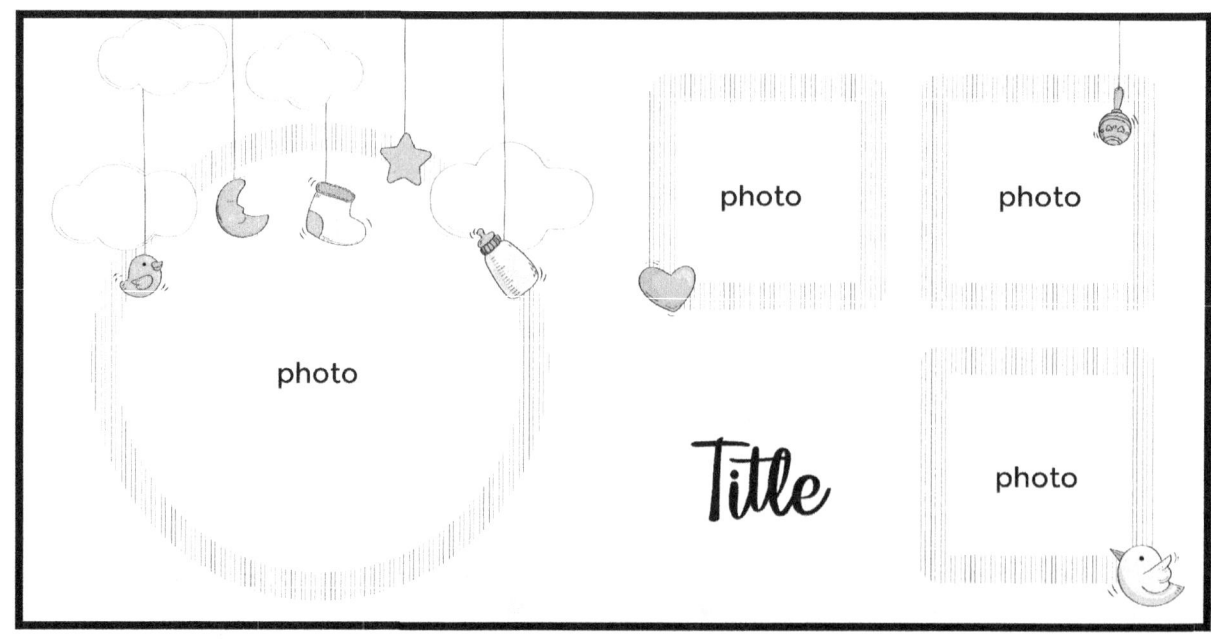

Title

photo
photo

Title

photo
photo
Journaling
photo

Title

photo
photo
photo
photo

42

43

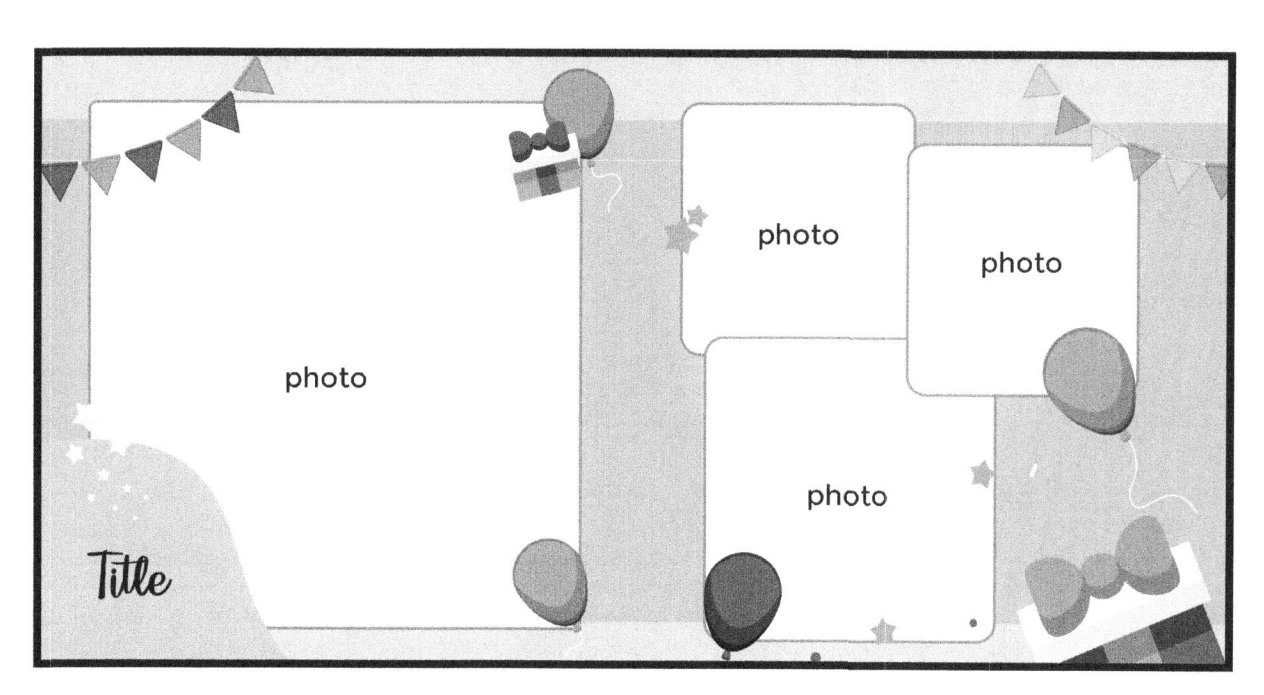

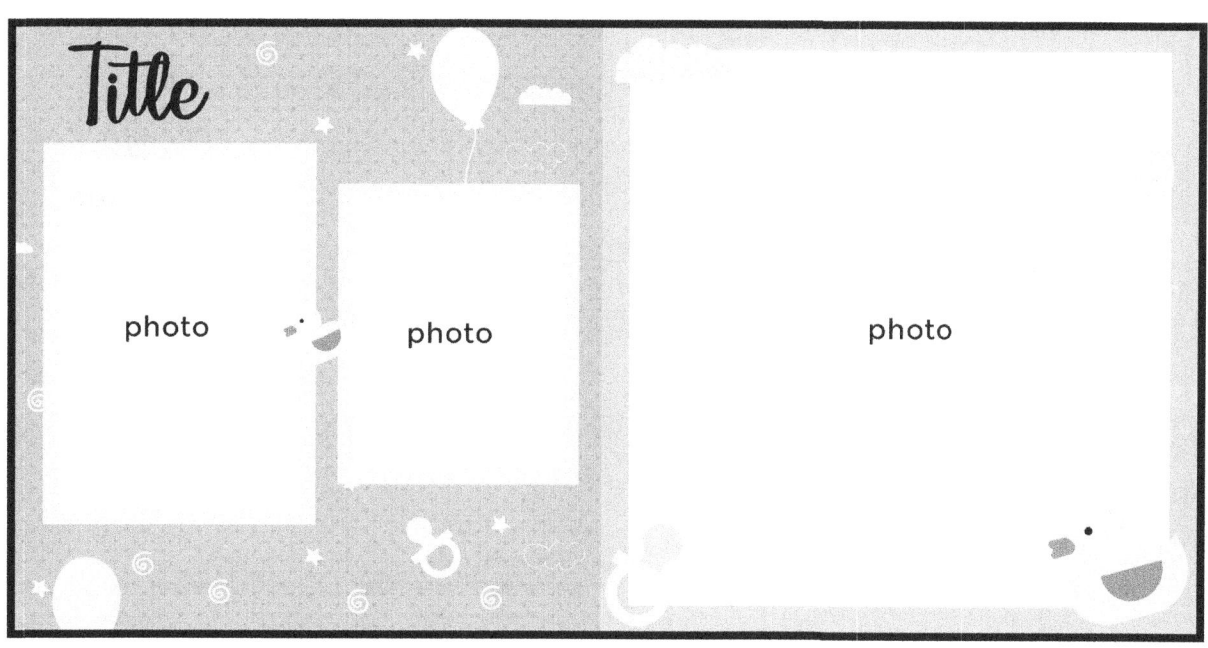

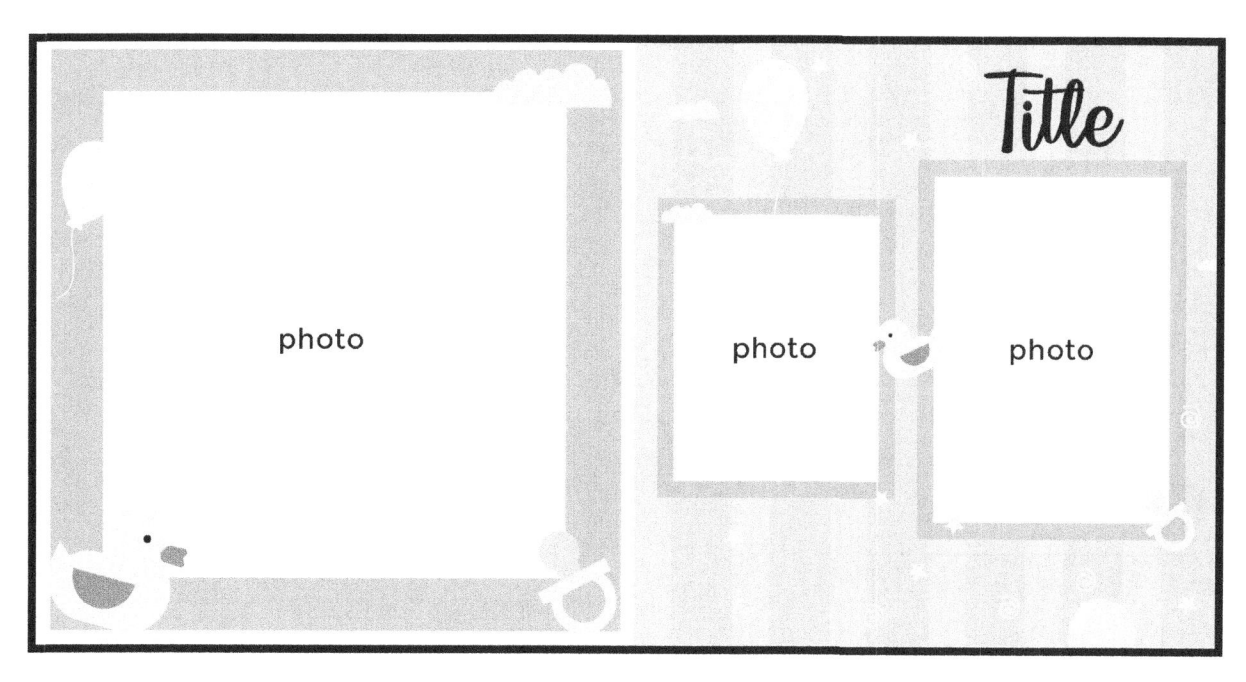

44

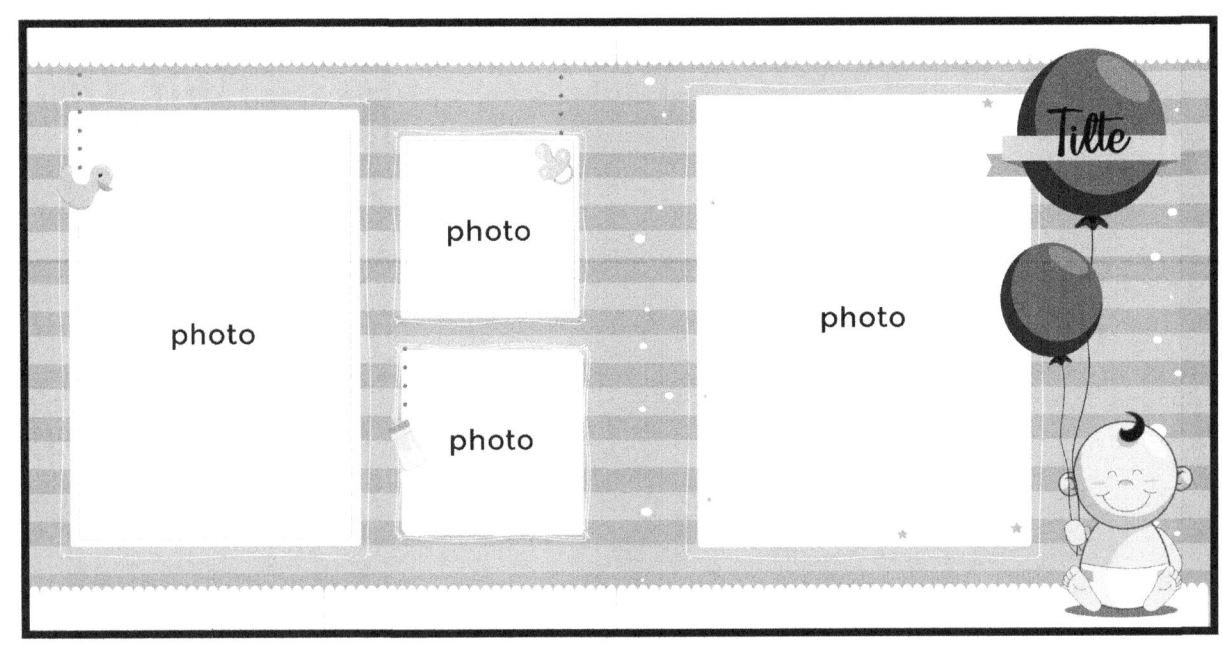

Title

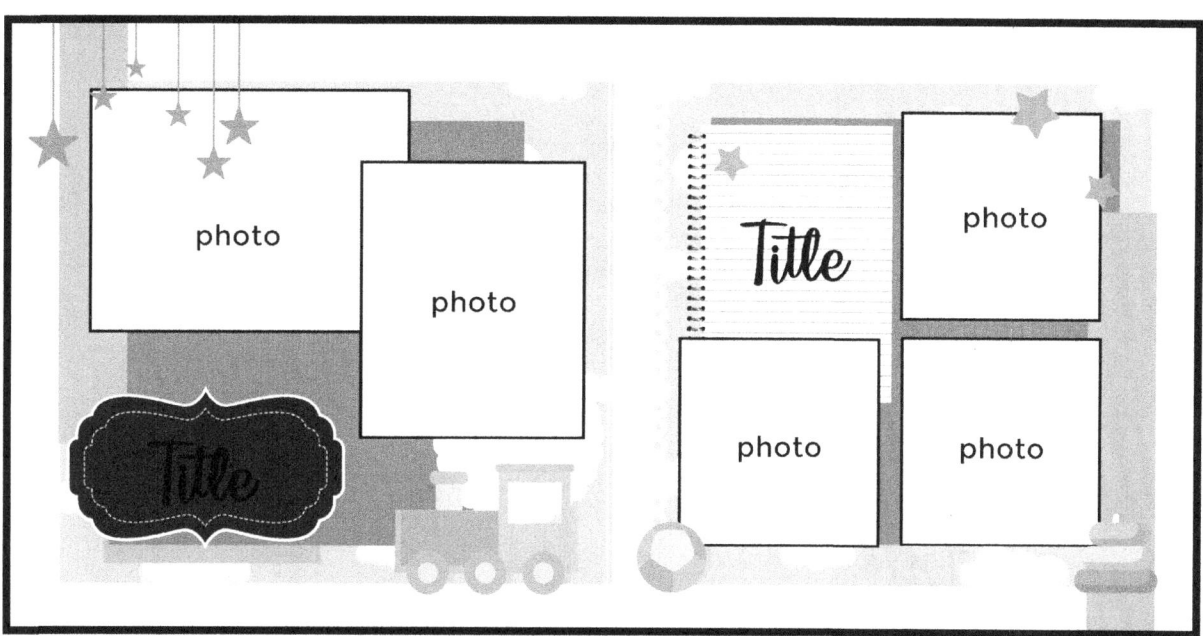

Title

Title

46

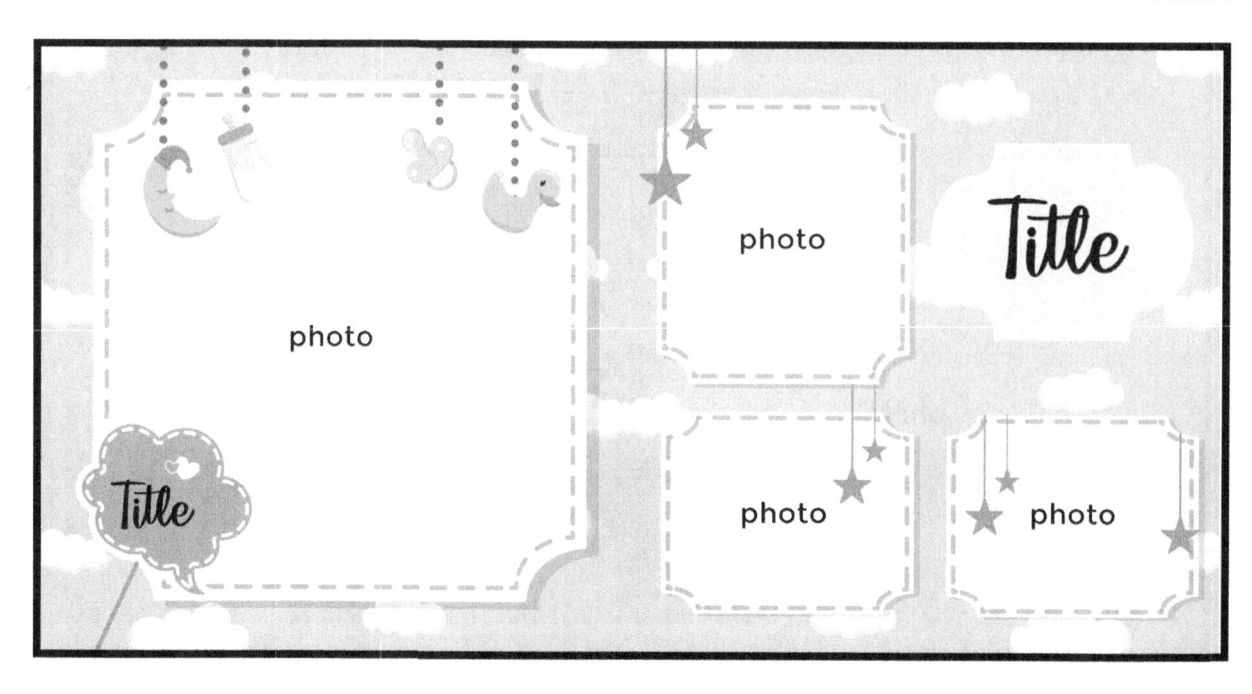

Happy *first* Birthday...

photo
photo
photo

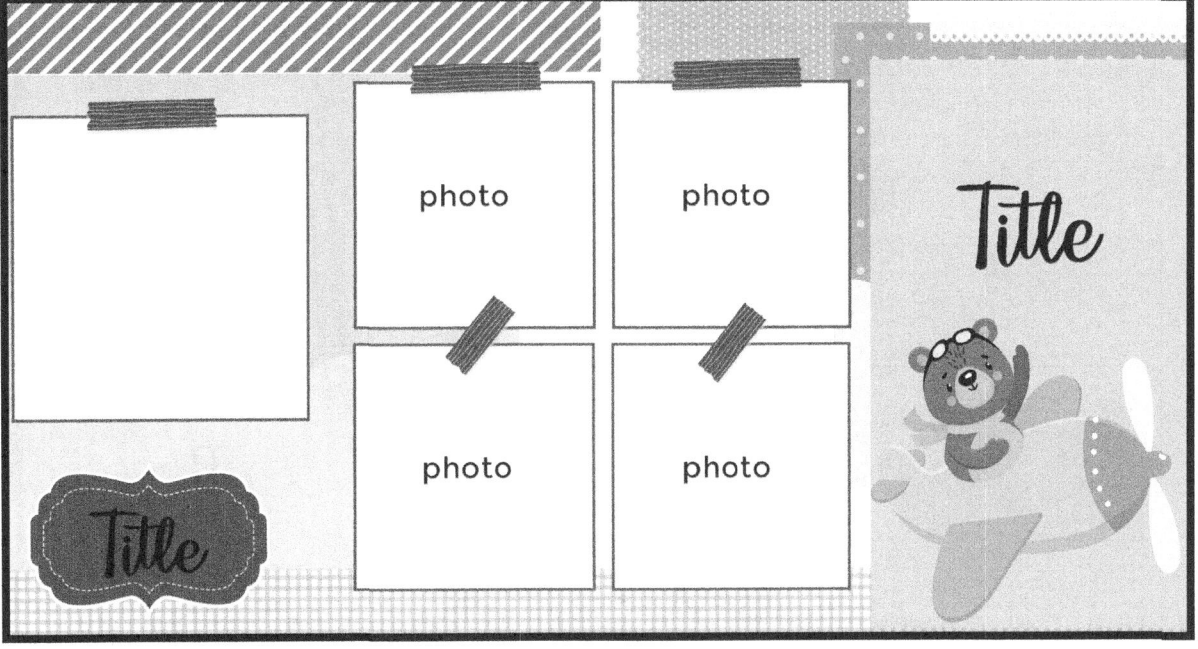

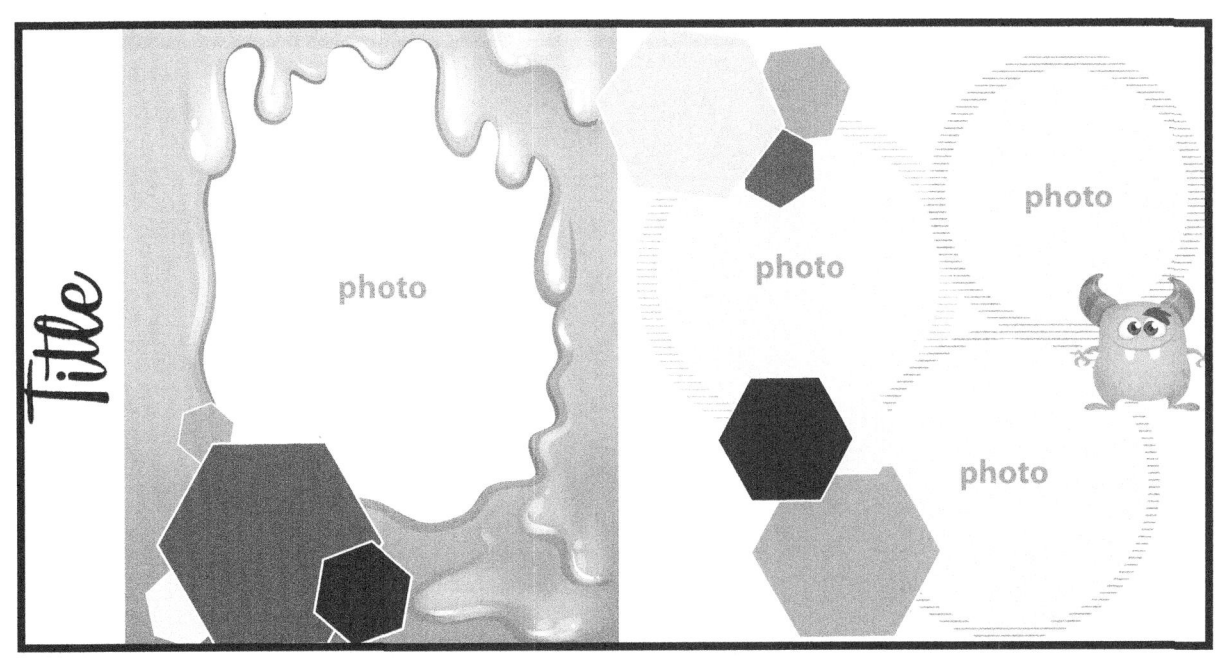

Title
photo
photo
photo
photo

Title
photo
photo
photo

photo

photo

photo

Title

Journaling

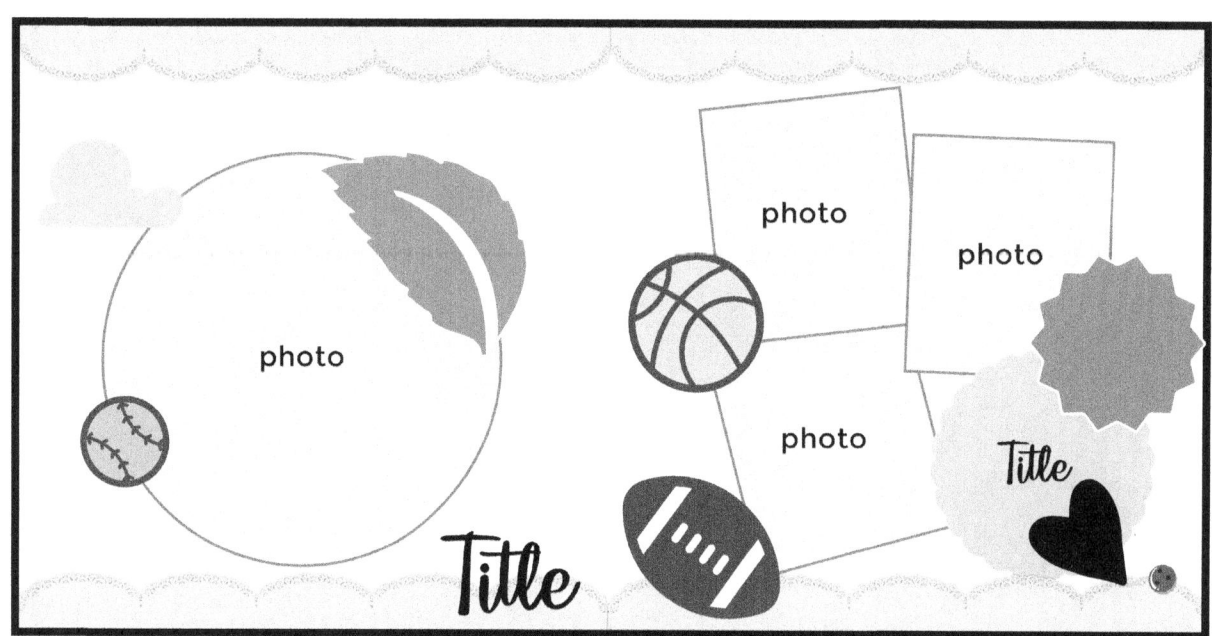

photo

photo

photo

Title

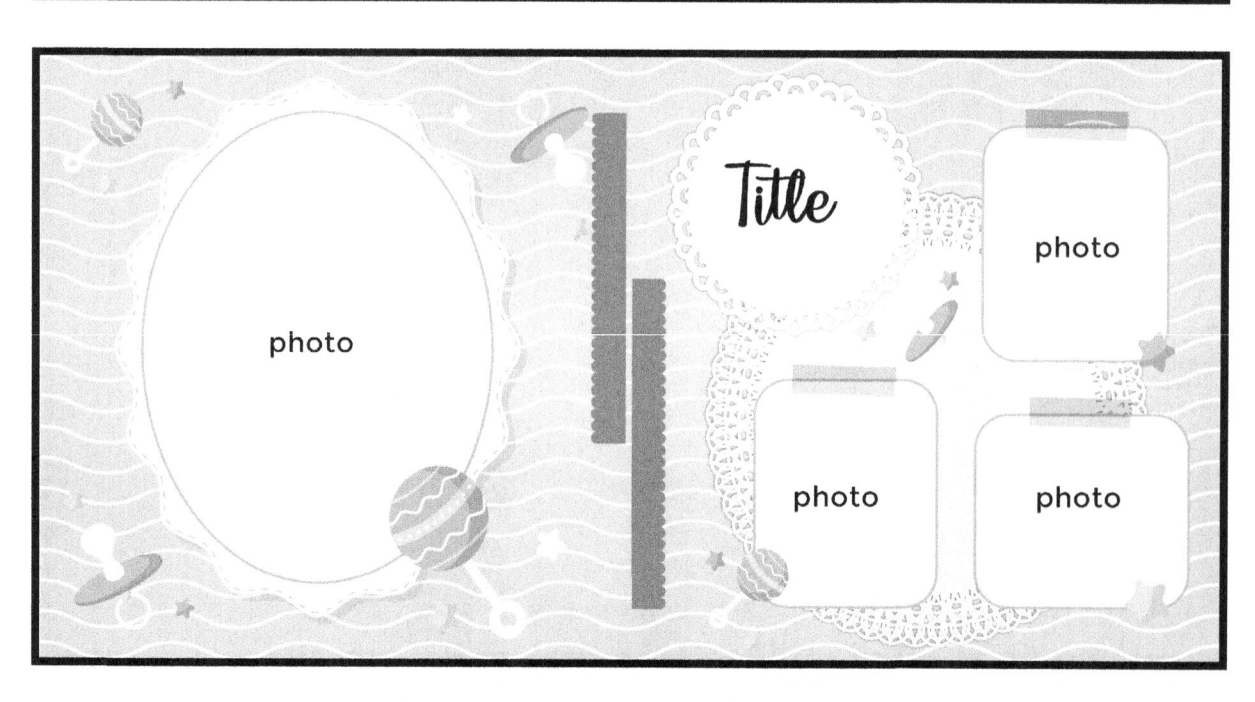

Title

photo

photo

photo

Title

photo

48

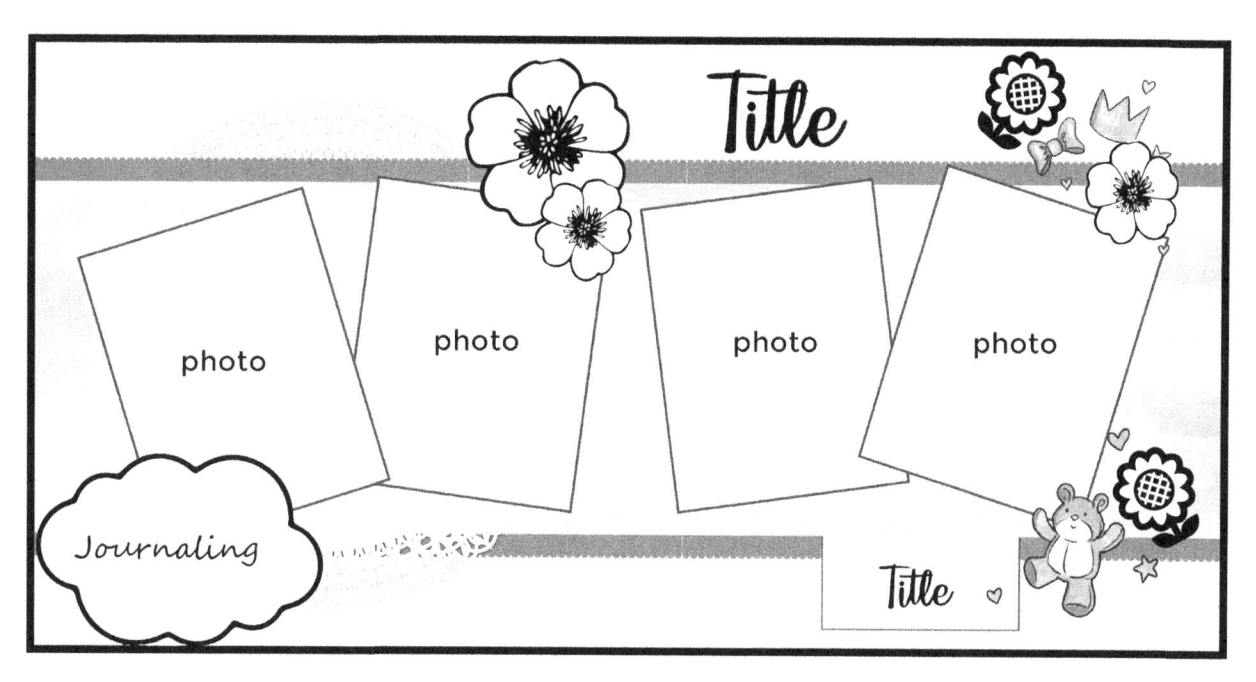

Title

photo photo photo photo

Journaling

Title

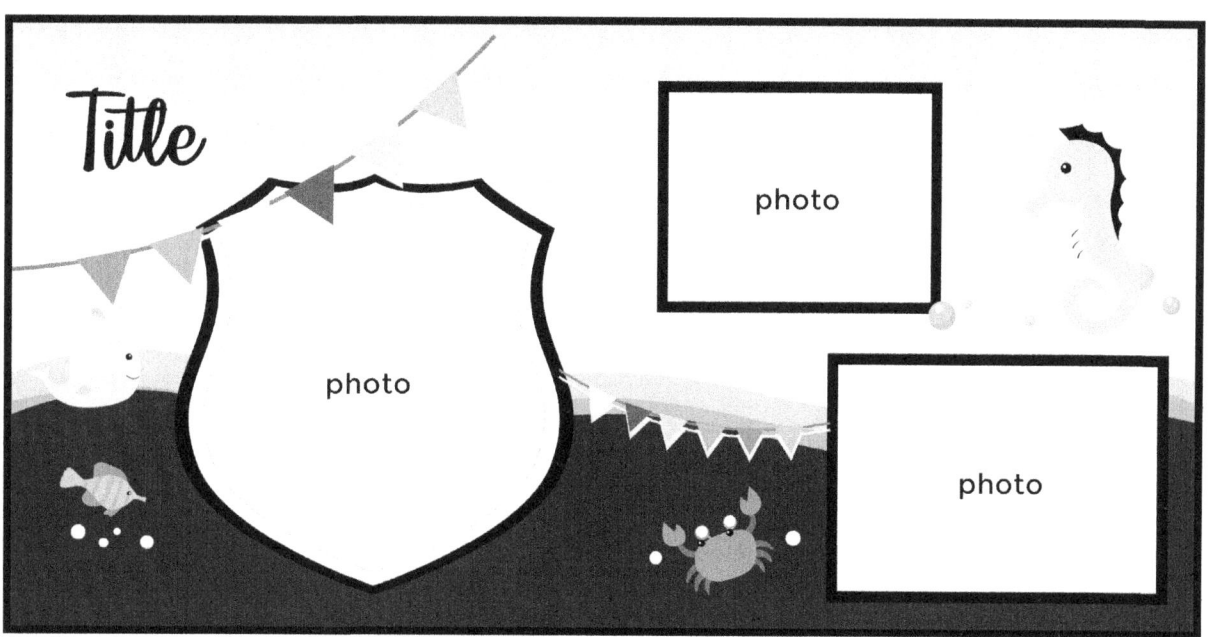

Title

photo

photo

photo

Title

photo

photo

photo

49

50

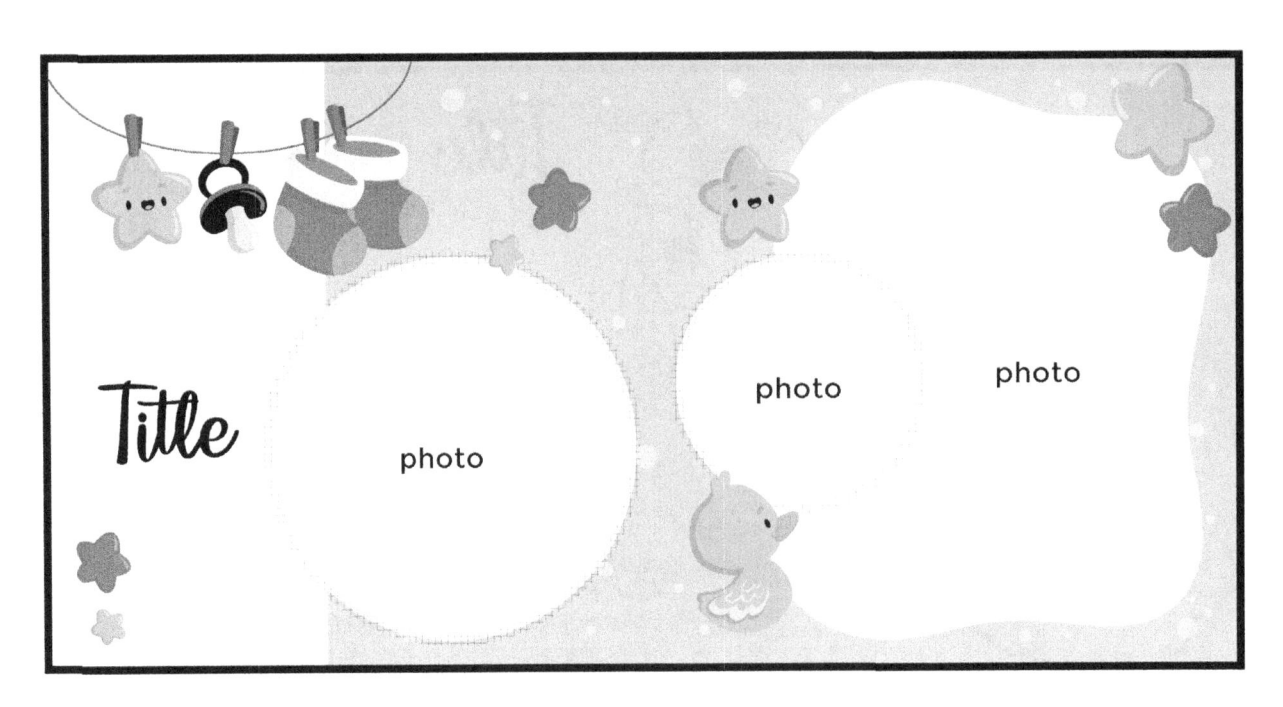

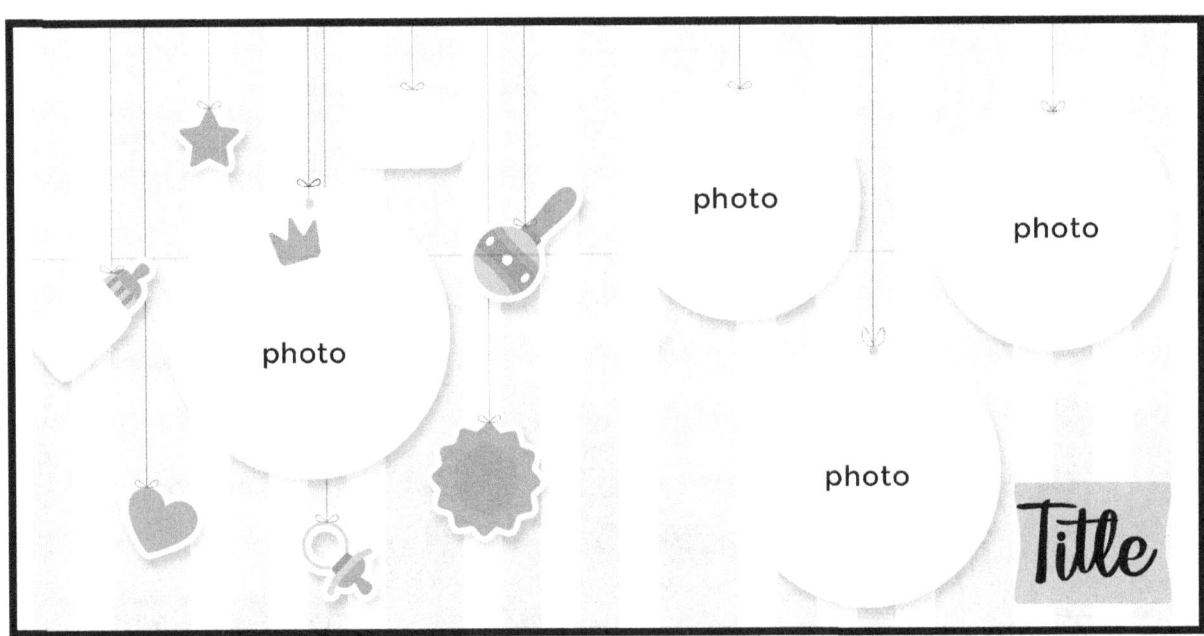

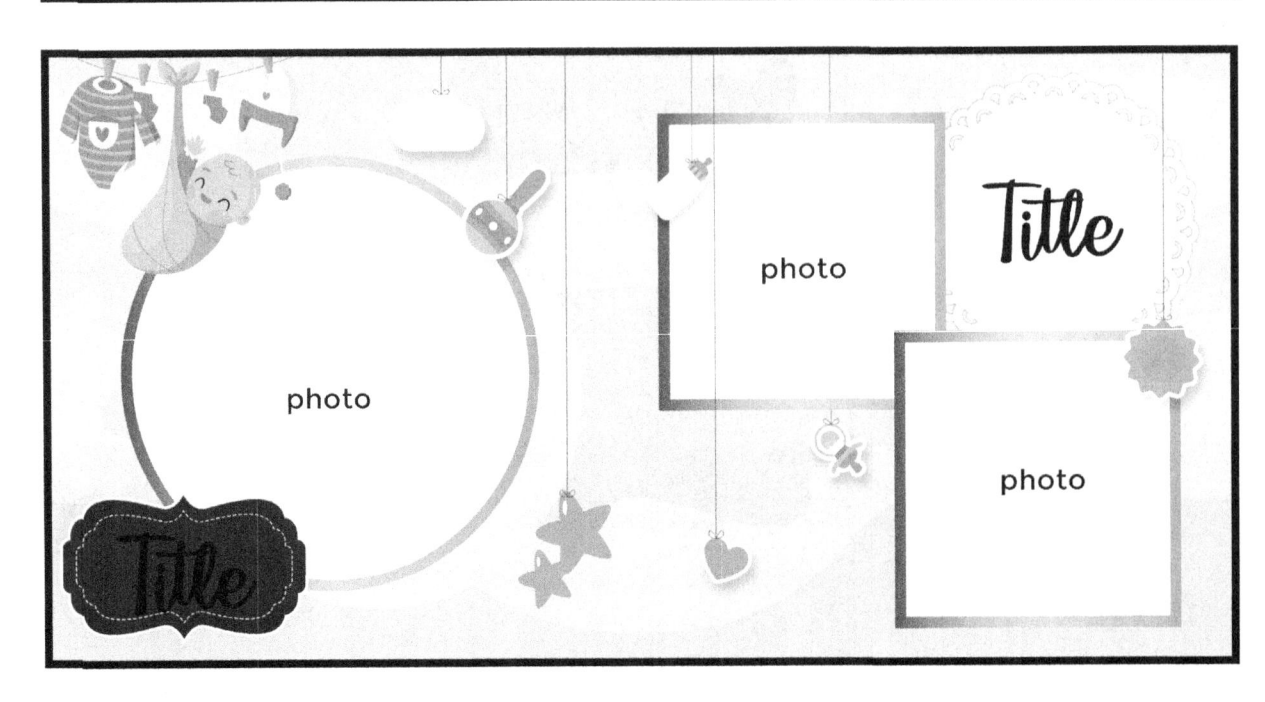

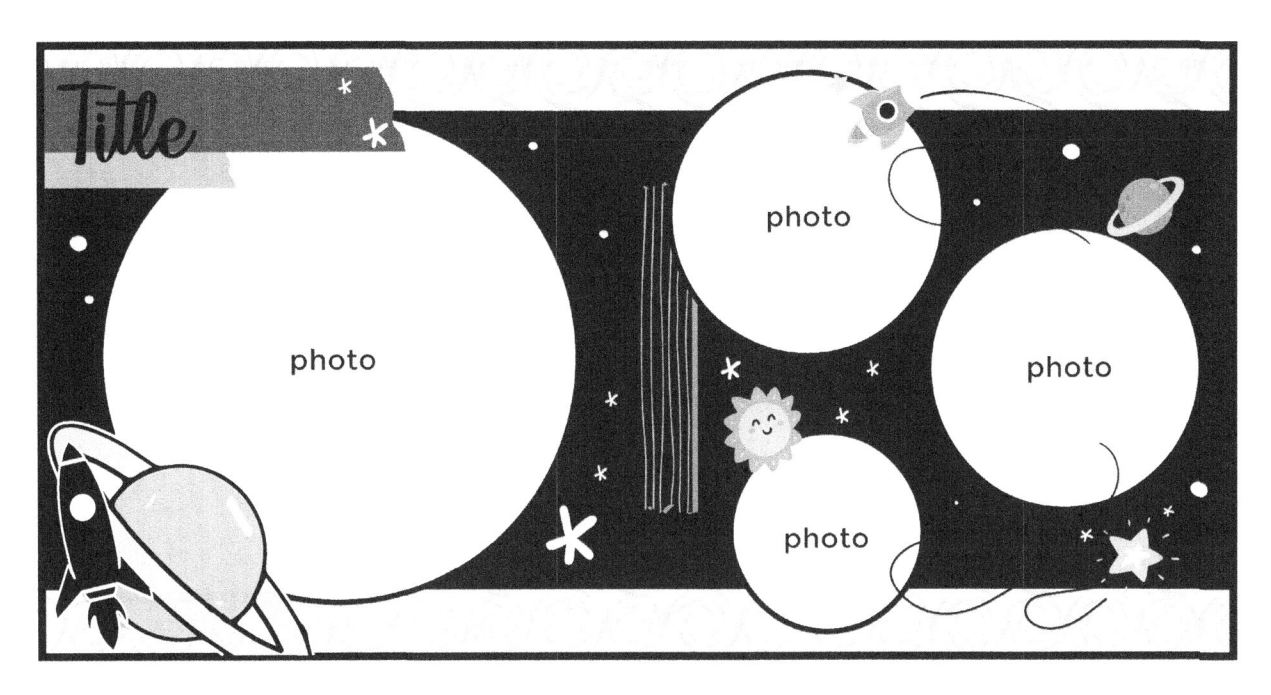

Title

photo
photo
photo
photo

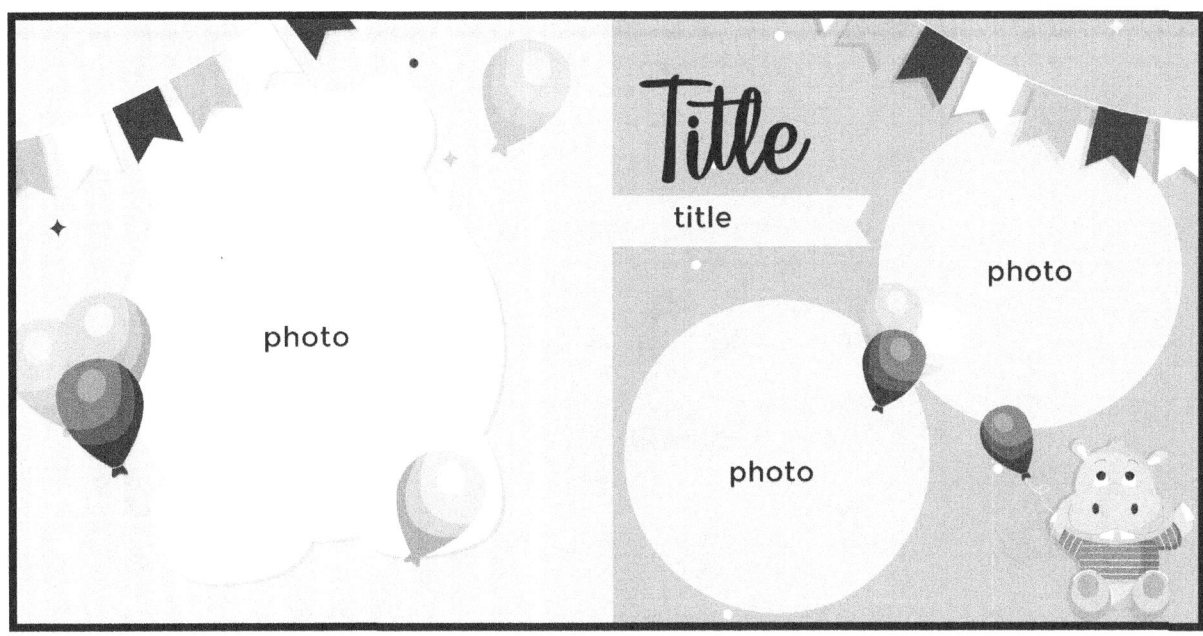

Title
title
photo
photo

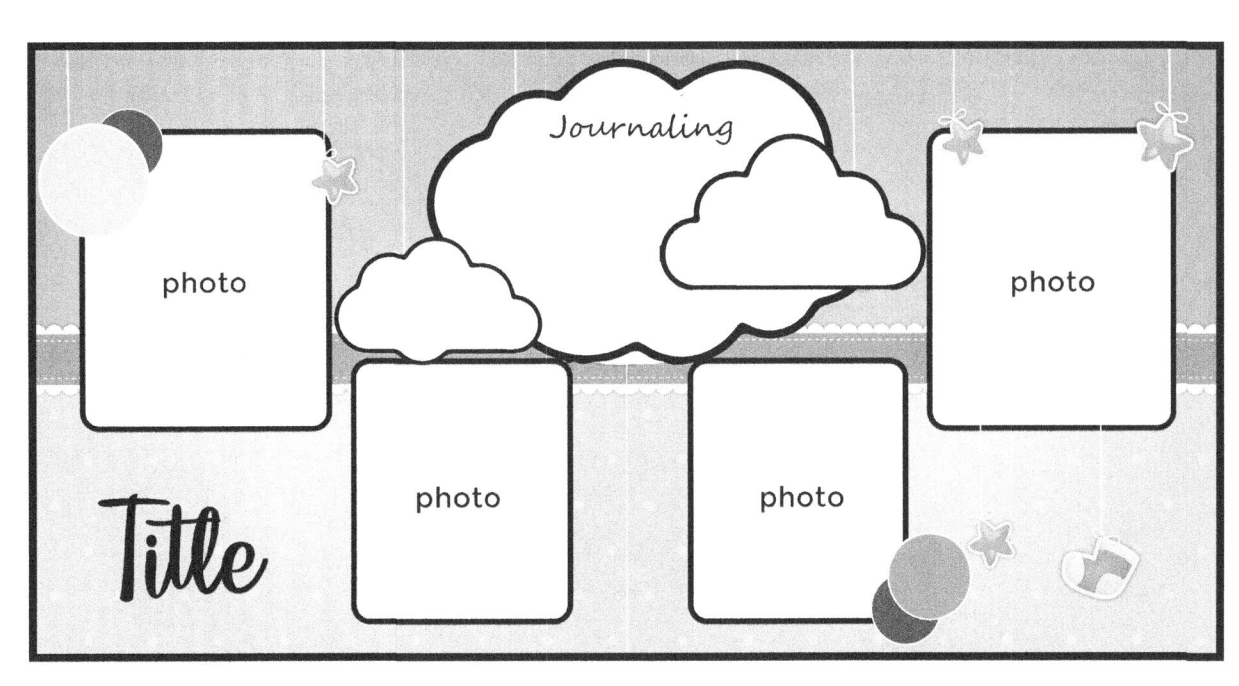

Journaling
photo
photo
photo
photo
Title

51

52

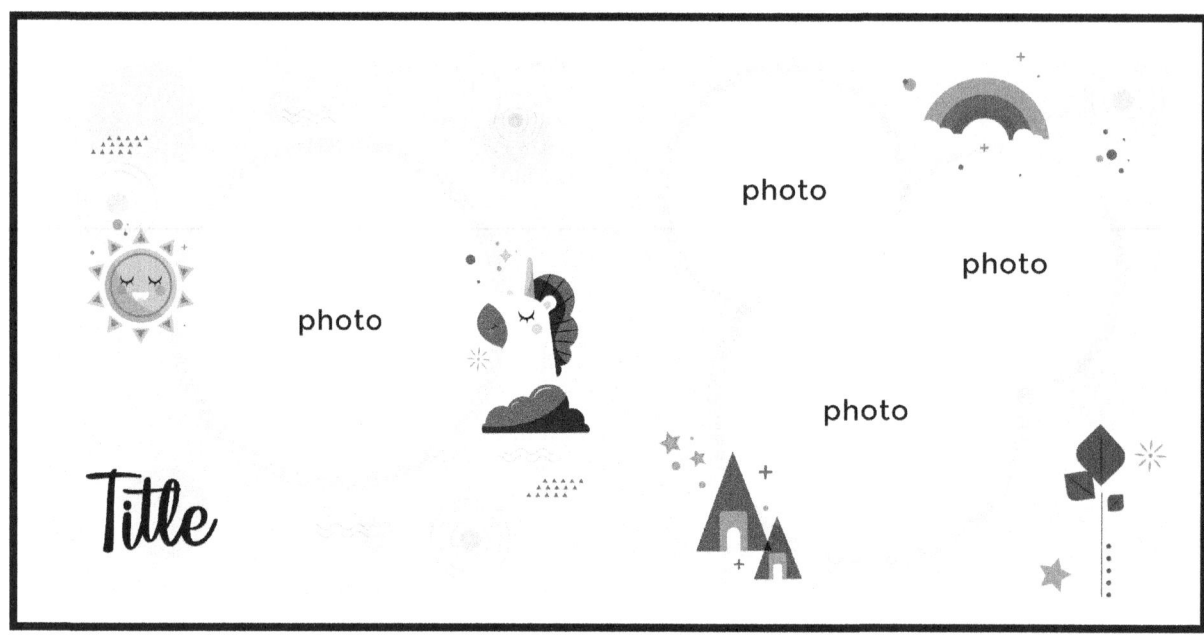

Boy

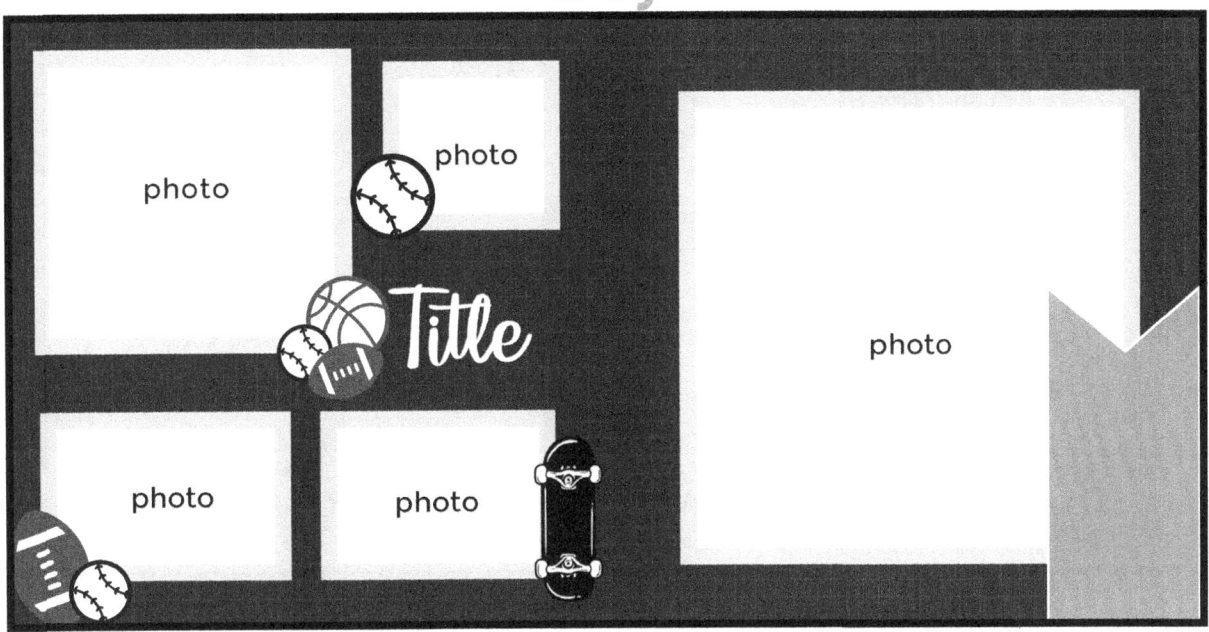

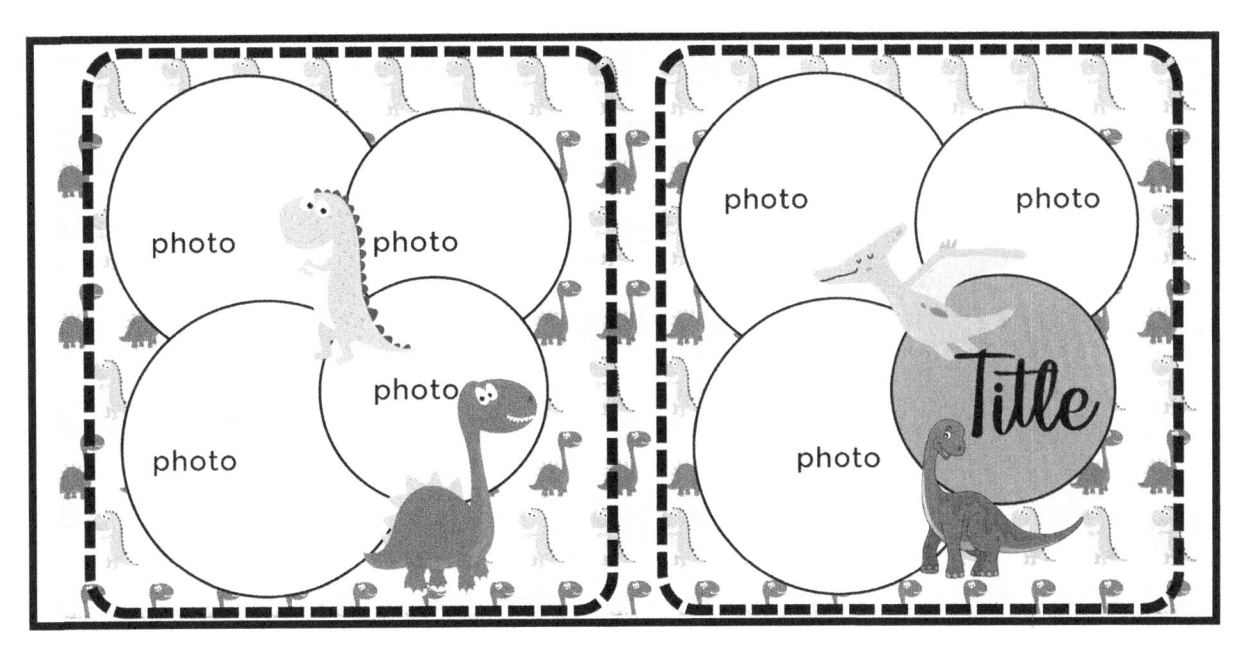

photo
photo
photo
photo
Title
photo
photo
photo

photo
Title
photo
photo
photo

Title
Title
photo
photo
photo
photo
photo
photo

55

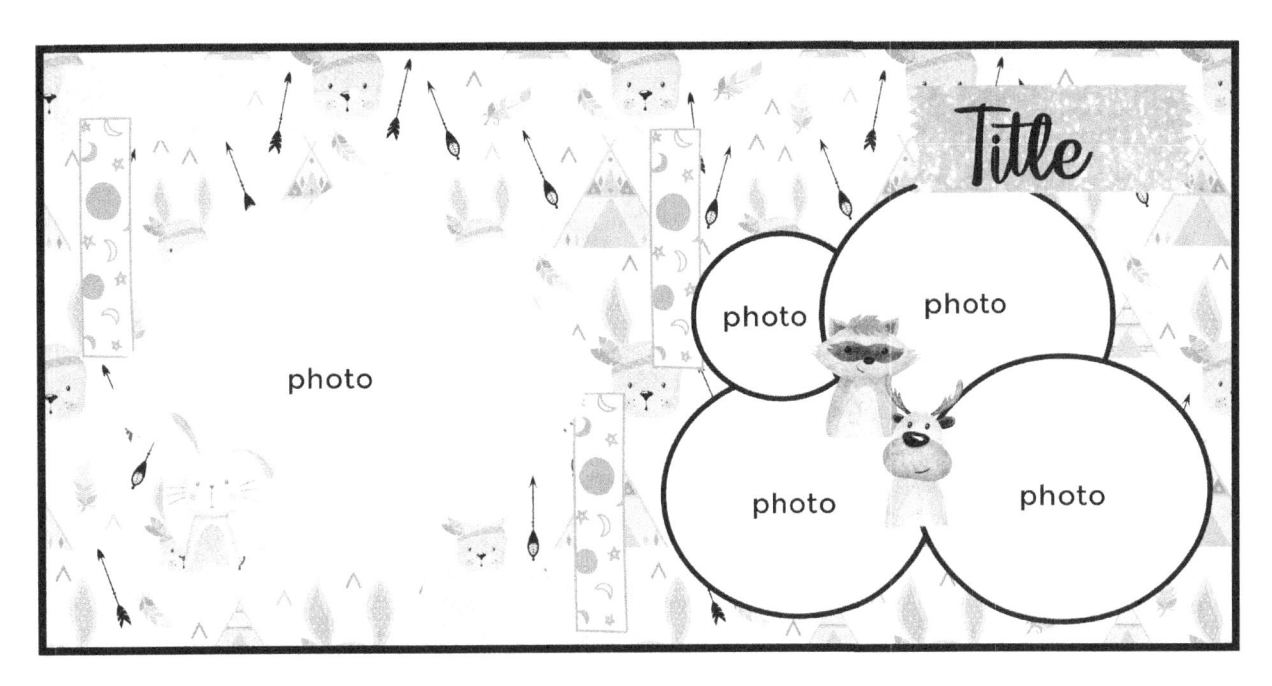

56

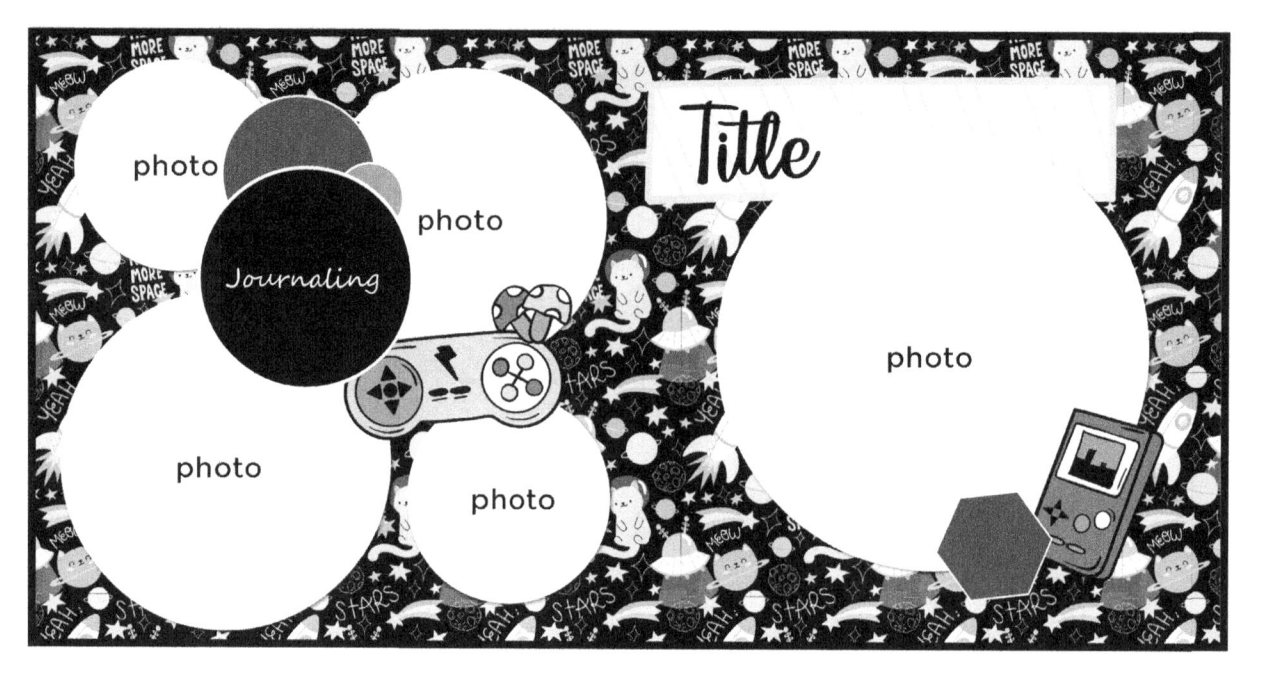

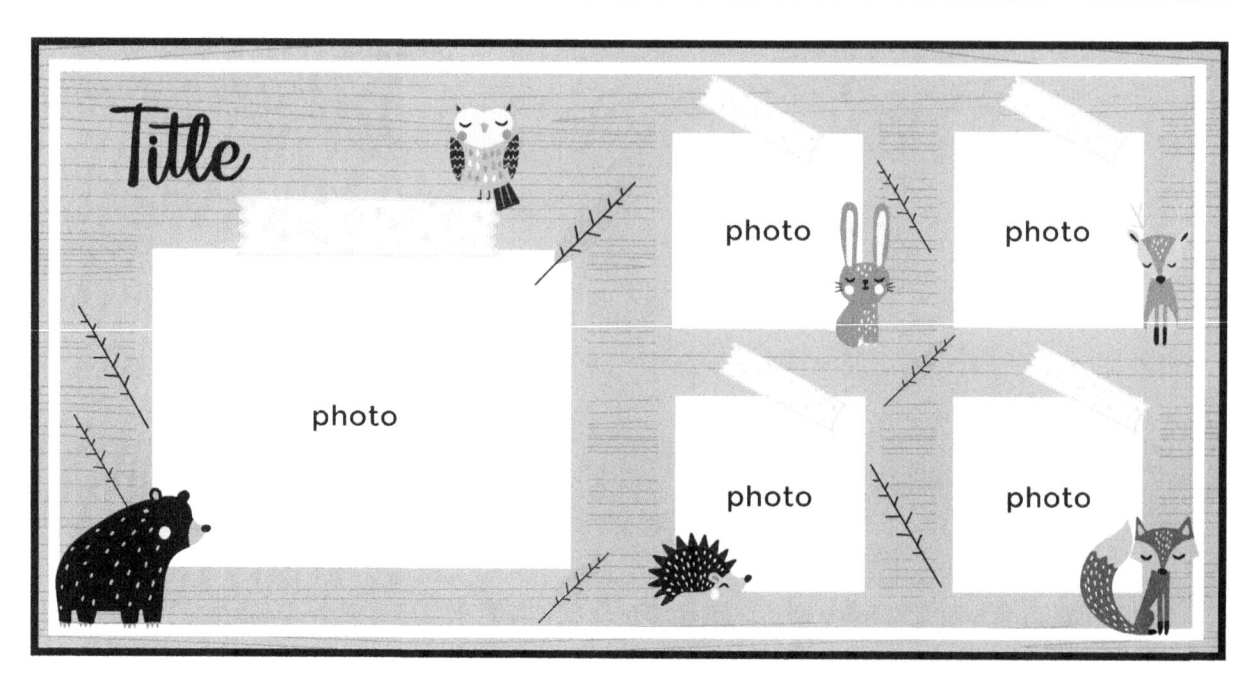

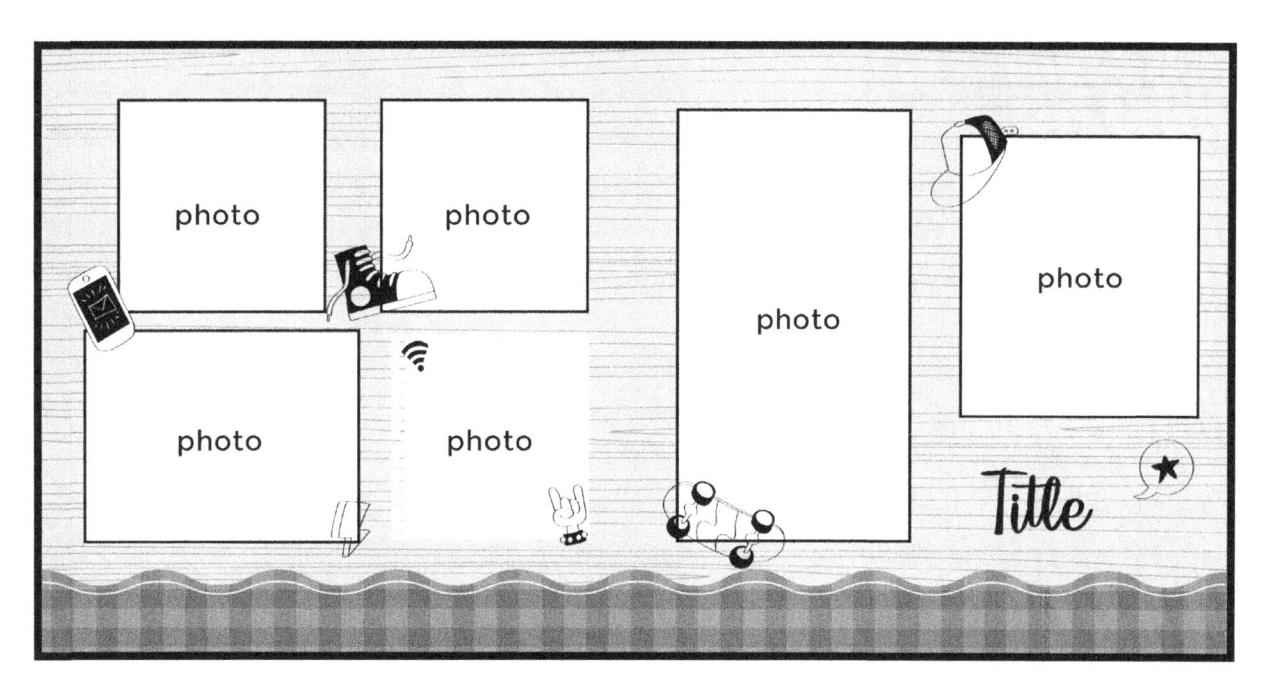

photo photo photo photo
photo photo
Title

photo photo photo
photo Title photo

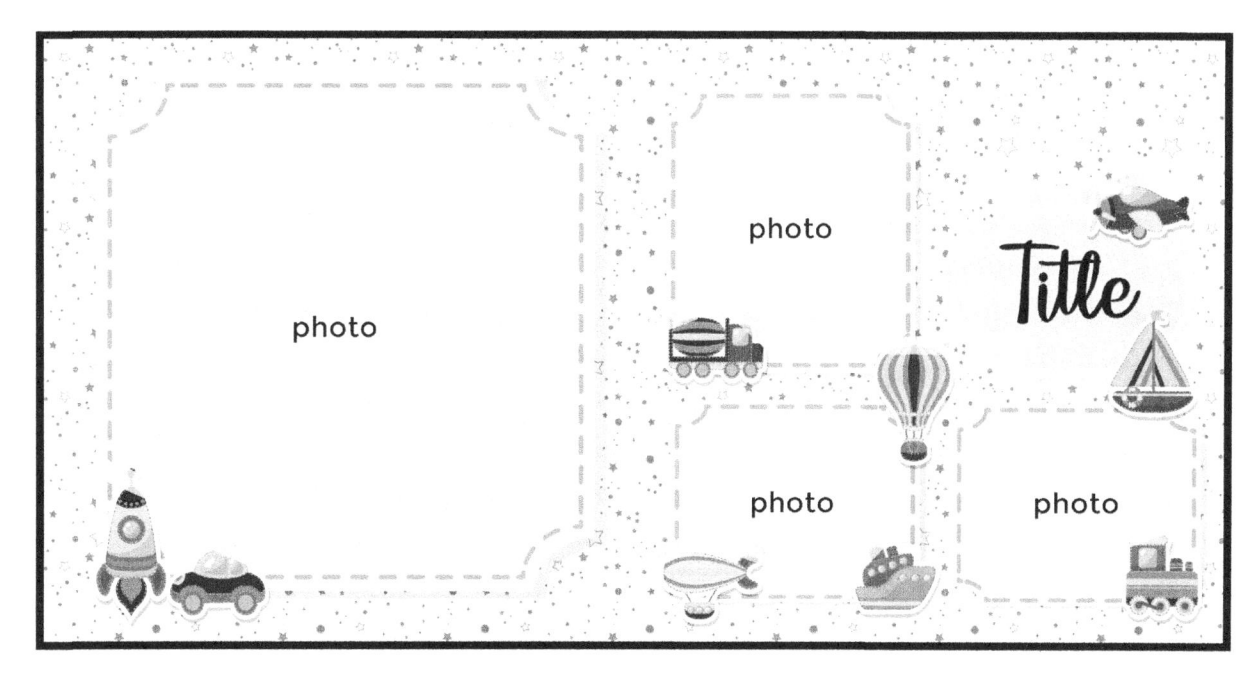

photo
photo
Title
photo photo

57

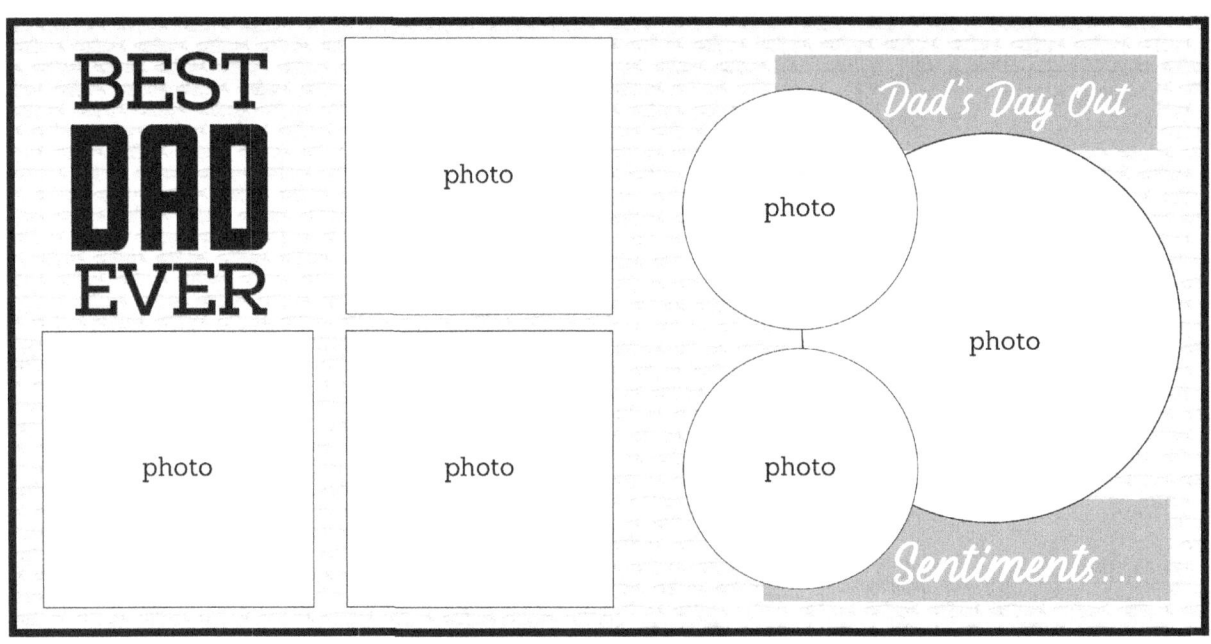

BEST DAD EVER

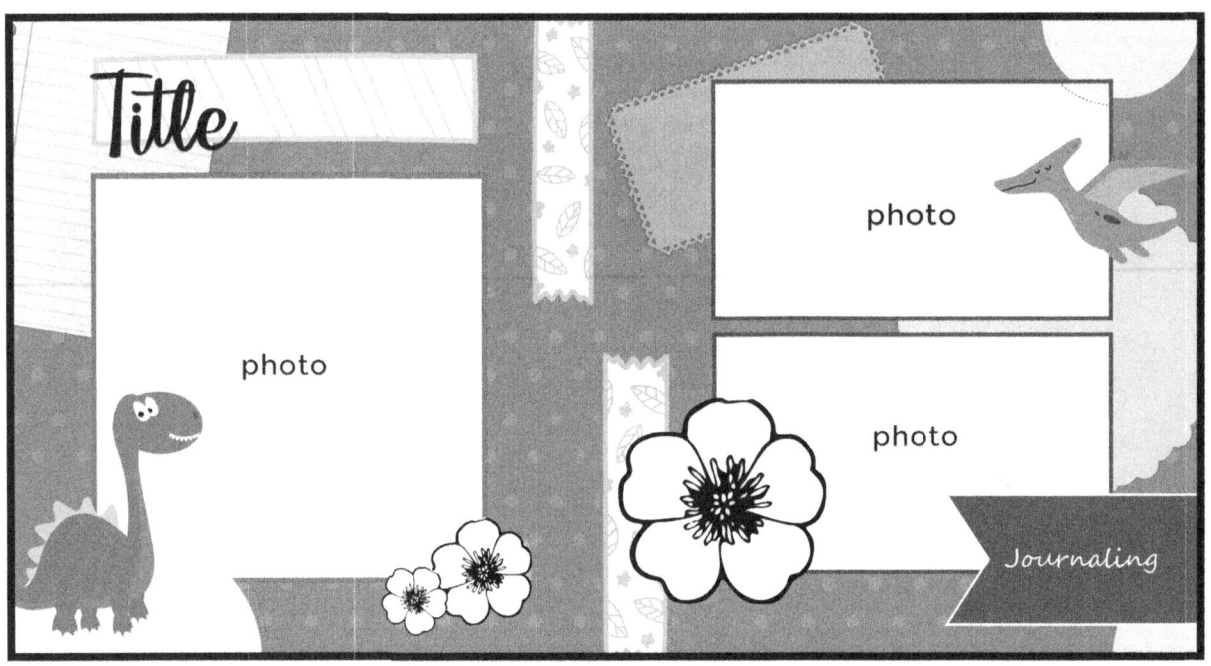

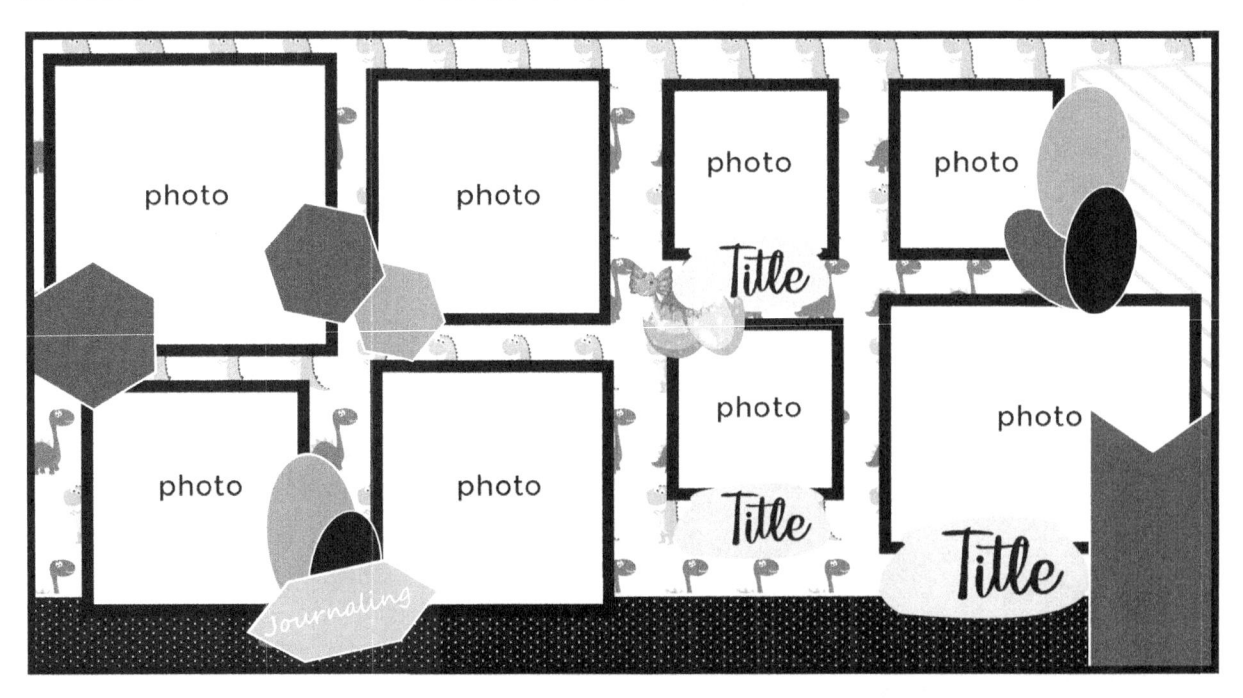

Dad's Day Out

Sentiments...

Title

Journaling

Title

Title

Title

Journaling

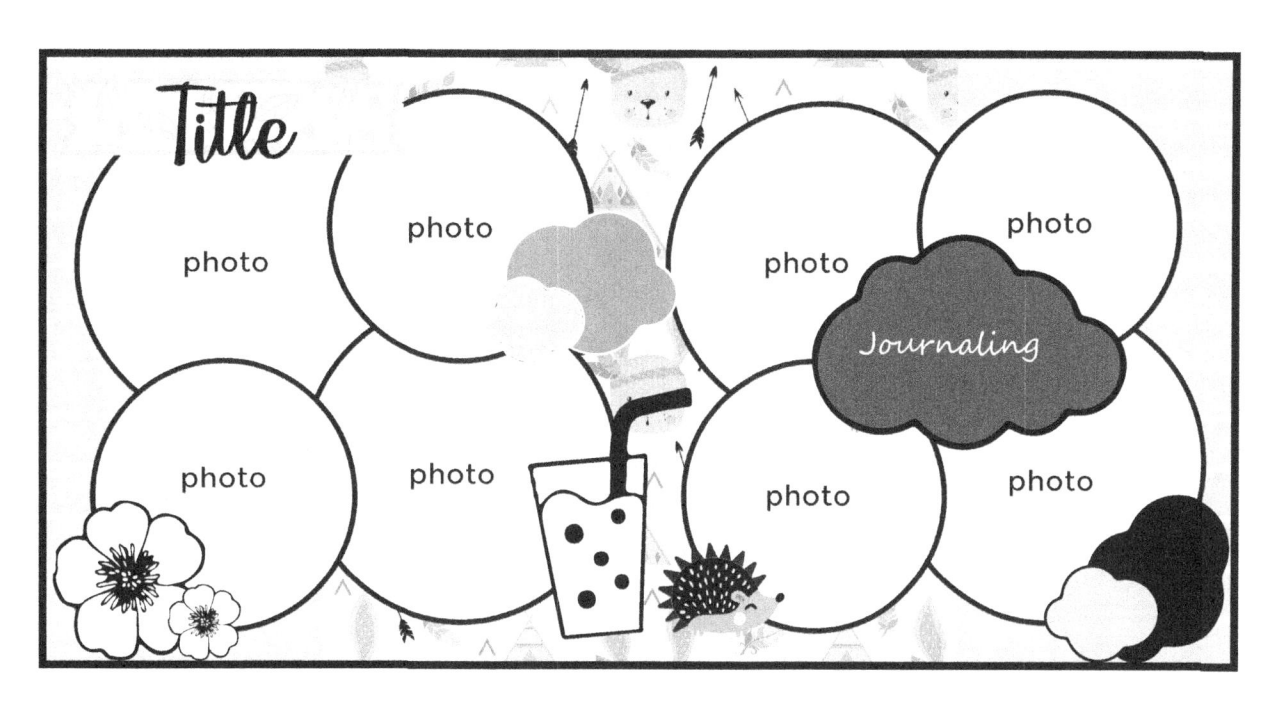

Title

photo photo photo photo

Journaling

photo photo photo photo

It's a Boy

photo

Name:
Born on:
Length:
Weight:
Feet stamp:

photo
photo

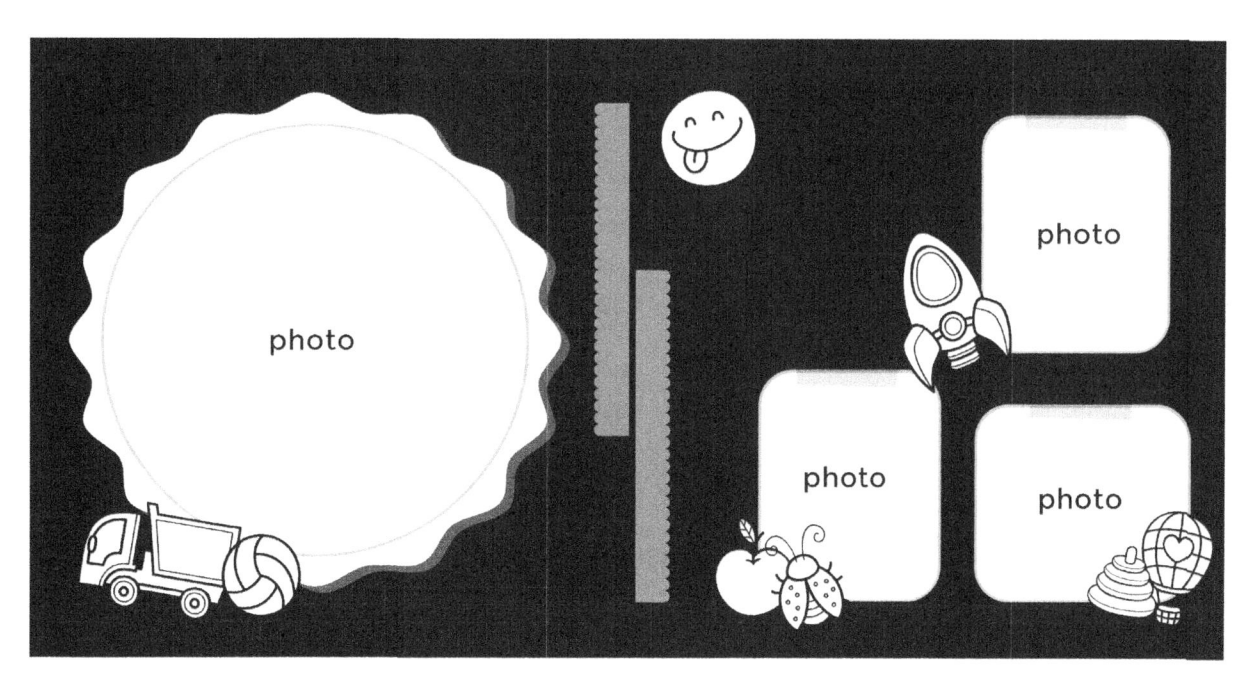

photo

photo
photo
photo

59

photo photo photo photo photo Title

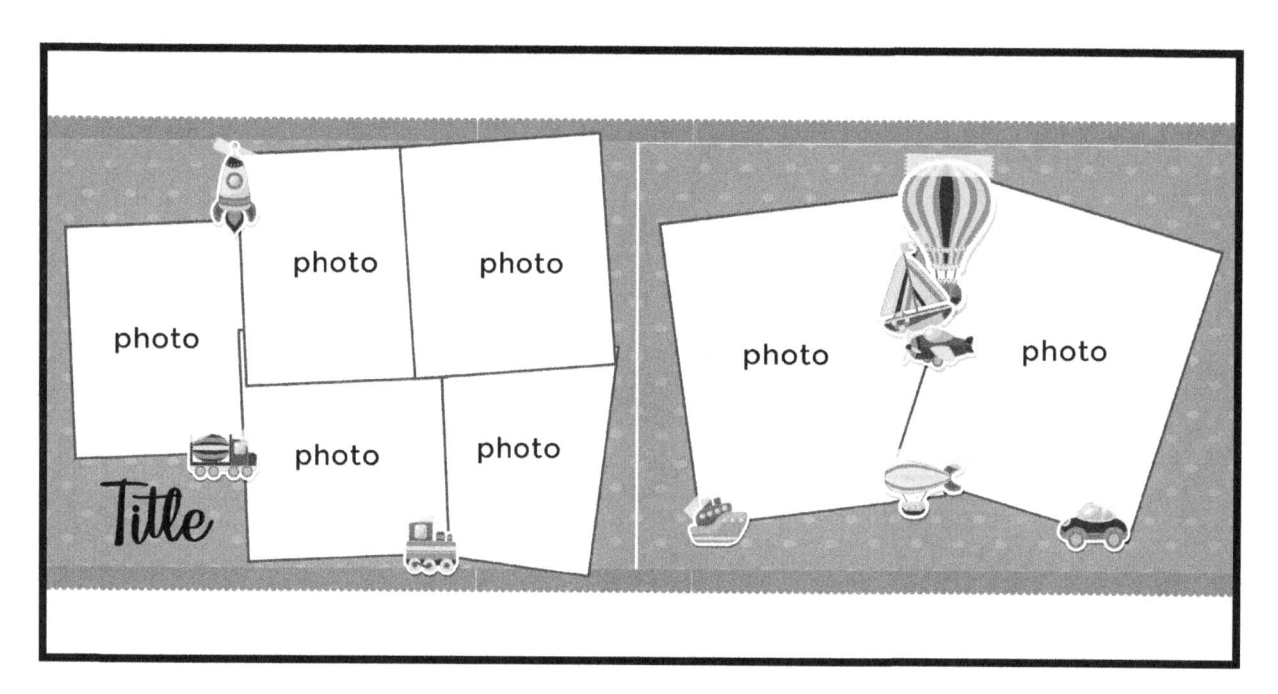

photo photo

Title journalling photo photo photo photo Game photo photo photo

photo Title photo photo photo journalling

60

61

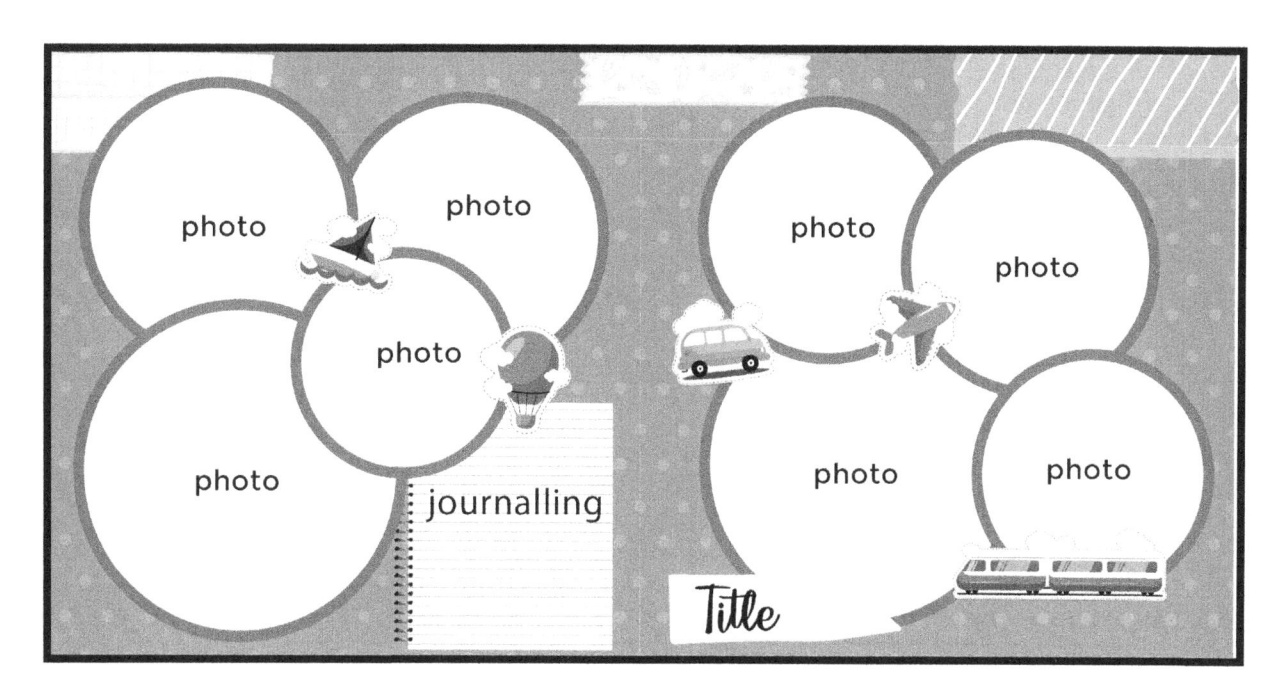

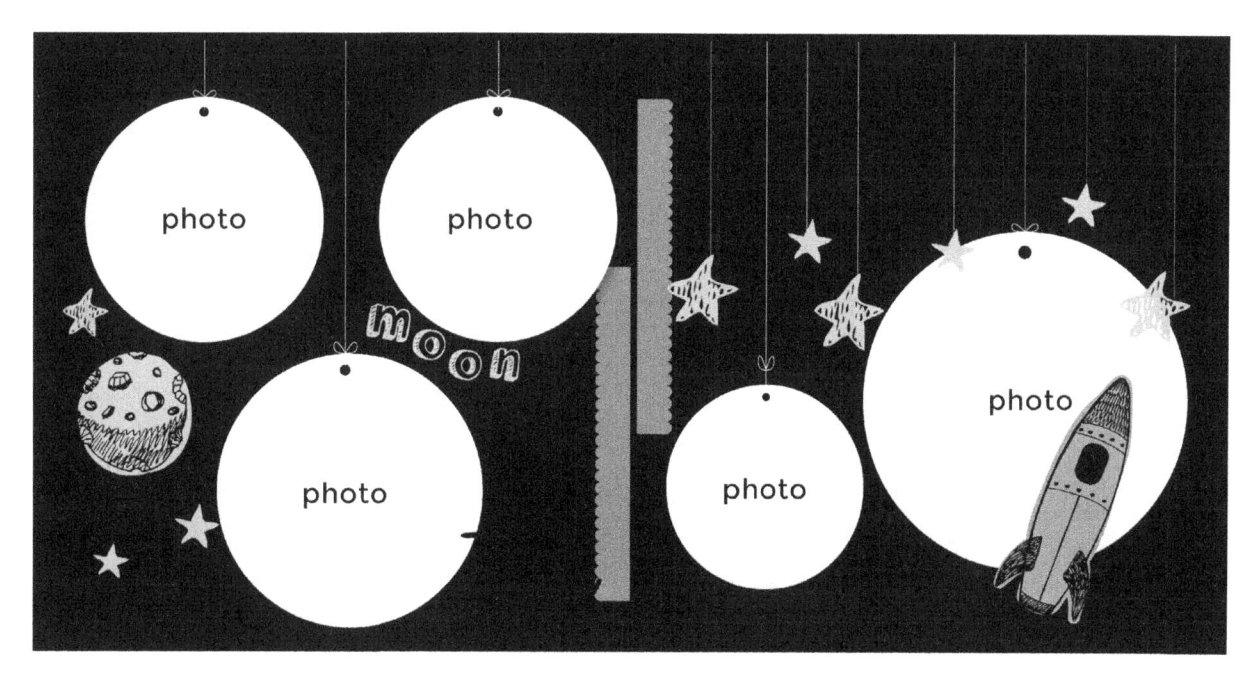

62

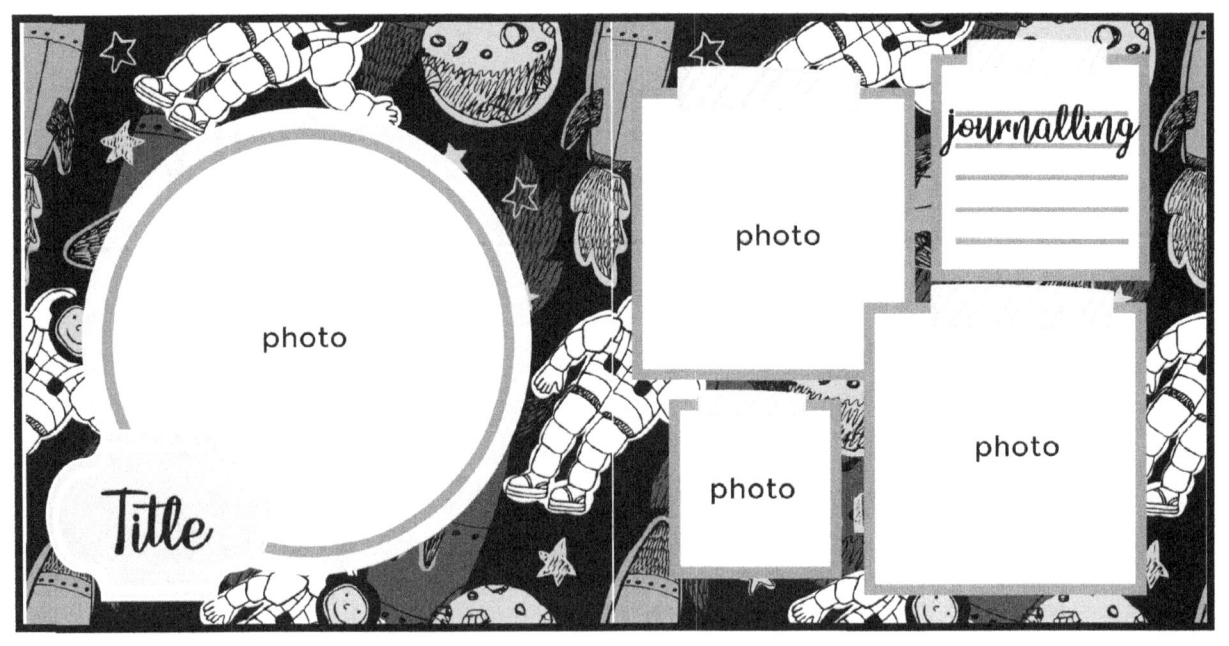

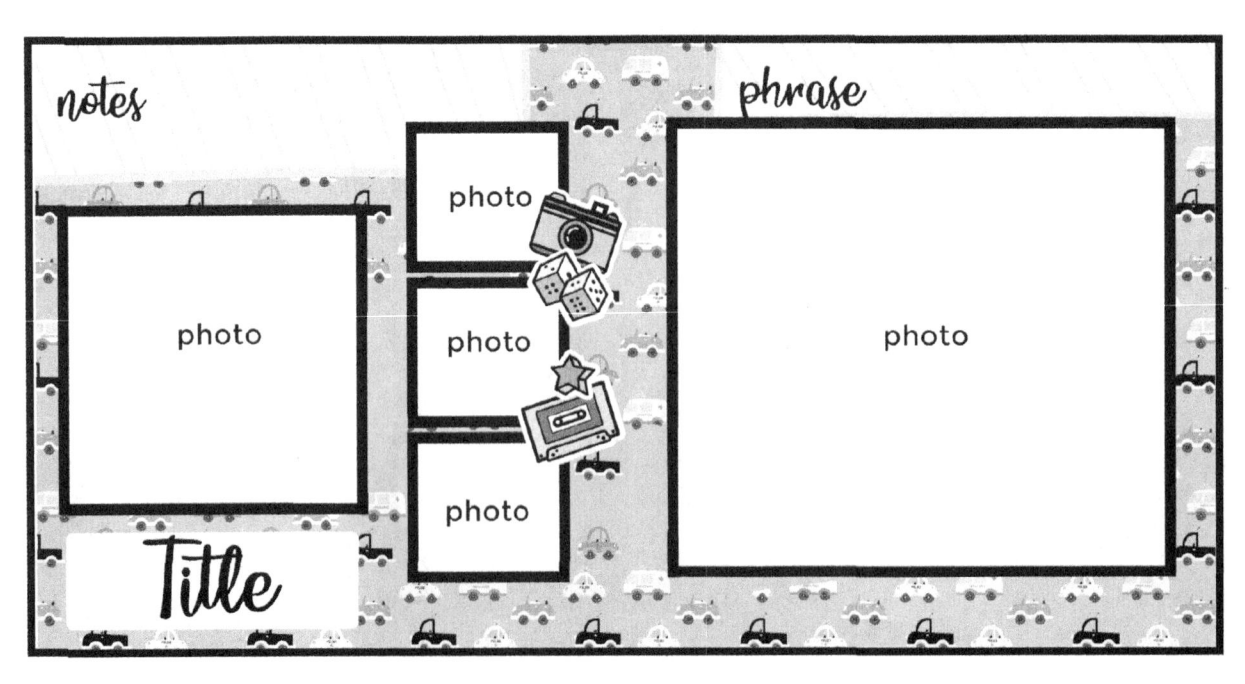

63

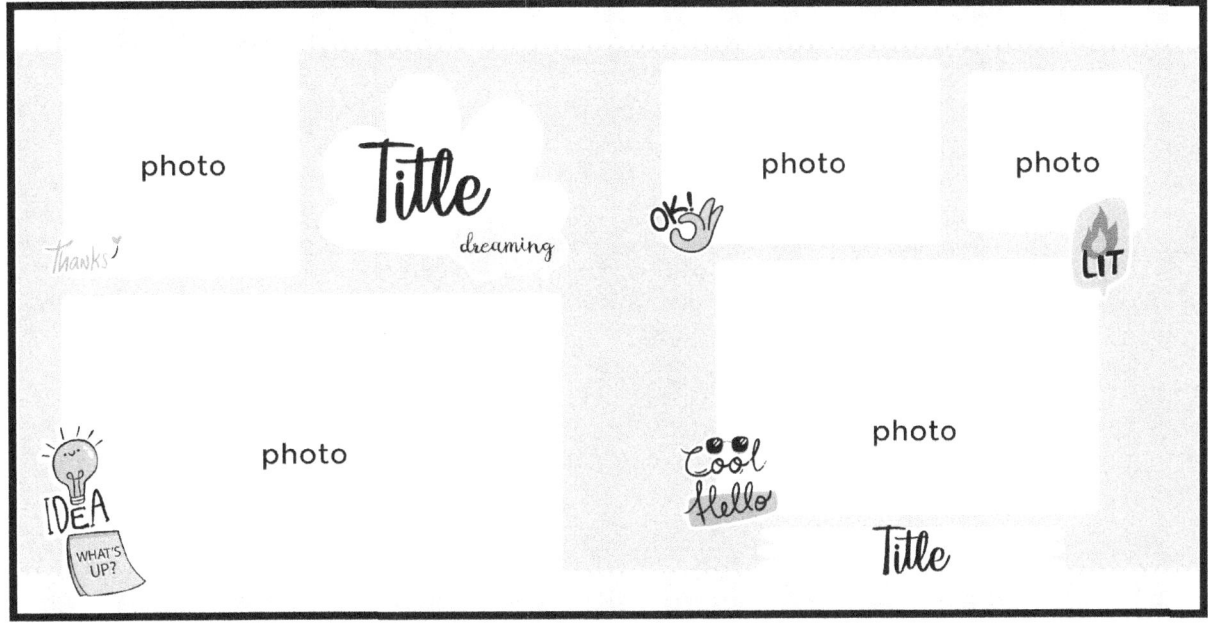

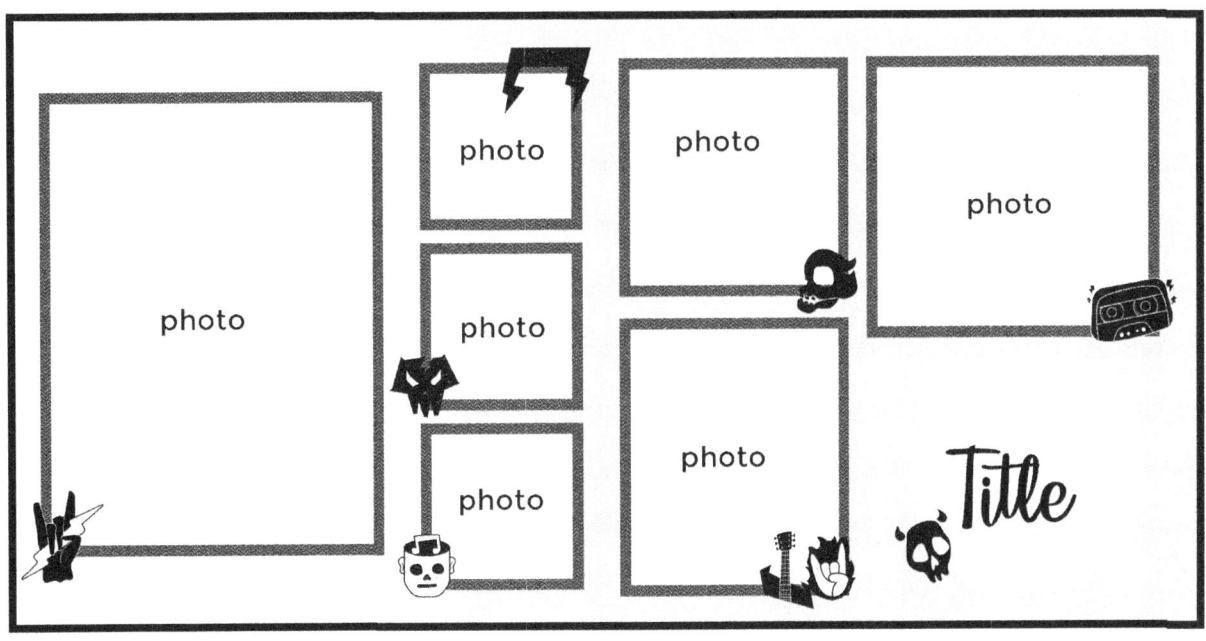

photo

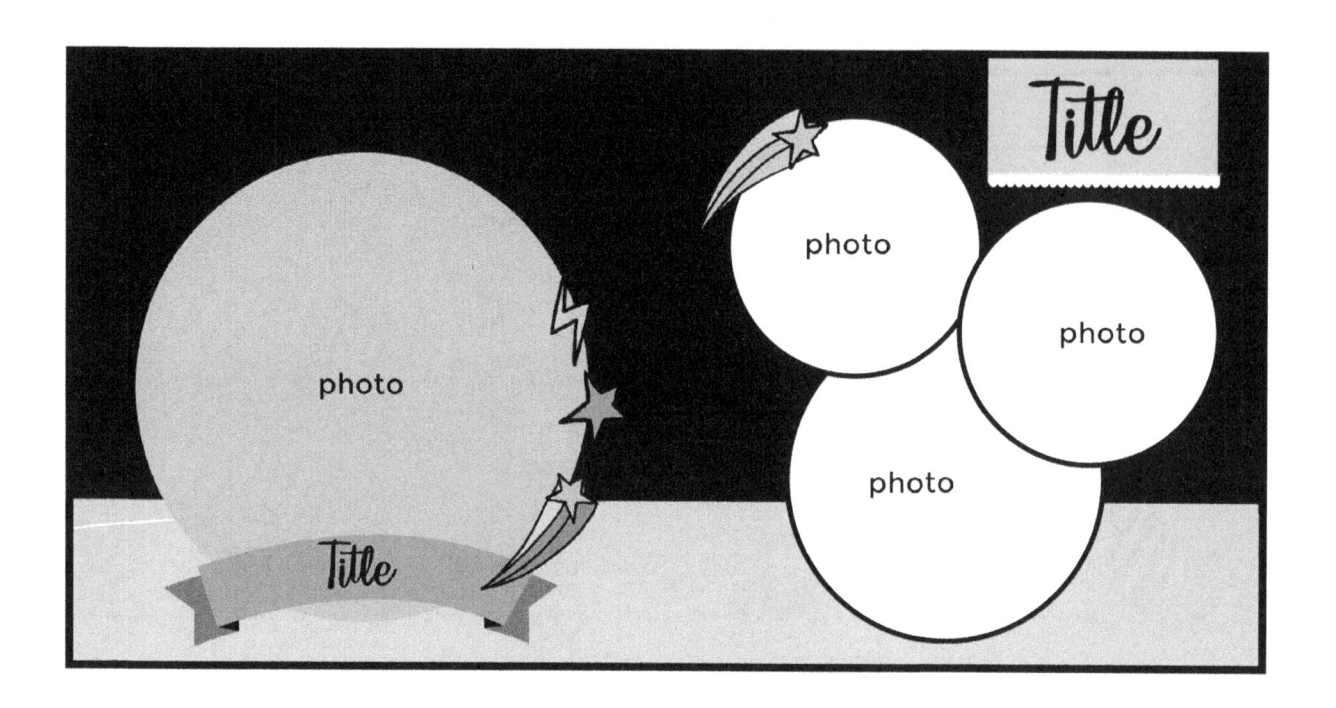

Title

photo

photo

photo

Title

Christmas

Title Here

Merry Christmas

HOLLY JOLLY

65

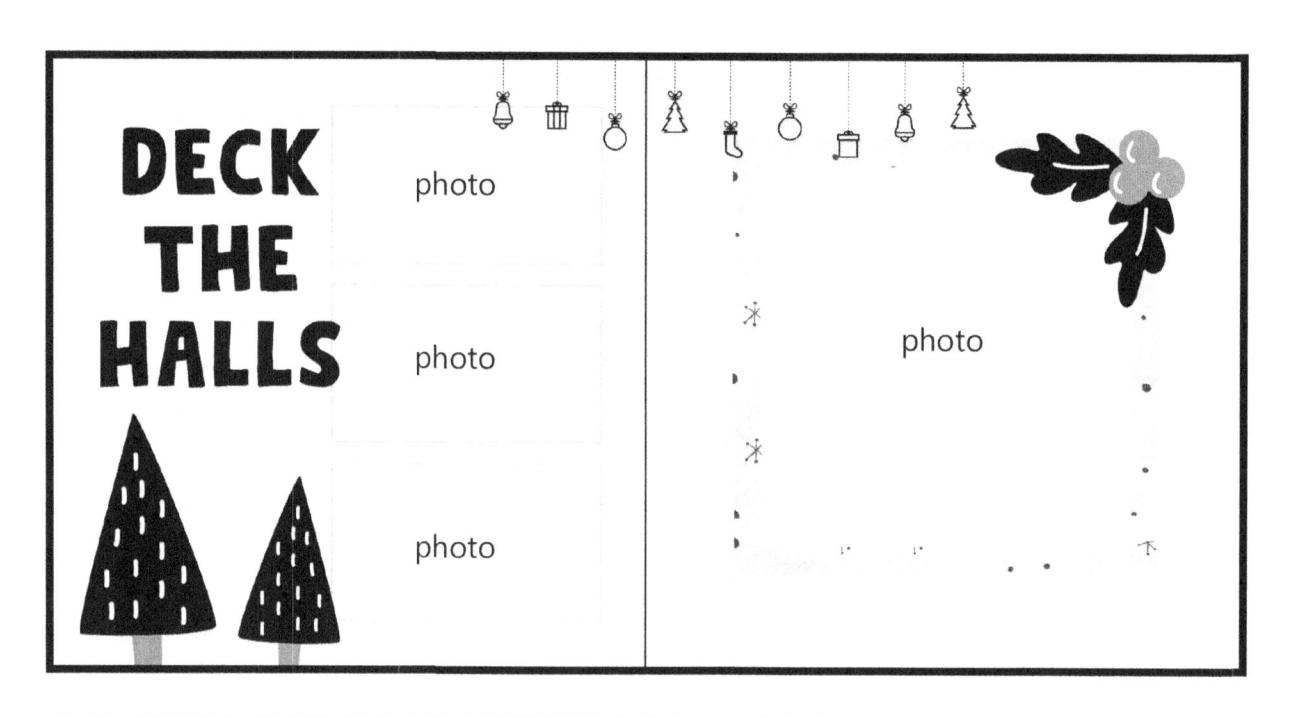

DECK THE HALLS

photo

photo

photo

photo

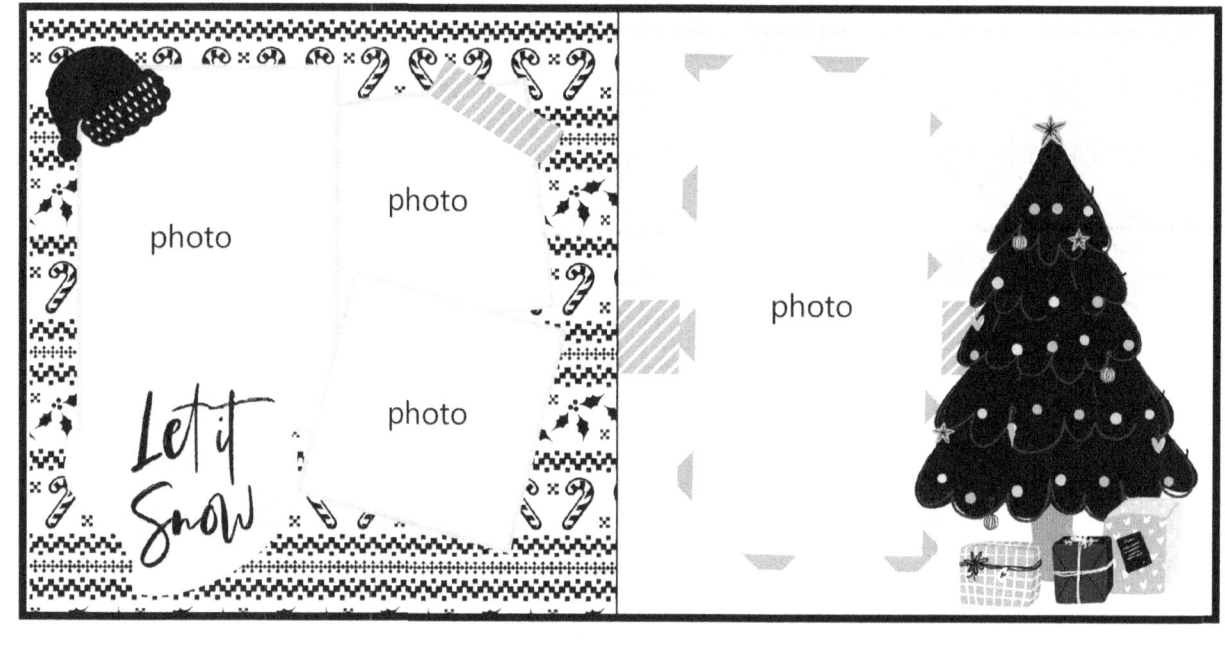

photo

photo

photo

Let it Snow

photo

photo

photo

photo

Title Here

66

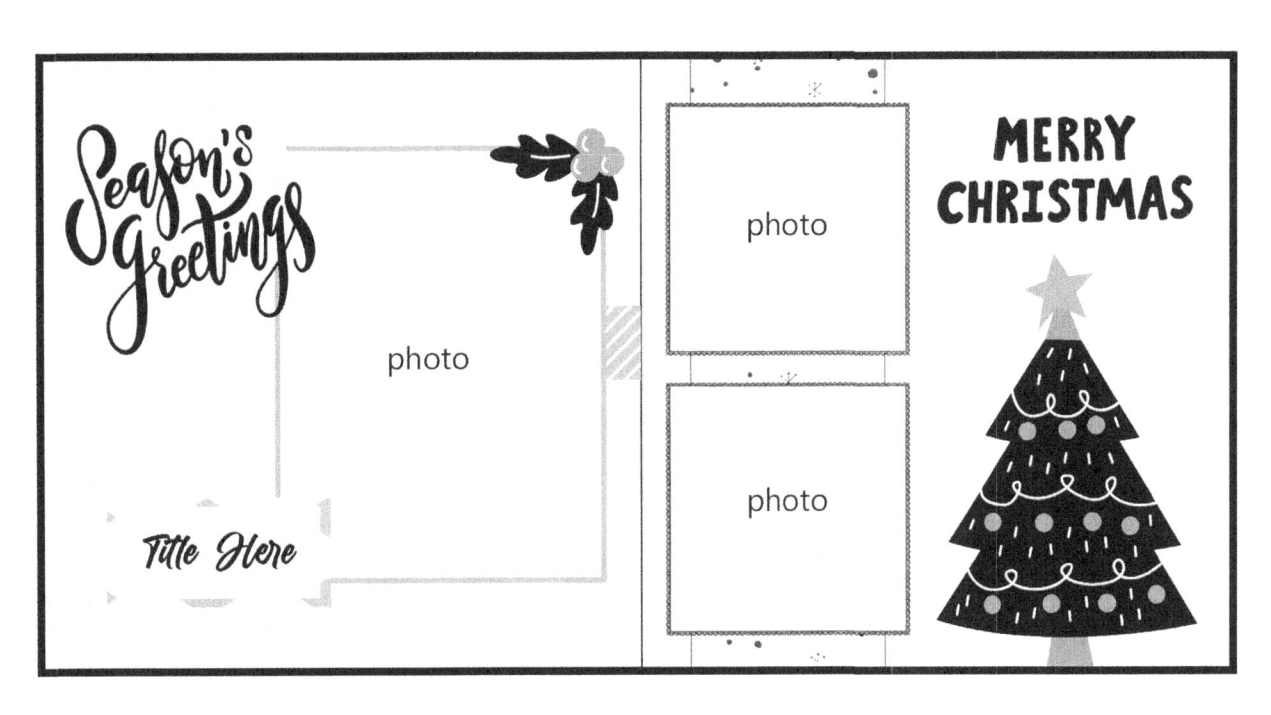

Season's Greetings

Title Here

photo

MERRY CHRISTMAS

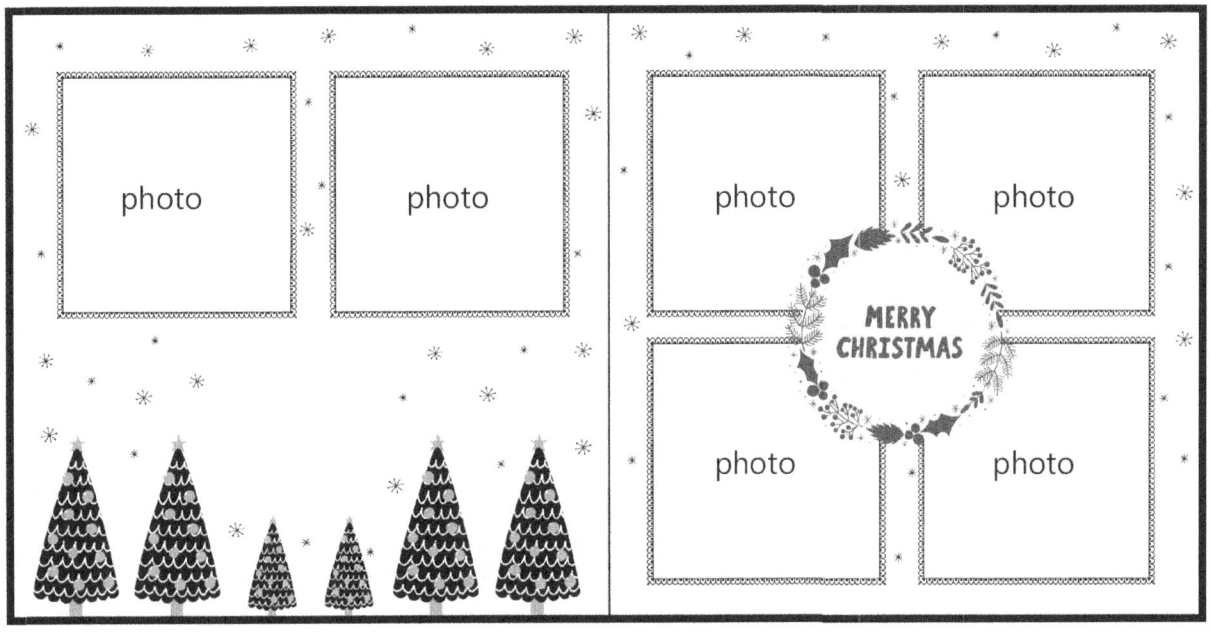

photo

photo

photo

photo

MERRY CHRISTMAS

photo

photo

photo

photo

DECEMBER 25th

photo

photo

MERRY CHRISTMAS

photo

photo

MERRY X-MAS

photo

photo

photo

HO HO HO

photo

photo

photo

photo

photo

Title here

HOLLY JOLLY

photo

Title here

photo

Journaling

photo

68

Season's Greetings

photo

photo photo photo

photo

MERRY CHRISTMAS

photo photo photo

photo photo

photo

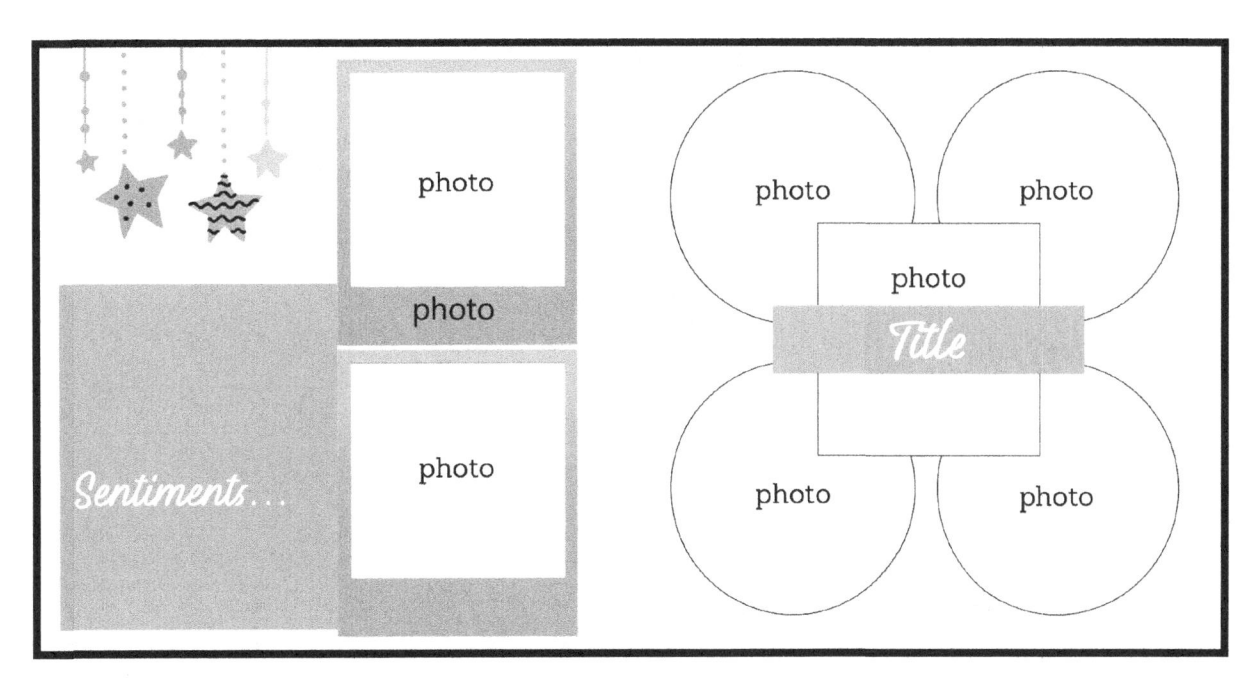

photo

photo

Sentiments...

photo photo

photo

Title

photo photo

69

CHRISTMAS

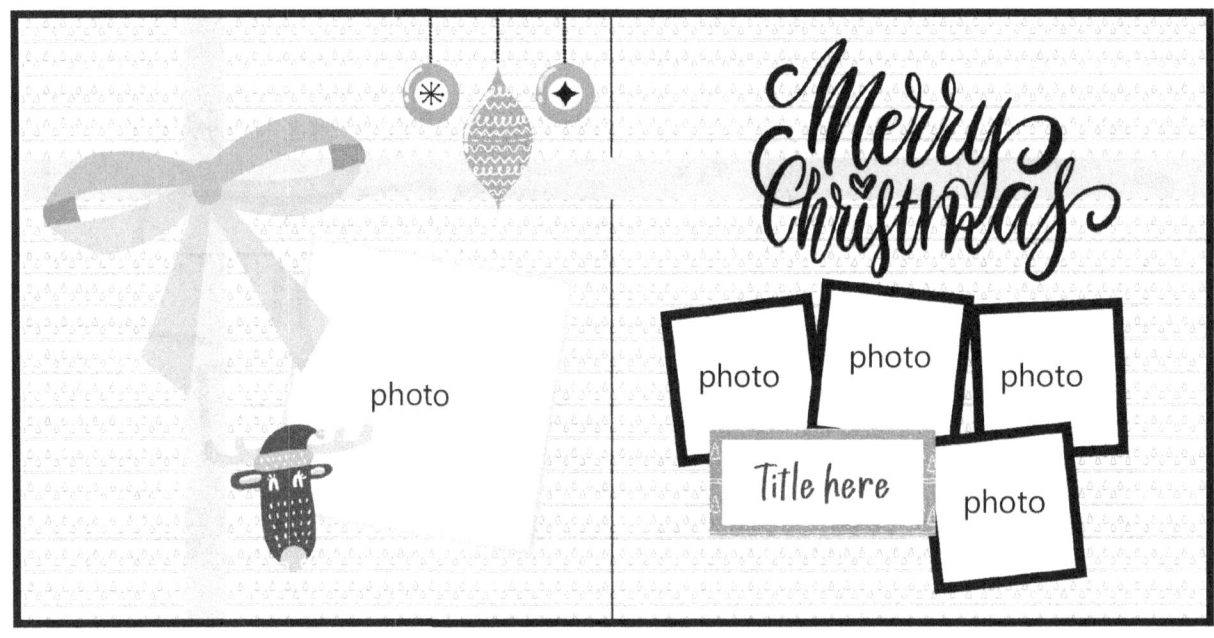

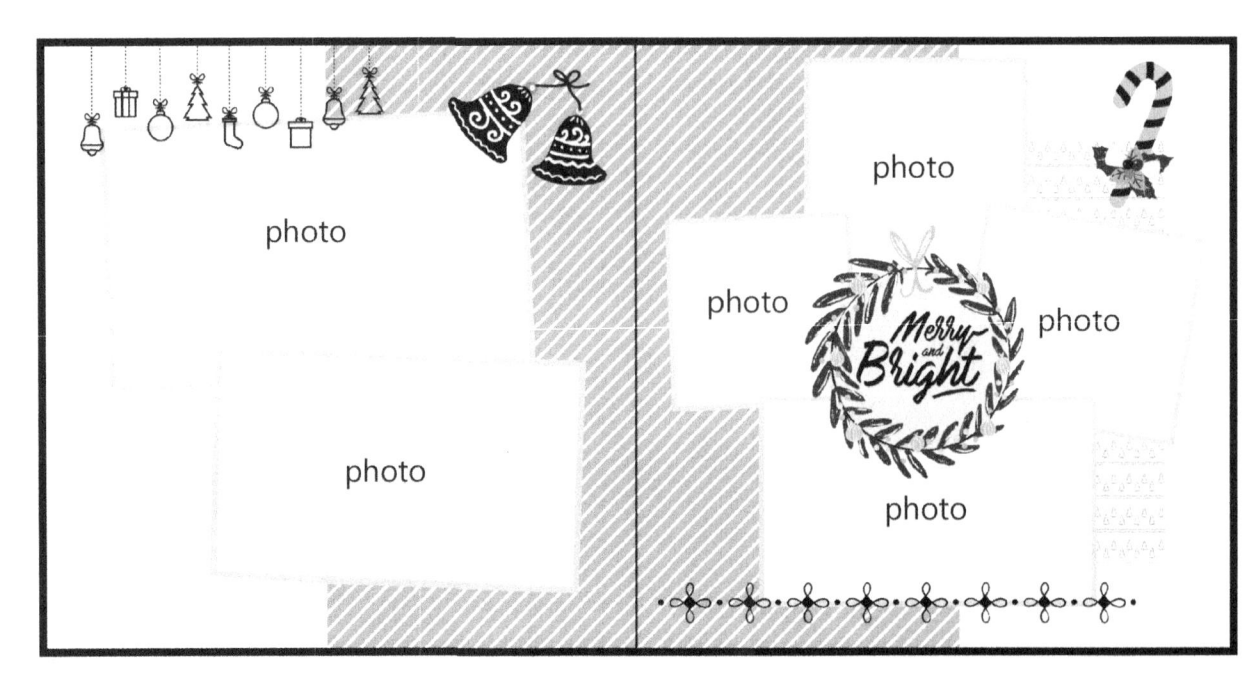

photo

Title

photo

photo

photo

Merry Christmas

photo photo photo

Title here

photo

photo

photo

photo

photo

photo

Merry and Bright

photo

photo

HO HO HO

photo
photo

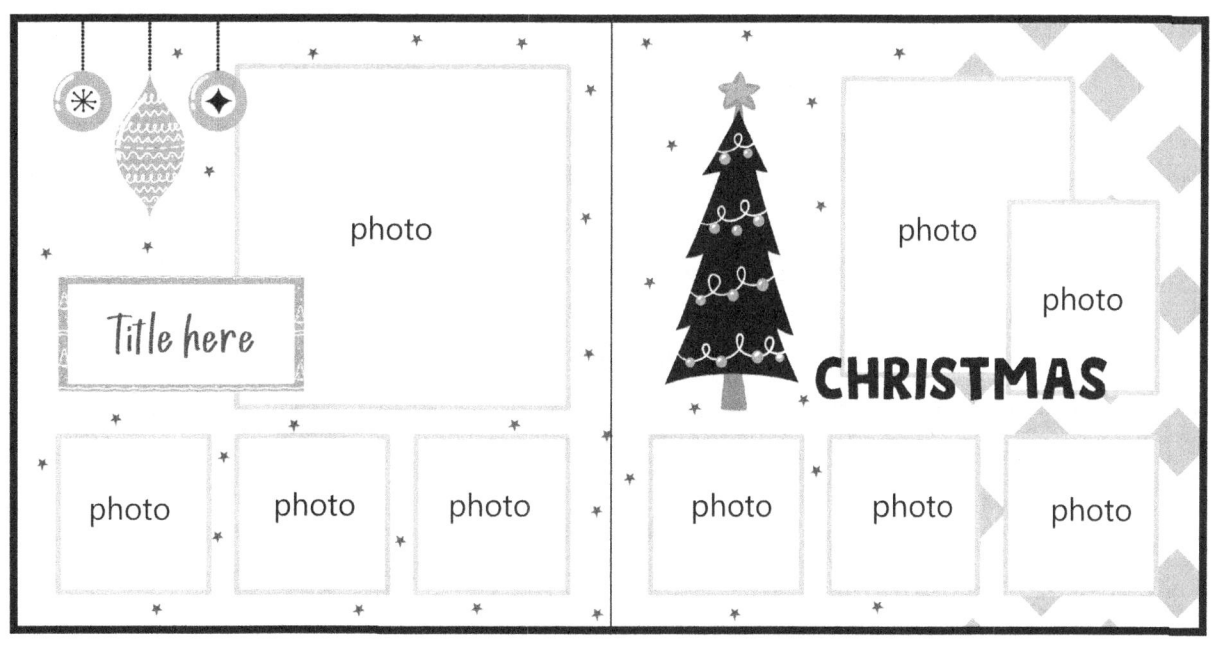

photo

Title here
photo
photo photo photo

CHRISTMAS
photo
photo
photo photo photo

photo

Merry Christmas
photo
photo

71

Title here

photo photo photo

photo
photo
photo

photo
photo
photo

let it snow

photo
photo photo

photo

photo photo

MERRY CHRISTMAS

photo photo

photo photo
photo photo

MERRY CHRISTMAS

photo photo
photo photo

Title here

photo
photo
photo

photo

MERRY CHRISTMAS

73

74

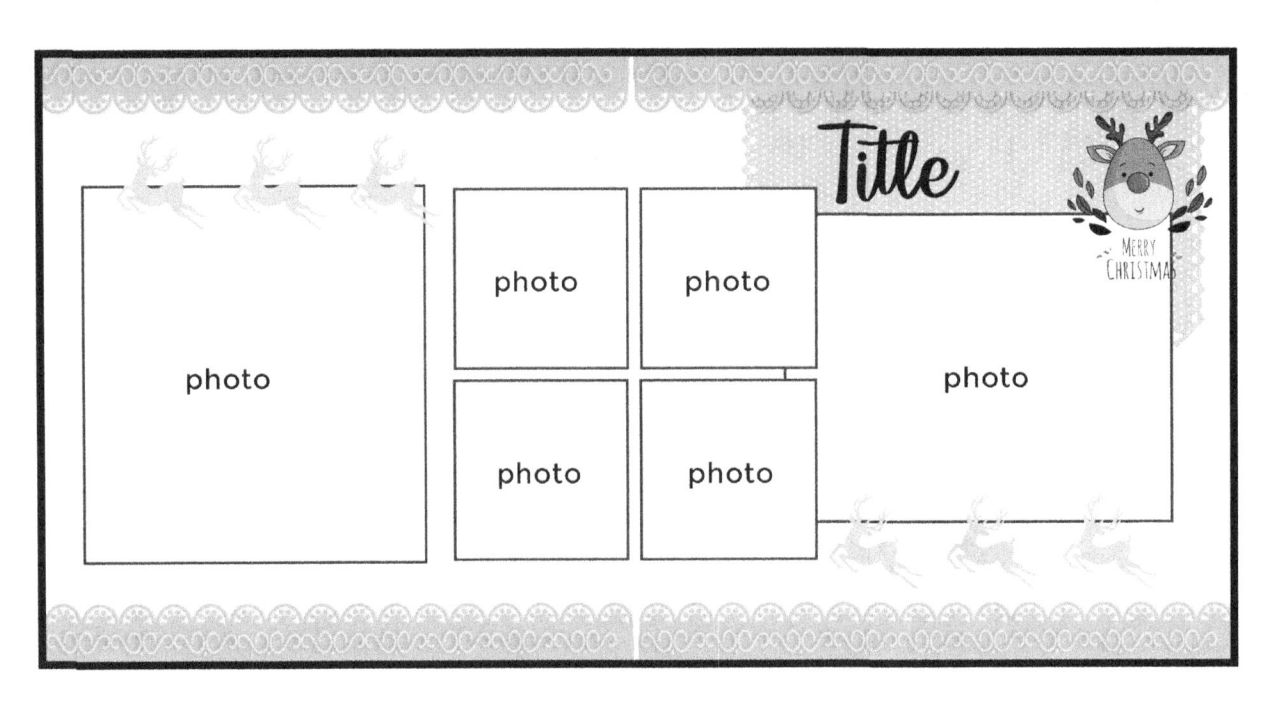

photo

photo photo

Title

Title

Merry Christmas

photo

Wishlist:

photo photo

75

Easter

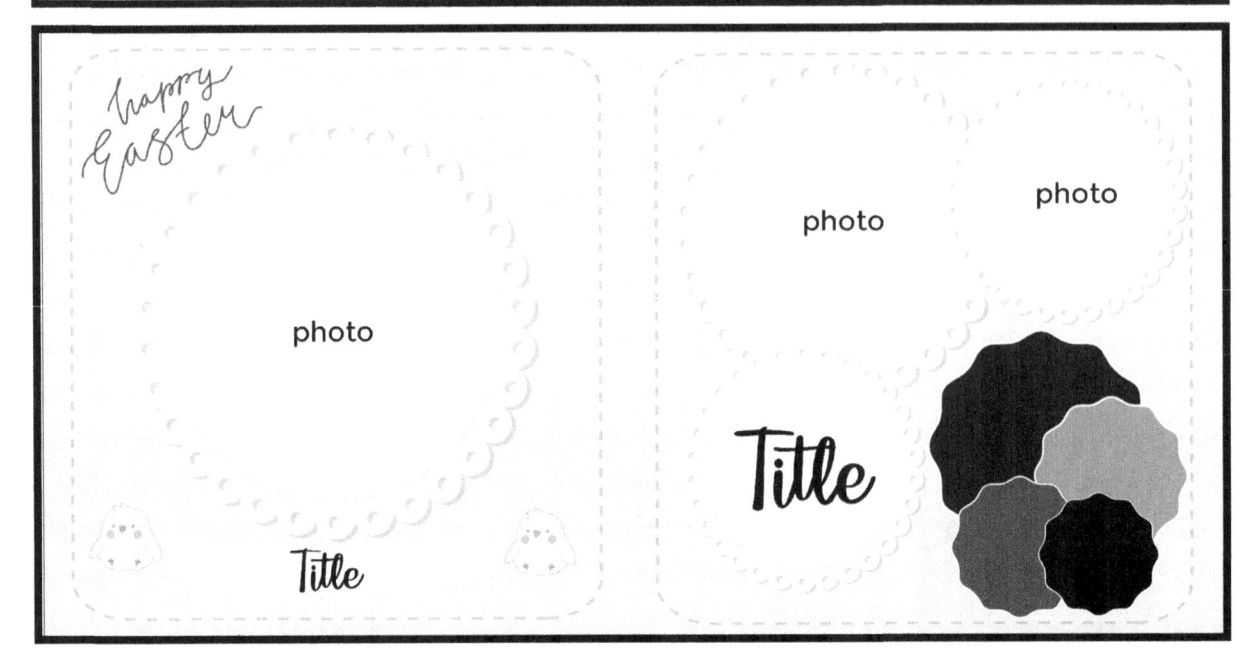

77

78

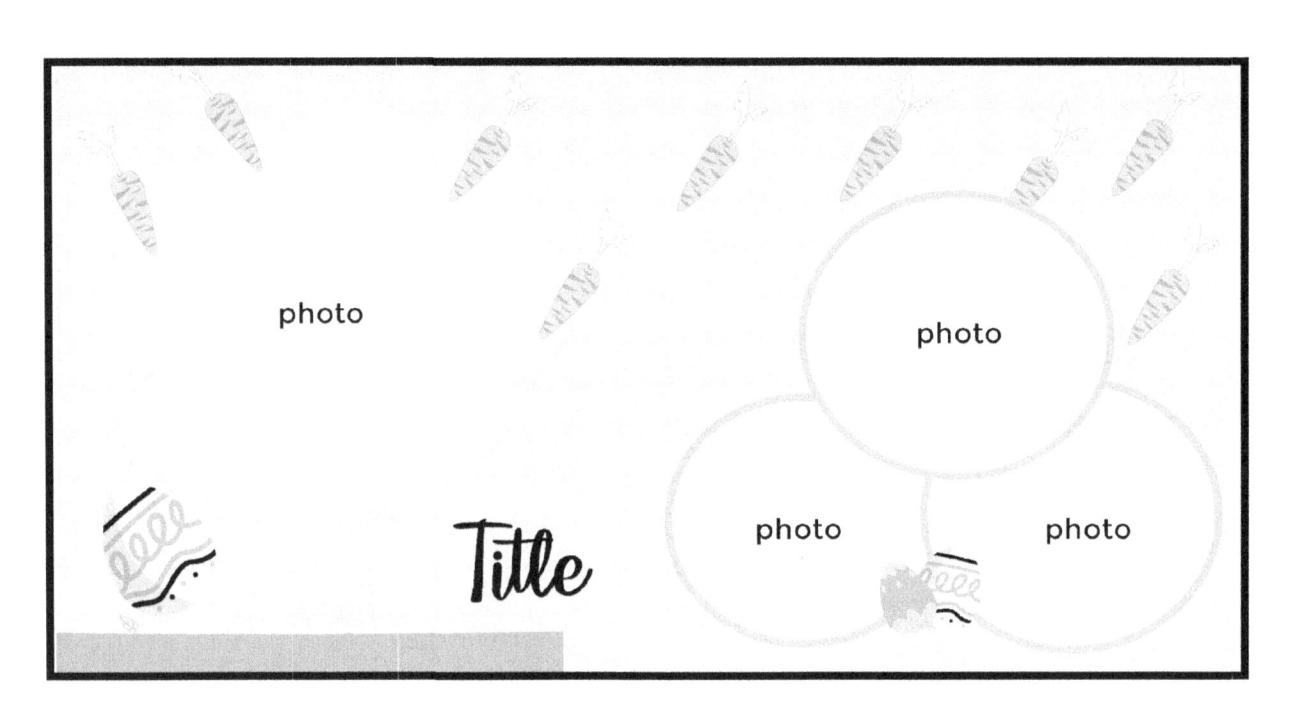

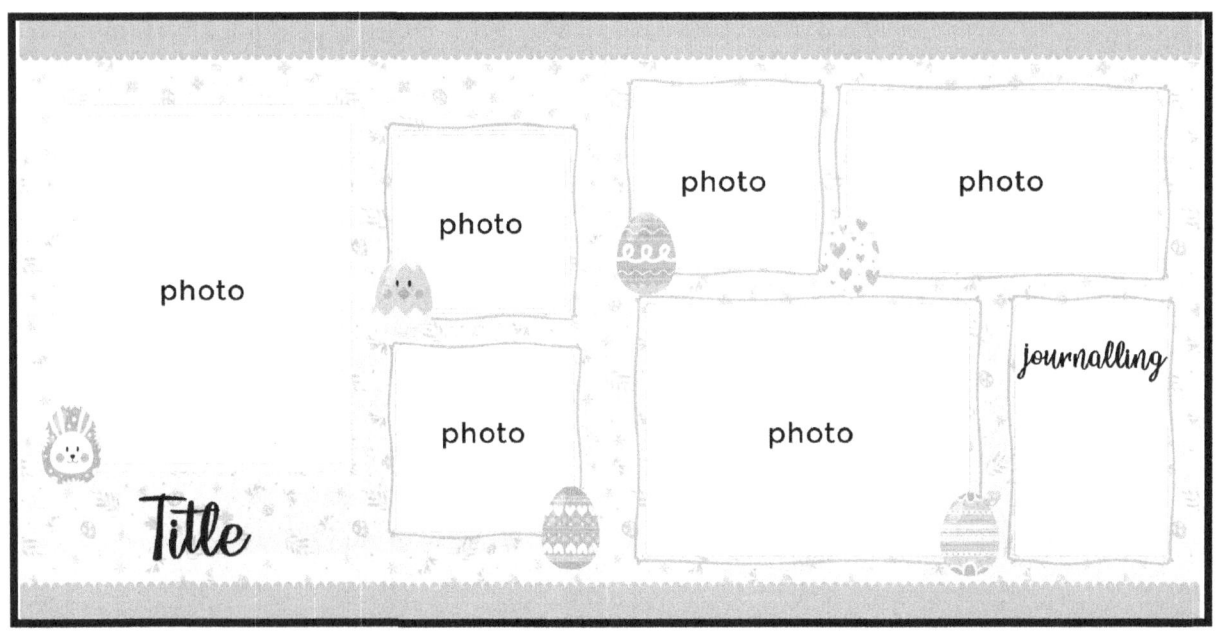

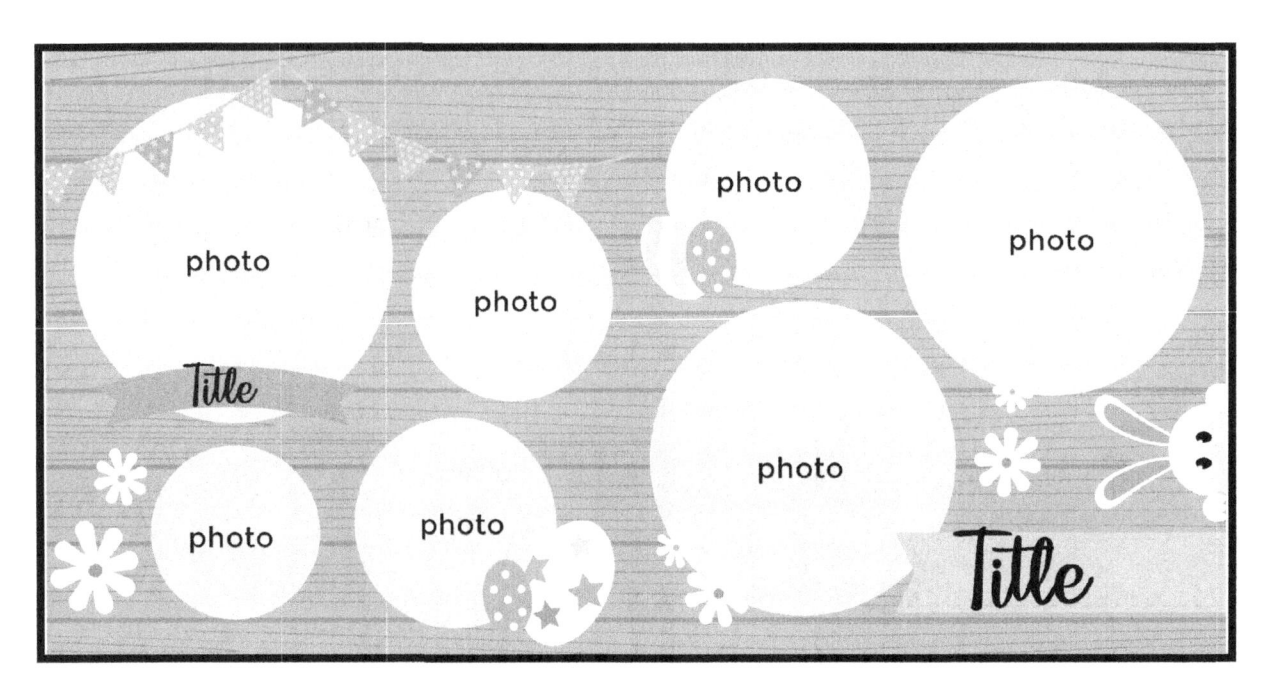

79

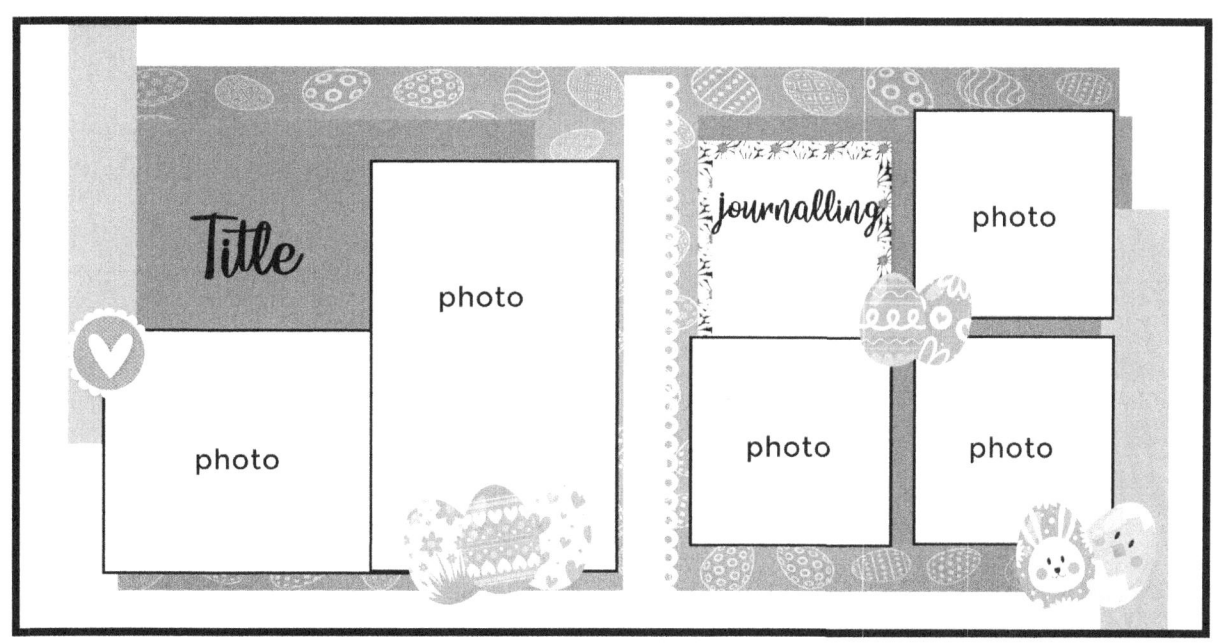

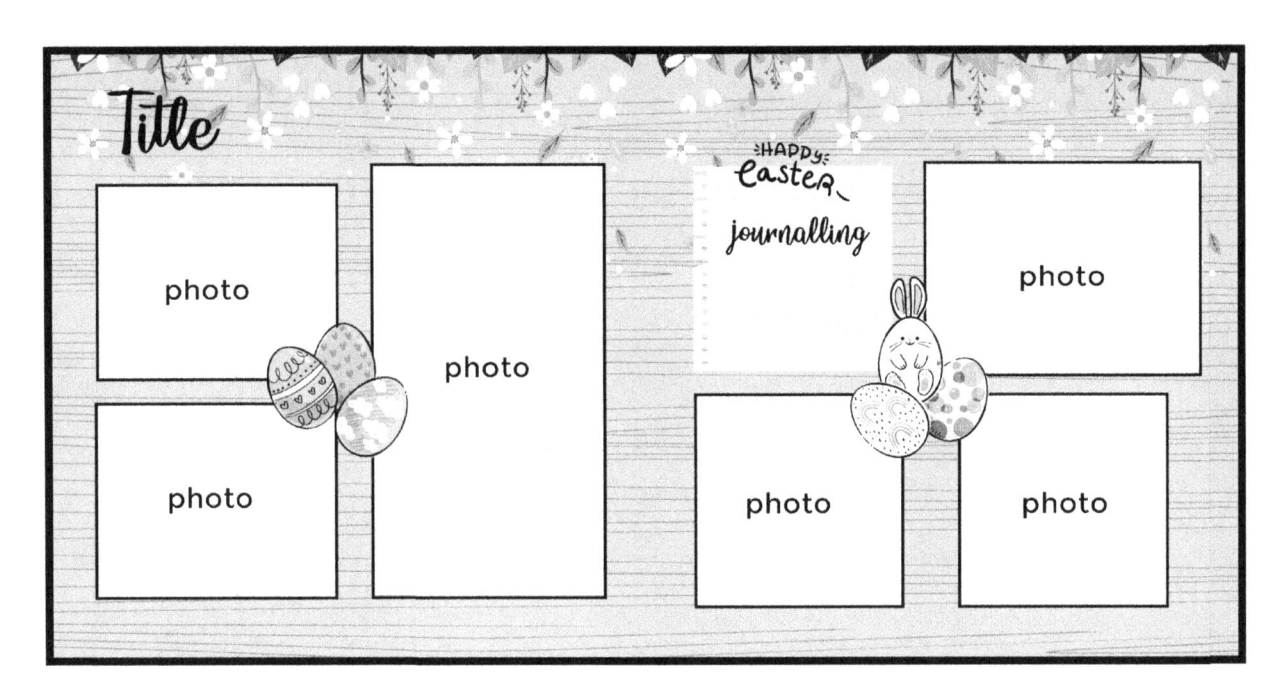

Title

Happy Easter journalling

photo · photo · photo · photo · photo · photo

---

photo · photo · photo · photo

journalling

HAPPY EASTER

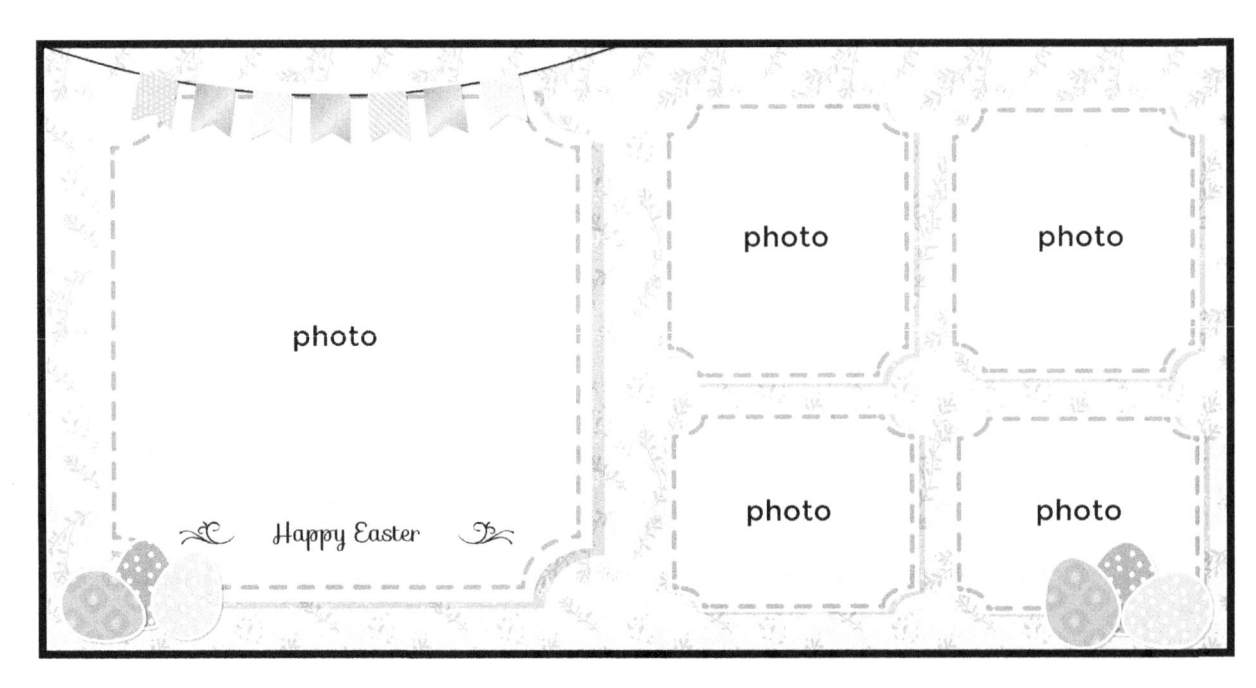

---

photo

Happy Easter

photo · photo · photo · photo

80

Title

photo
photo
photo
photo

photo
photo
photo
photo
photo
photo
Title
Title
Title

Title

photo
photo
photo
photo
photo
photo
photo

81

happy easter

I found Easter Eggs

He has risen!

Easter Sunday

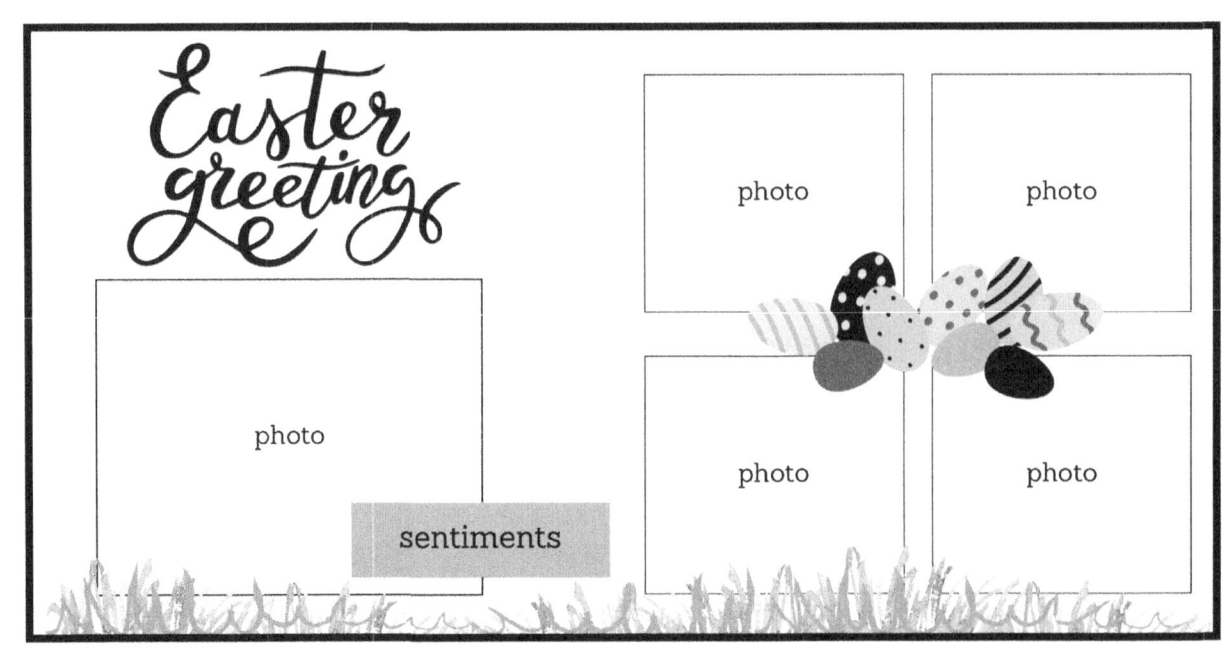

Easter greeting

sentiments

83

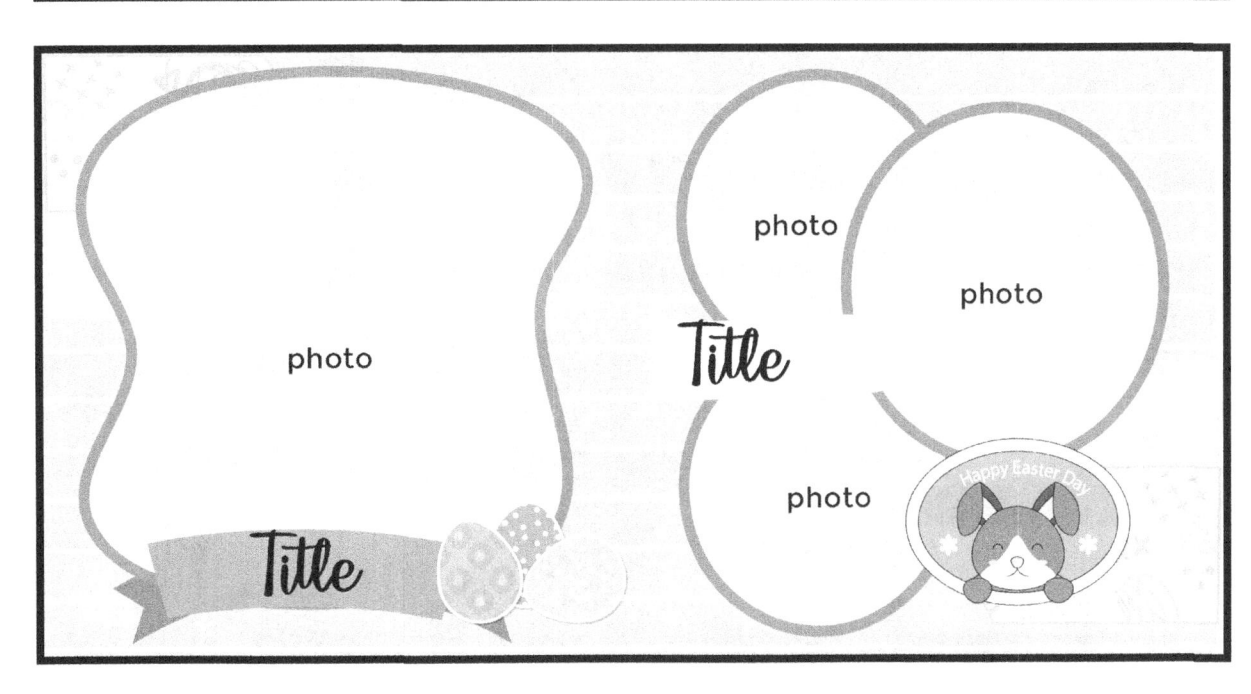

Title

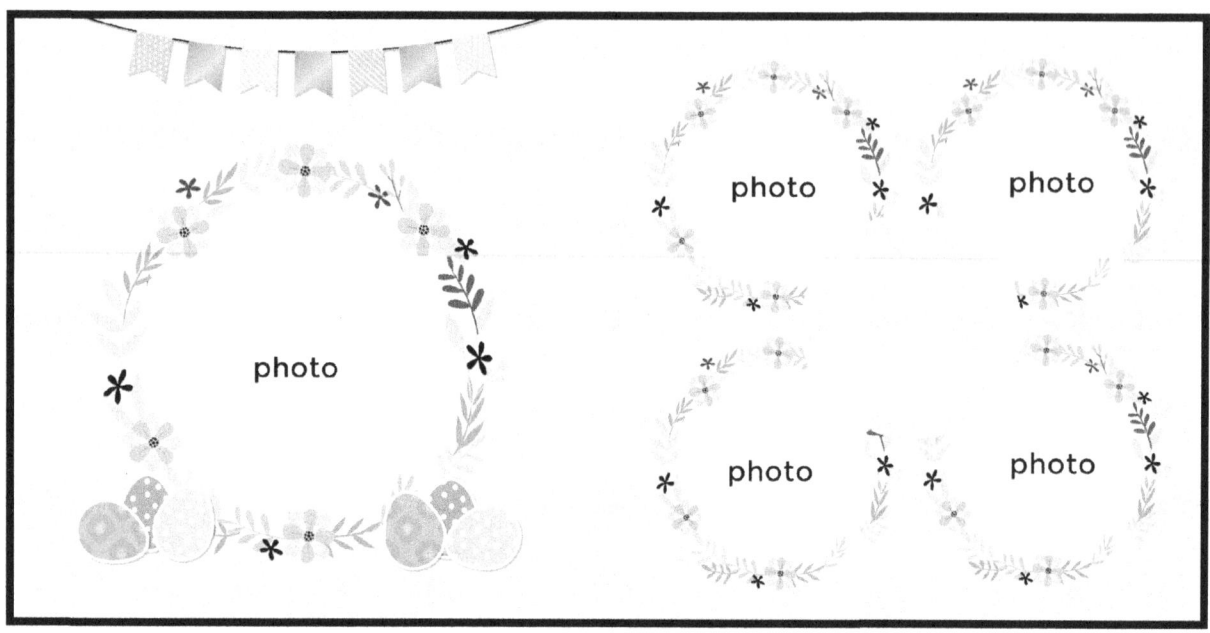

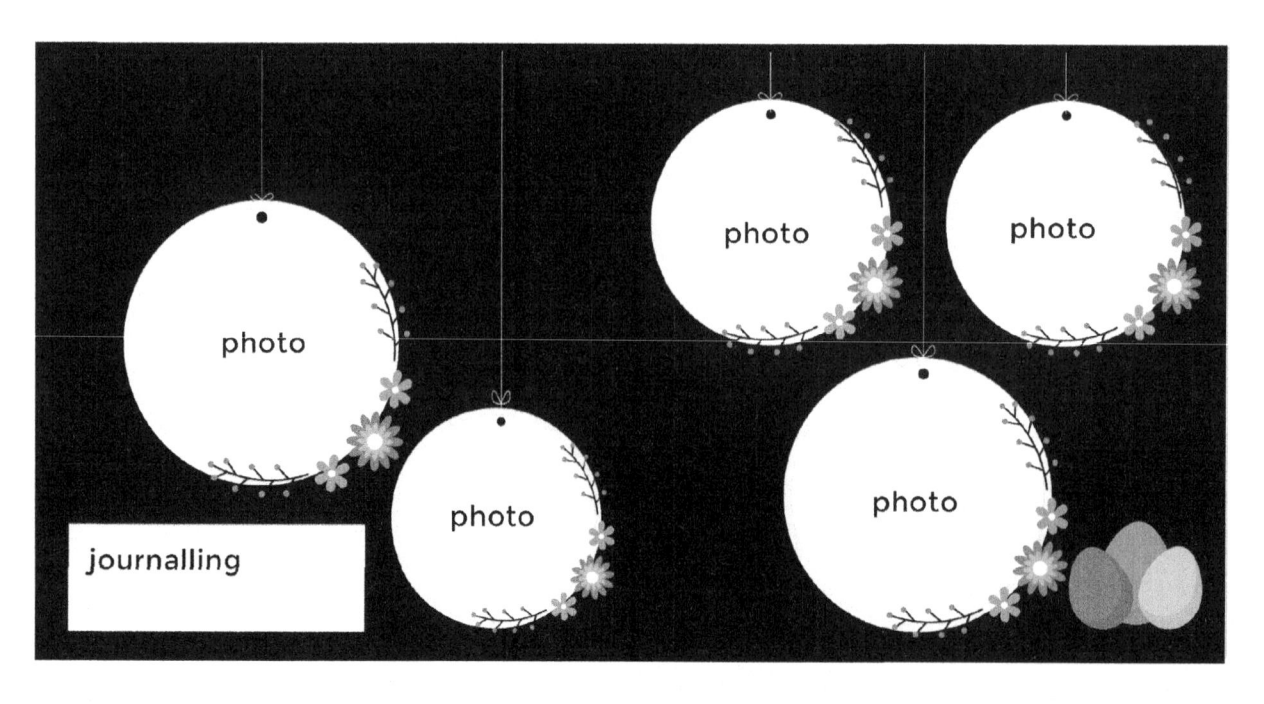

photo

journalling

85

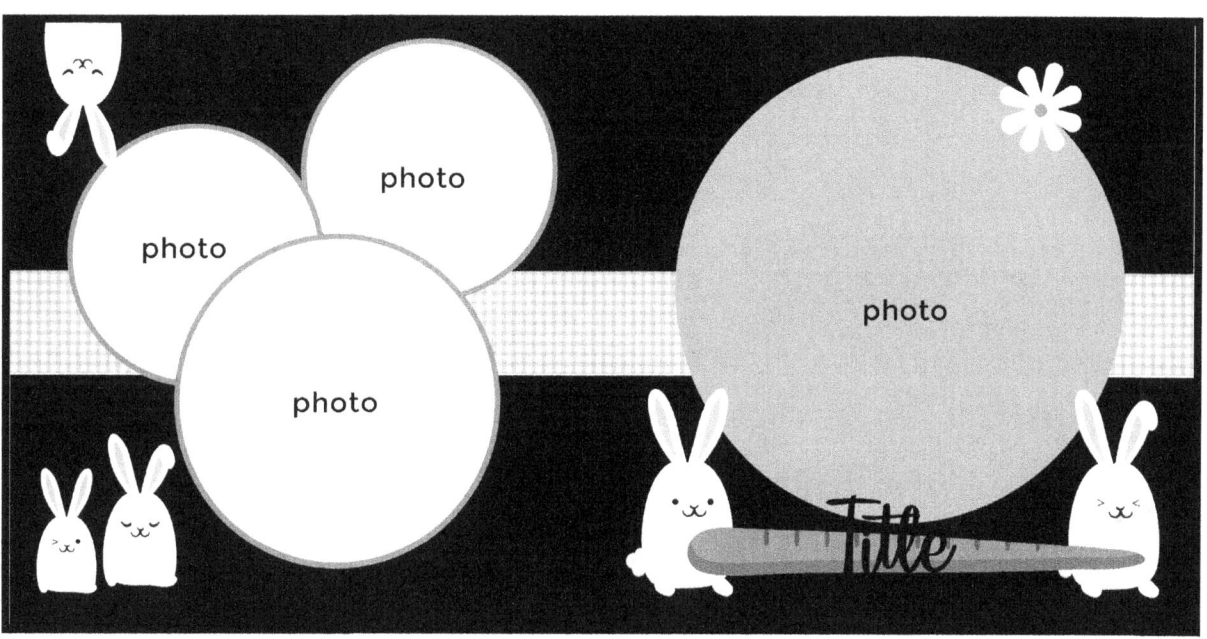

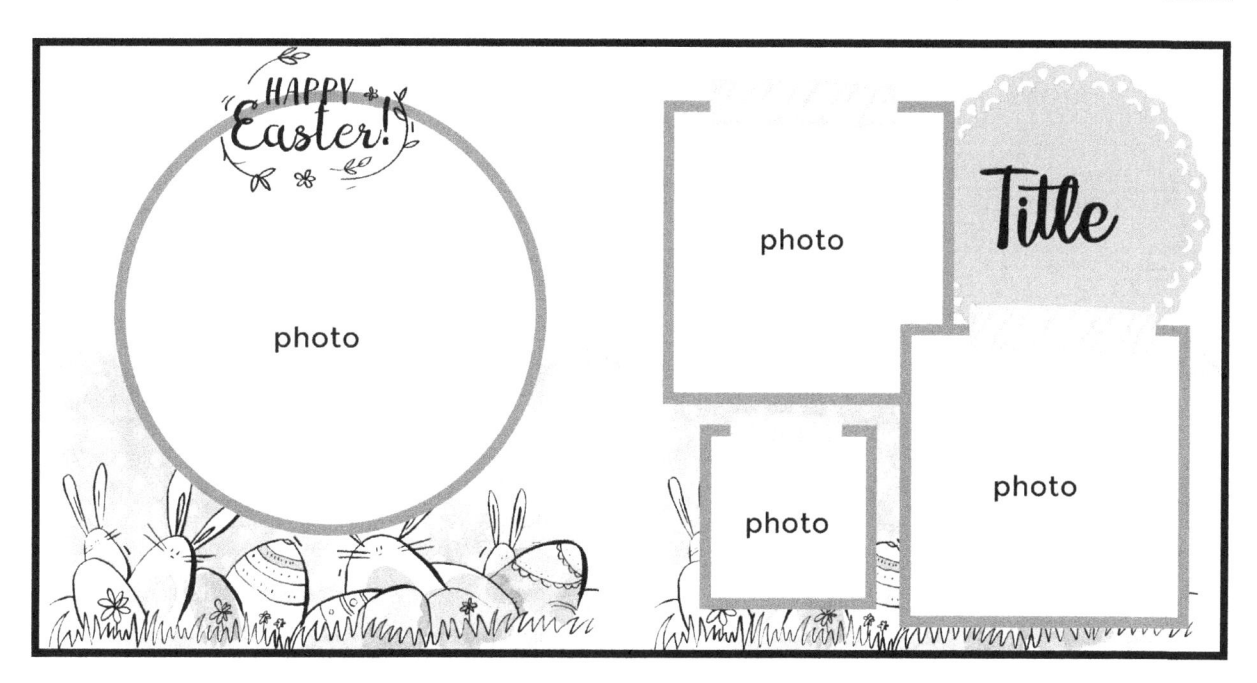

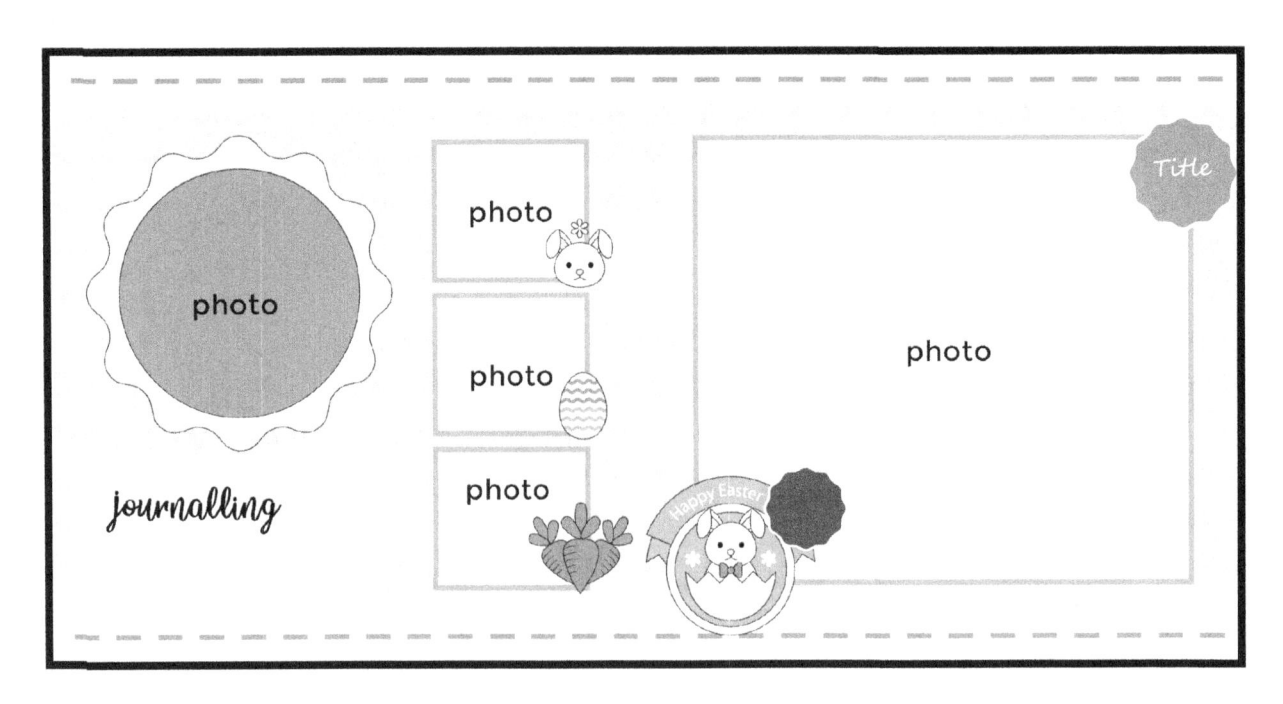

Layout 1

- photo (circle) — journalling
- photo
- photo
- photo
- photo
- Title

Layout 2

- photo
- HAPPY EASTER / Happy
- Title
- Title
- photo
- photo
- photo

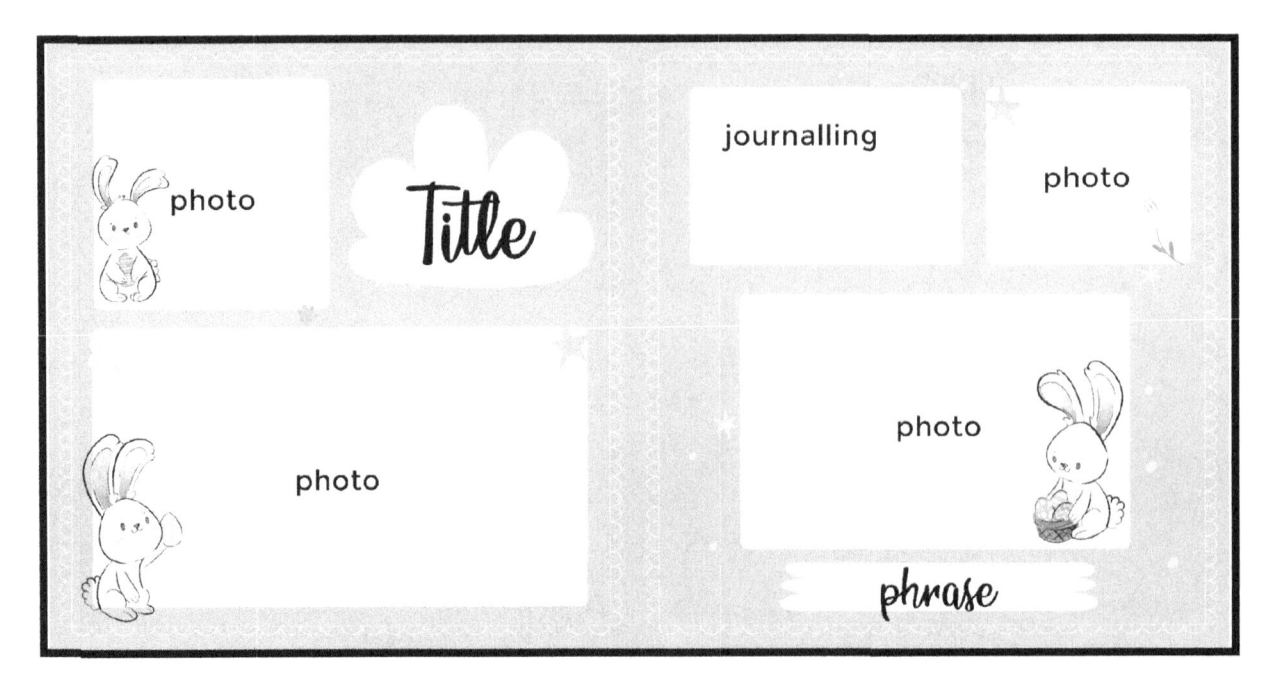

Layout 3

- photo
- Title
- journalling
- photo
- photo
- photo
- phrase

87

Family

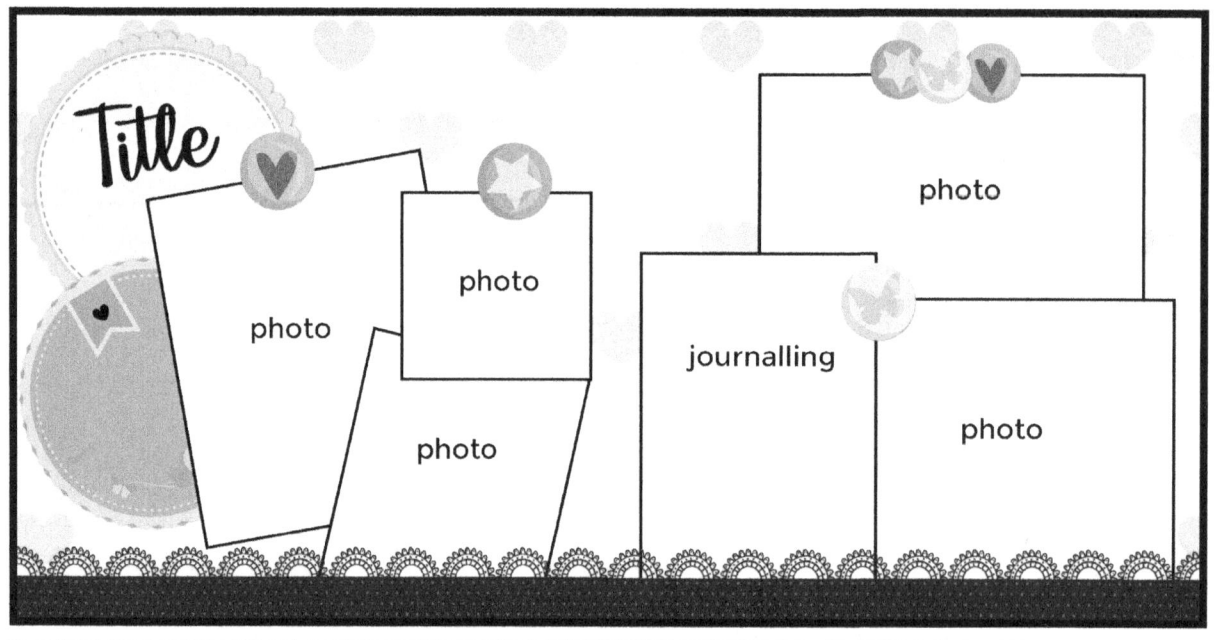

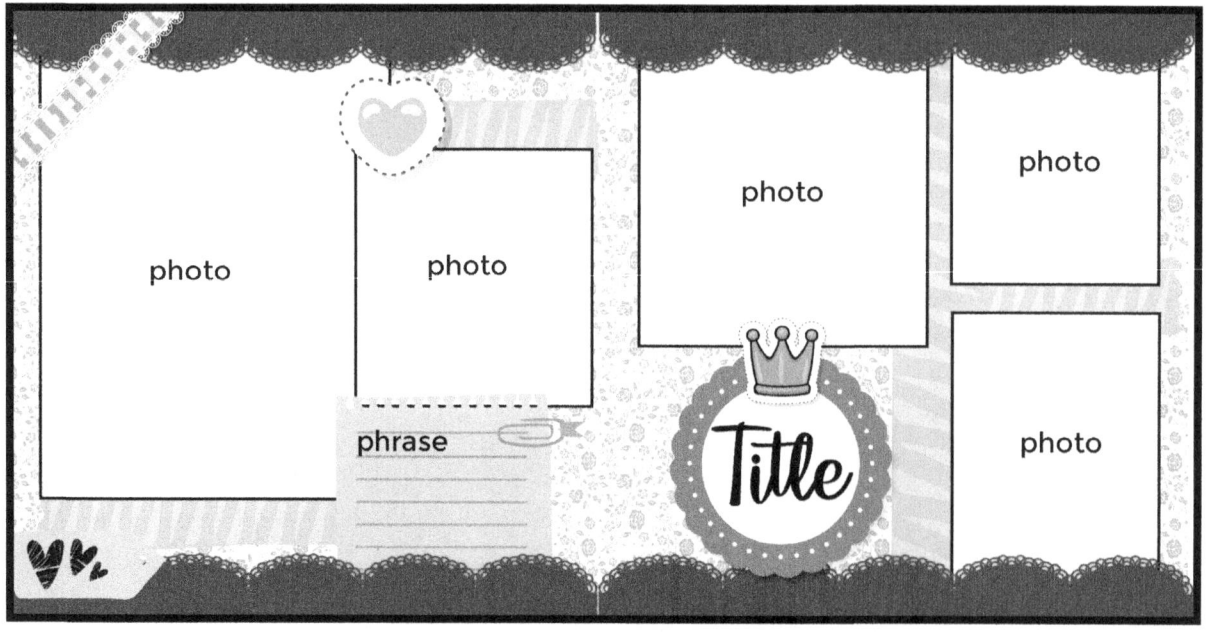

89

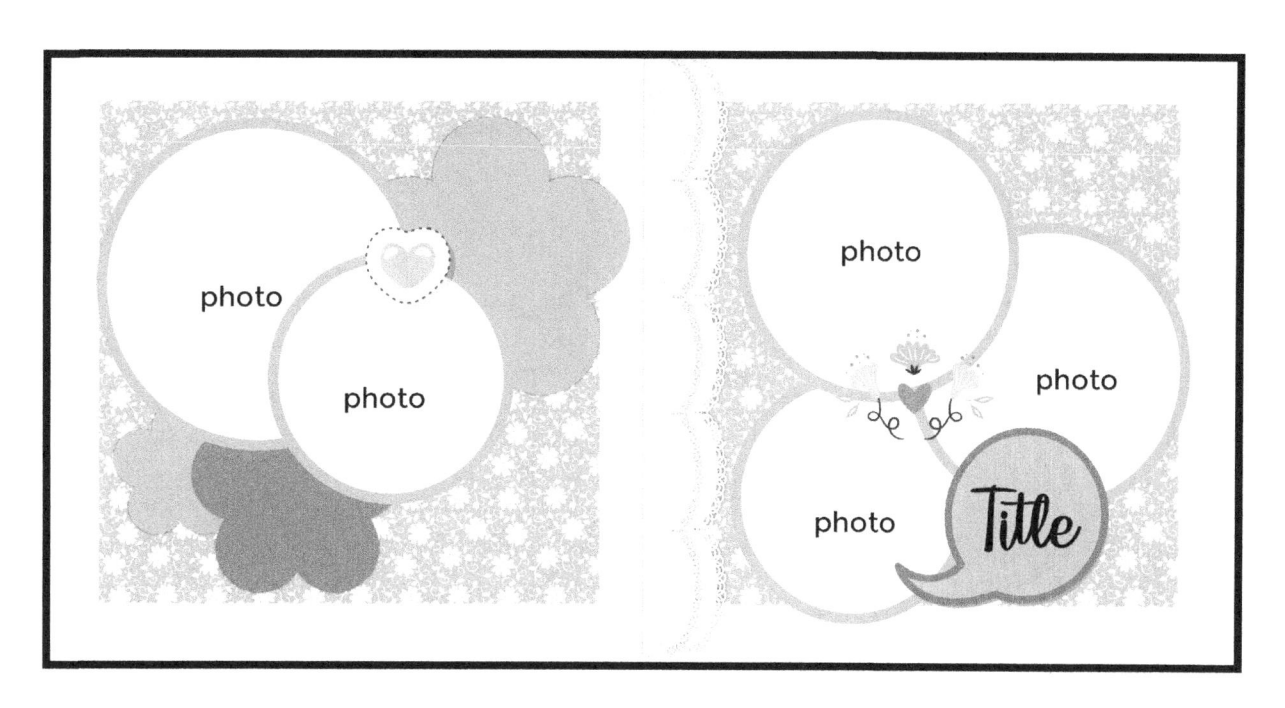

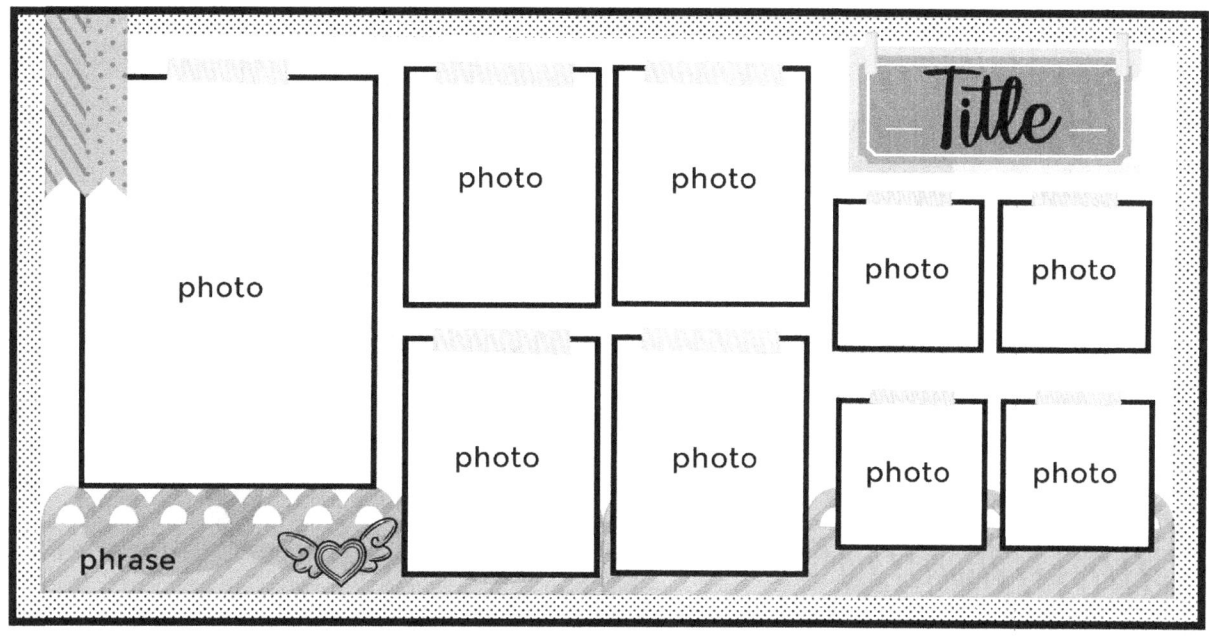

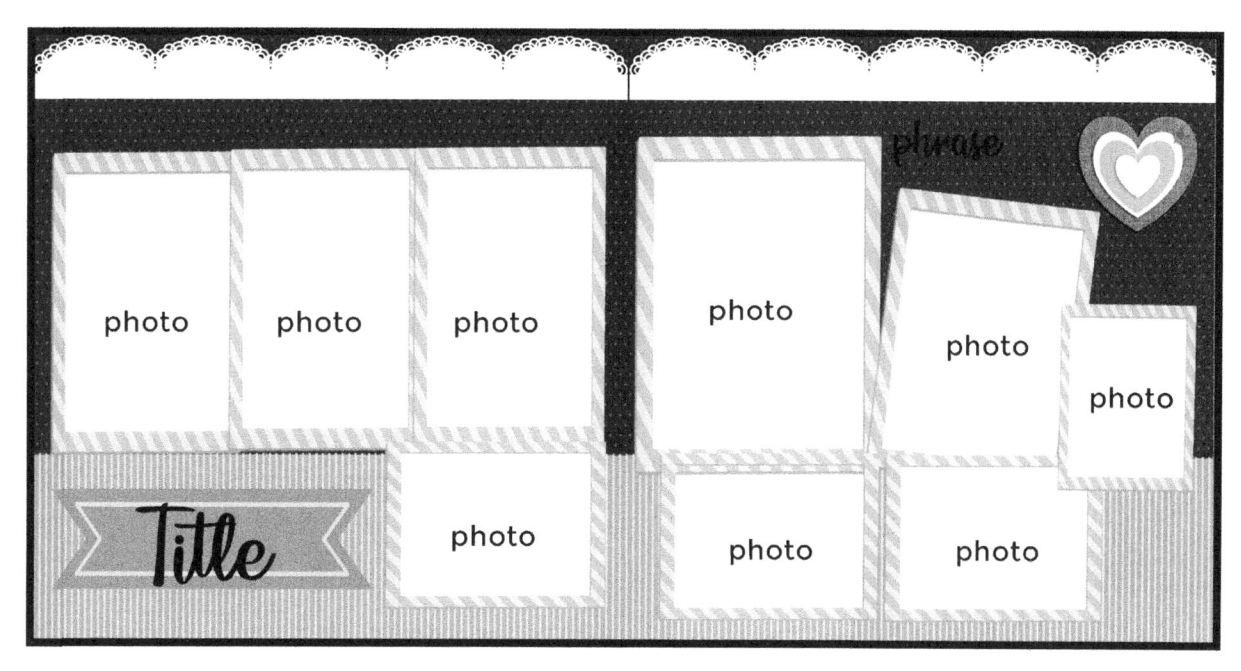

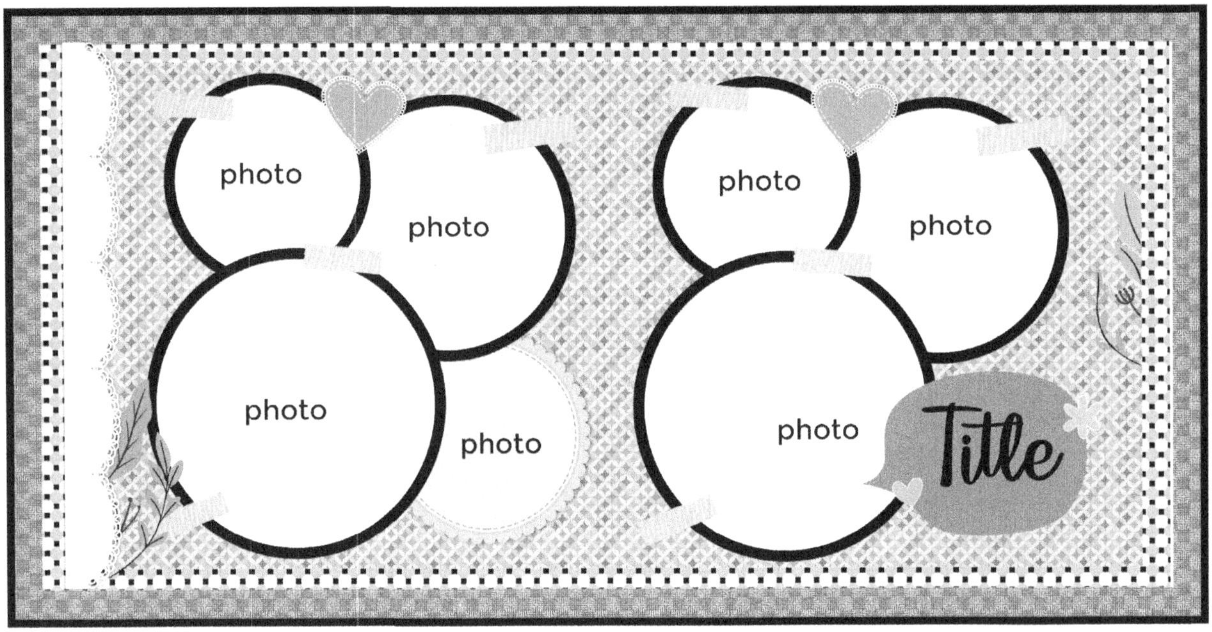
photo
photo
photo
photo
photo
photo
photo
photo
Title

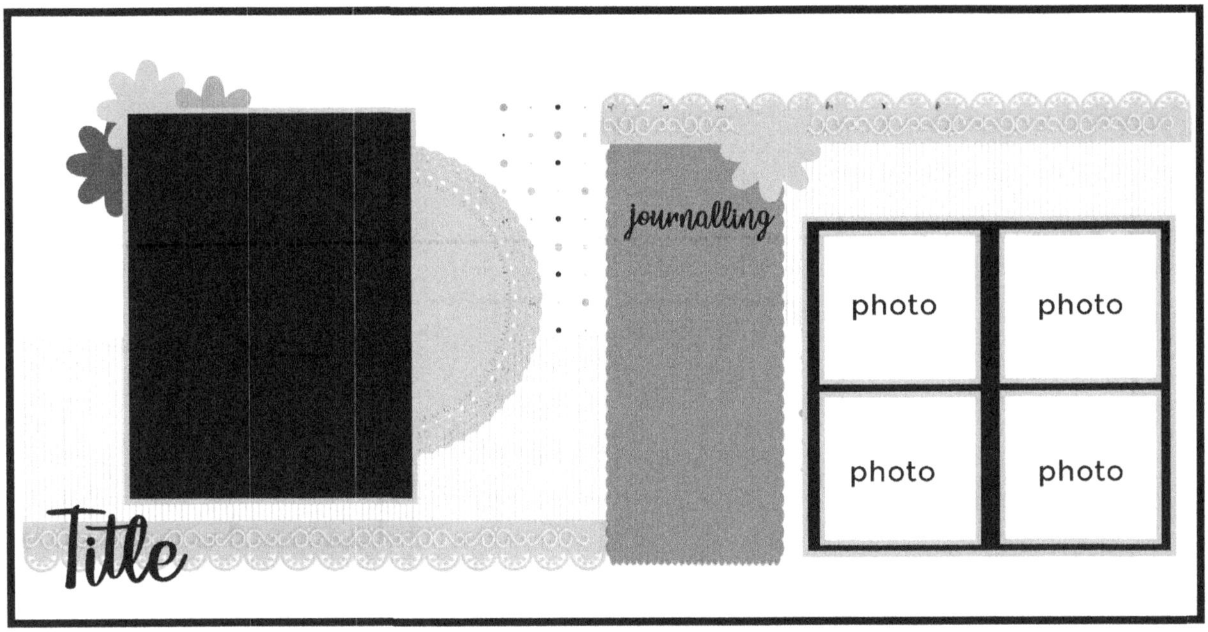
journalling
photo
photo
photo
photo
Title

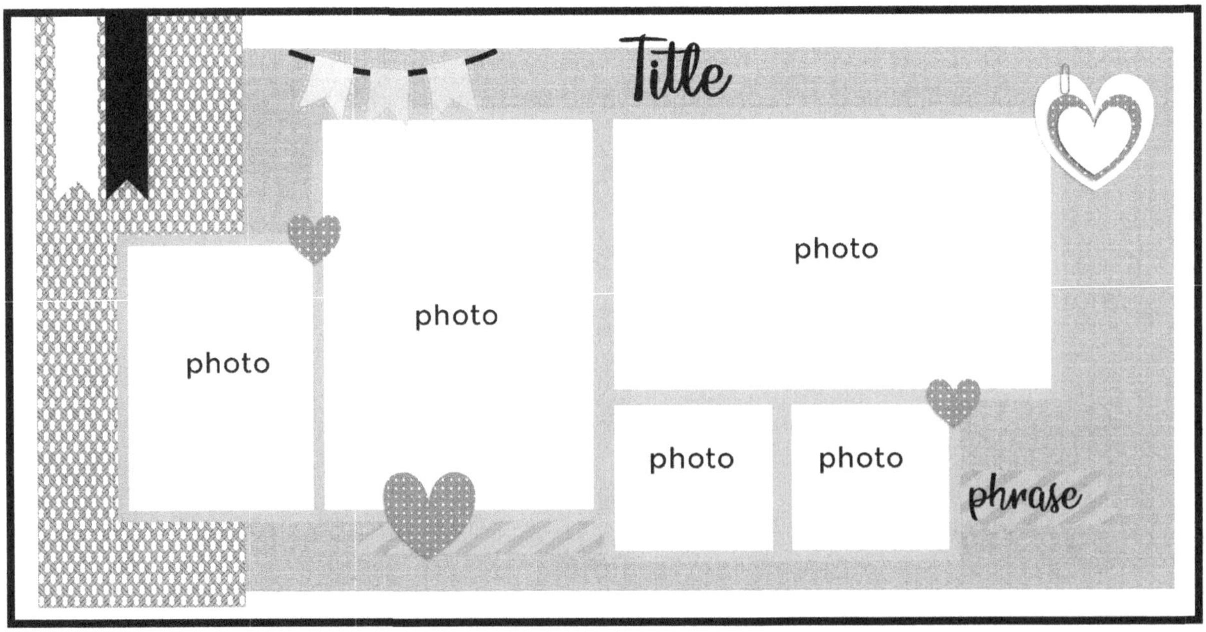
Title
photo
photo
photo
photo
photo
phrase

91

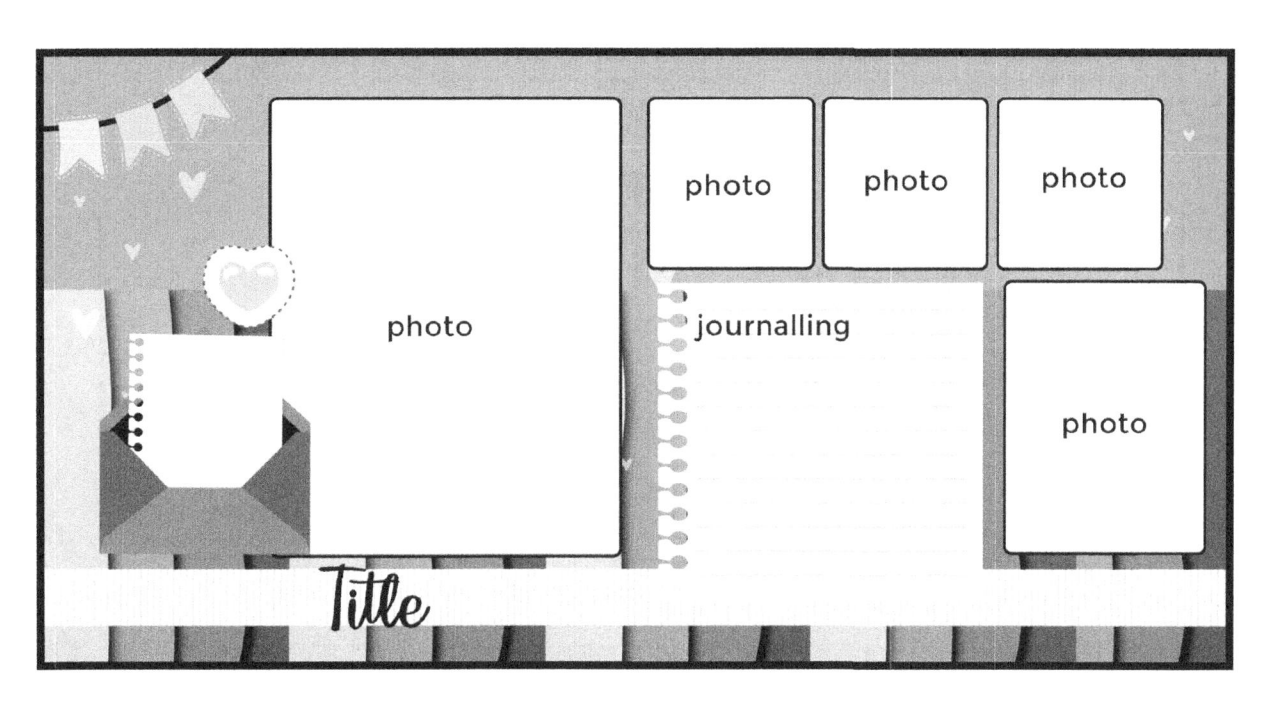

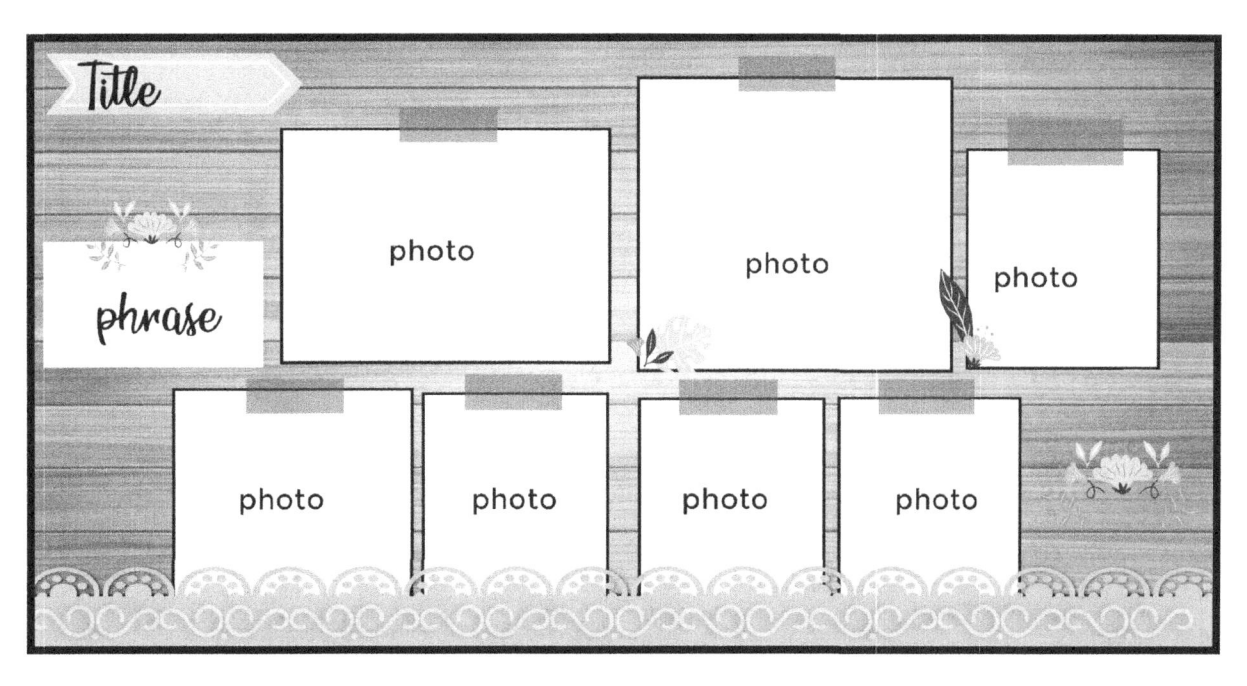

92

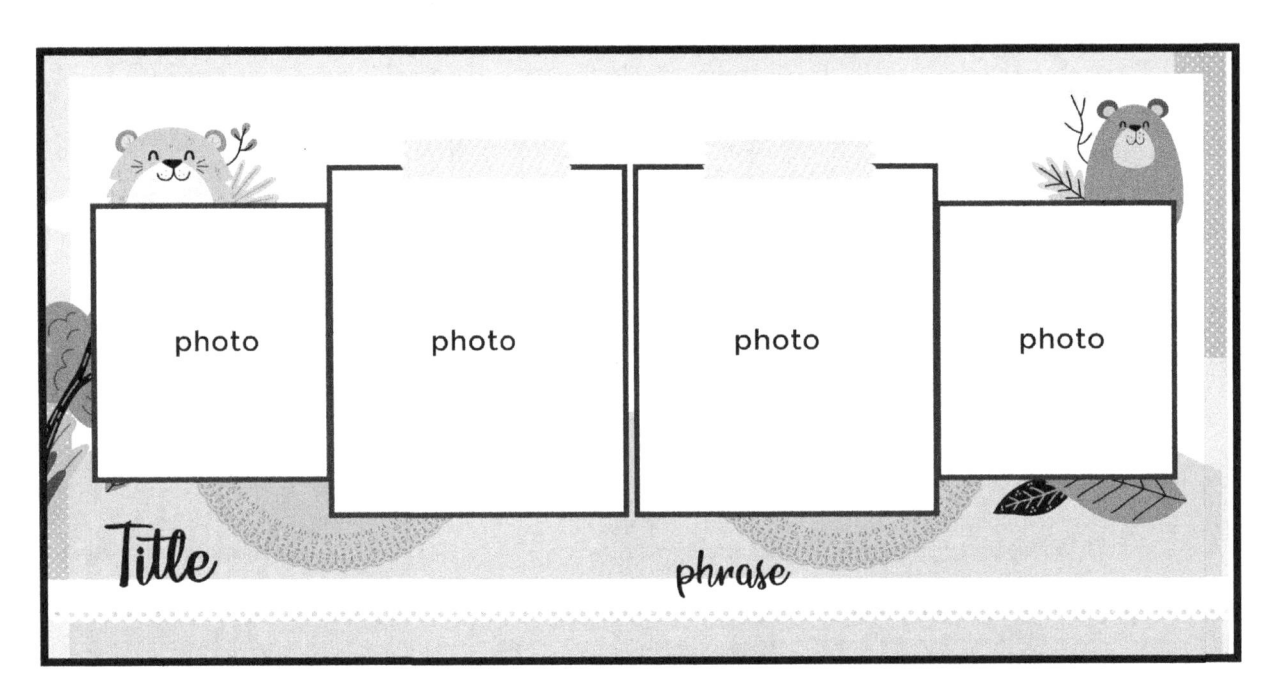

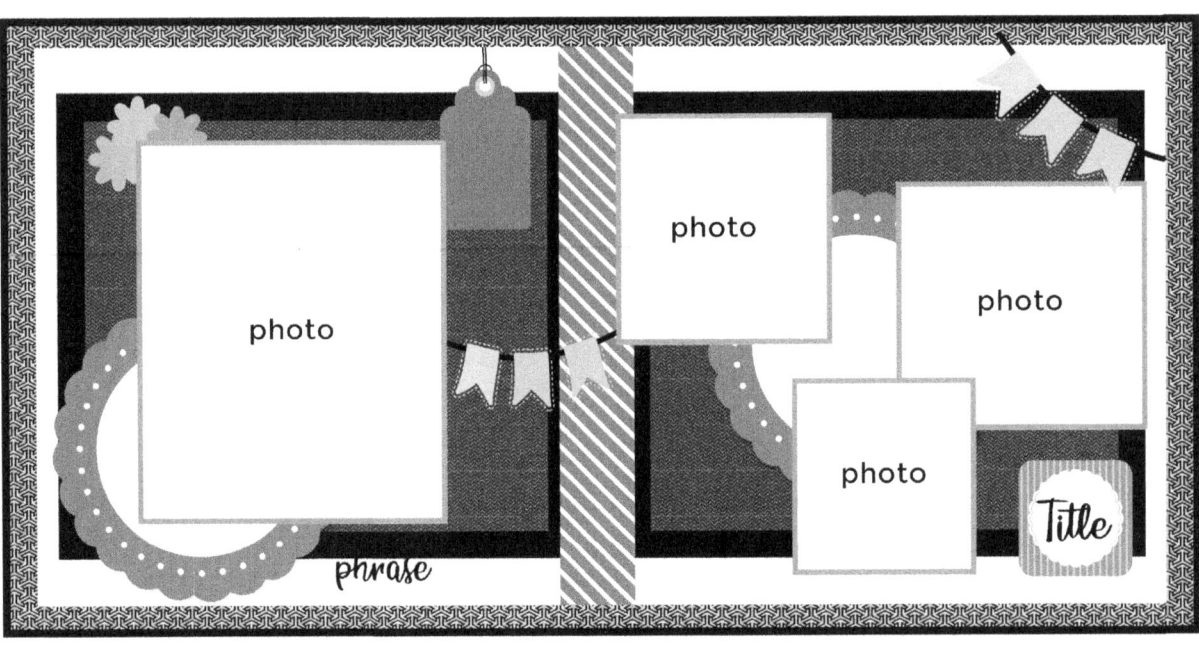

93

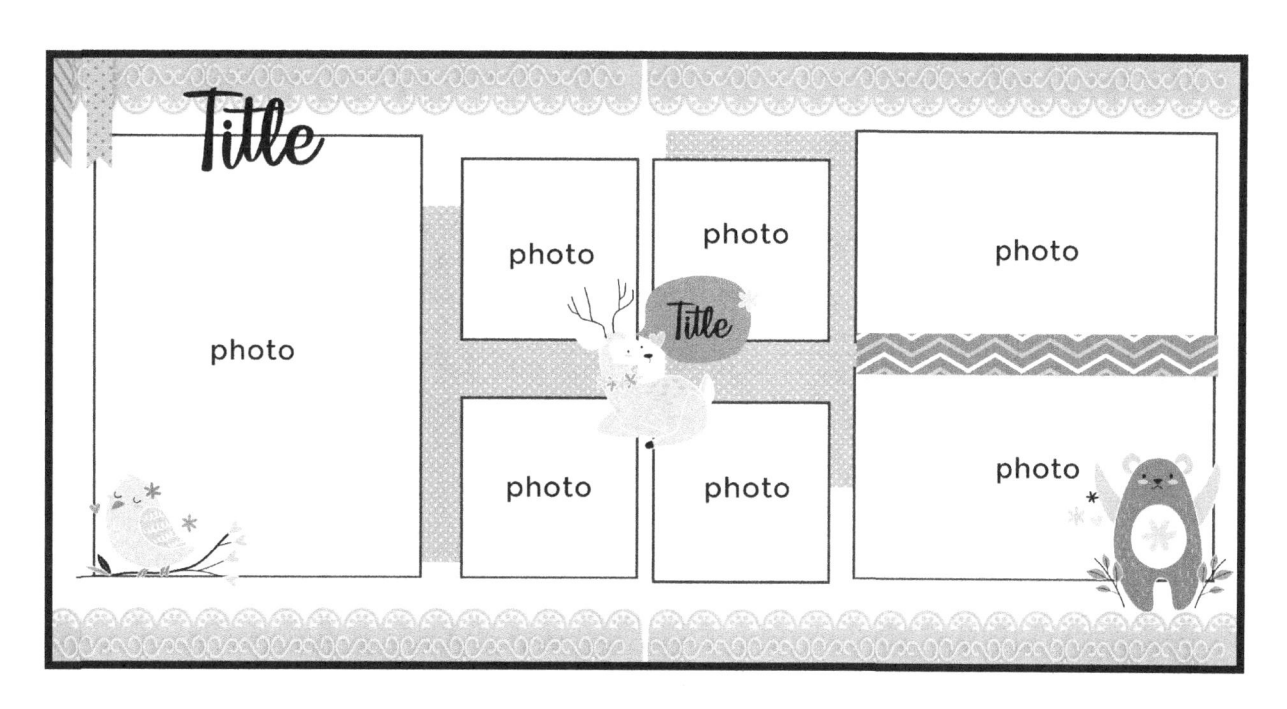

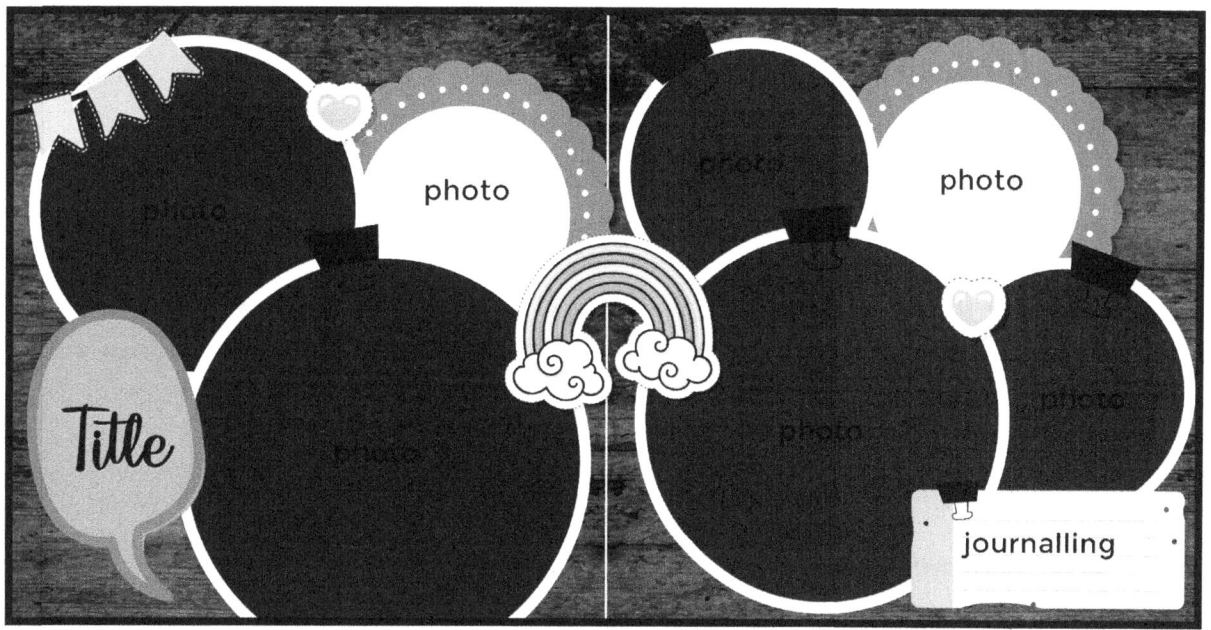

94

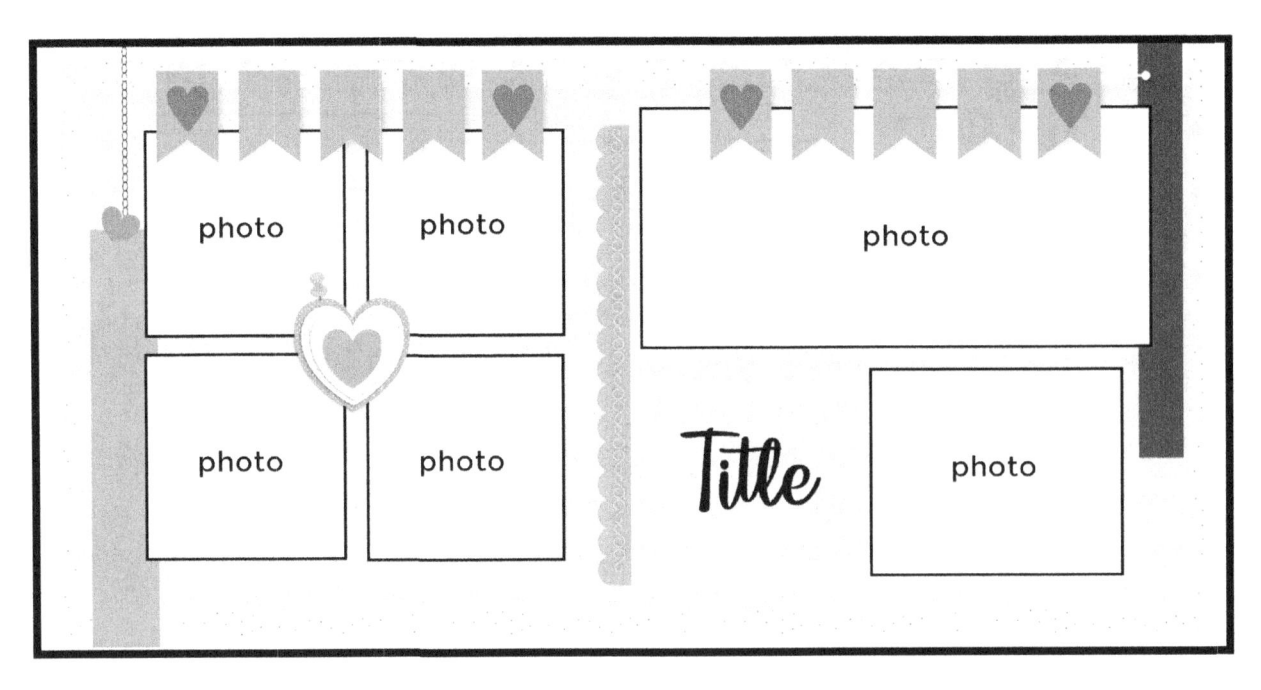

photo
photo
photo
Title
photo
photo
photo
photo

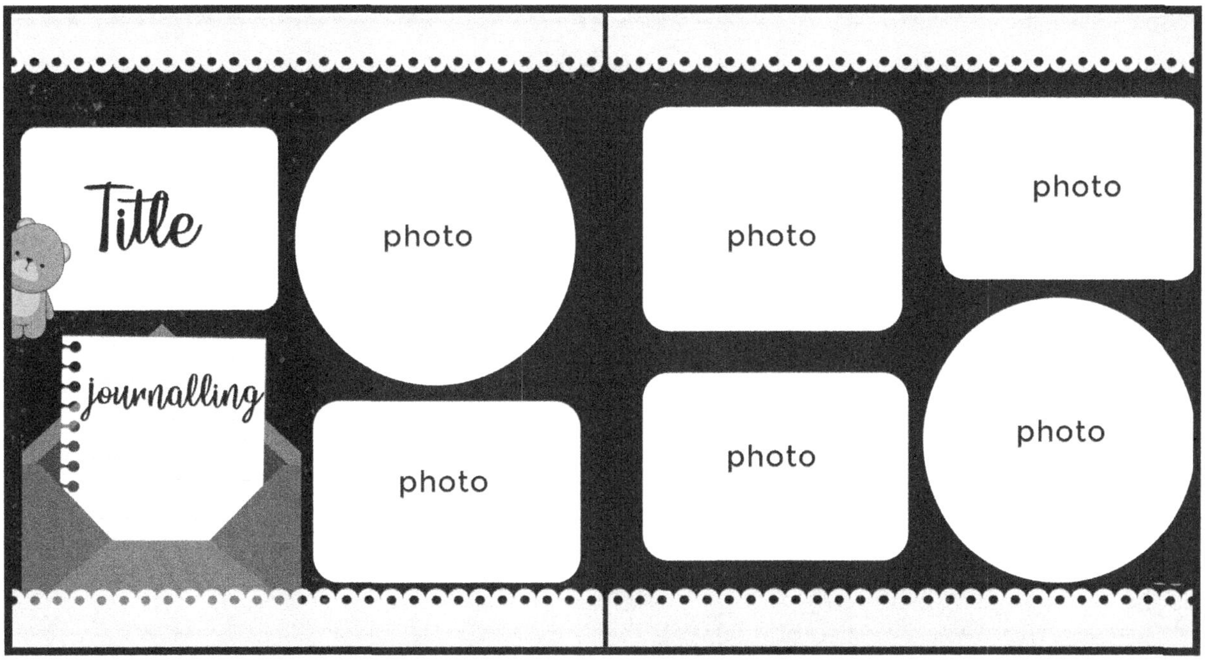
Title
photo
journalling
photo
photo
photo
photo
photo

phrase
Title

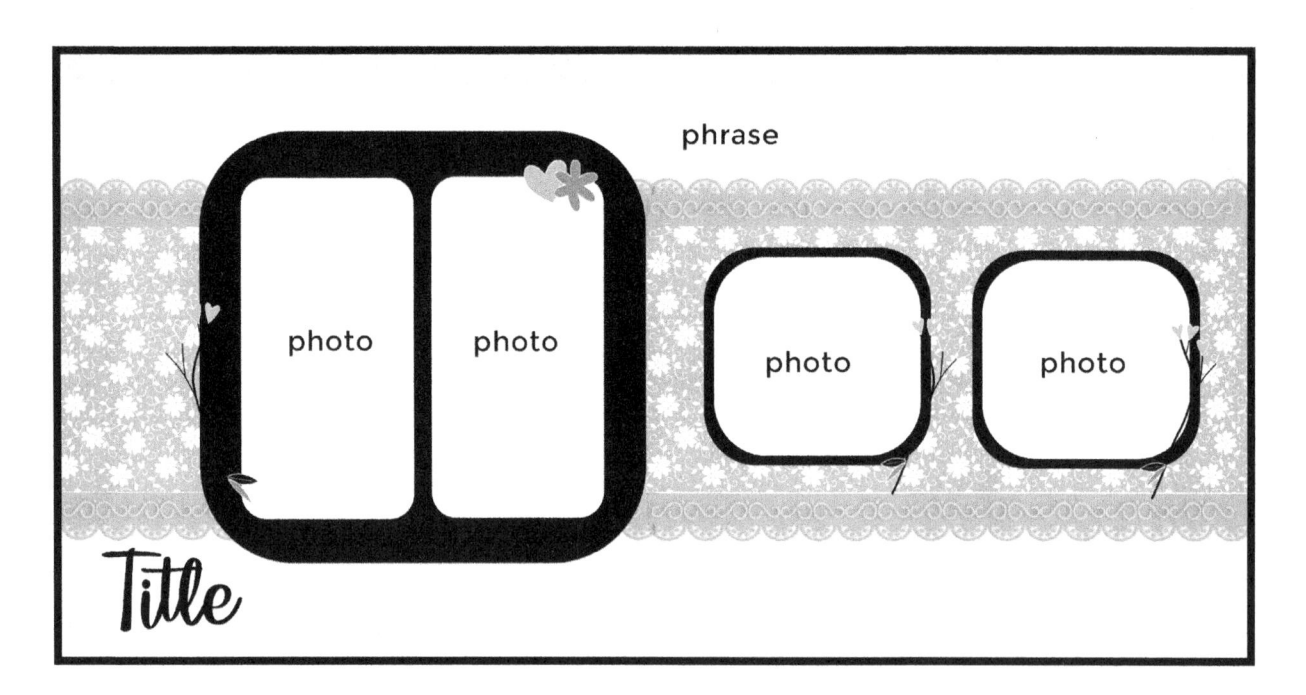

phrase

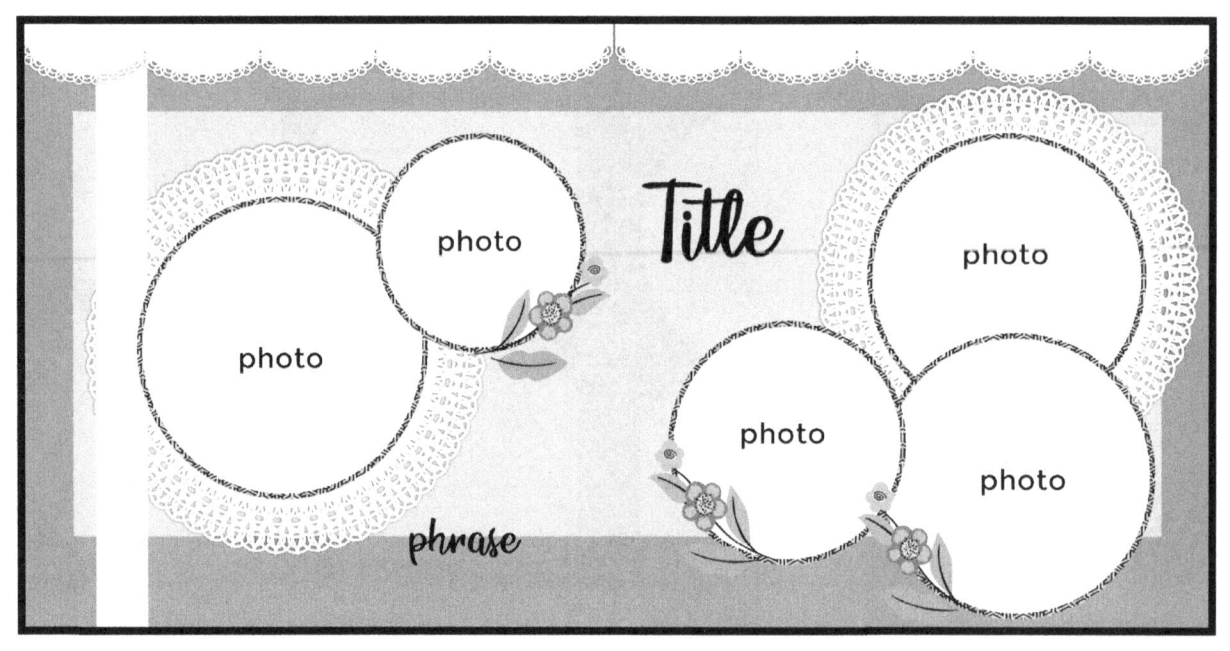

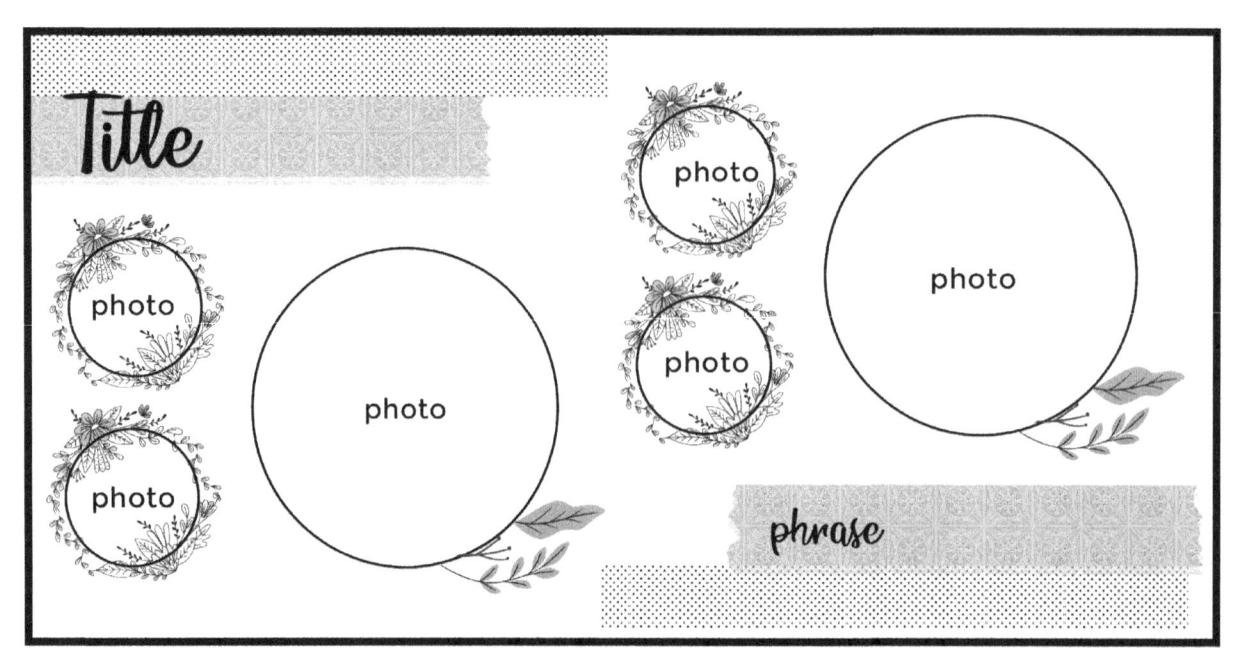

Title

Title

phrase

Title

phrase

96

97

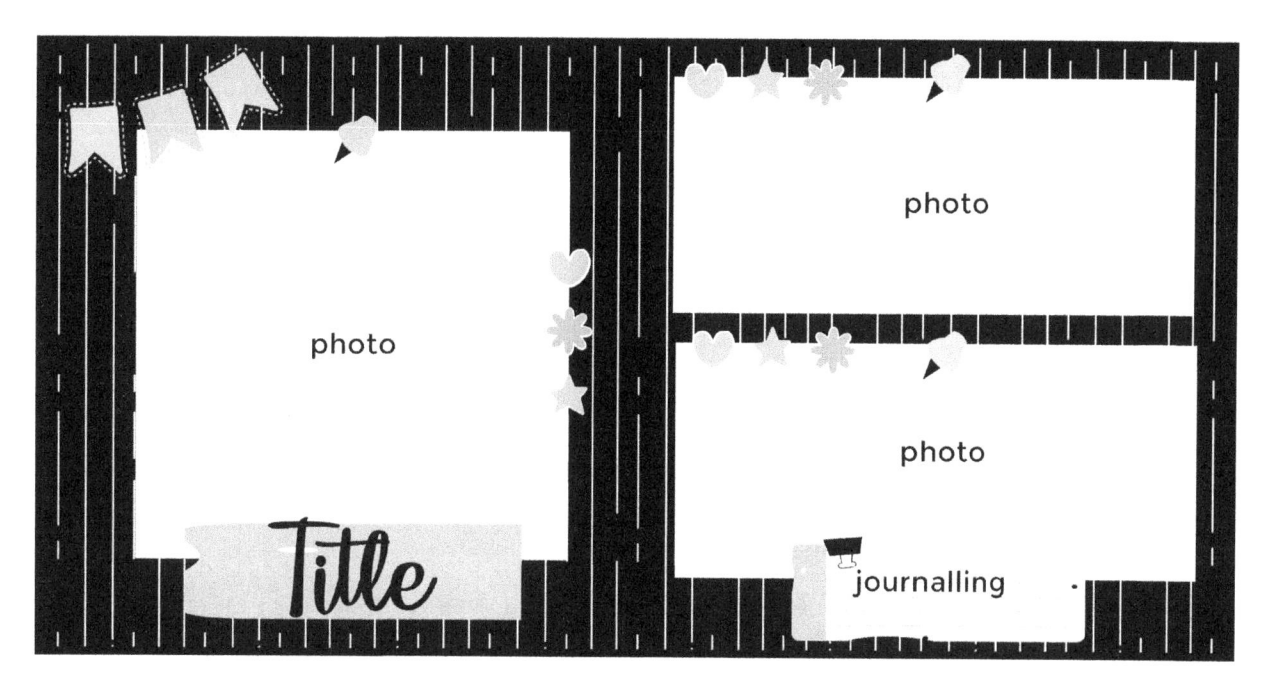

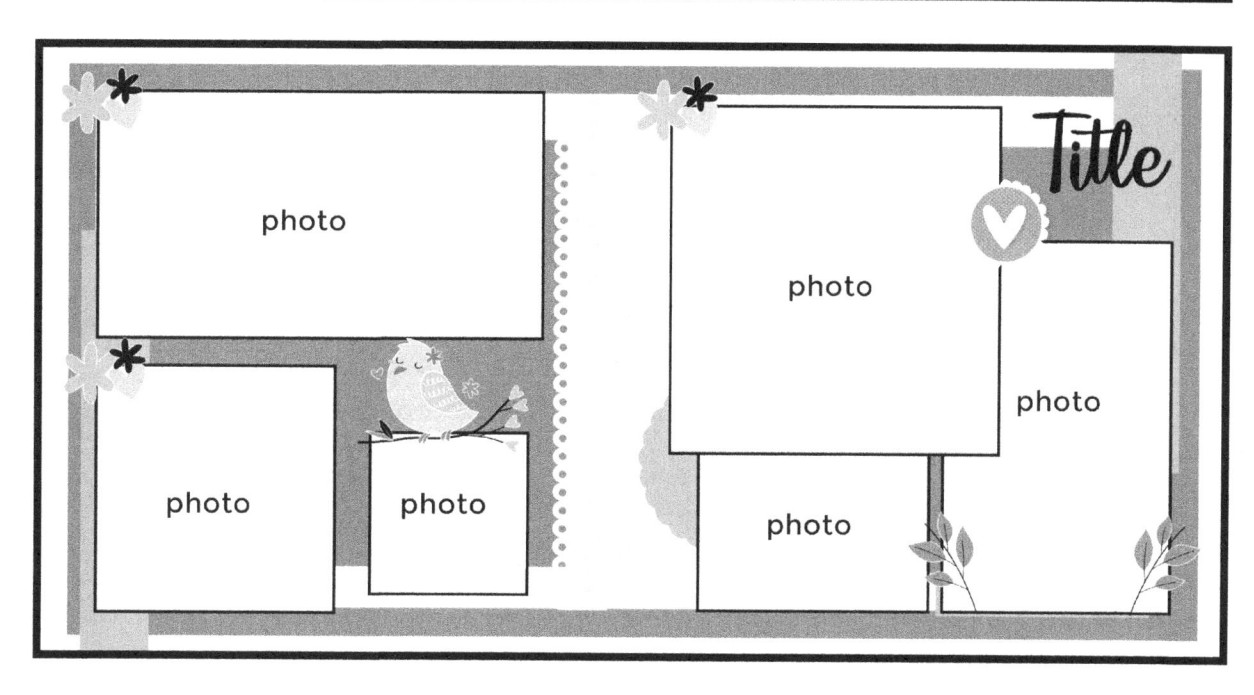

98

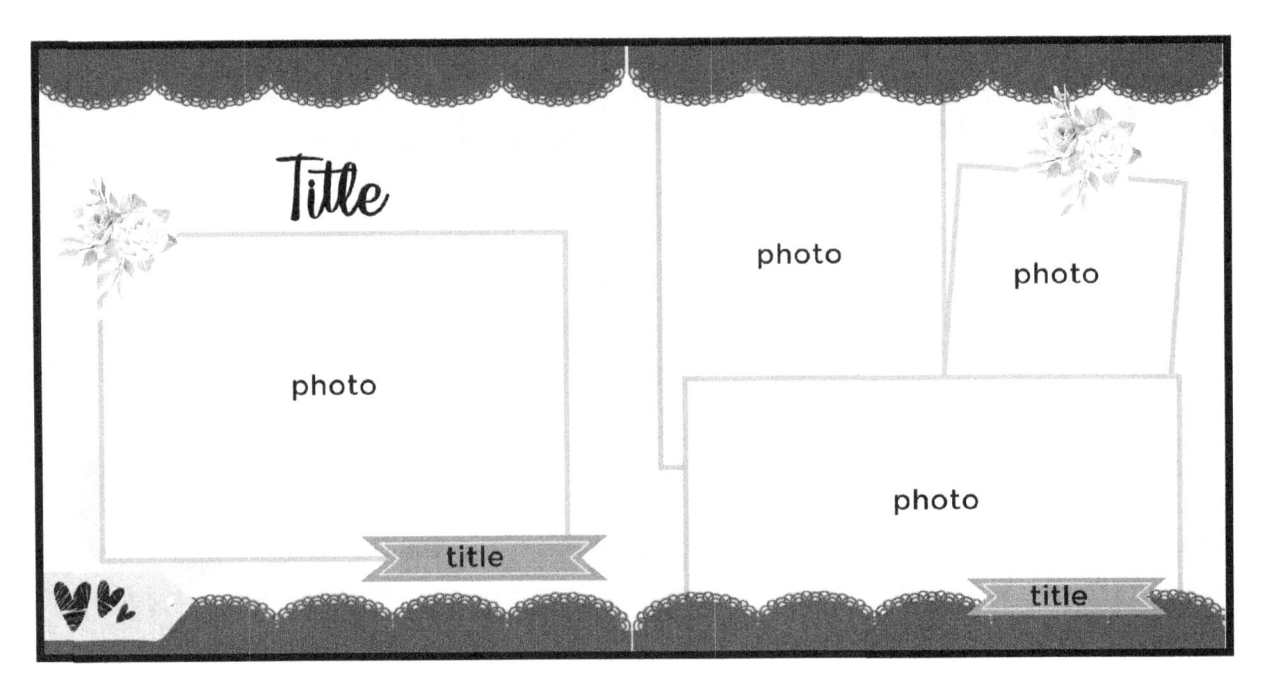

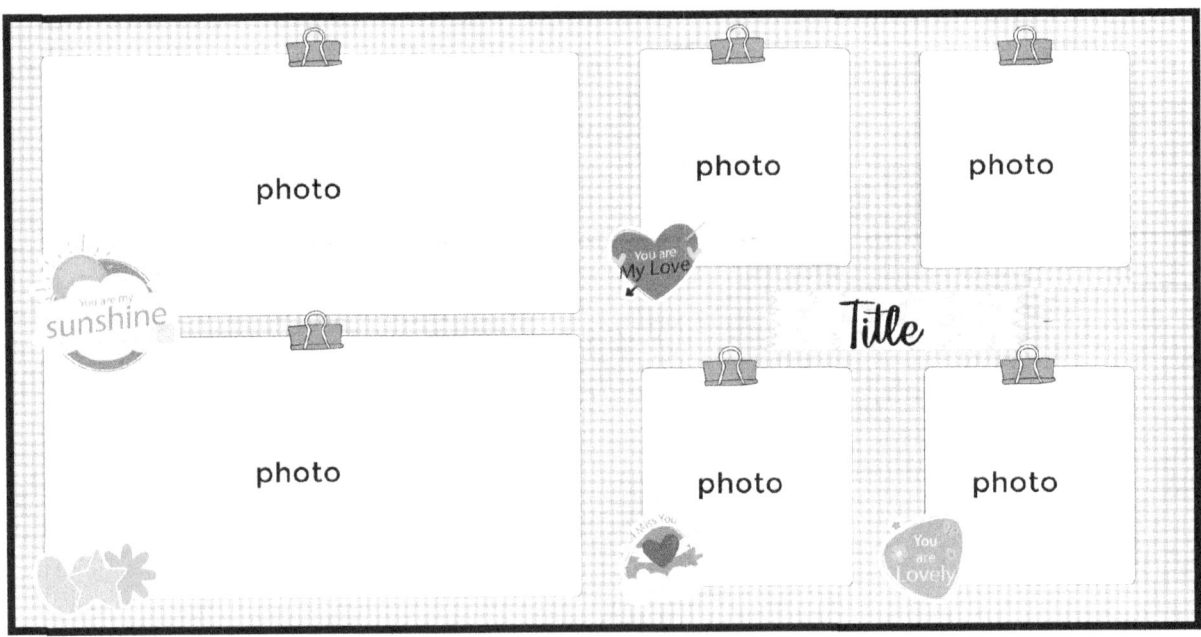

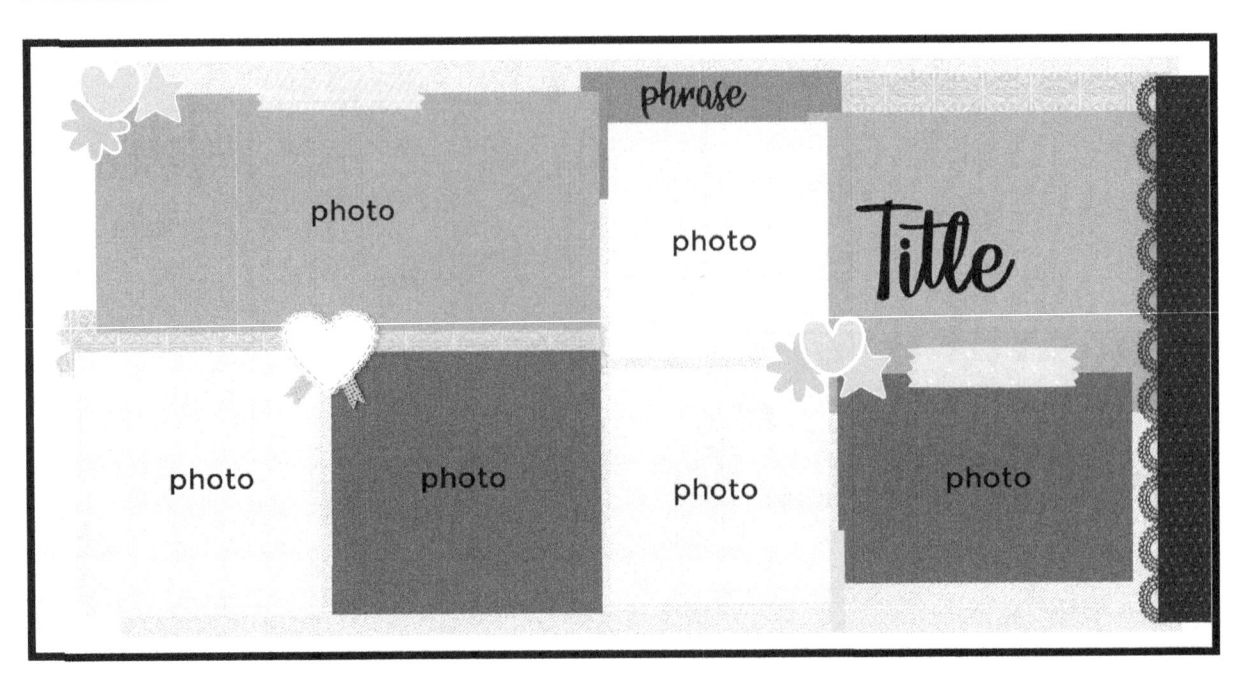

TOGETHER

photo

photo

photo

photo

photo

Title

MY FAMILY

phrase

photo

photo

Title

photo

photo

photo

photo

Title

99

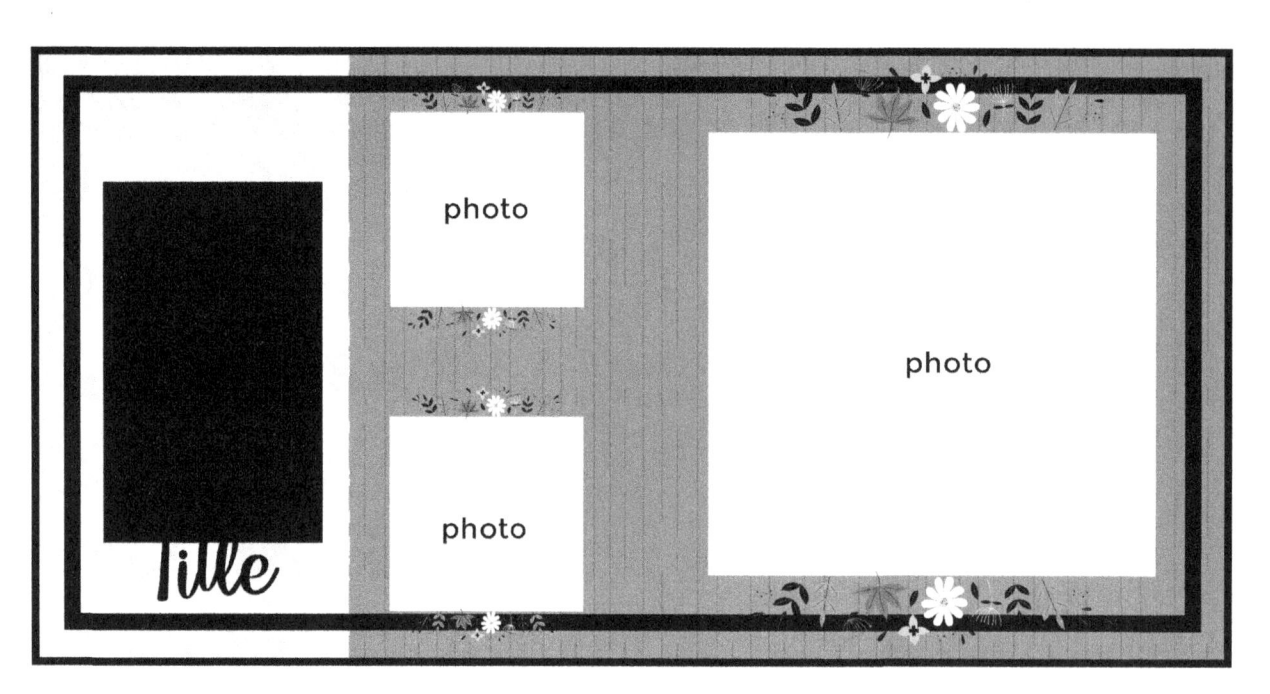

Title

photo

photo

photo

Family Camping Trip

photo | photo
photo | photo

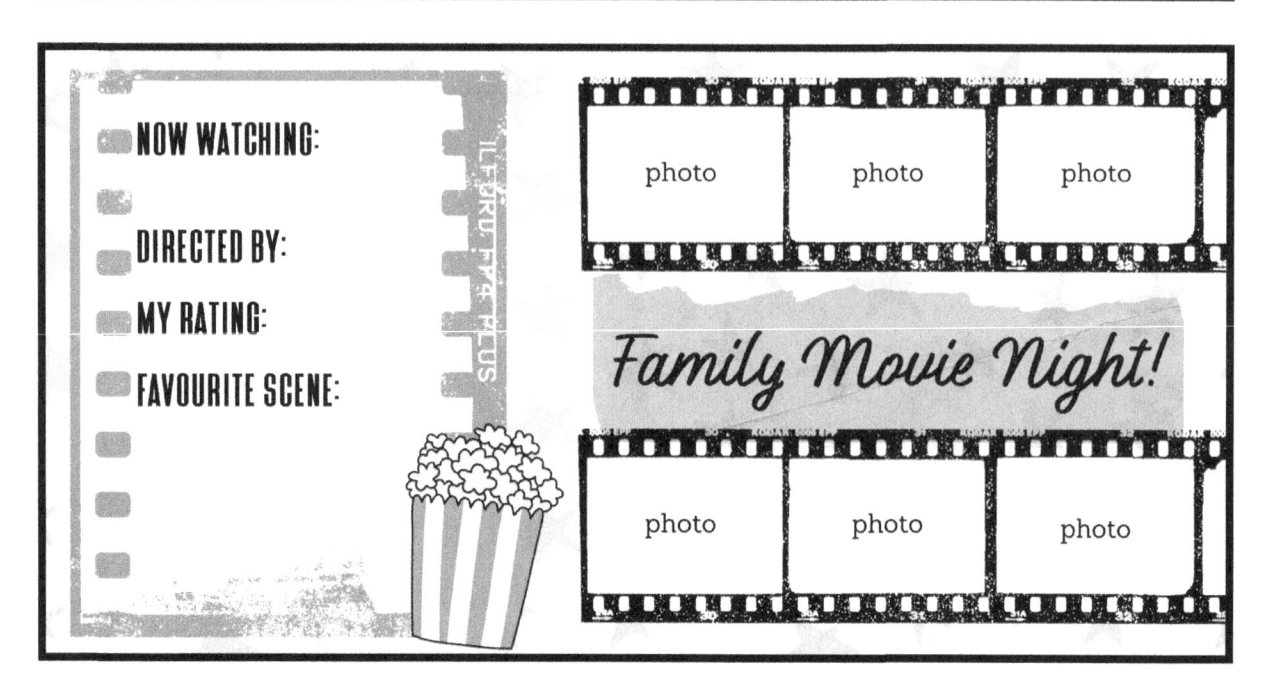

NOW WATCHING:

DIRECTED BY:

MY RATING:

FAVOURITE SCENE:

photo | photo | photo

Family Movie Night!

photo | photo | photo

Girl Birthday

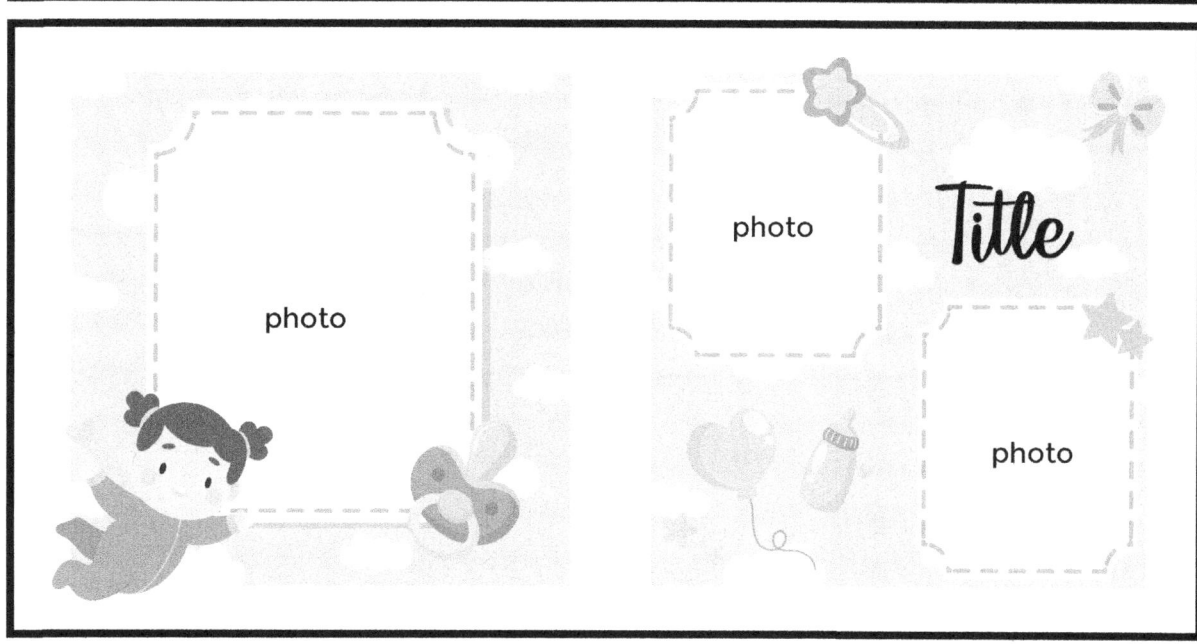

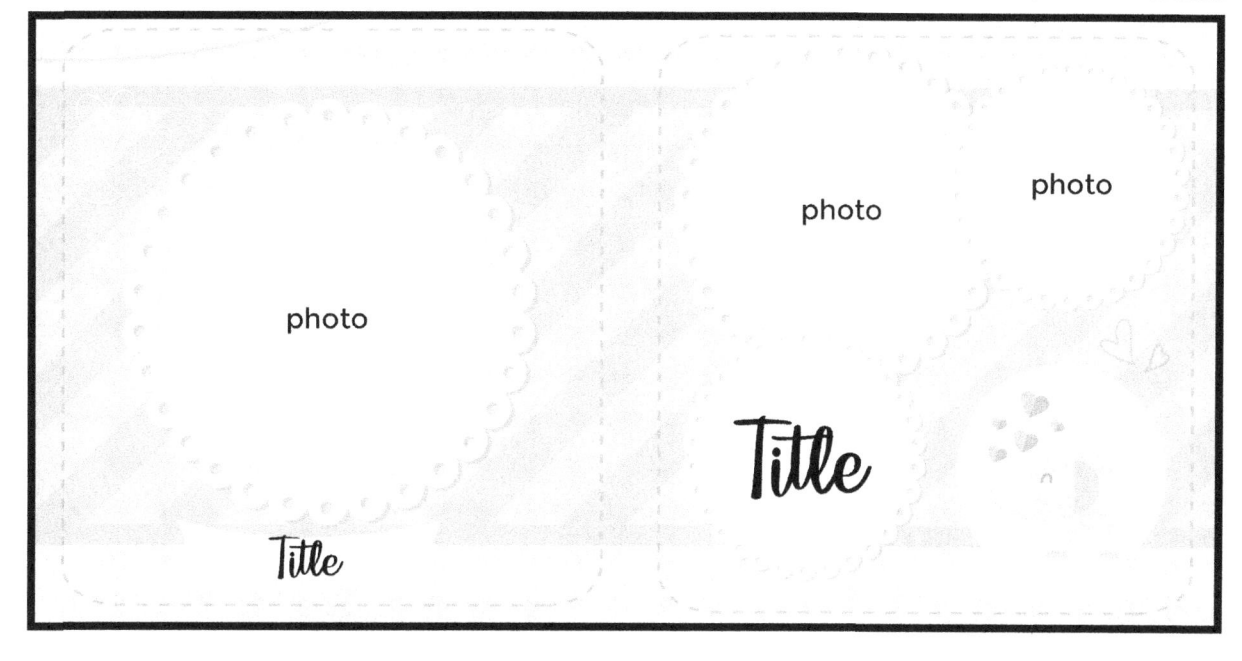

photo

photo

Title

photo

photo

Title

photo

photo

photo

photo

Title

Title

101

102

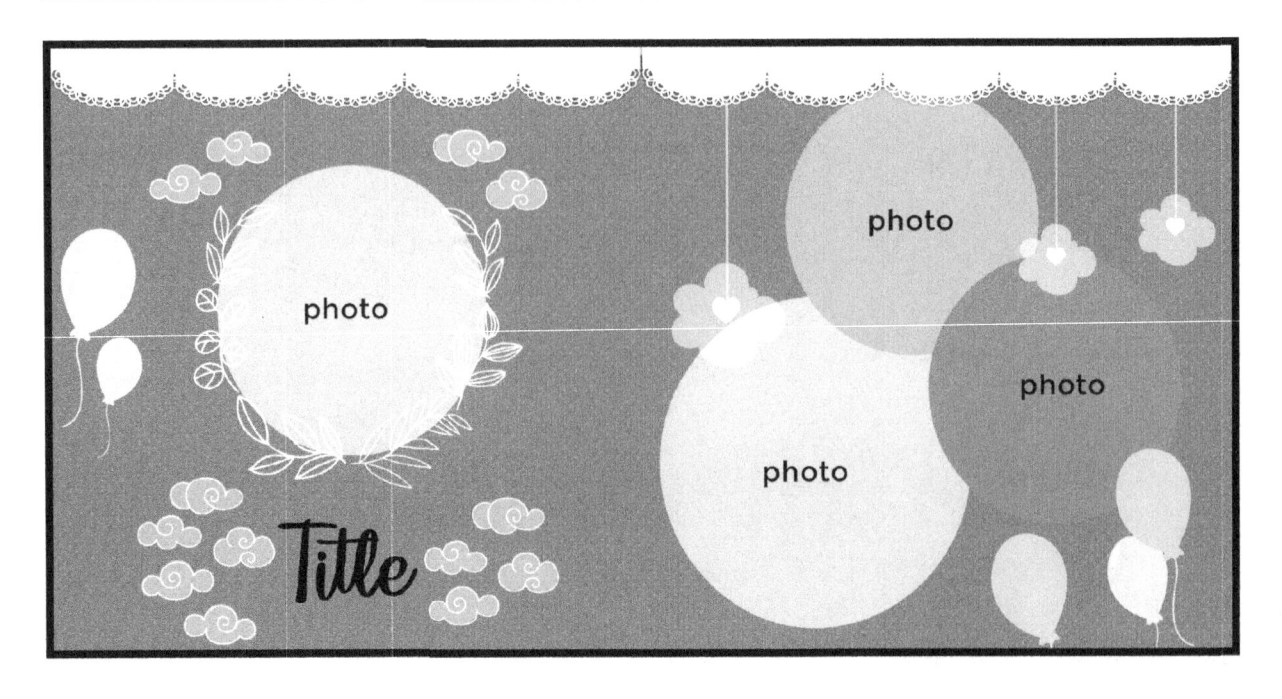

Title

photo
photo
photo

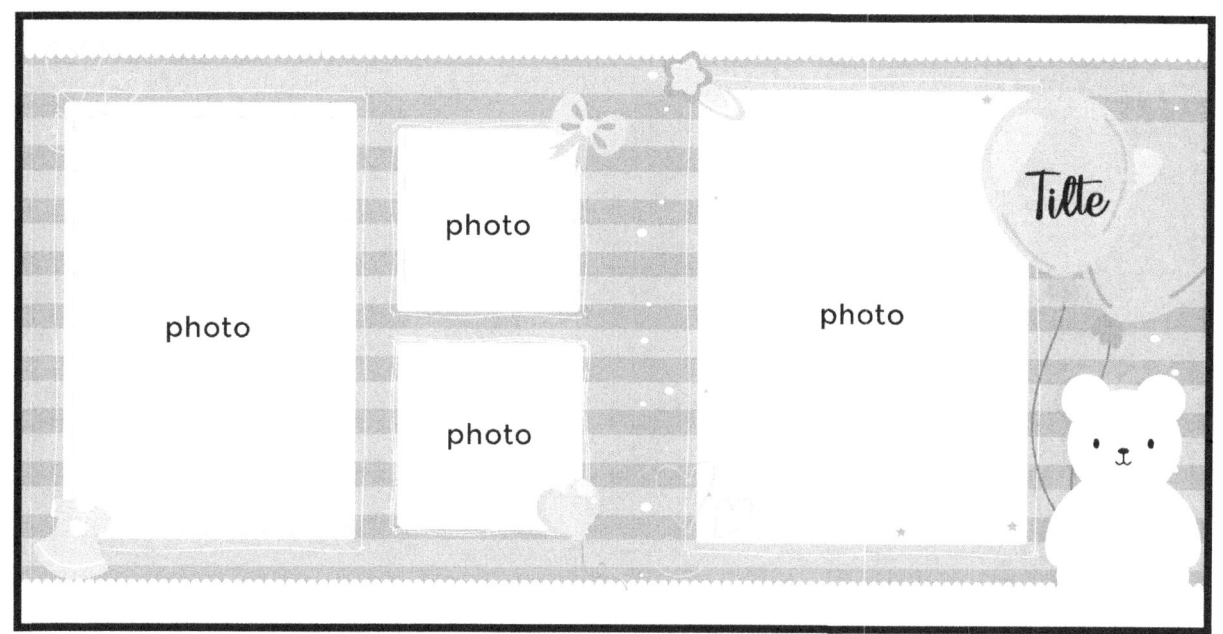

photo
photo
photo
photo
Tilte

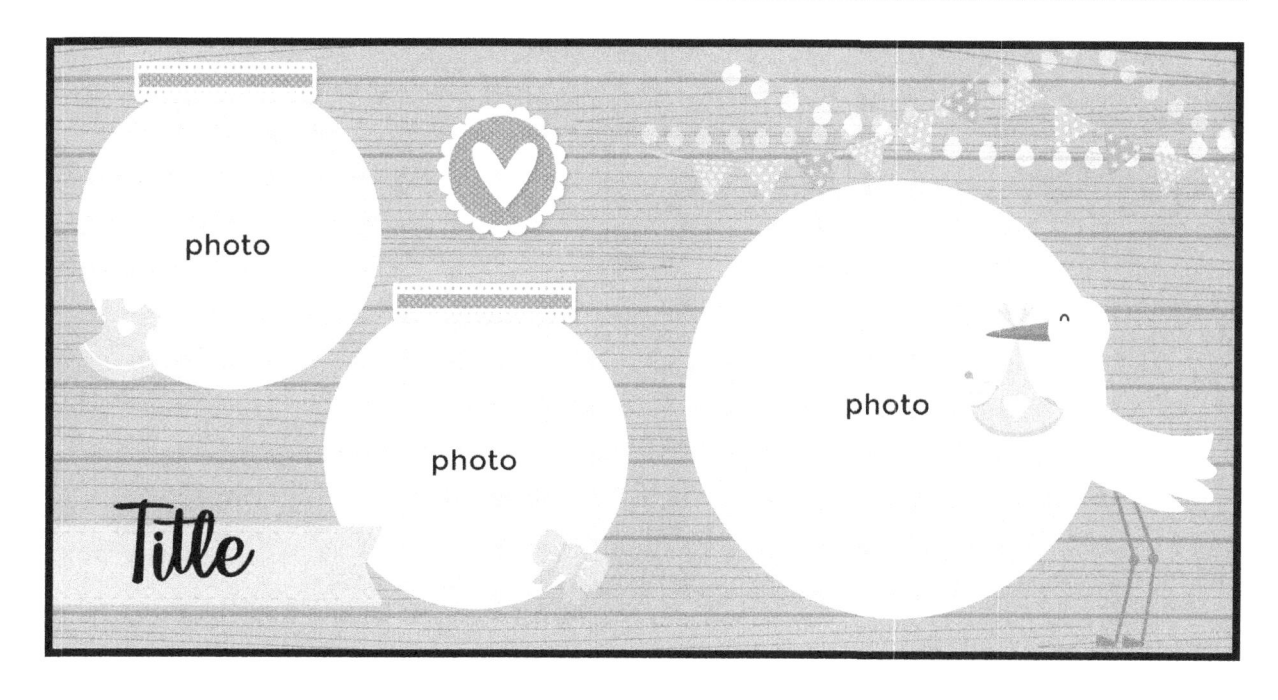

photo
photo
photo
Title

103

Title

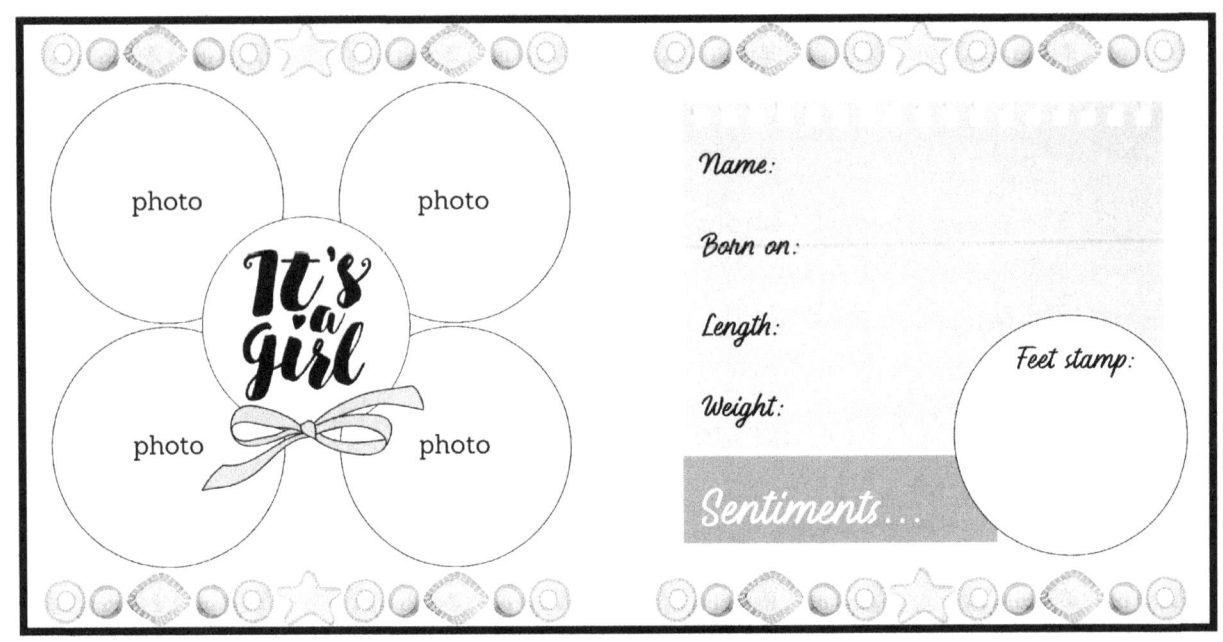

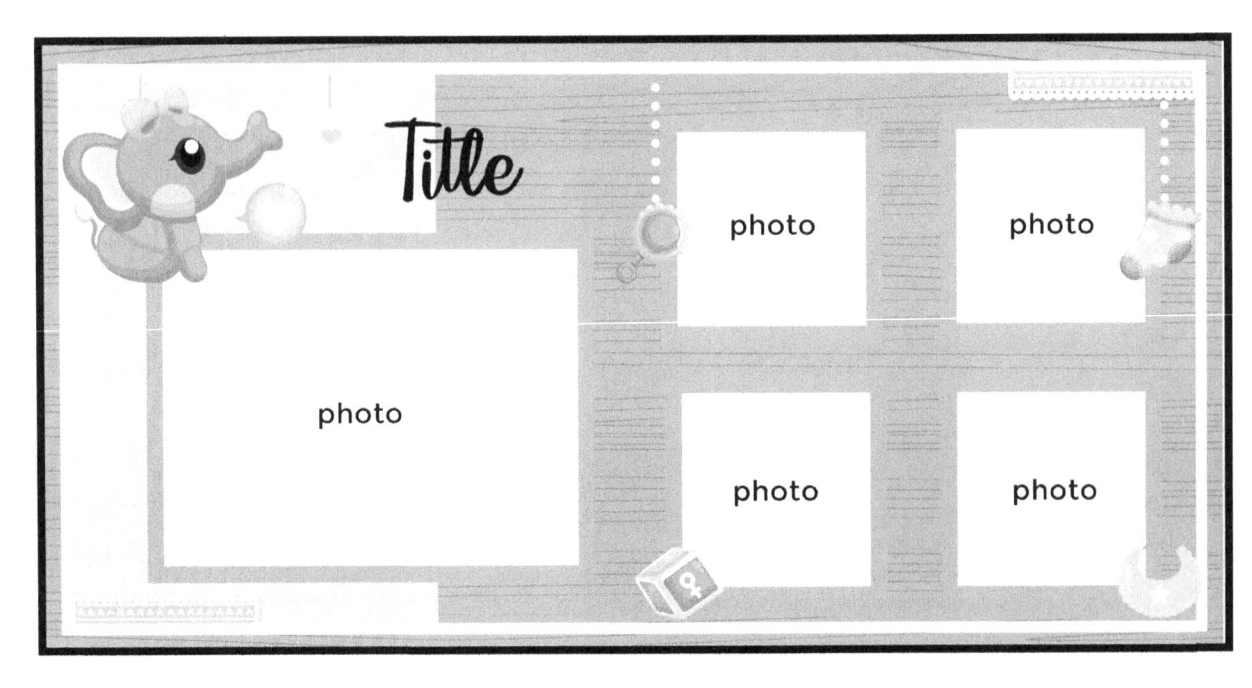

Name:
Born on:
Length:
Weight:

It's a girl

Feet stamp:

Sentiments...

Title

104

105

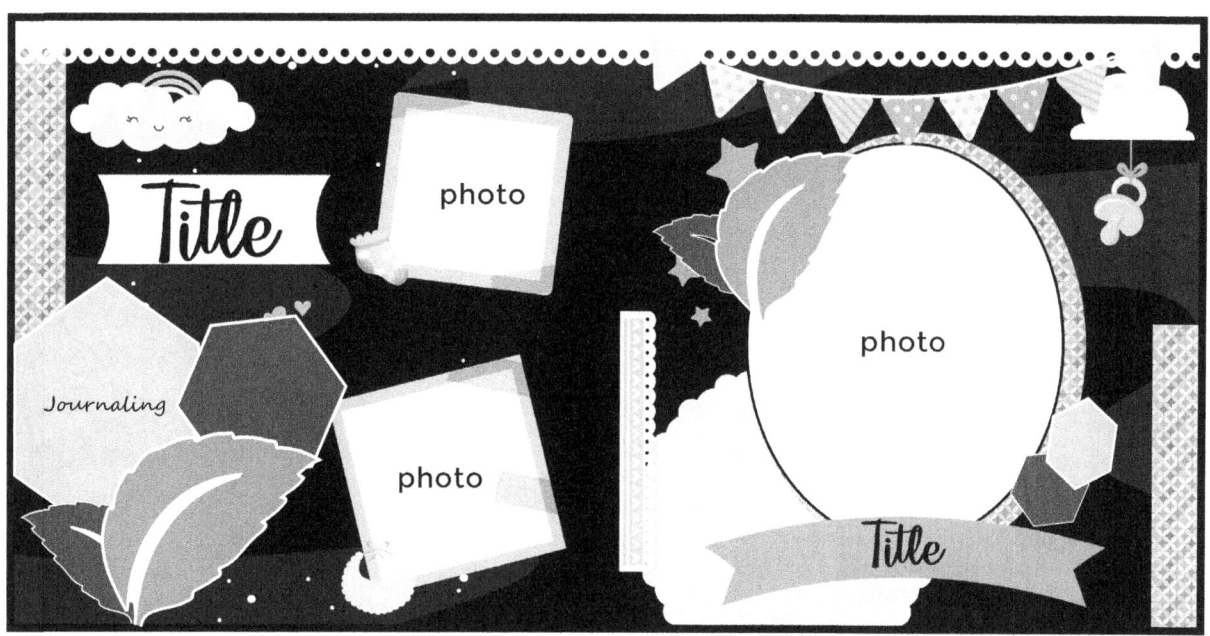

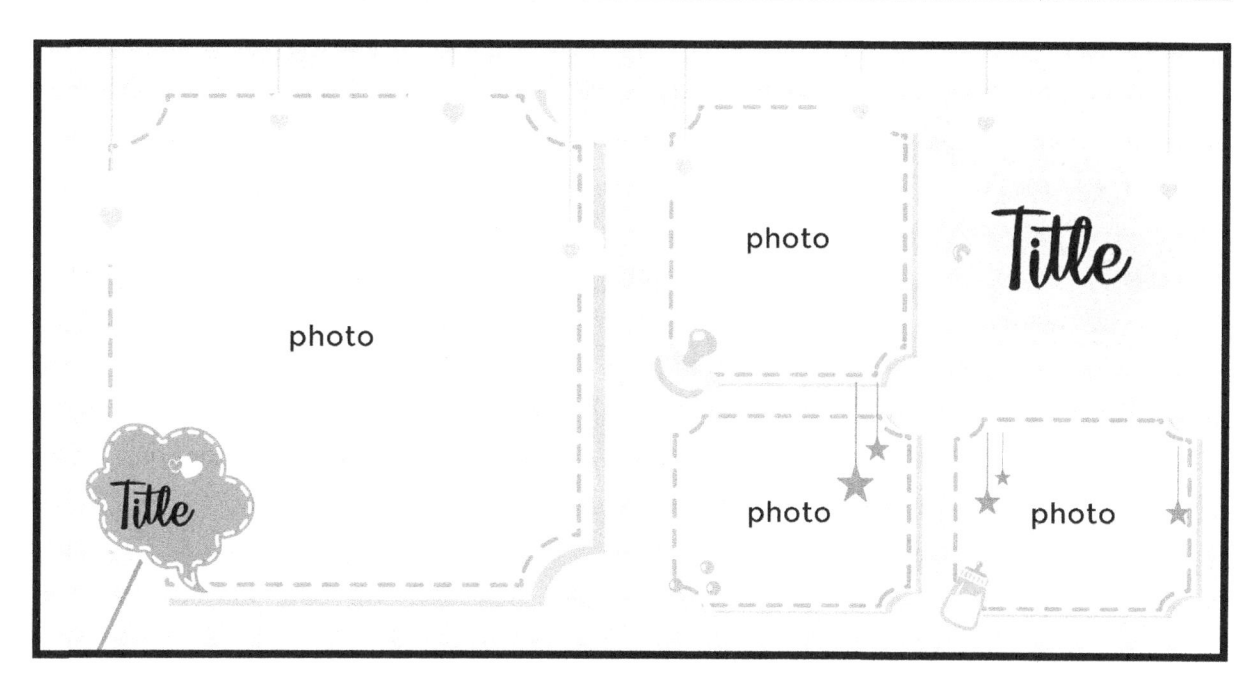

106

107

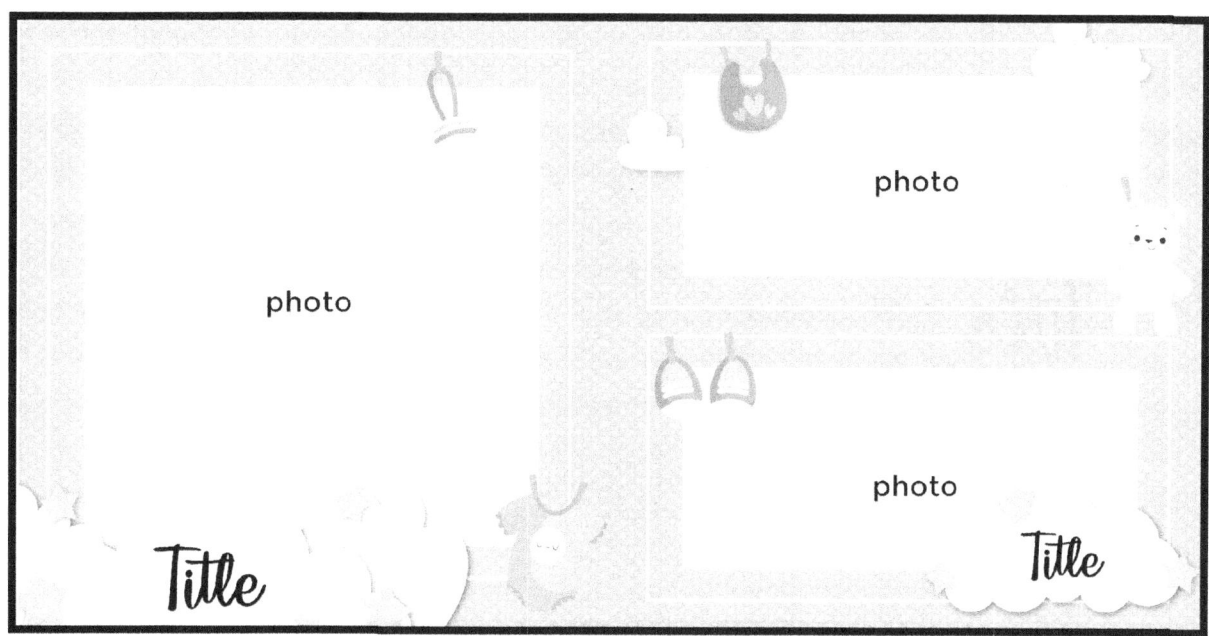

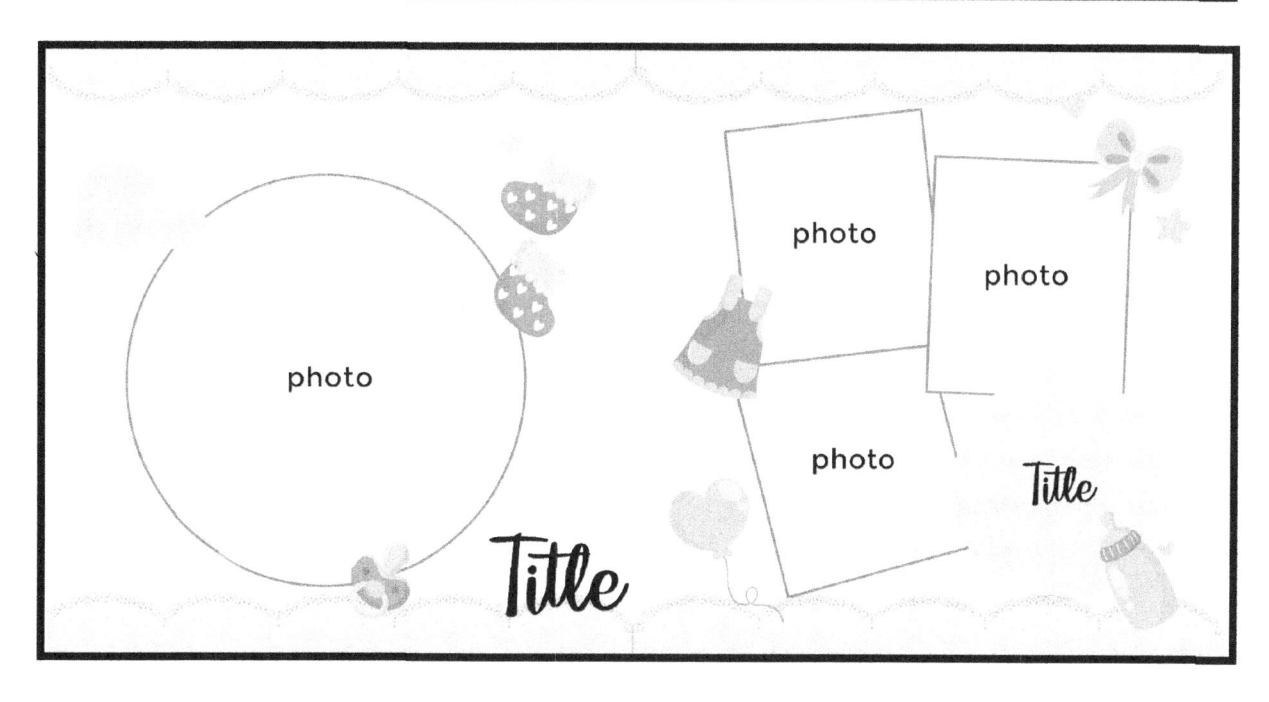

108

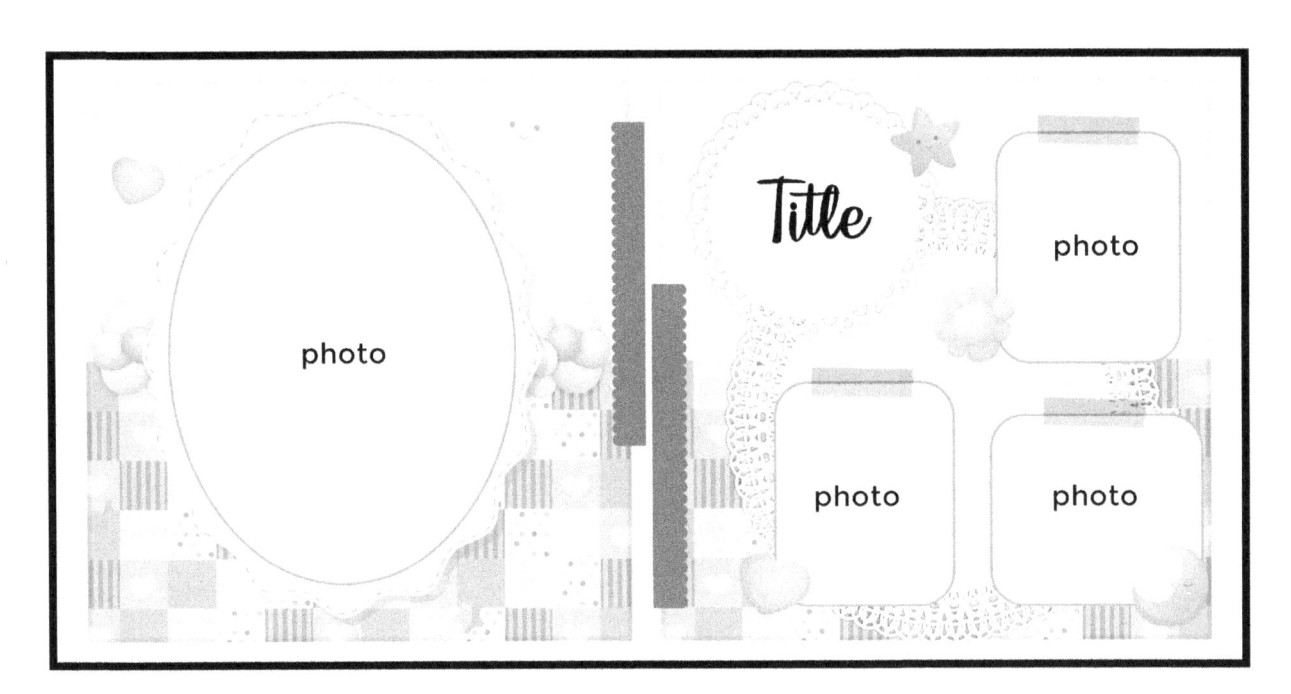

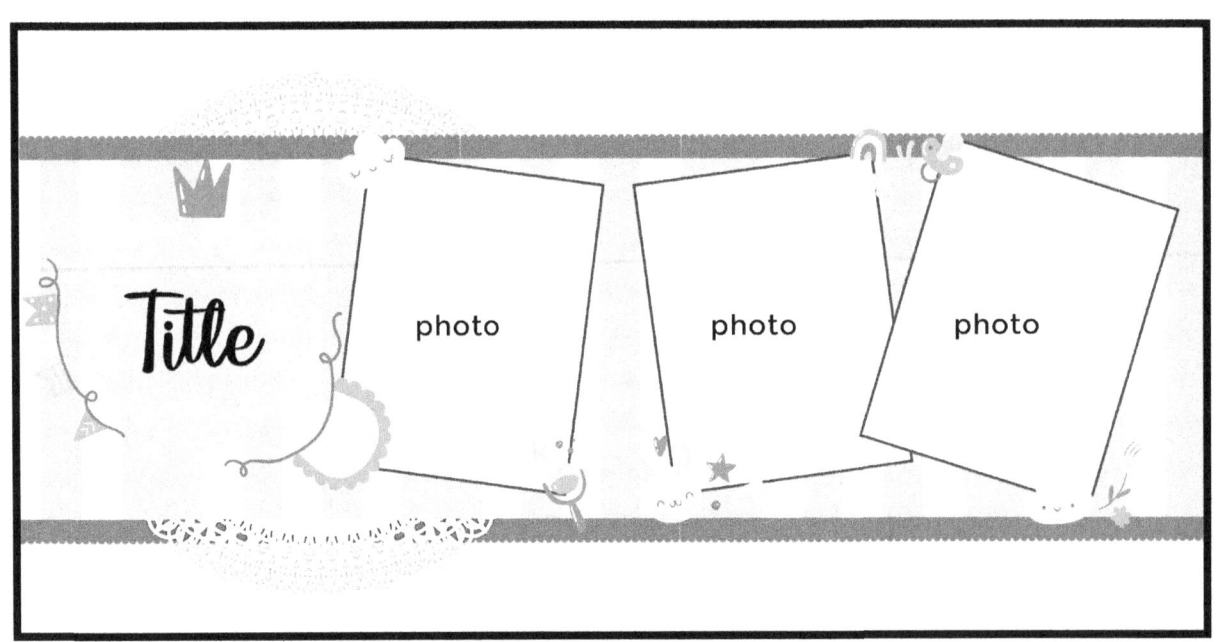

109

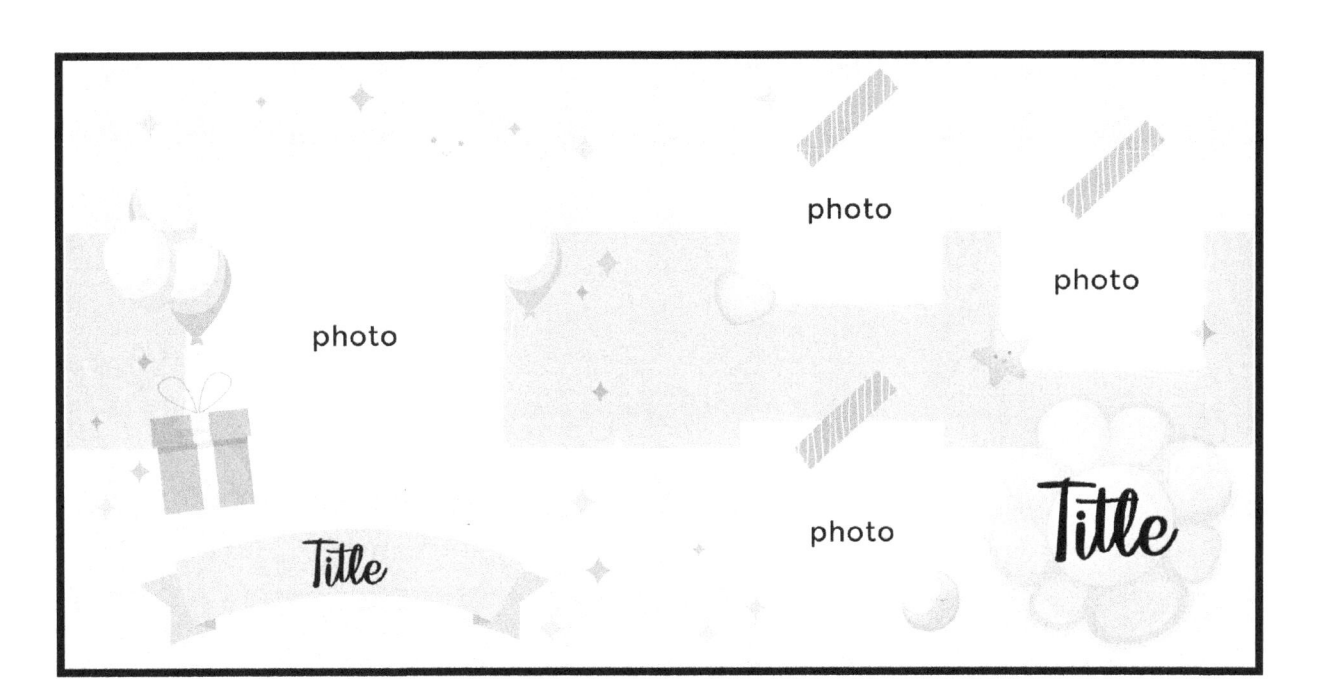

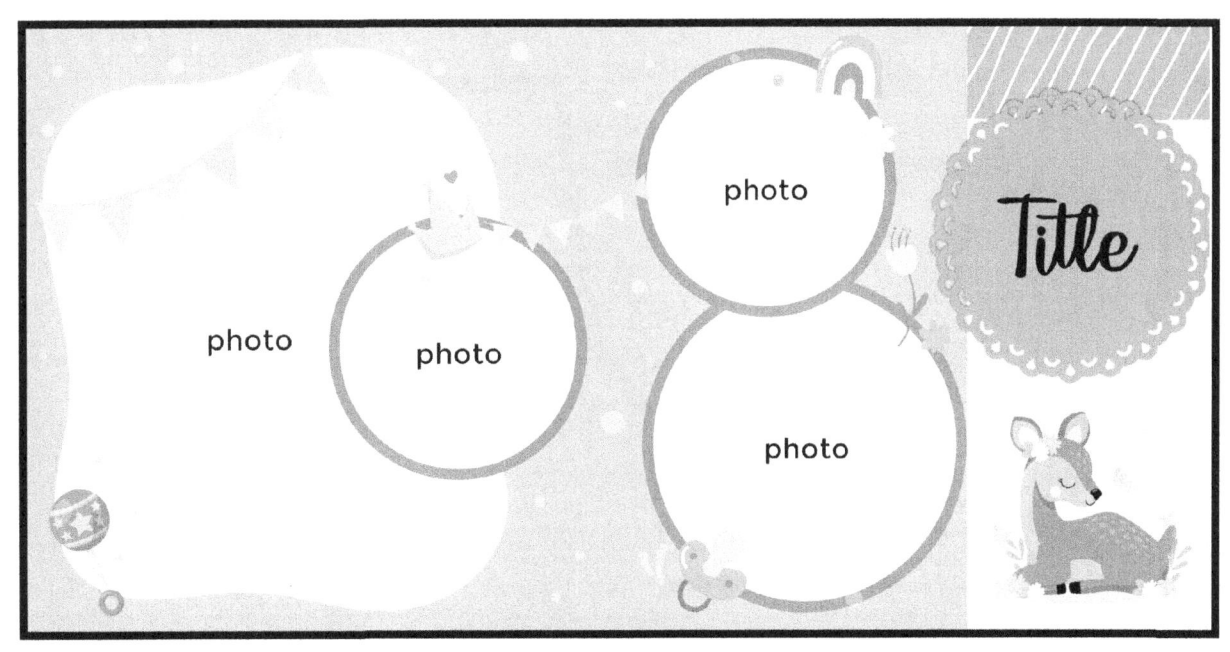

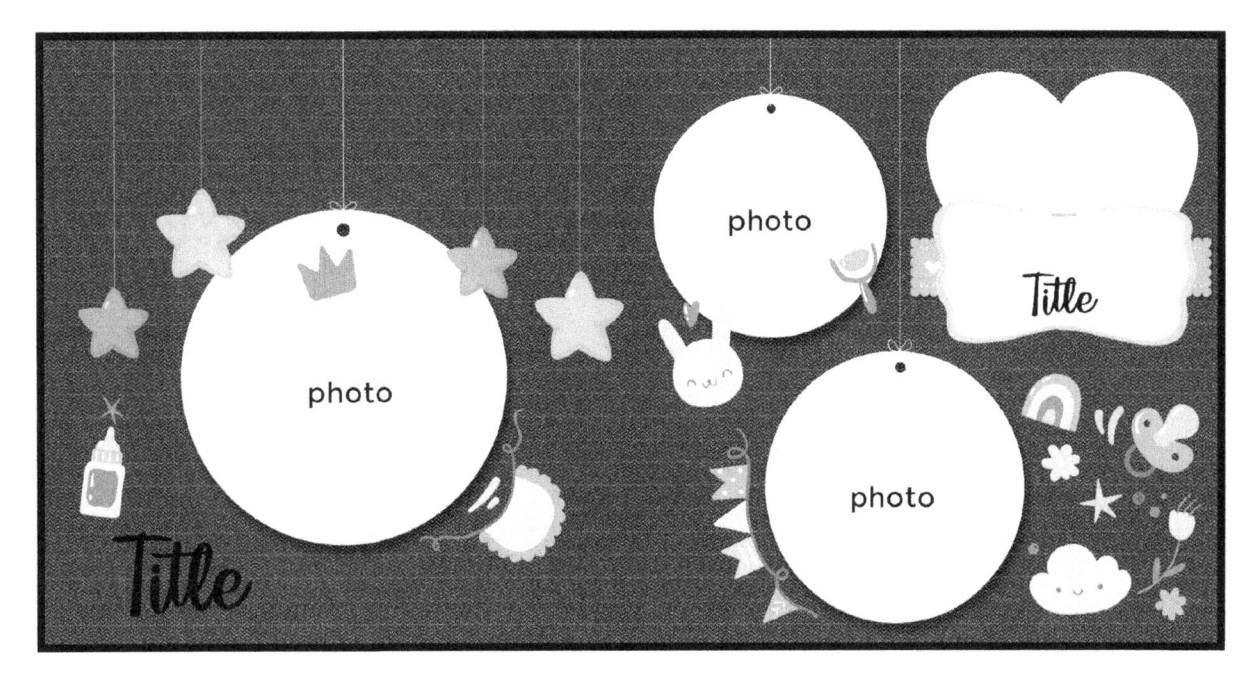

110

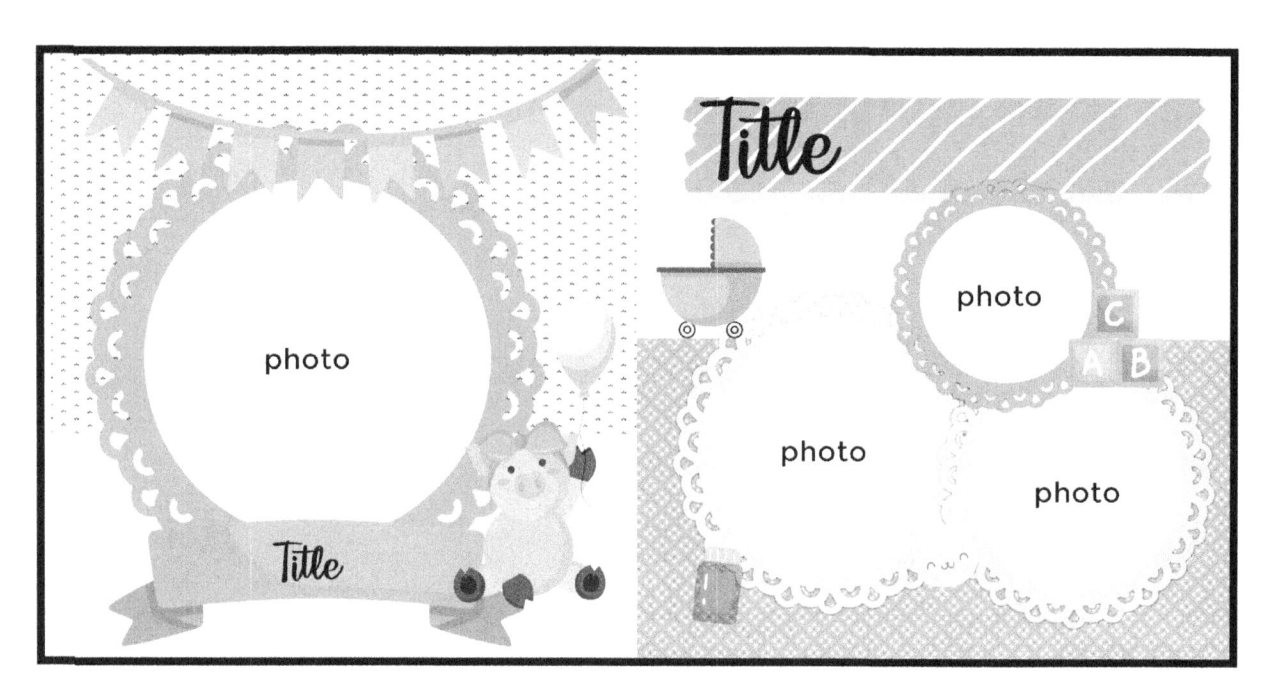

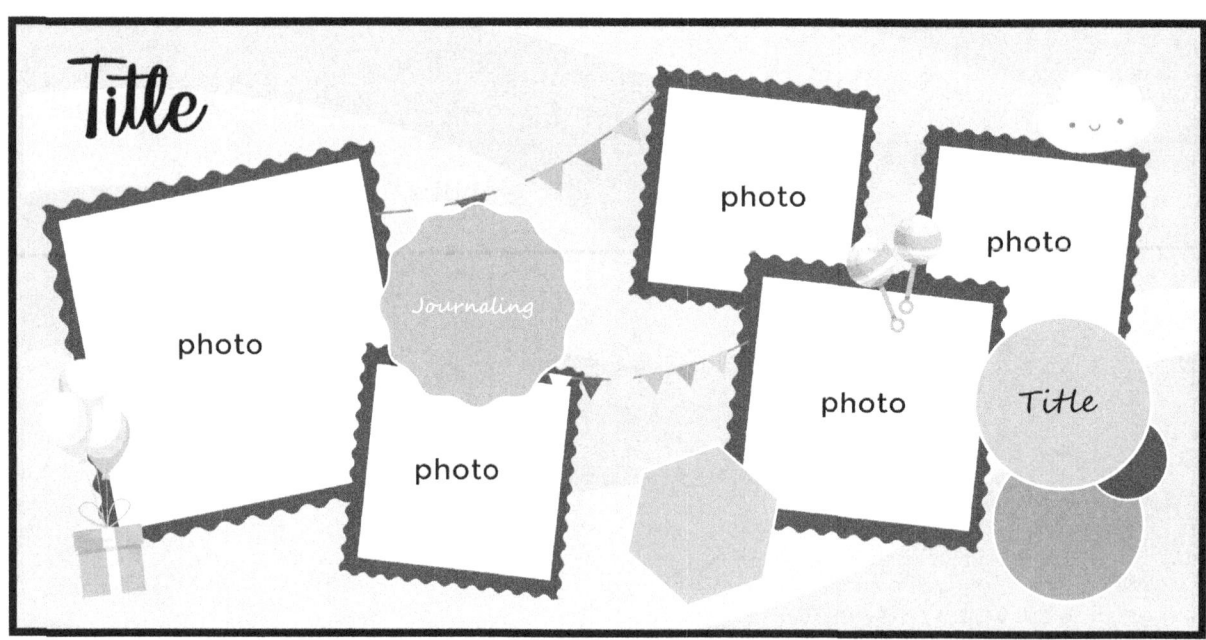

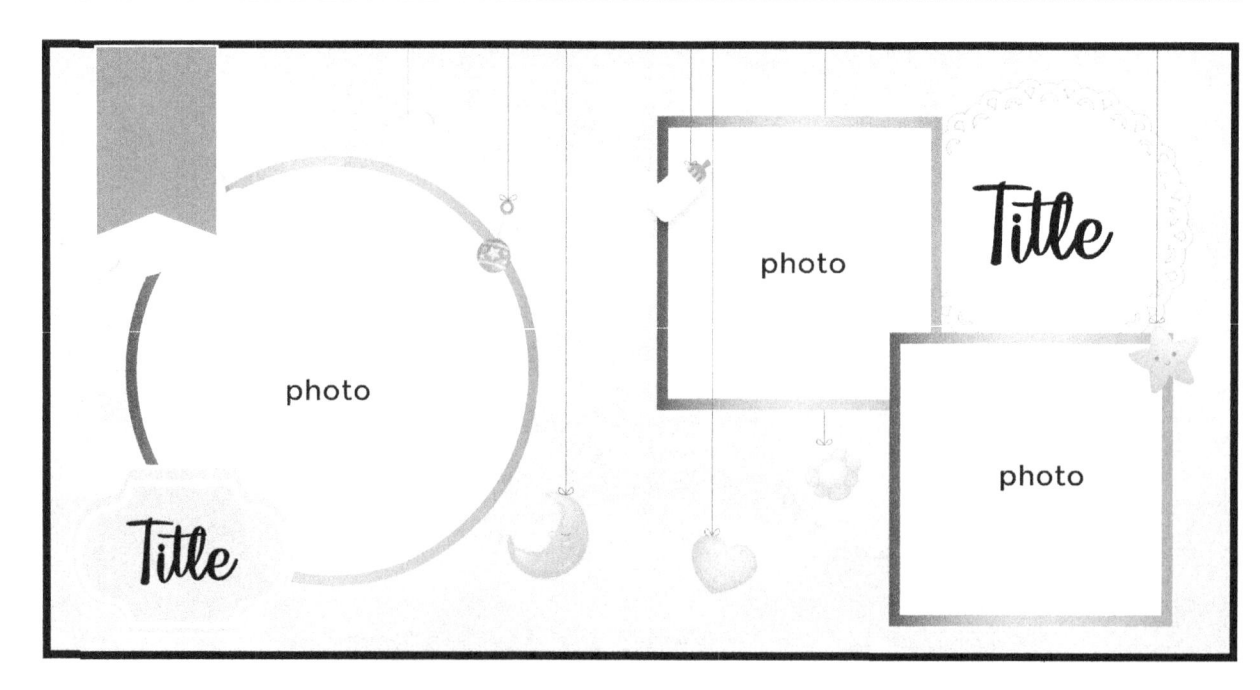

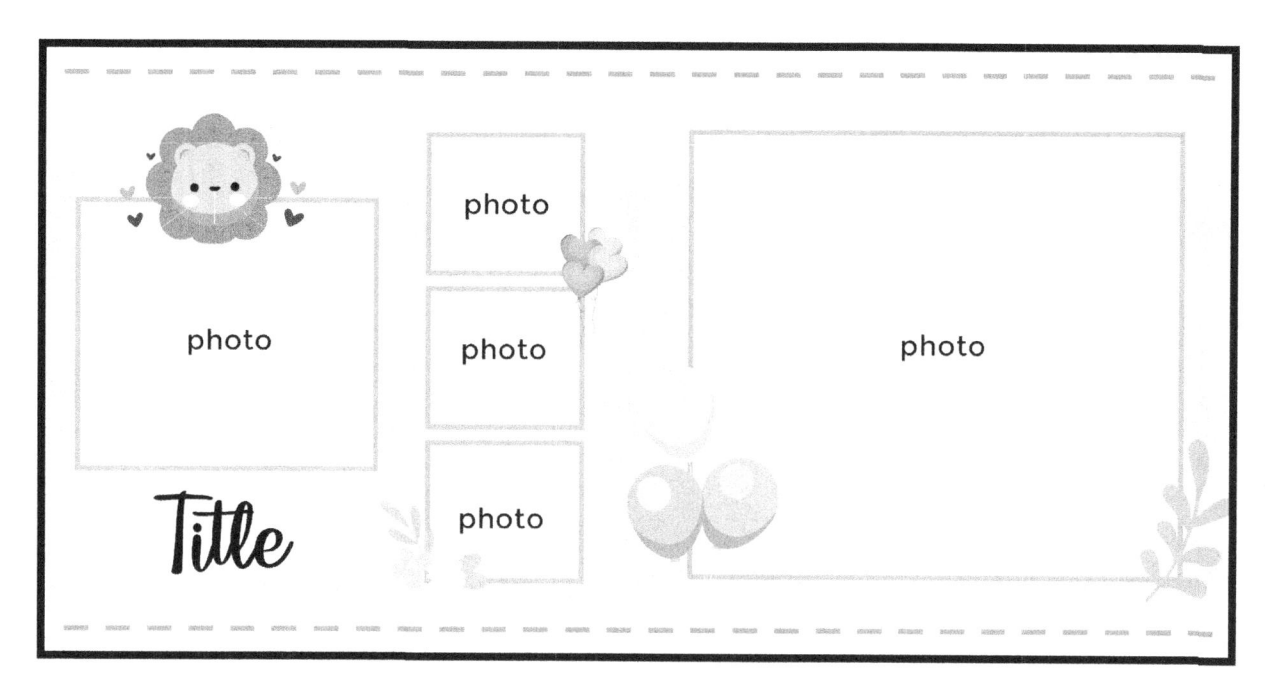

photo

photo

photo

photo

Title

photo

Title

title

photo

photo

photo

photo

Title

photo

photo

Title

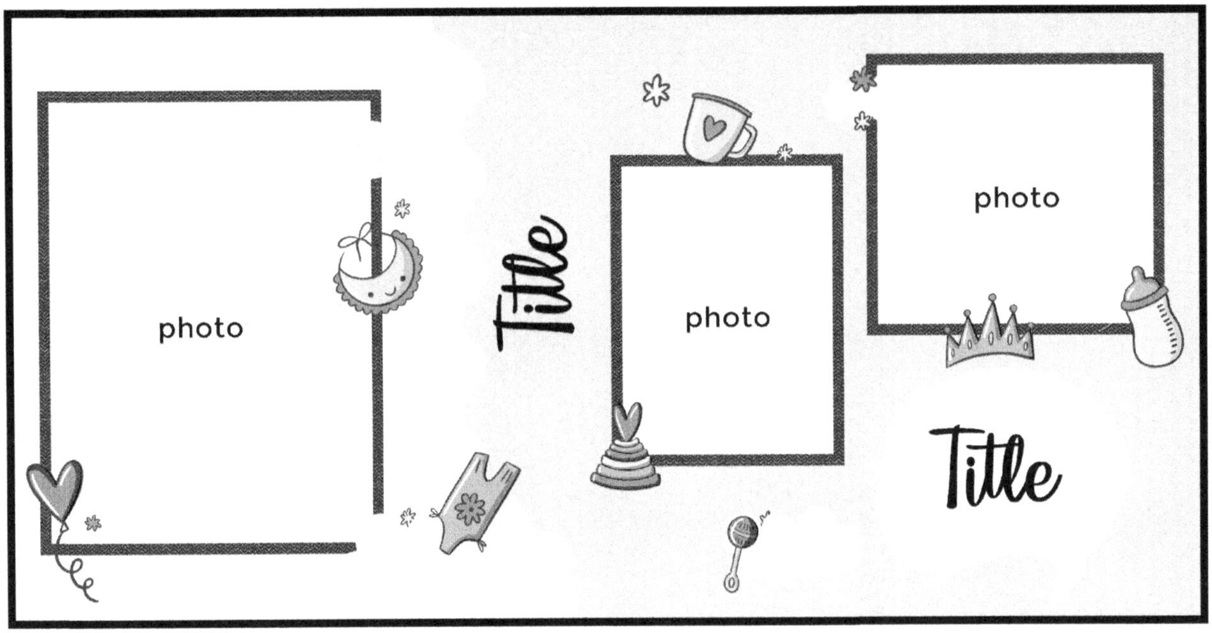
photo
Title
photo
photo
Title

Title
photo
photo
photo
photo
Title

Friend

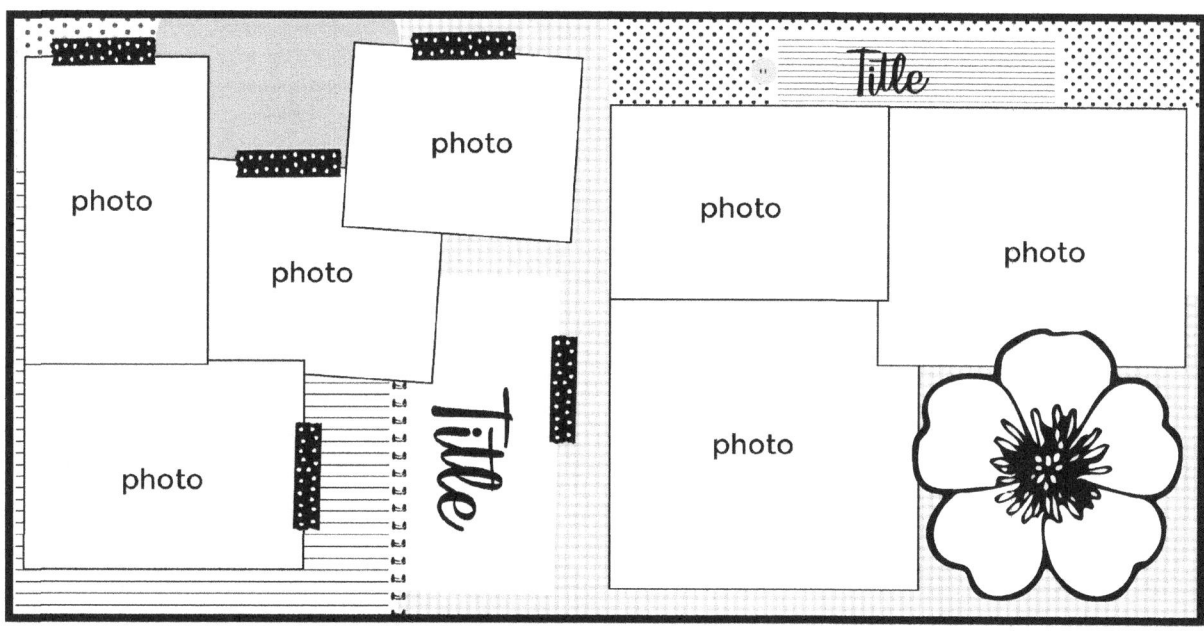

114

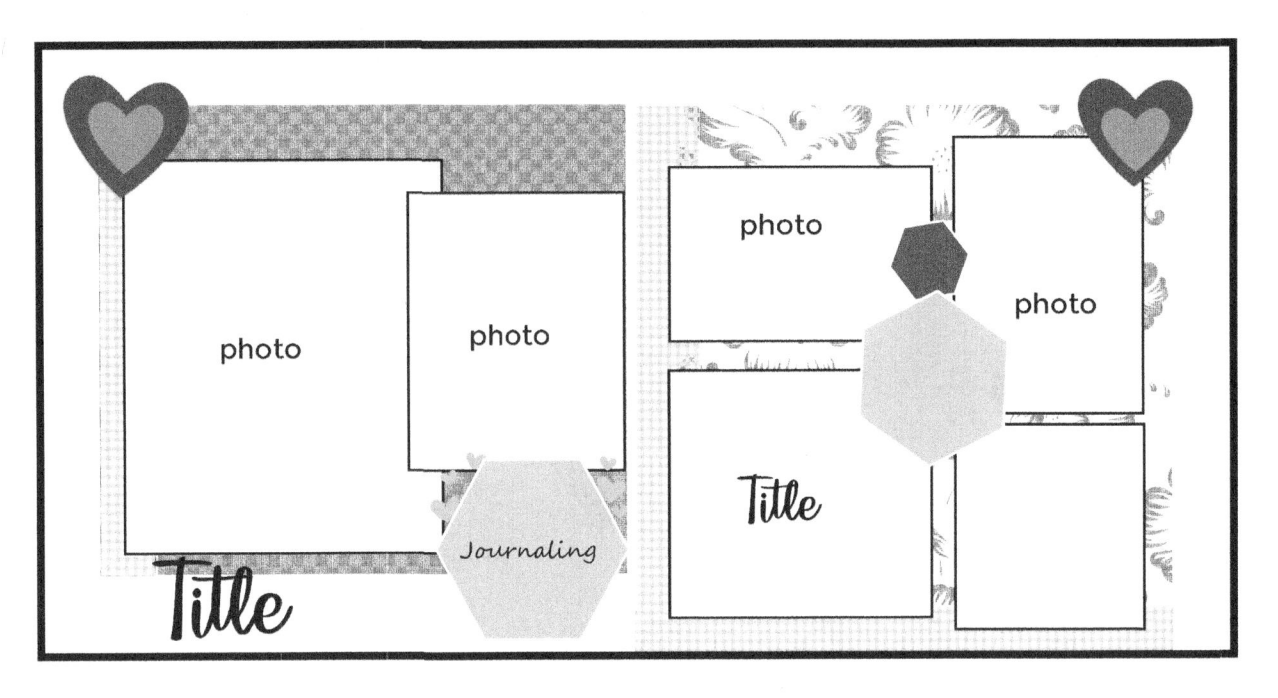

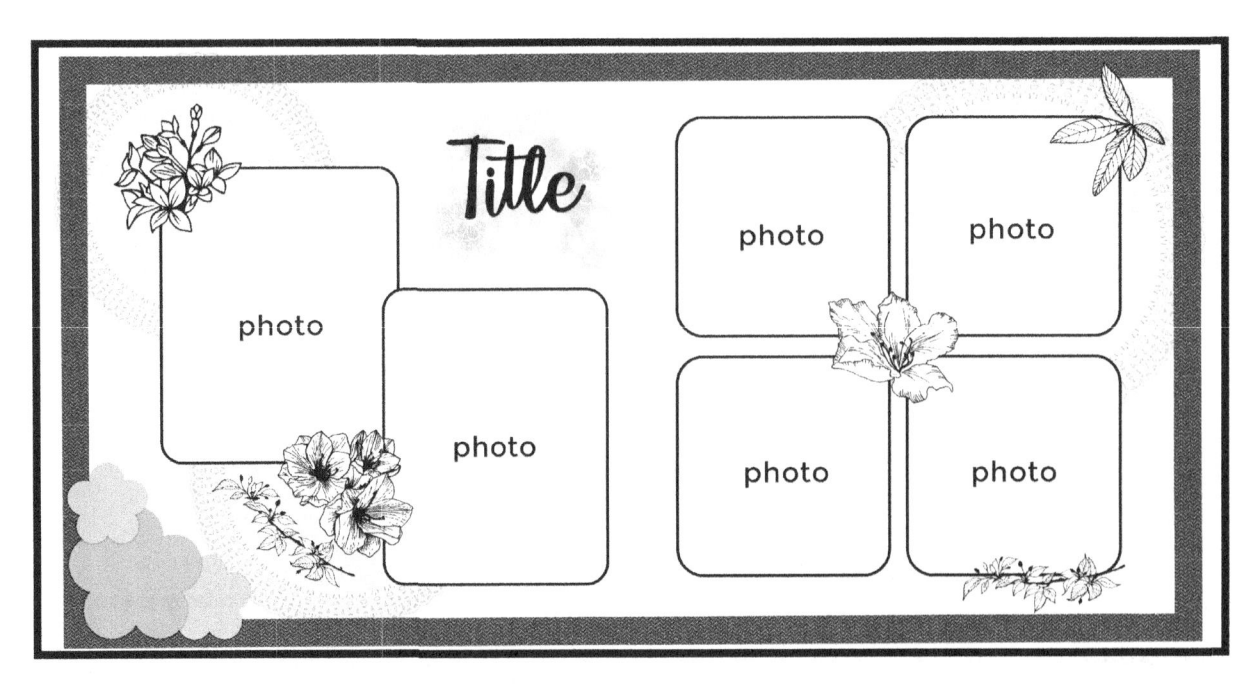

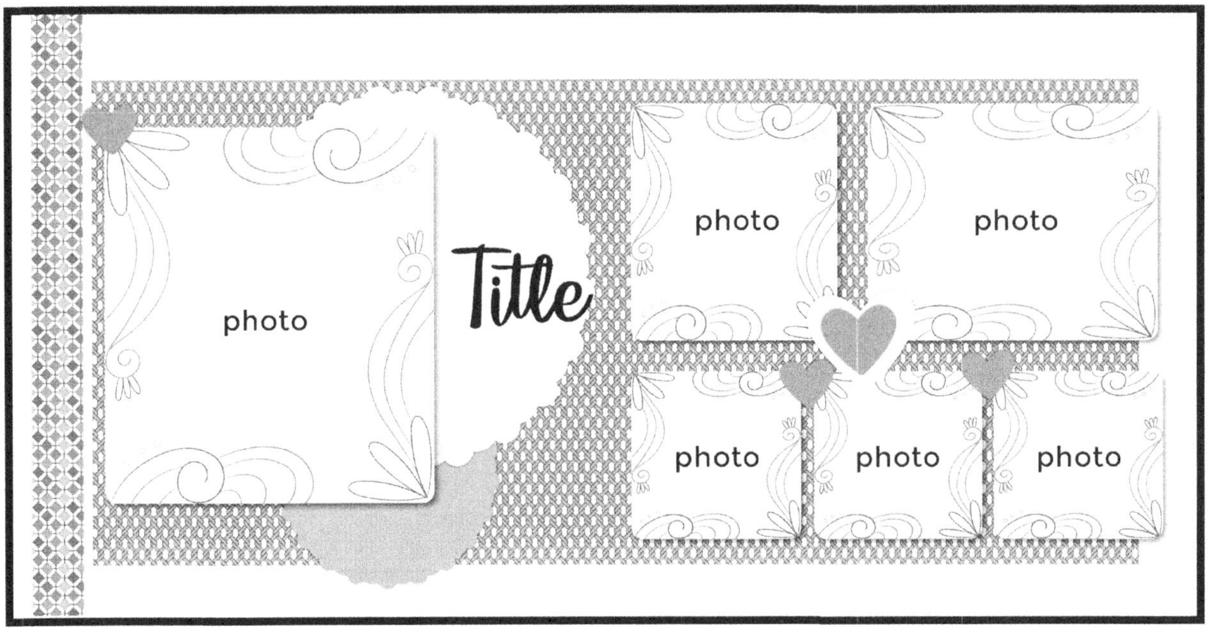
Title
photo
photo
photo
photo
photo
photo

photo
photo
Title
photo
photo
photo

photo
photo
Title
photo
photo
photo
photo
photo
photo
photo
photo

116

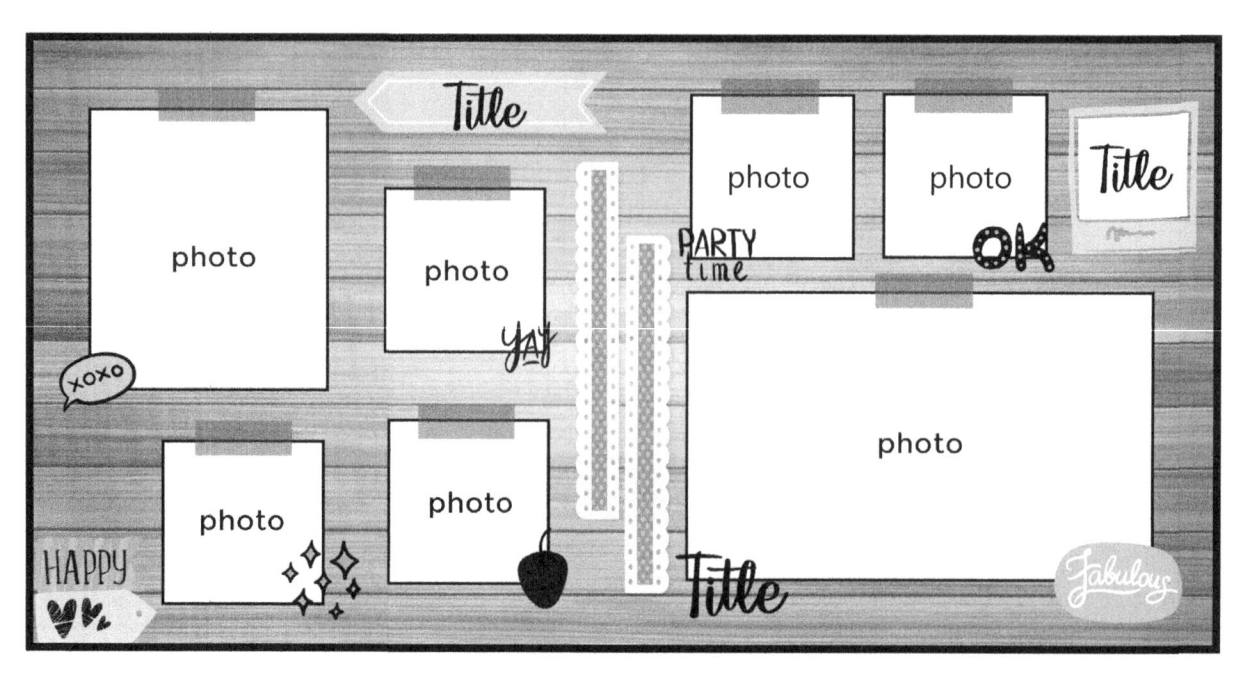

117

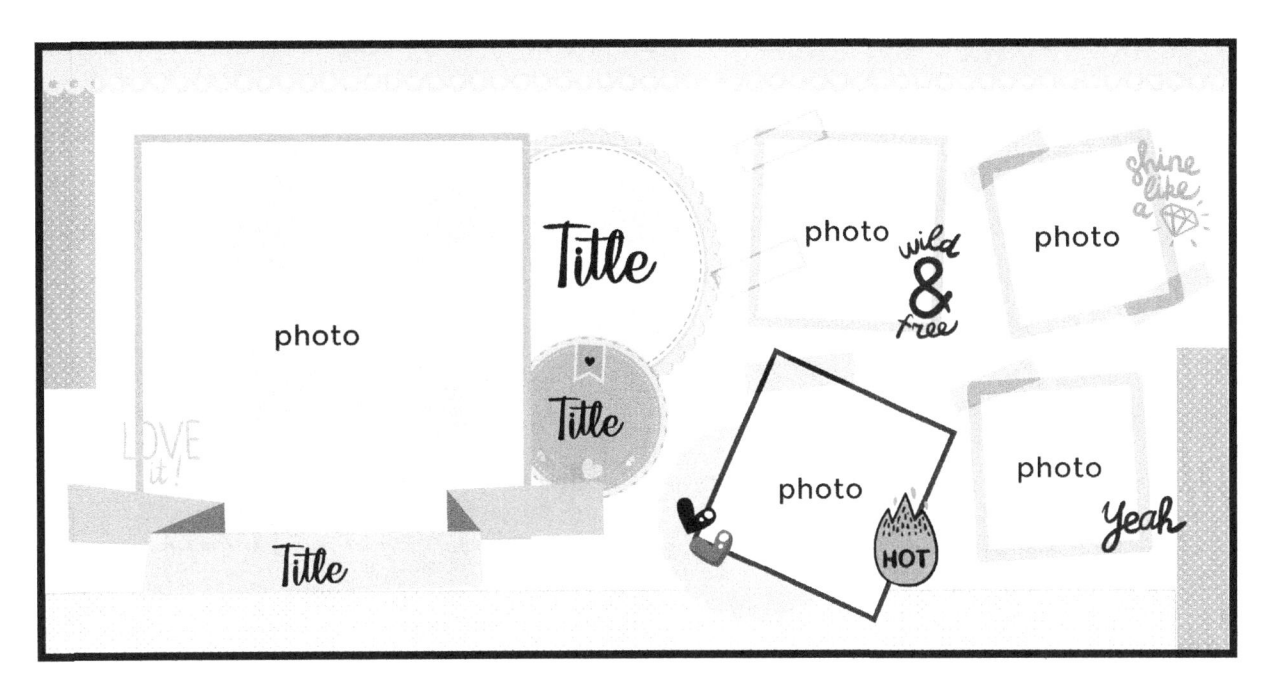

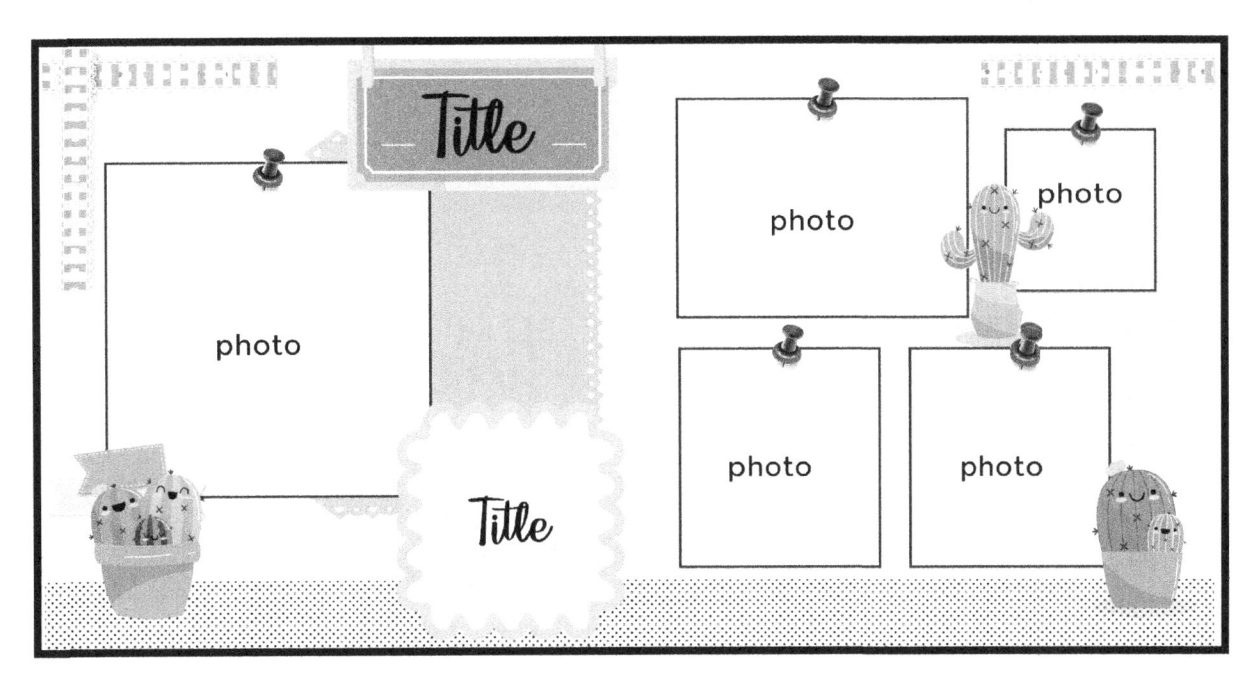

118

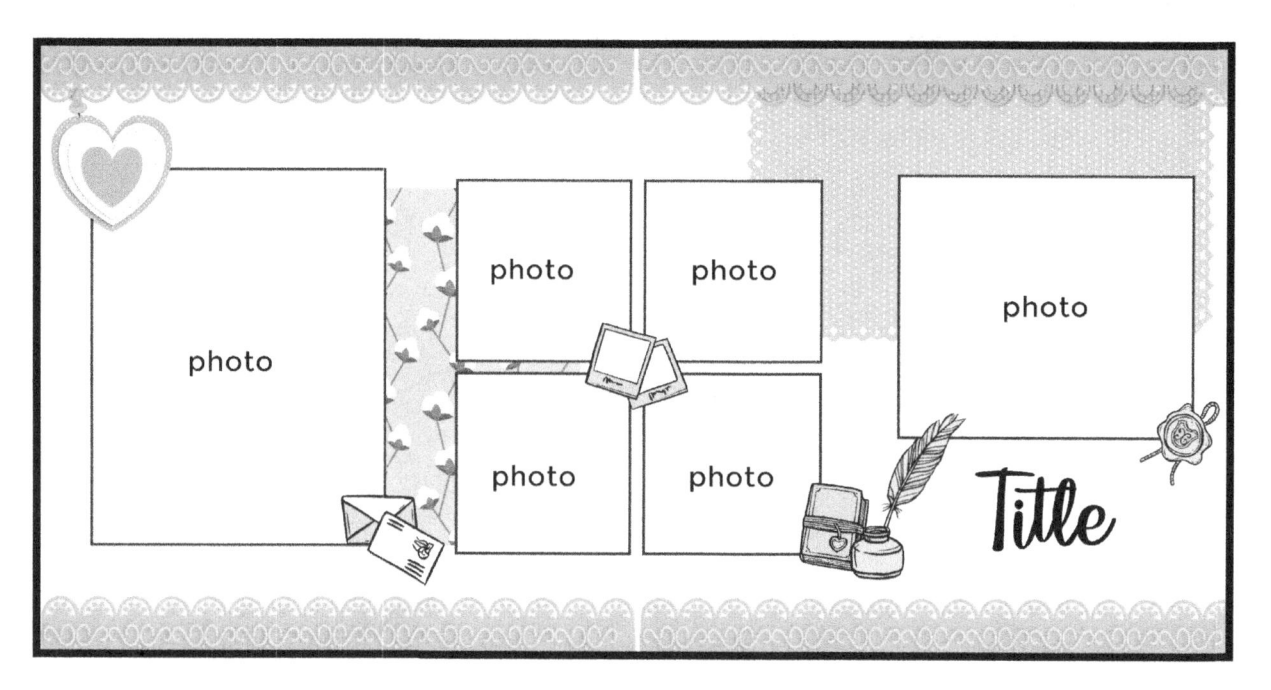

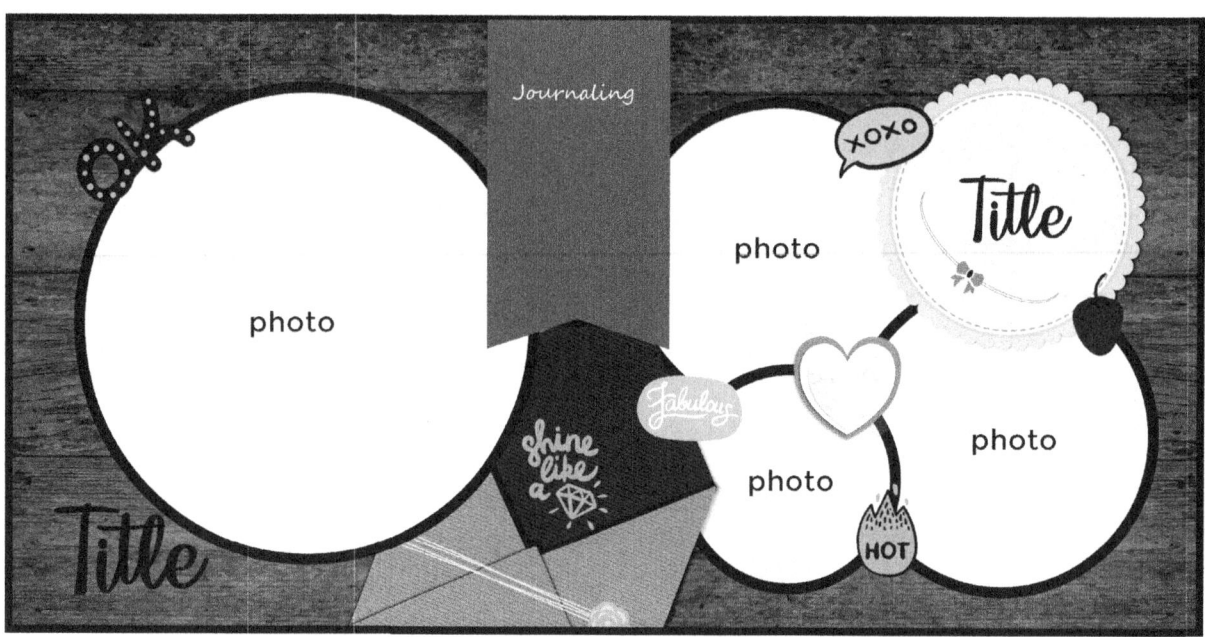

119

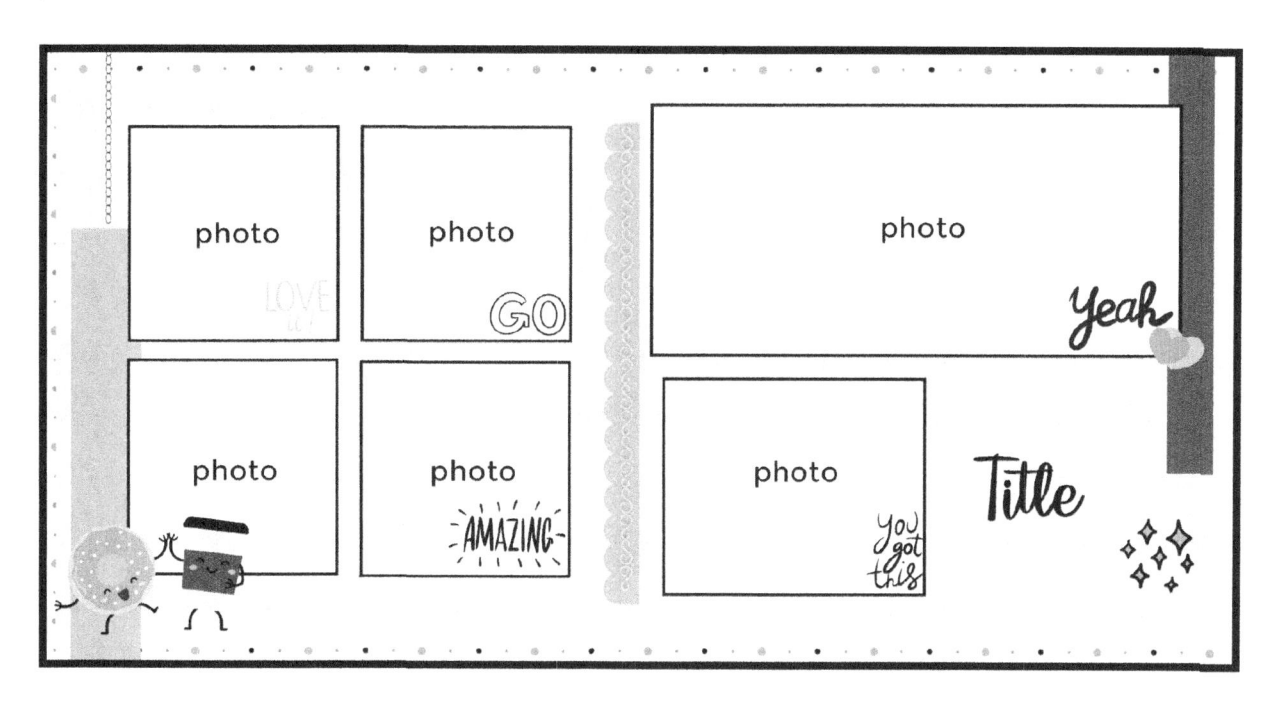

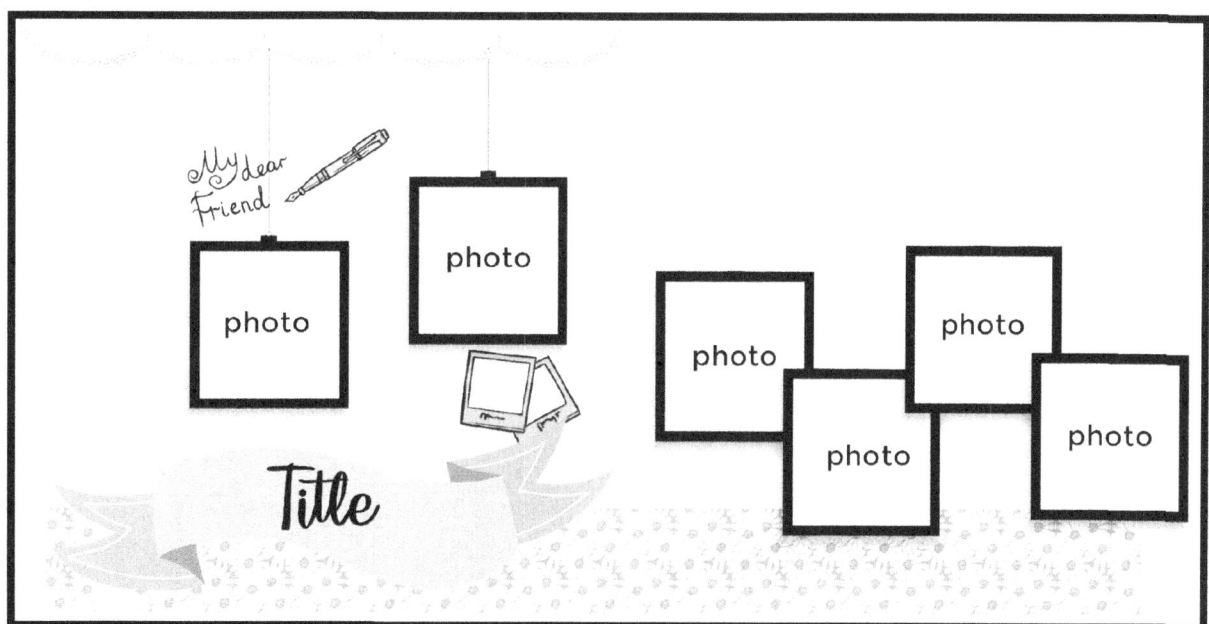

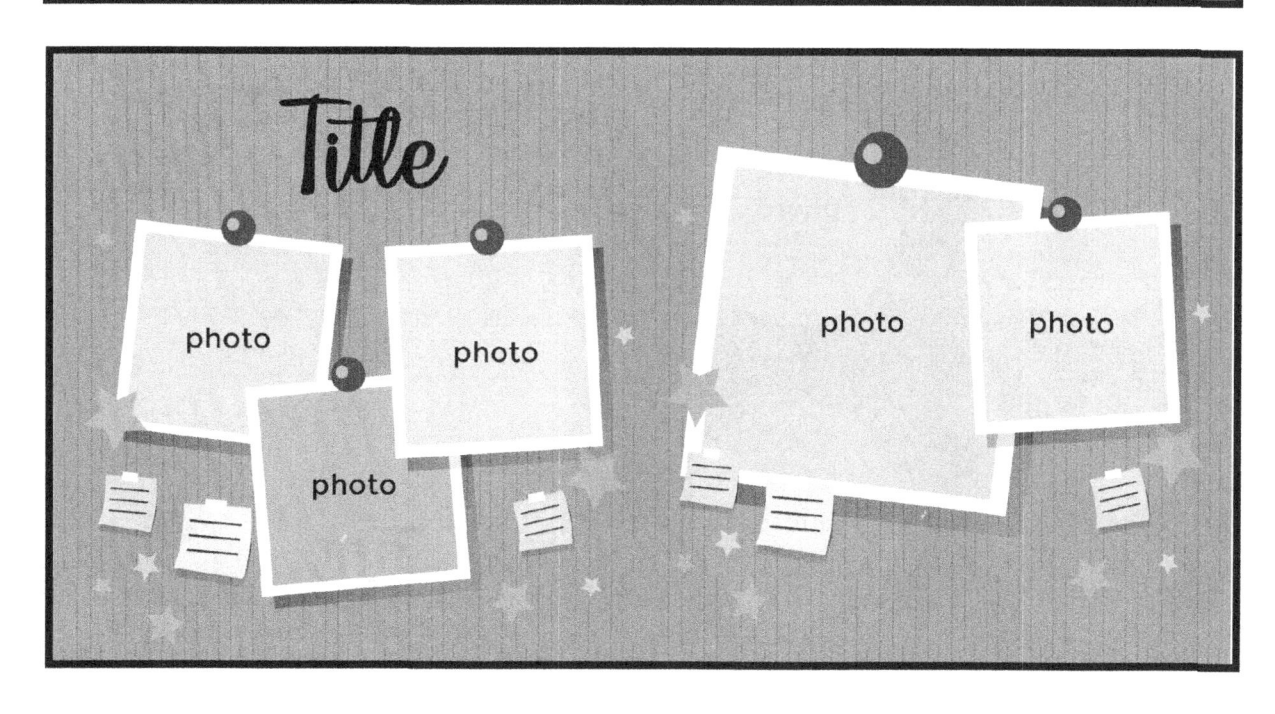

120

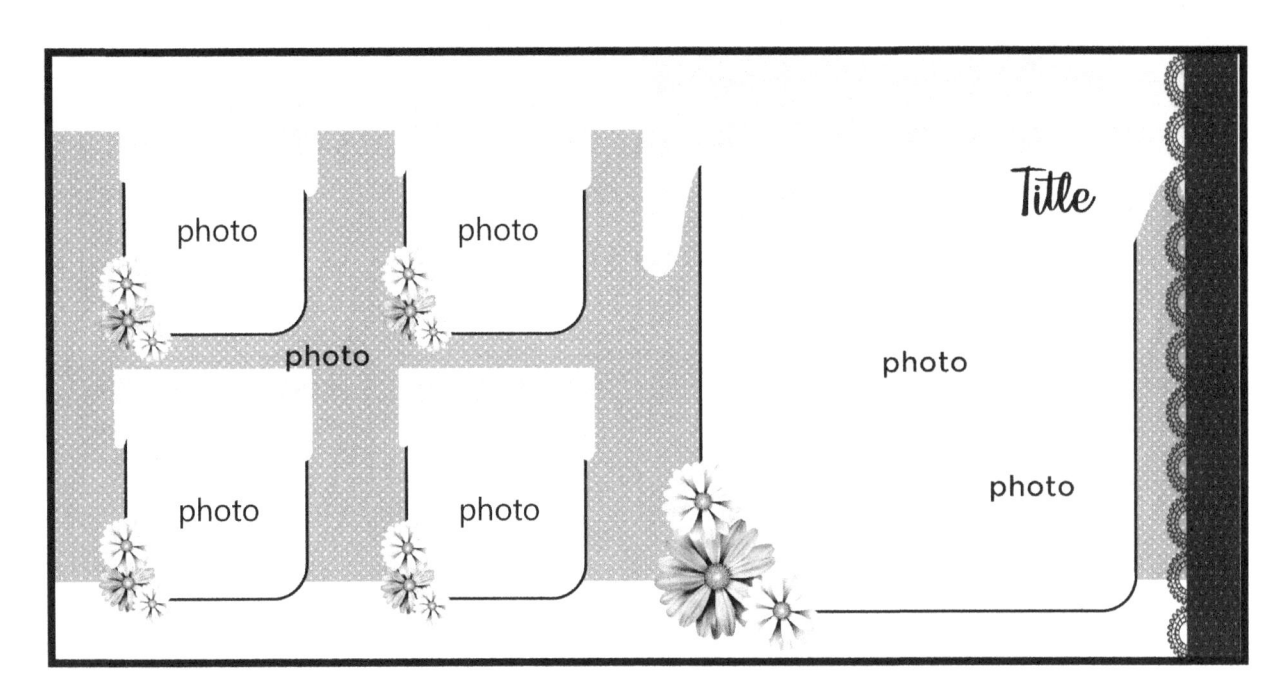

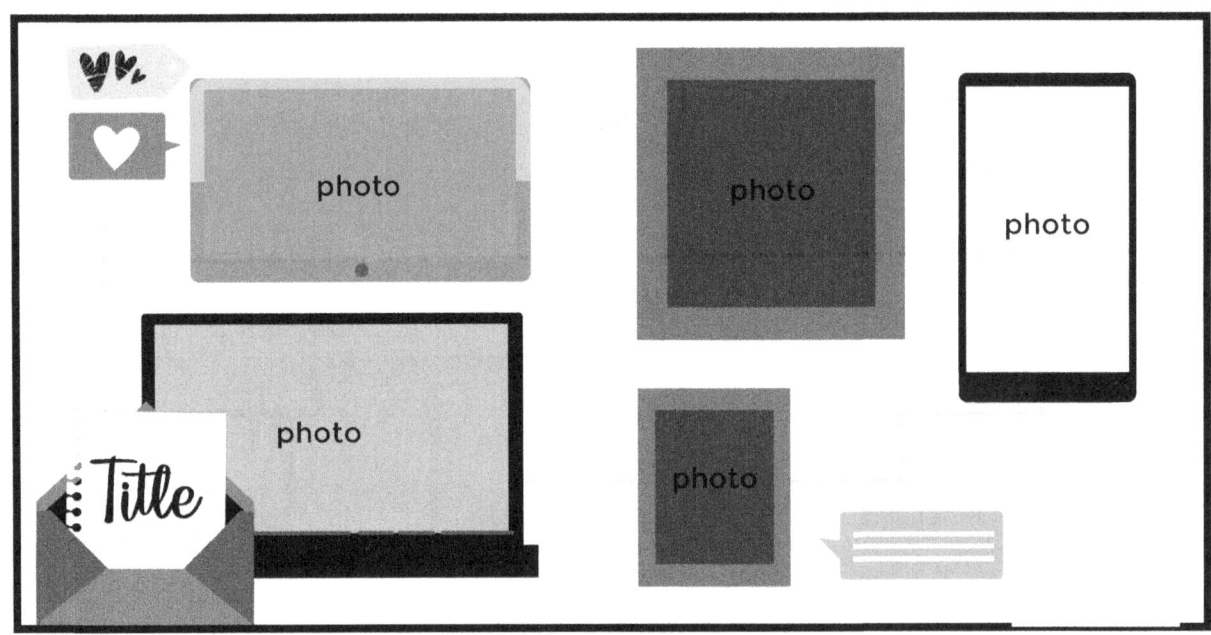

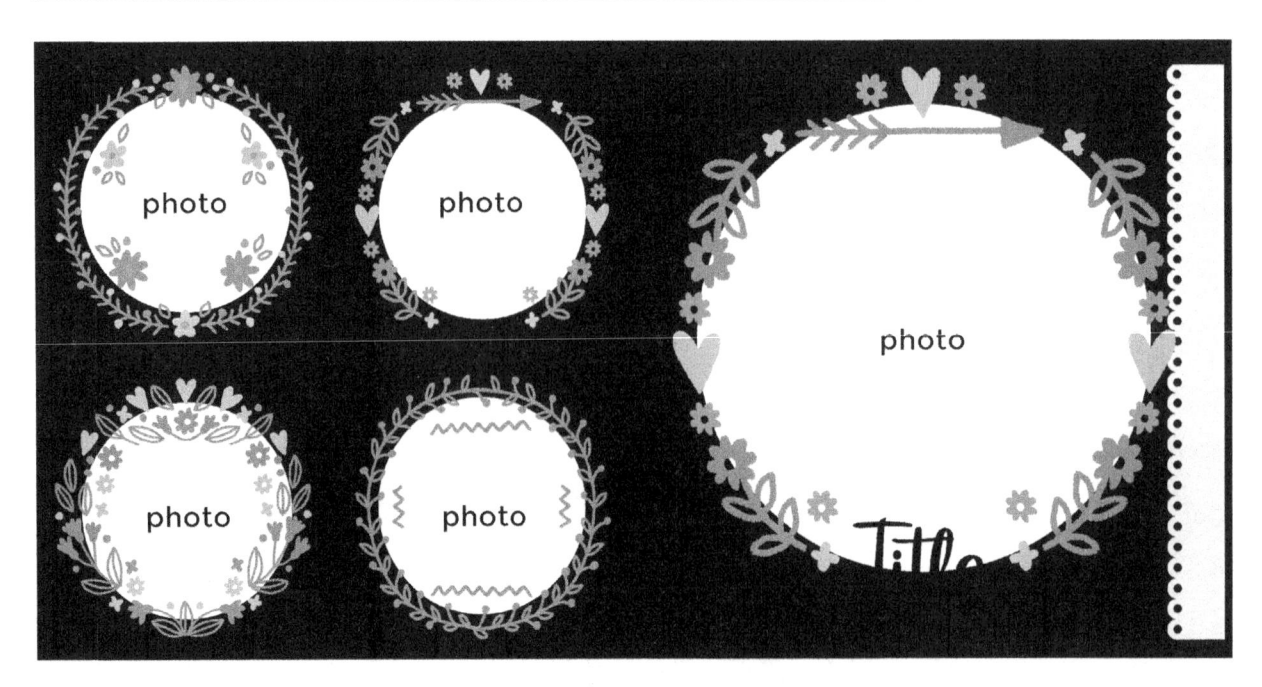

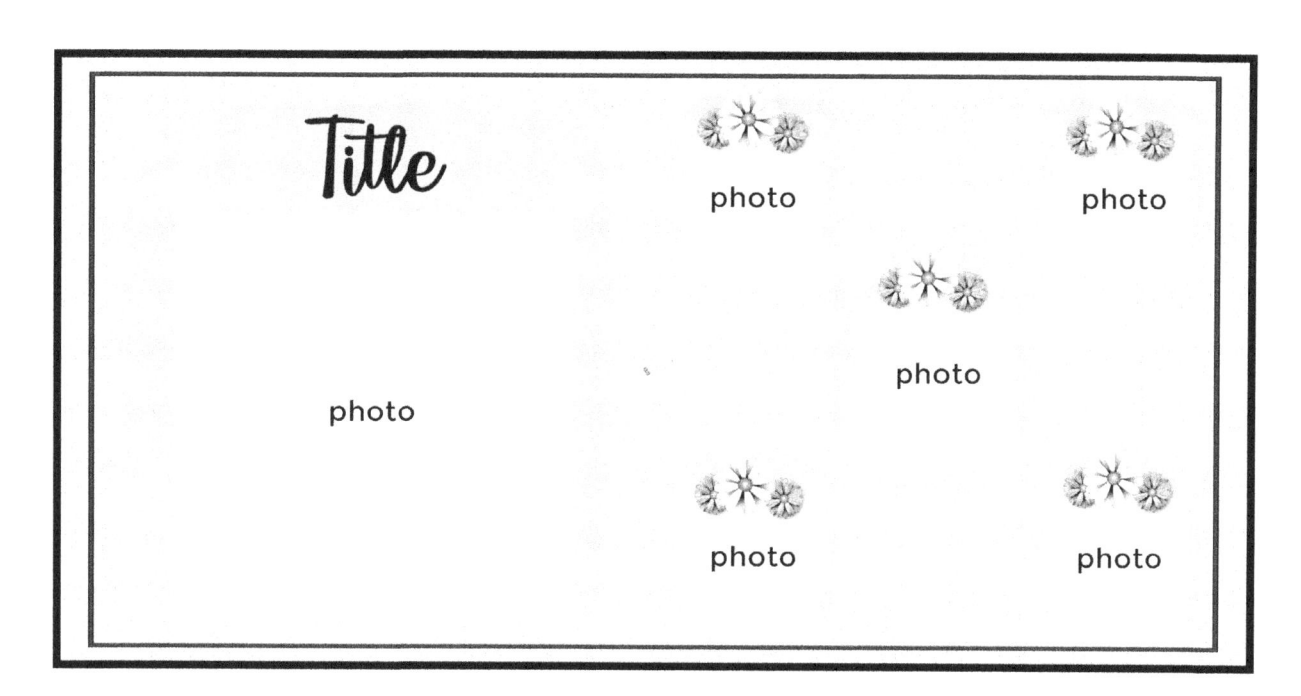

Title

photo

photo

photo

photo

photo

photo

photo

photo

photo

Title

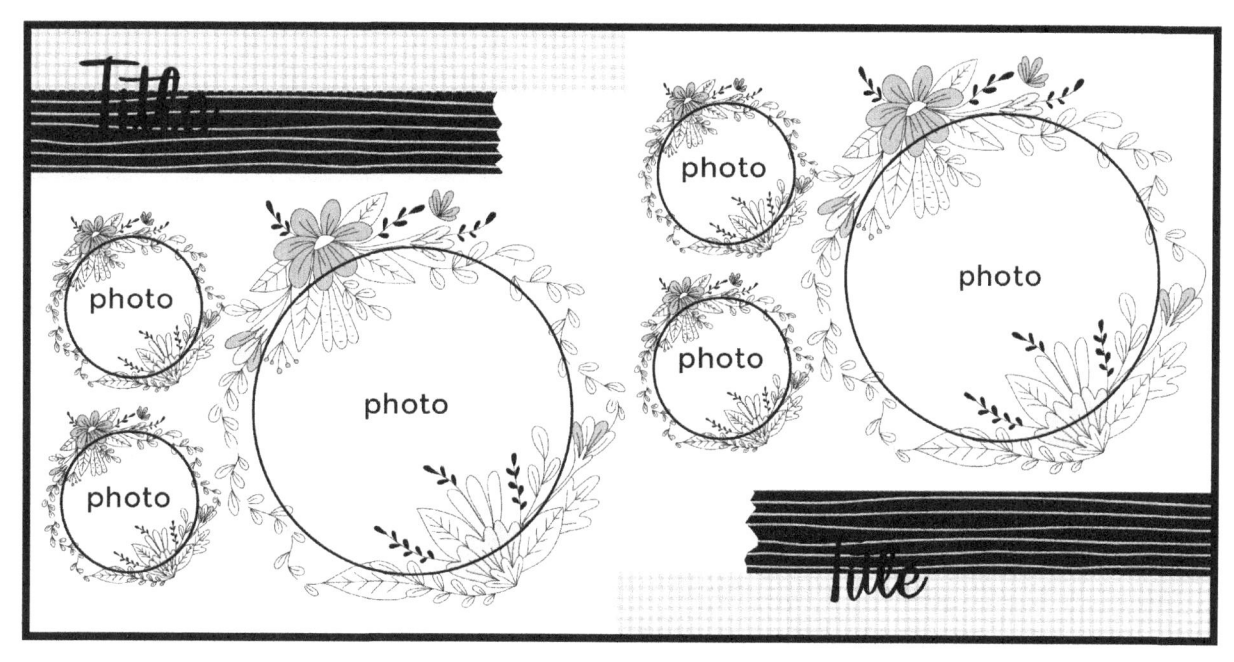

Title

photo

photo

photo

photo

photo

Title

122

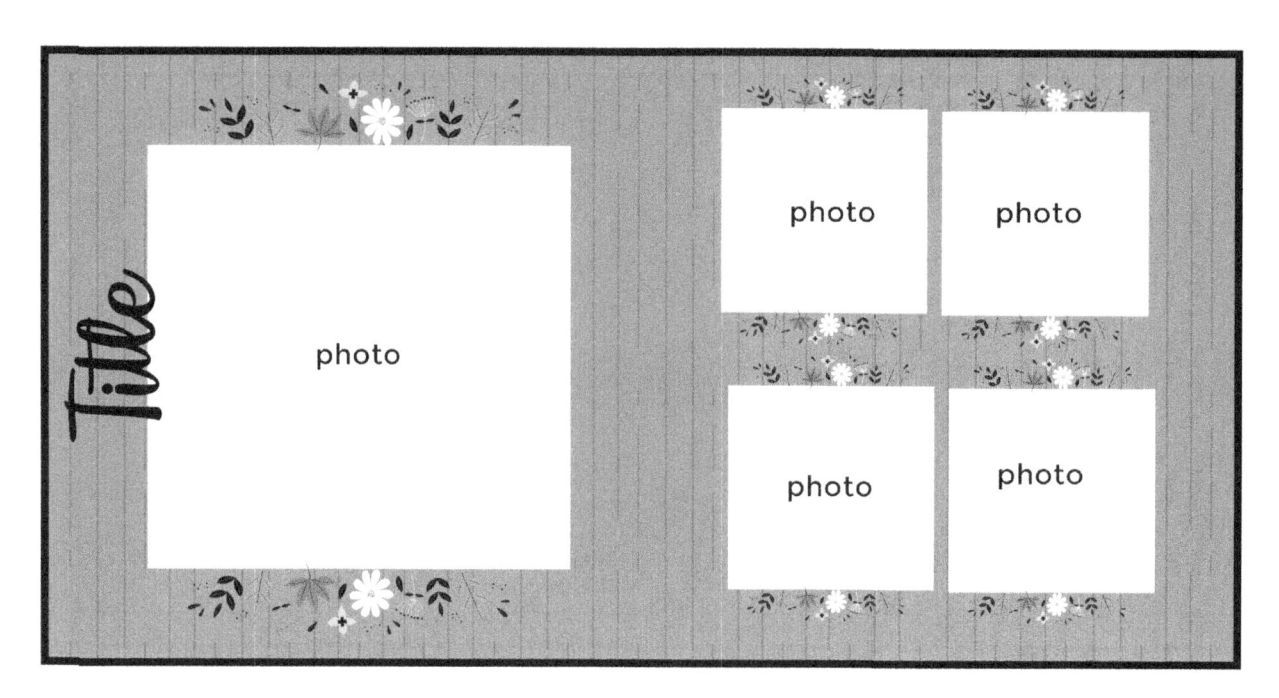

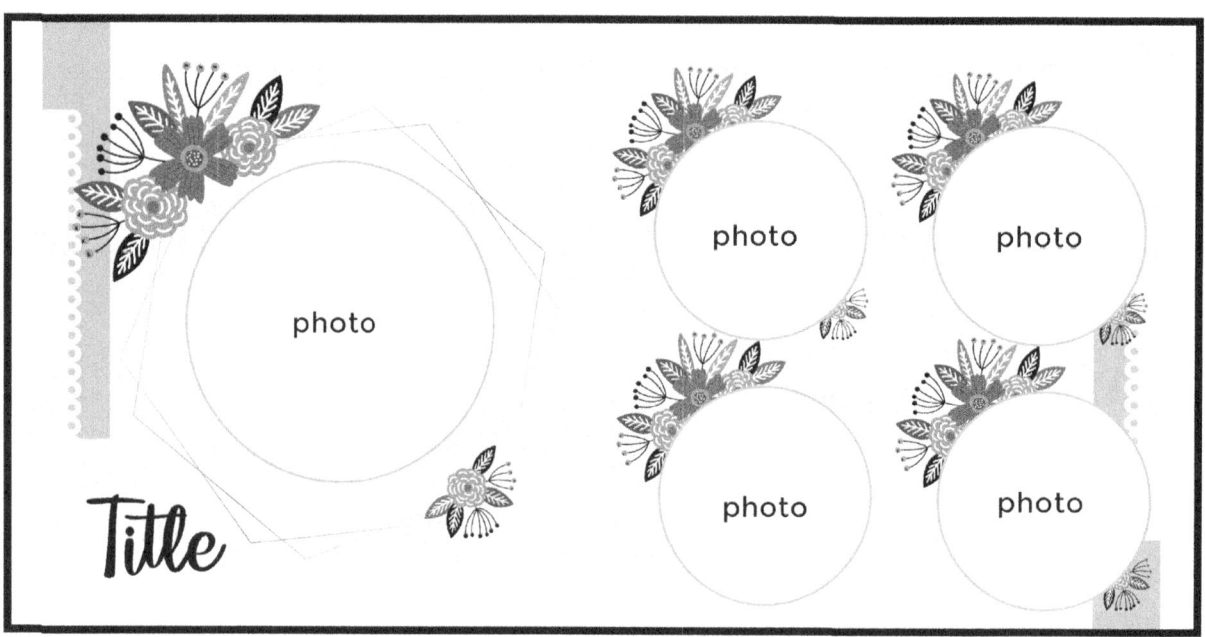

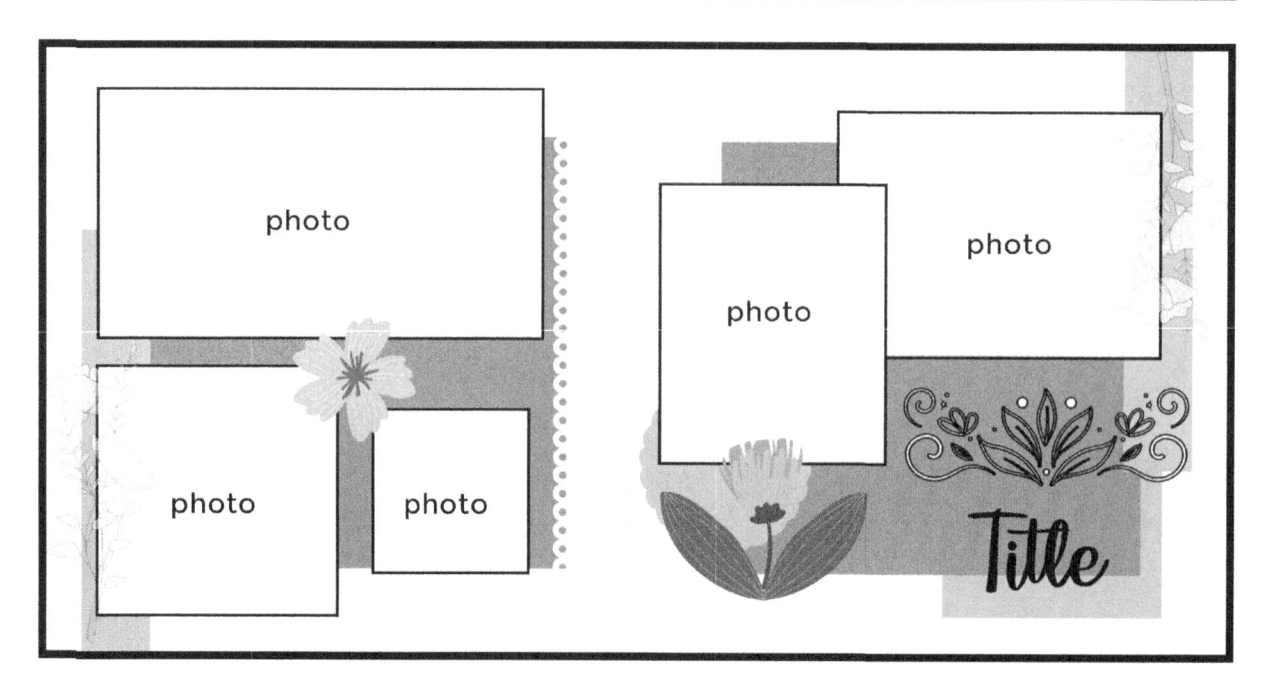

123

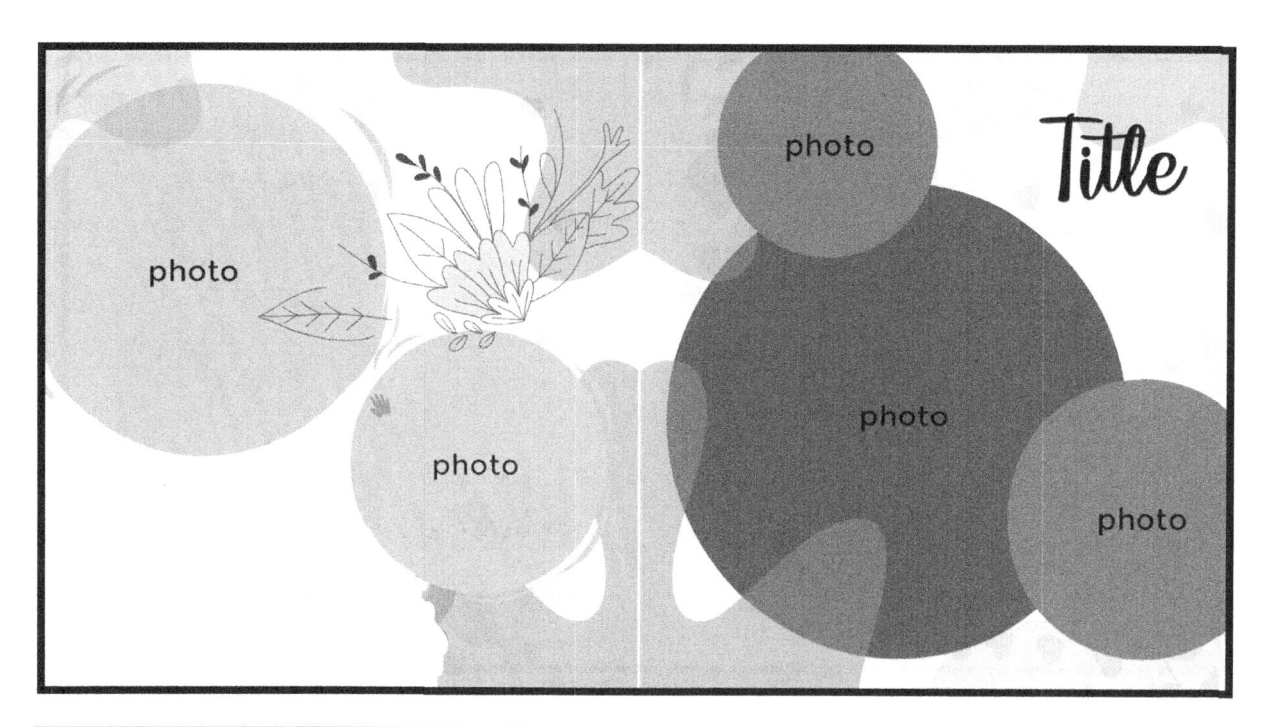

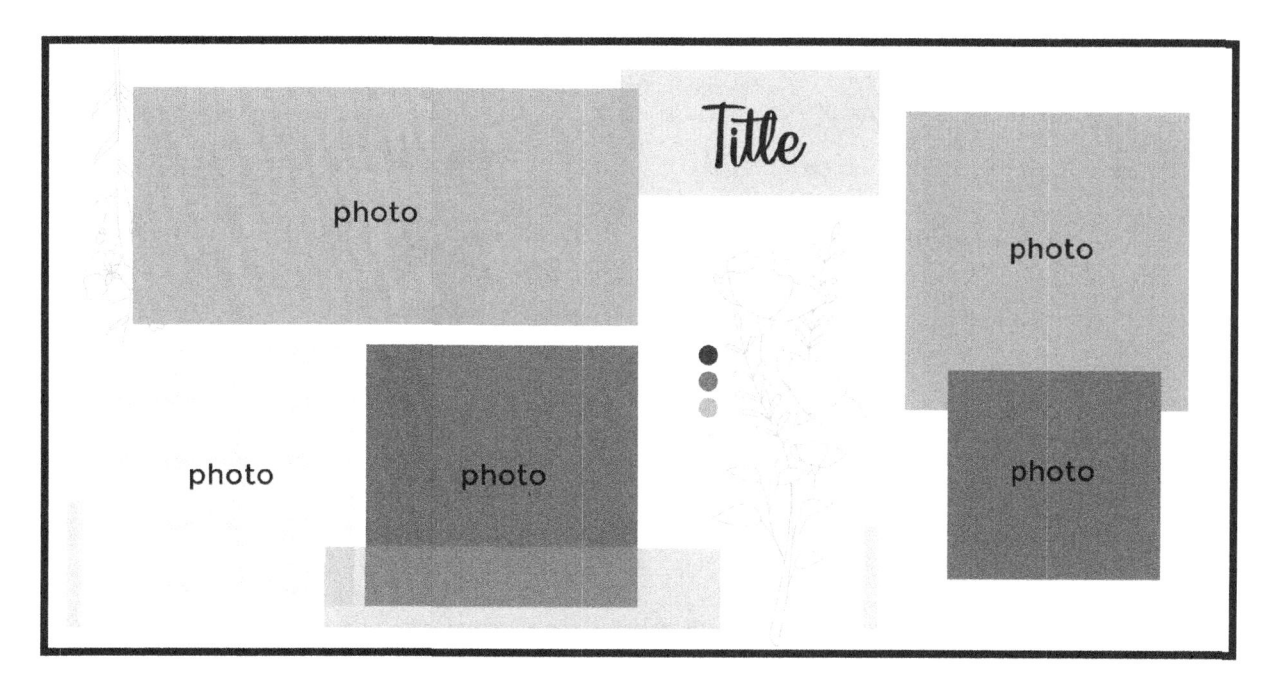

REMEMBER

photo

photo

photo

photo

photo

Title

BEST FRIENDS

Title

photo

photo

photo

photo

Childhood Friends

photo

photo

Sentiments...

photo

photo

photo

Sentiments...

Bff

Girl

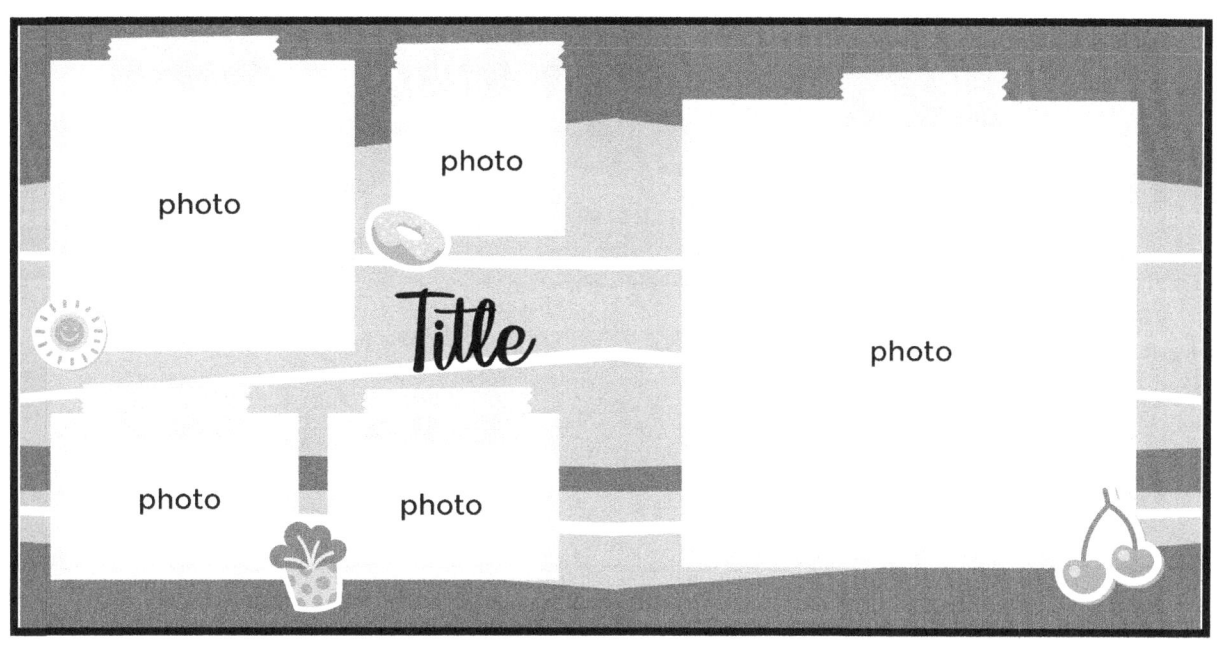

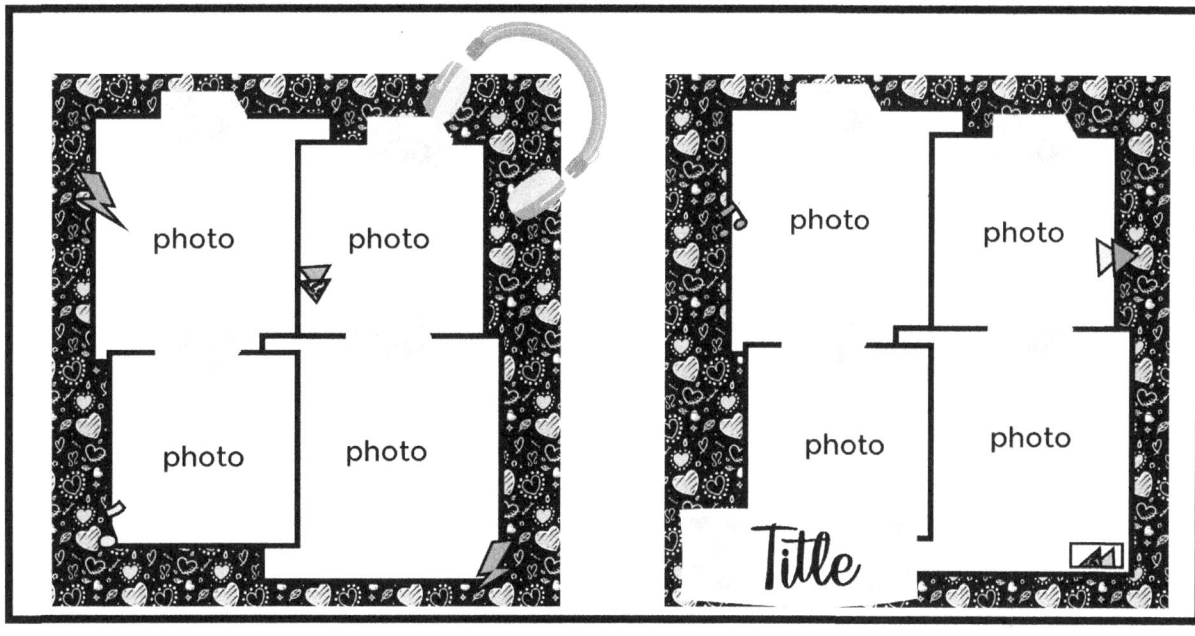

125

126

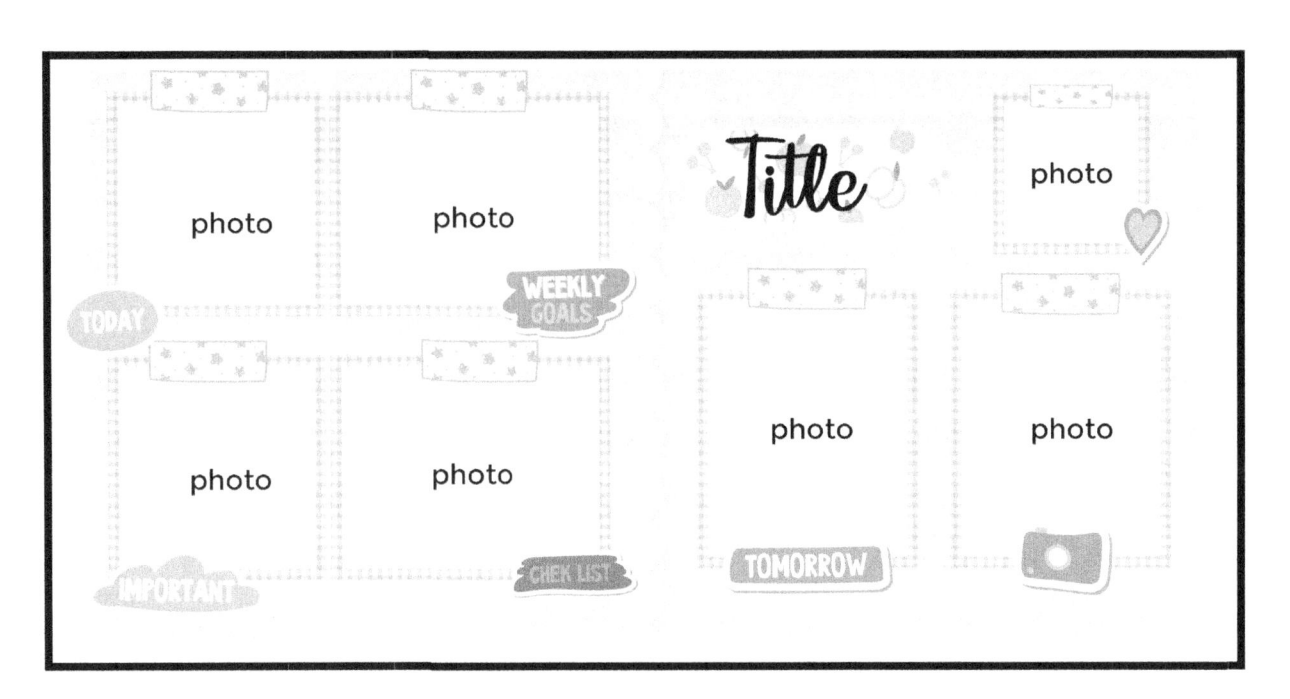

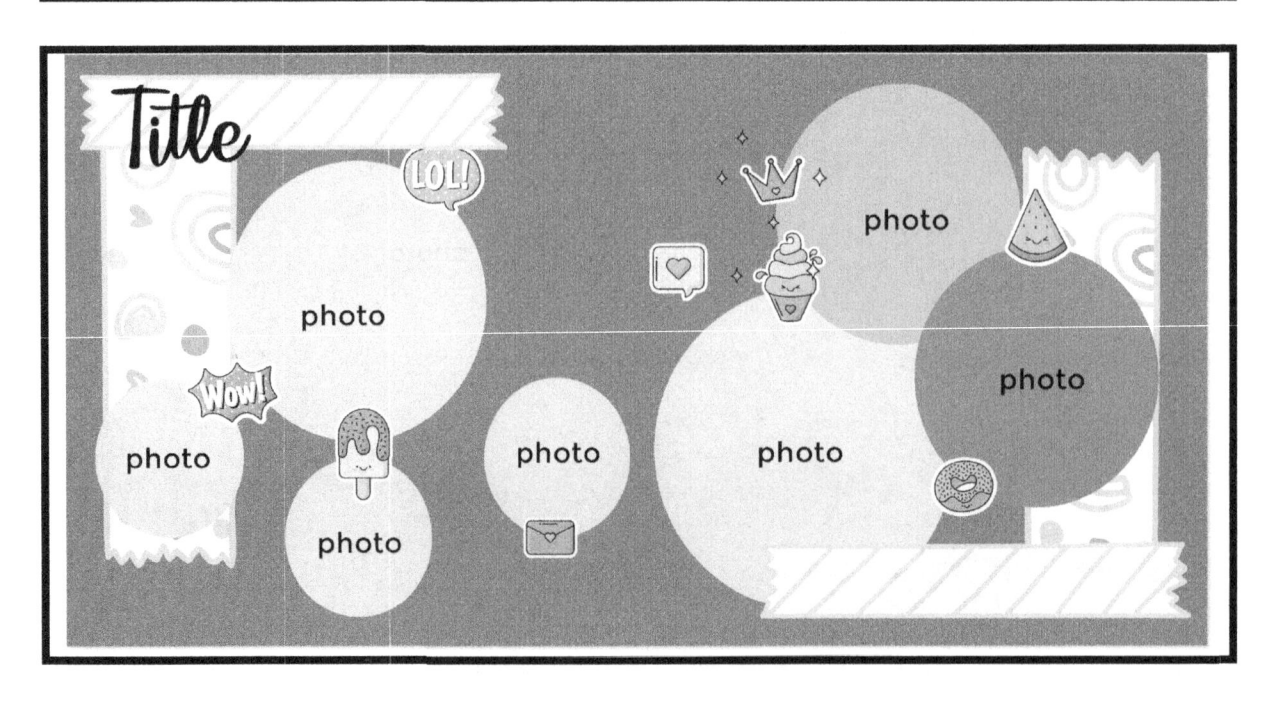

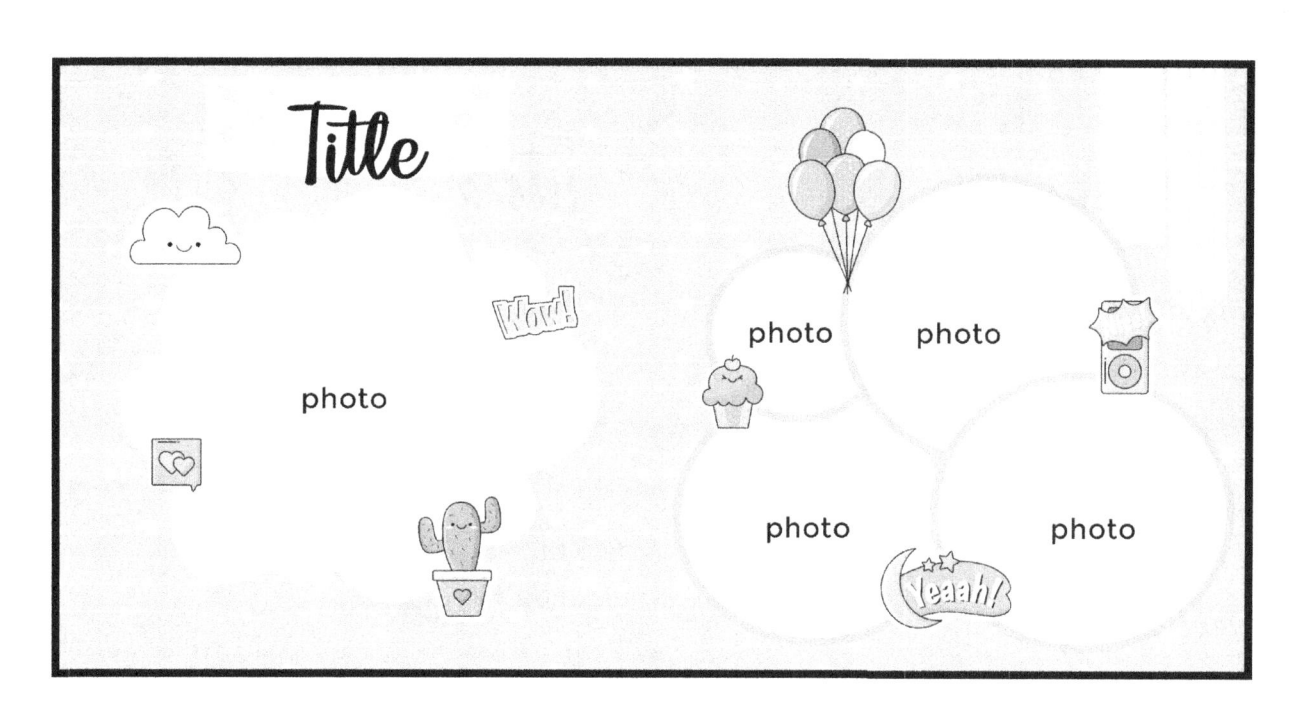

Title

photo
photo
photo
photo
photo

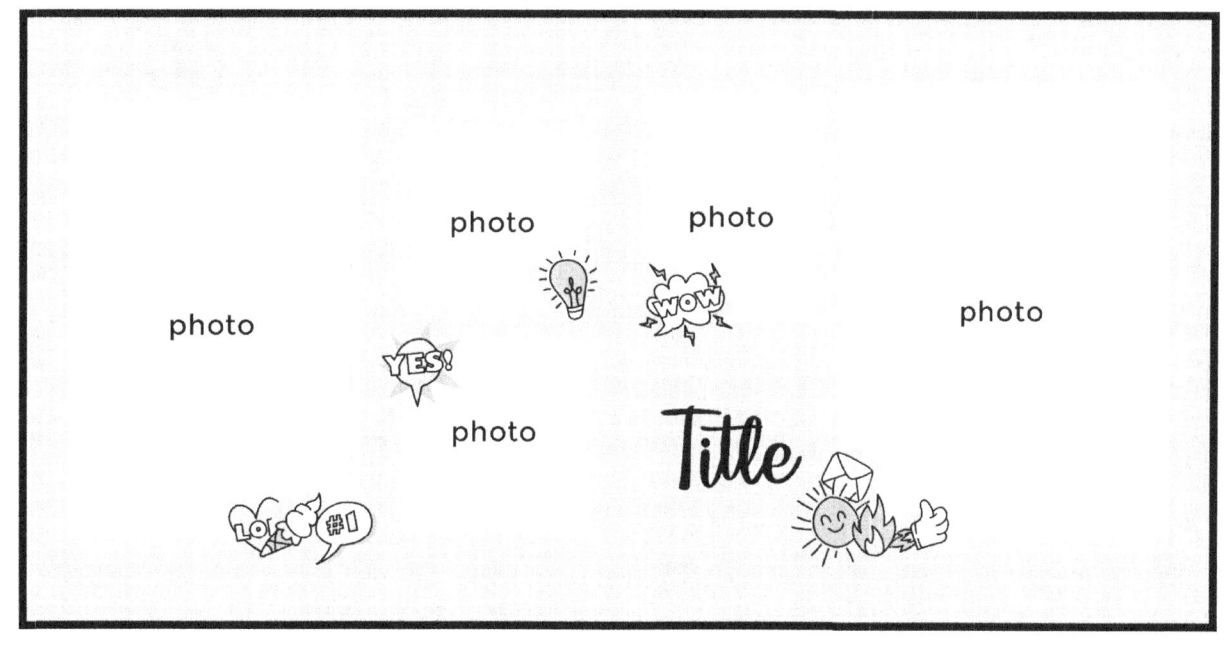

photo
photo
photo
photo
photo
Title

Title

photo
photo
photo
photo
photo
Title

127

128

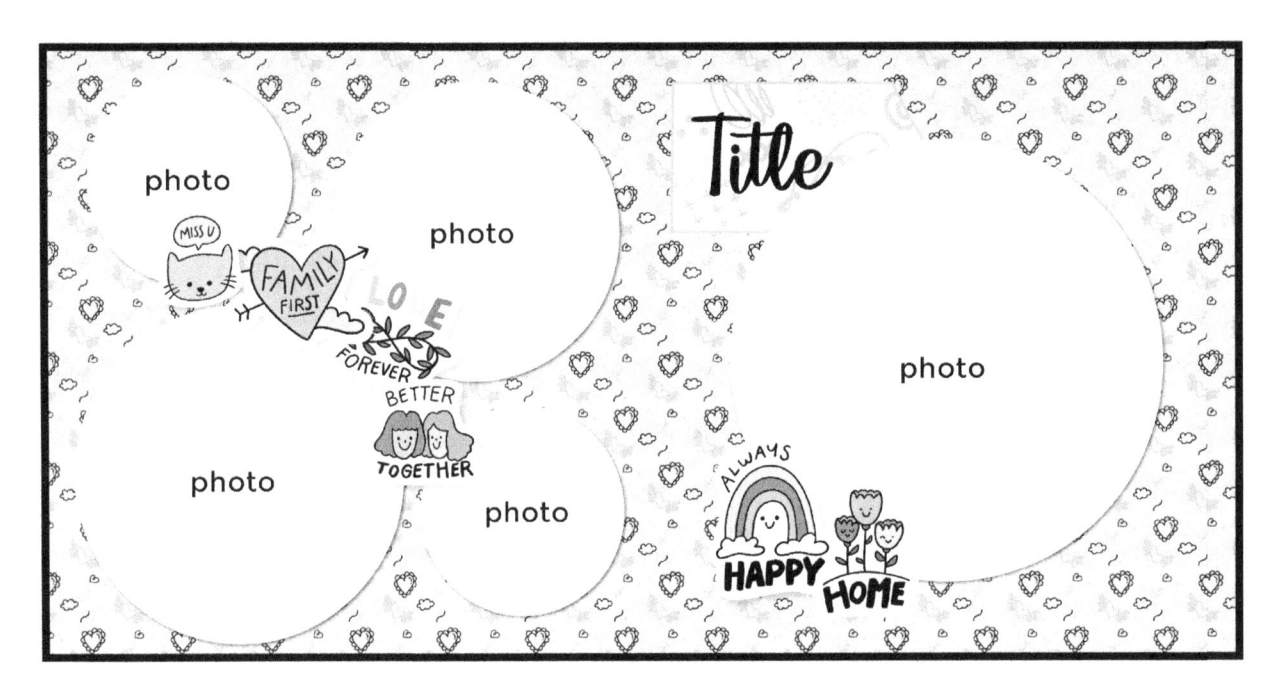

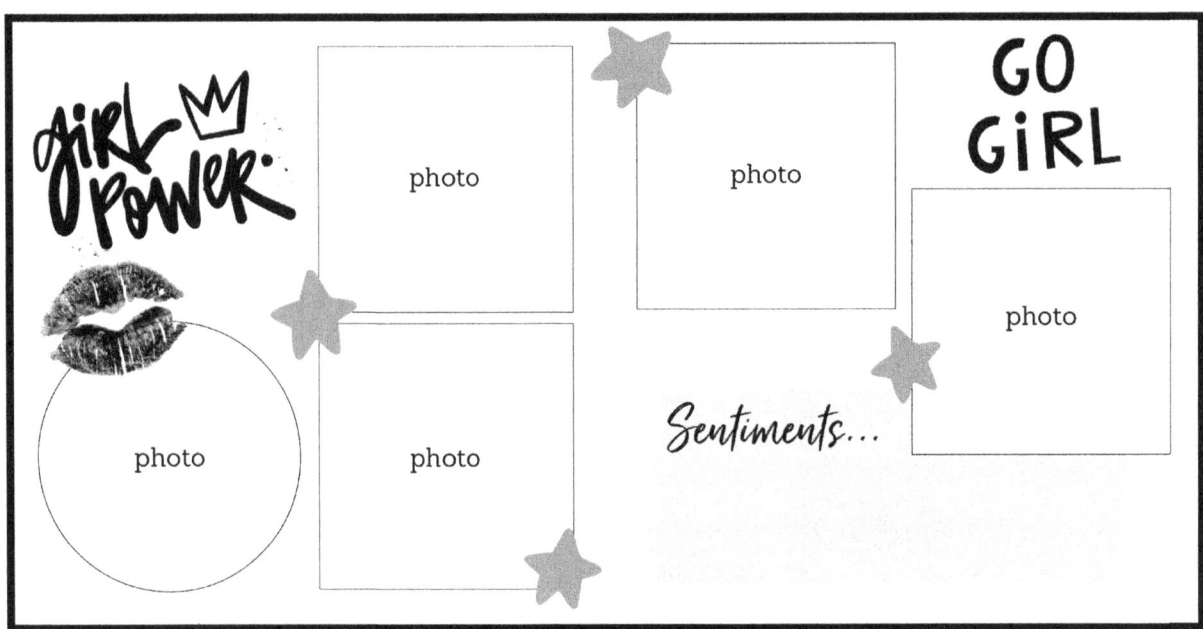

129

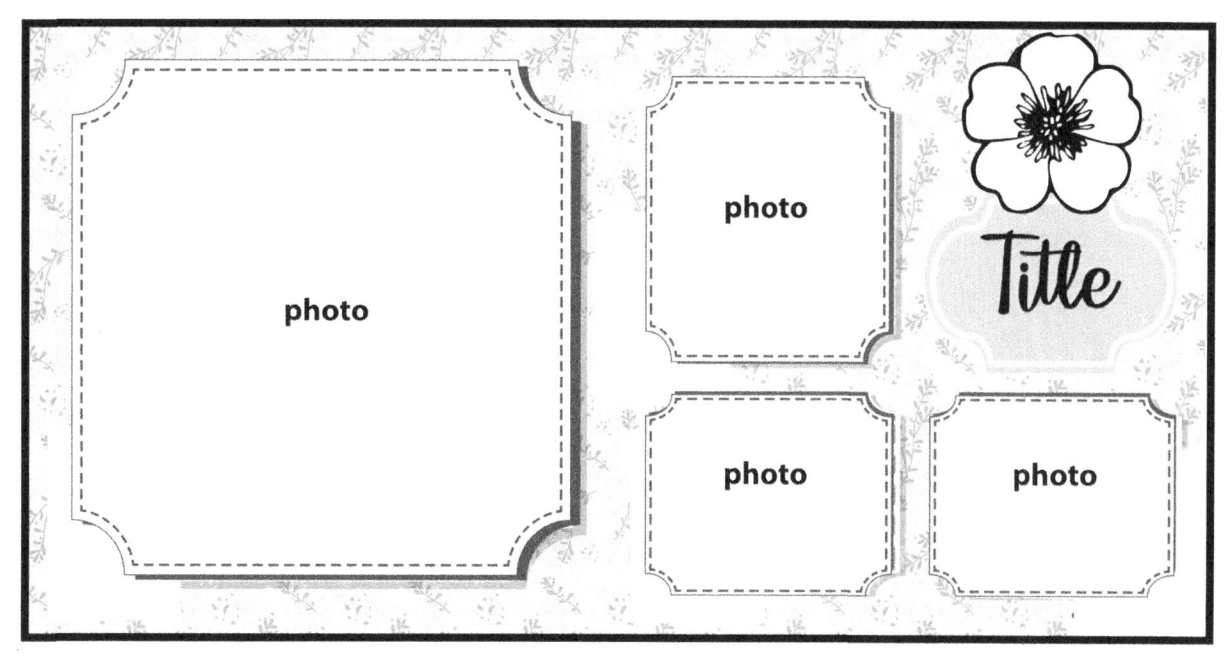

Title
photo
photo
photo

photo
photo
photo
photo
BETTER TOGETHER
Title
MISS U
photo
FOREVER
FAMILY FIRST
photo
Title
photo
HOME
Title
ALWAYS
Title
HAPPY

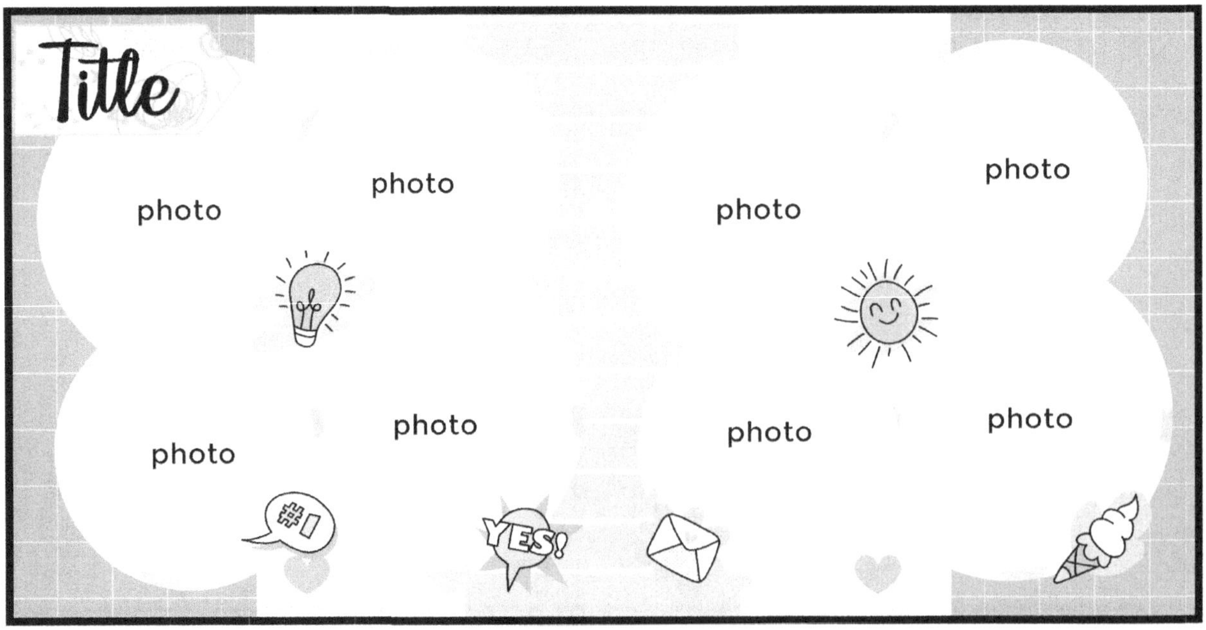
Title
photo
photo
photo
photo
photo
photo
photo
photo
#1
YES!

131

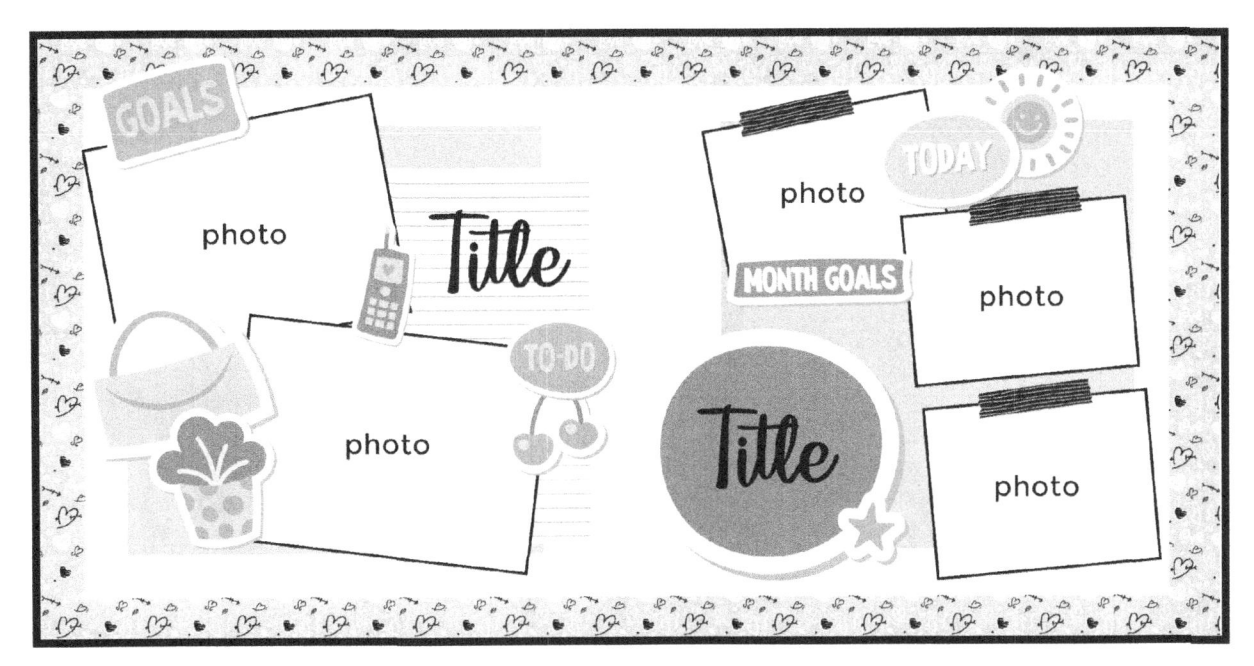

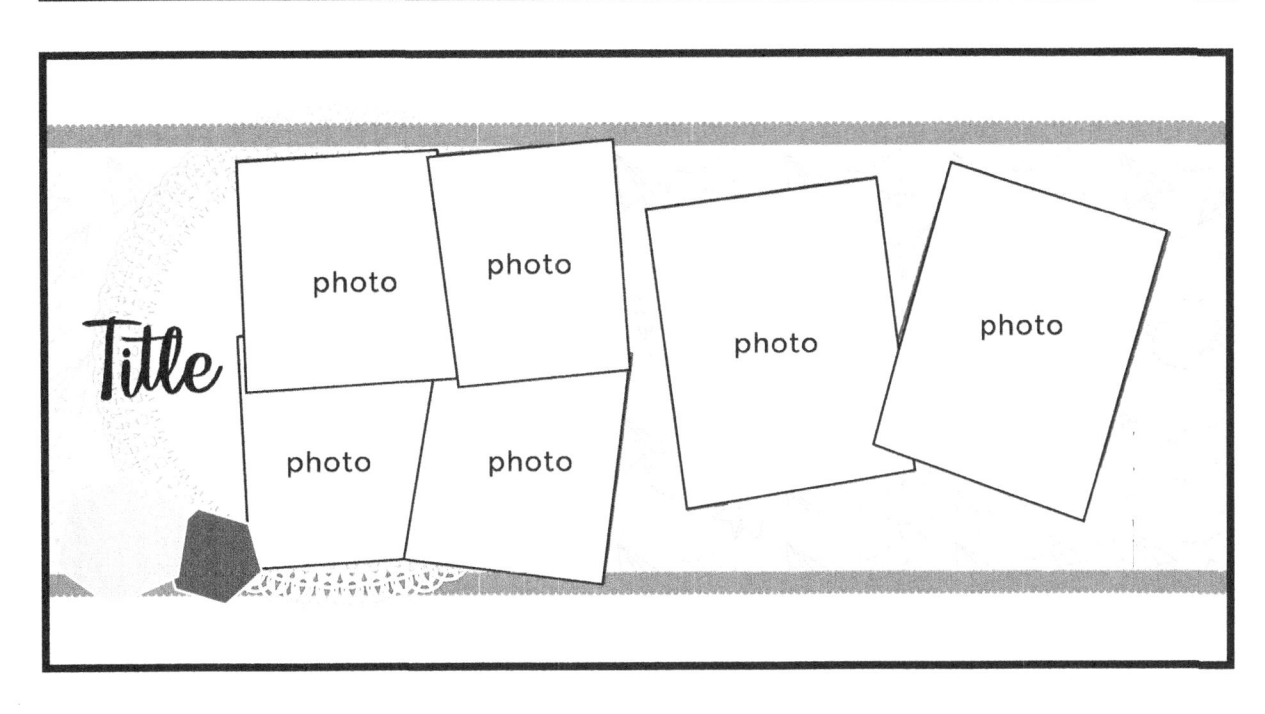

132

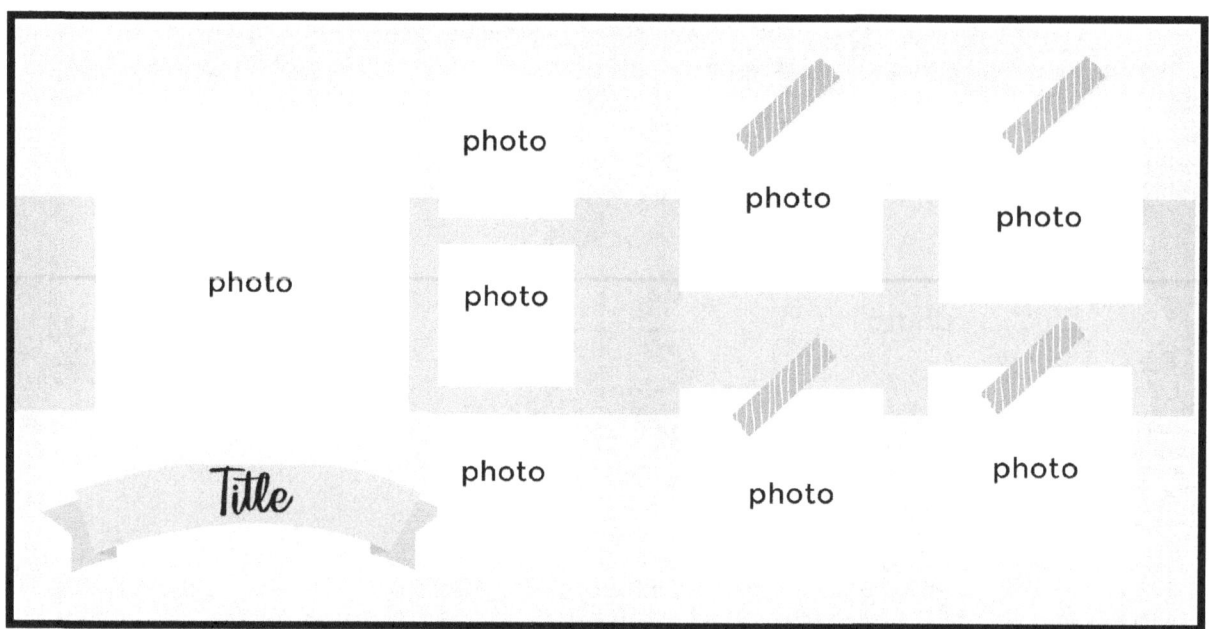

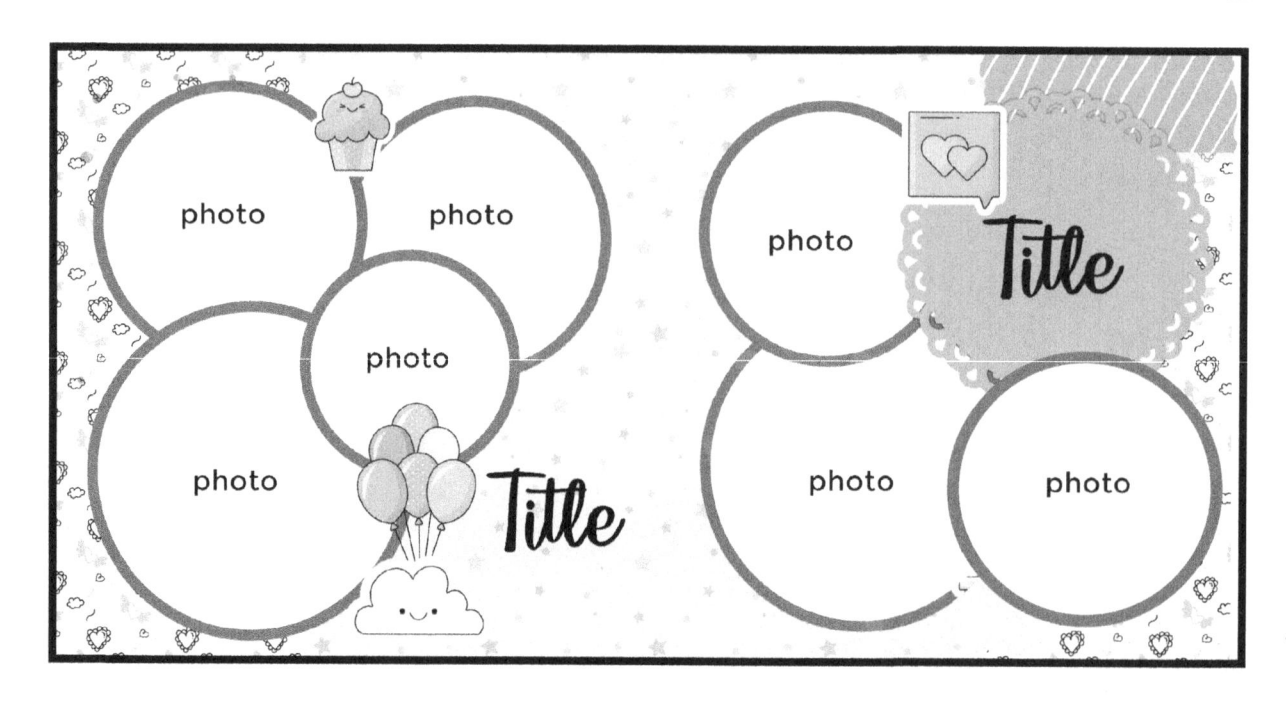

133

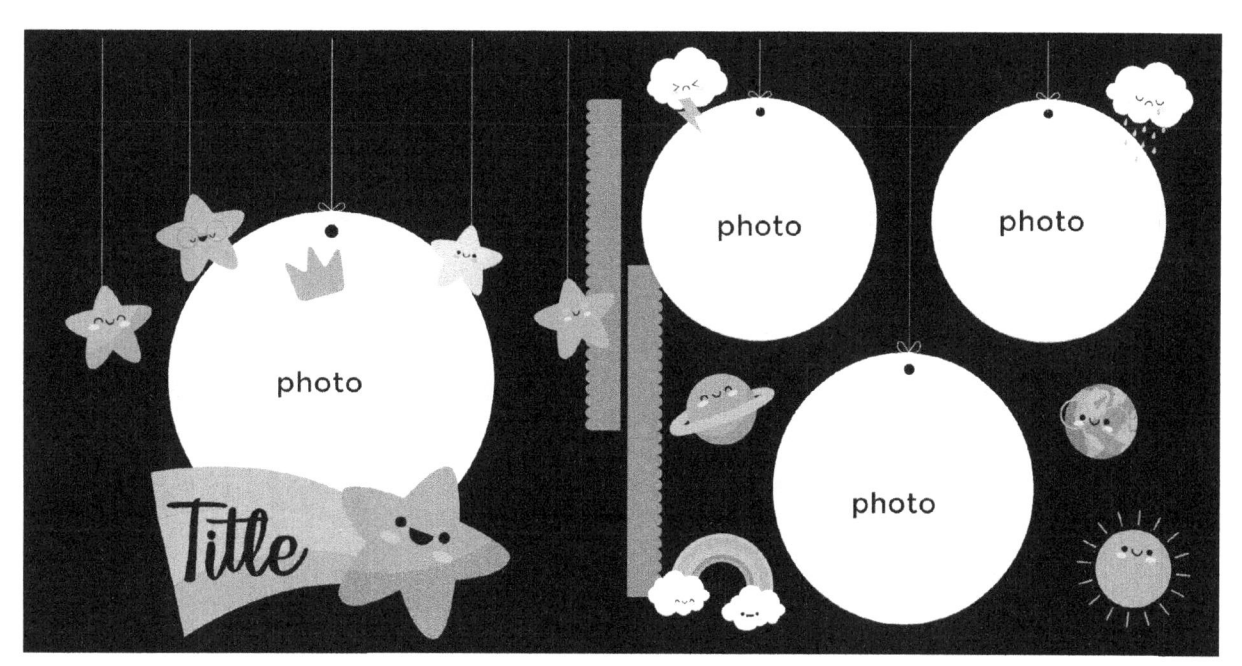

134

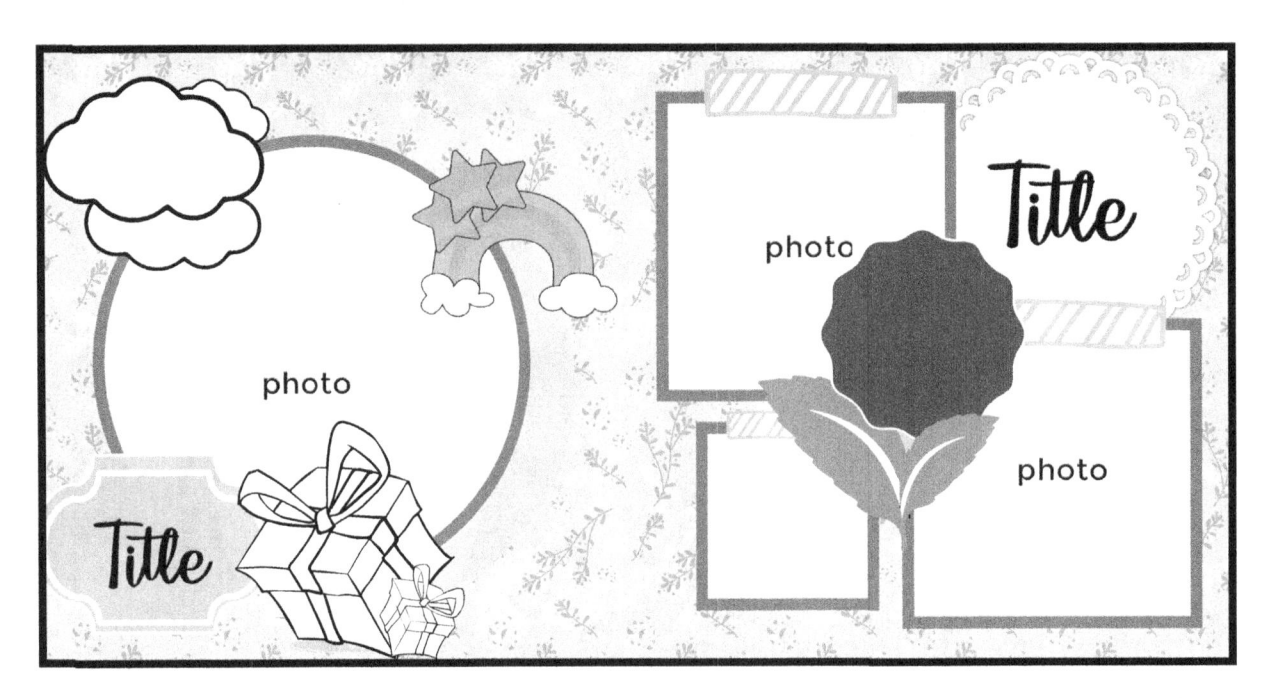

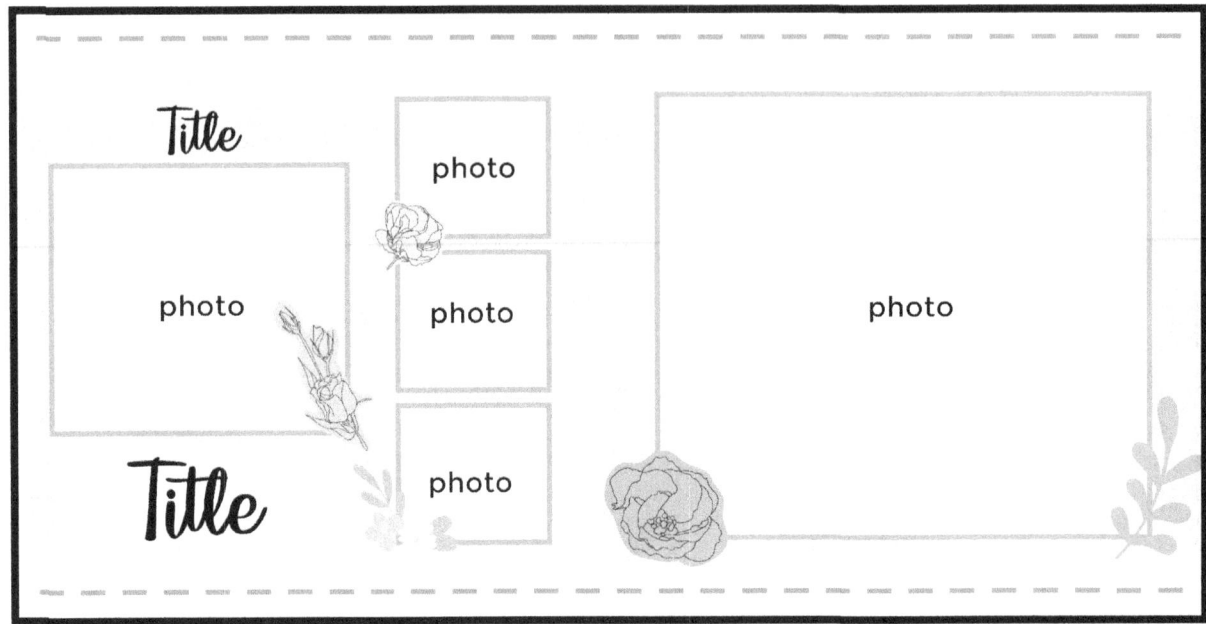

photo
Title
photo
photo
Title

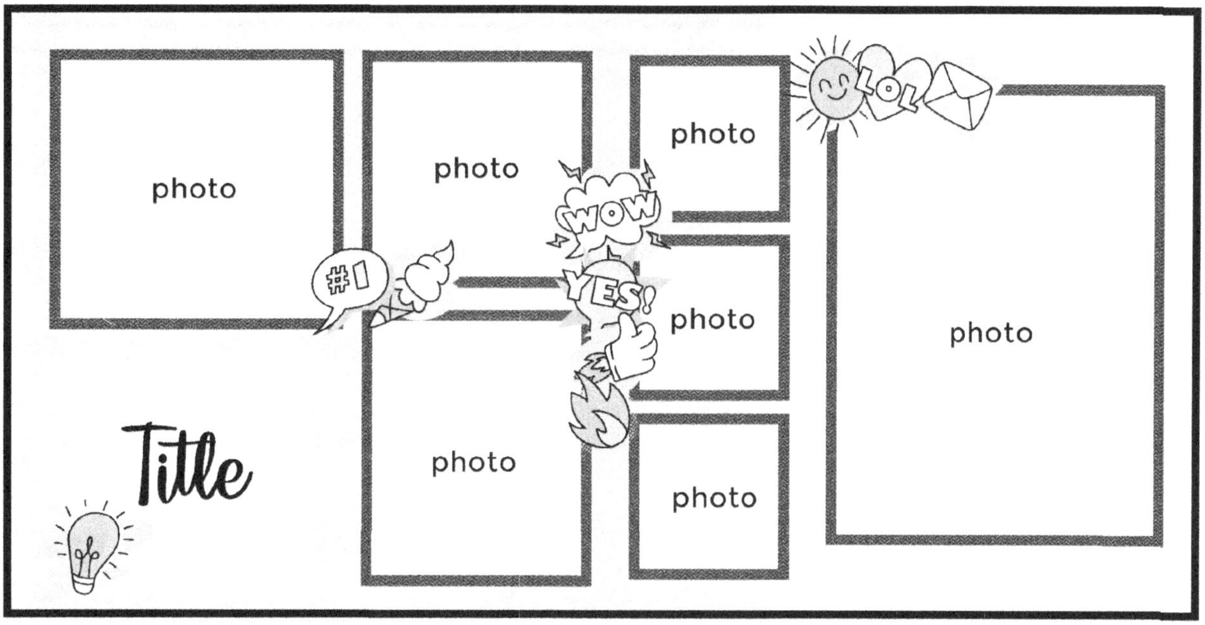
photo
photo
photo
LOL
WOW
#1
YES!
photo
photo
Title
photo
photo

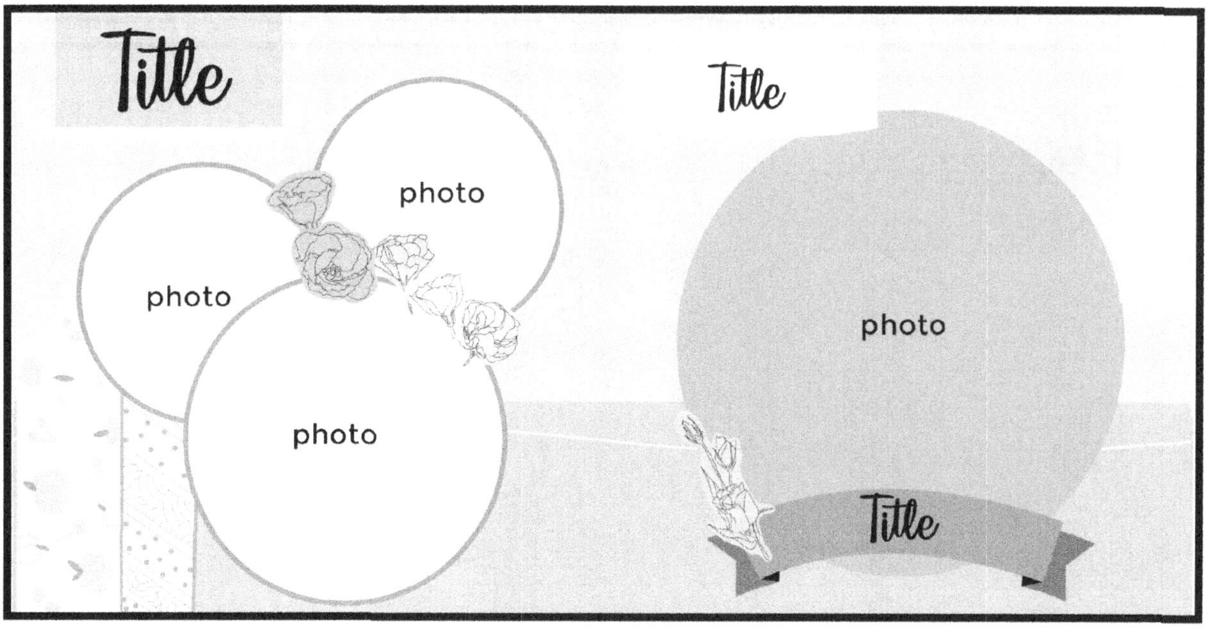
Title
Title
photo
photo
photo
photo
Title

Pet

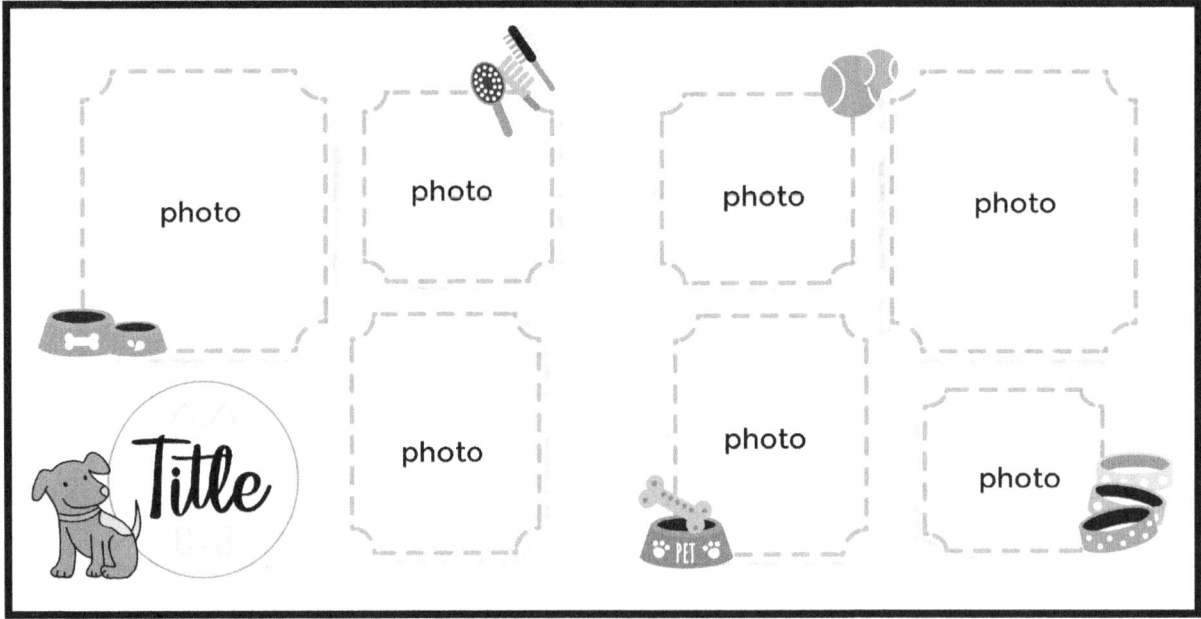

137

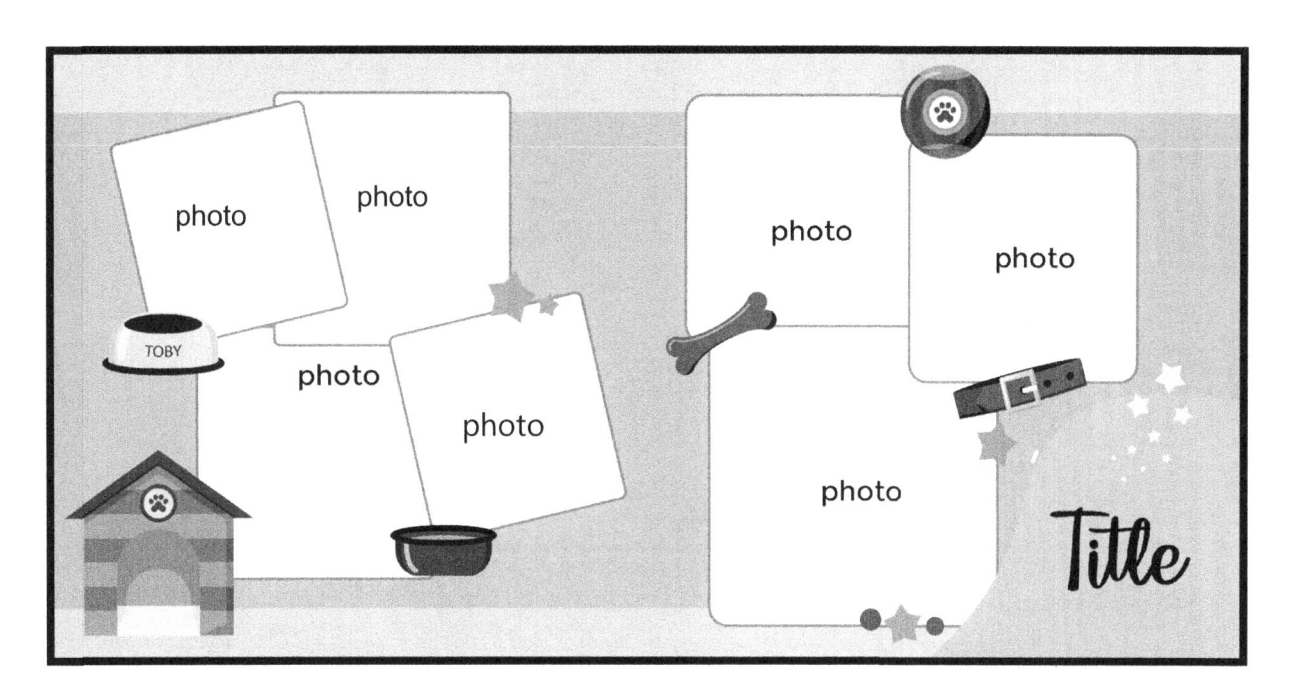

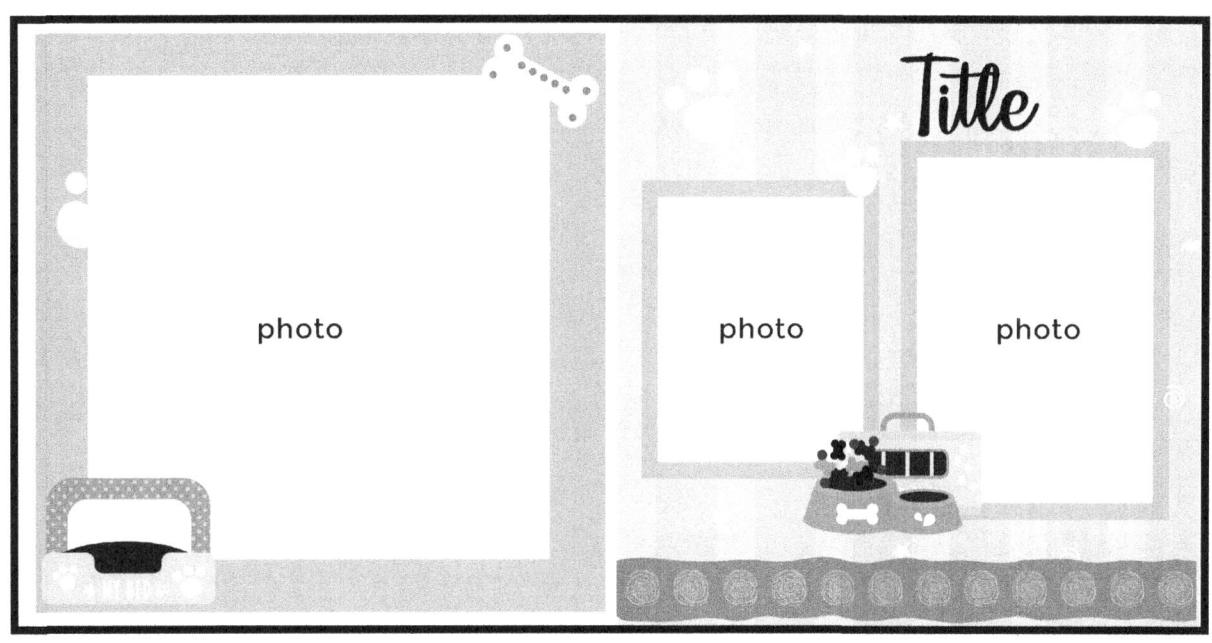

138

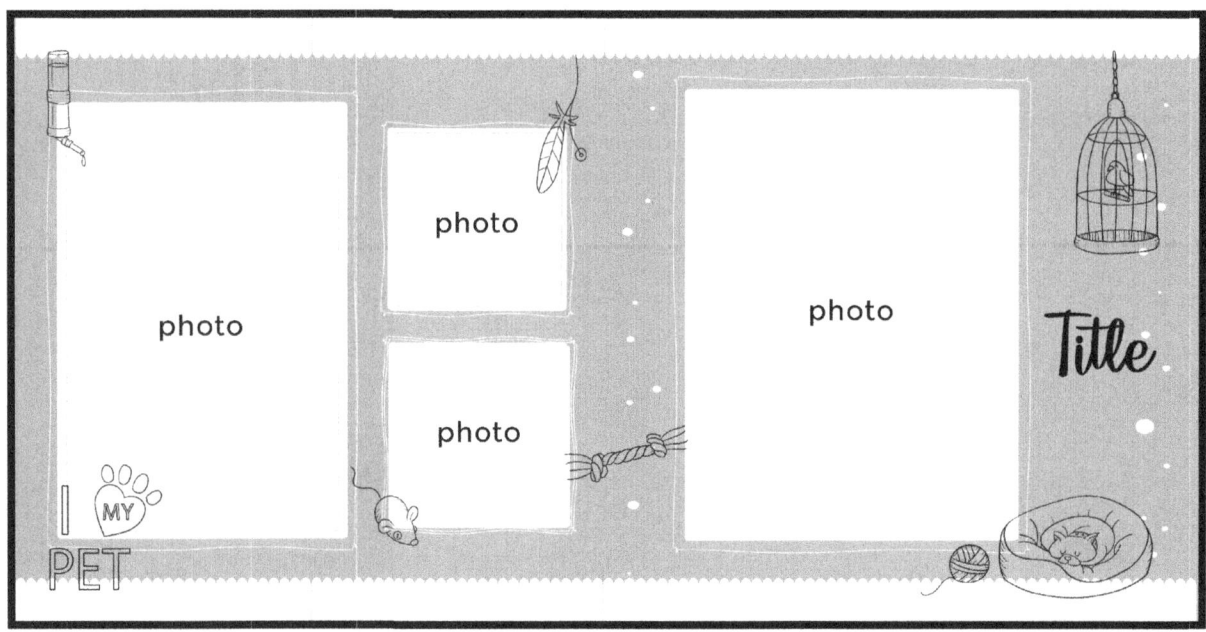

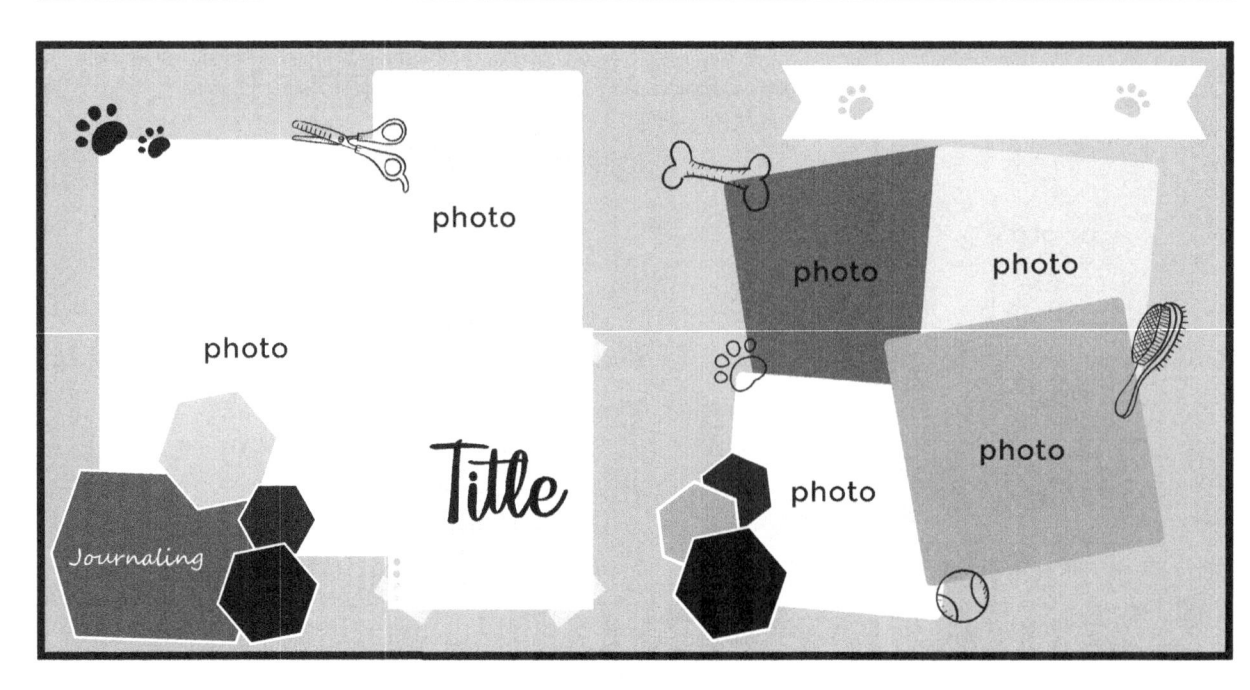

photo

Title

photo

photo

photo

photo

Title

photo

photo

Title

photo

photo

photo

139

Playtime with my favourite pal!

photo
photo
photo
photo
photo 

Title
photo
photo
photo
photo
photo
photo
photo
photo
photo

Title
photo
Title
photo
photo
photo
photo

141

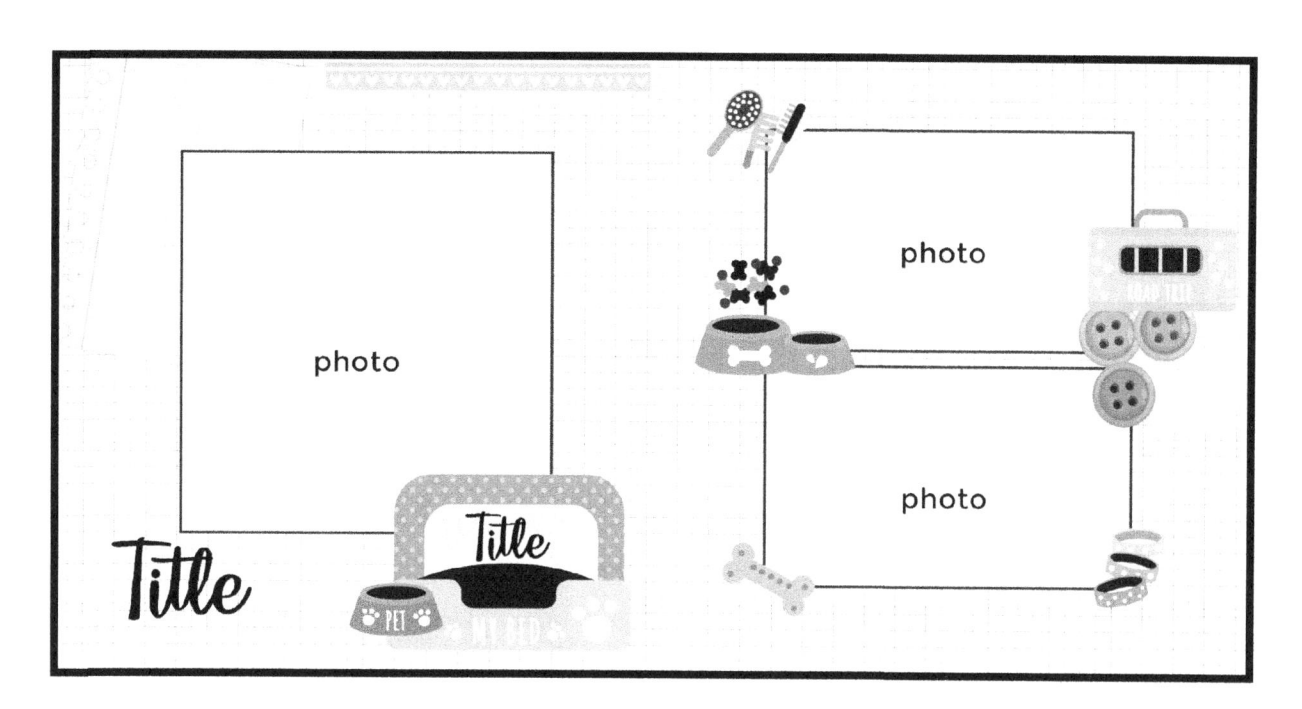

It's Cat-urday!

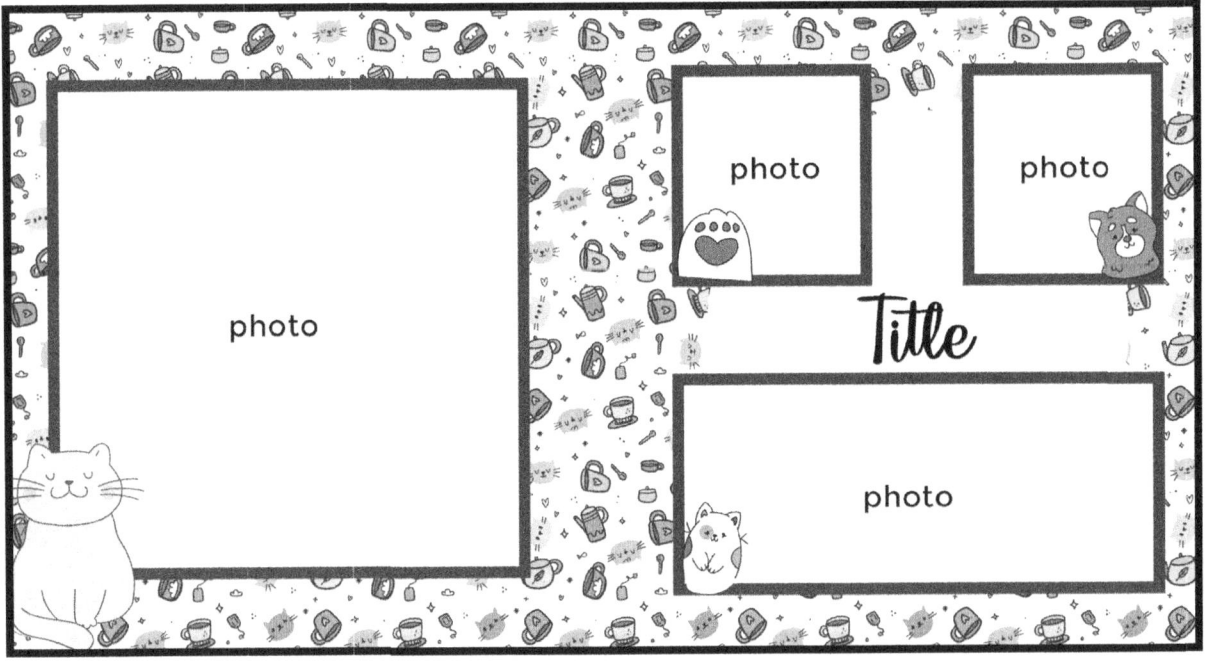

Title

Title

Title

142

143

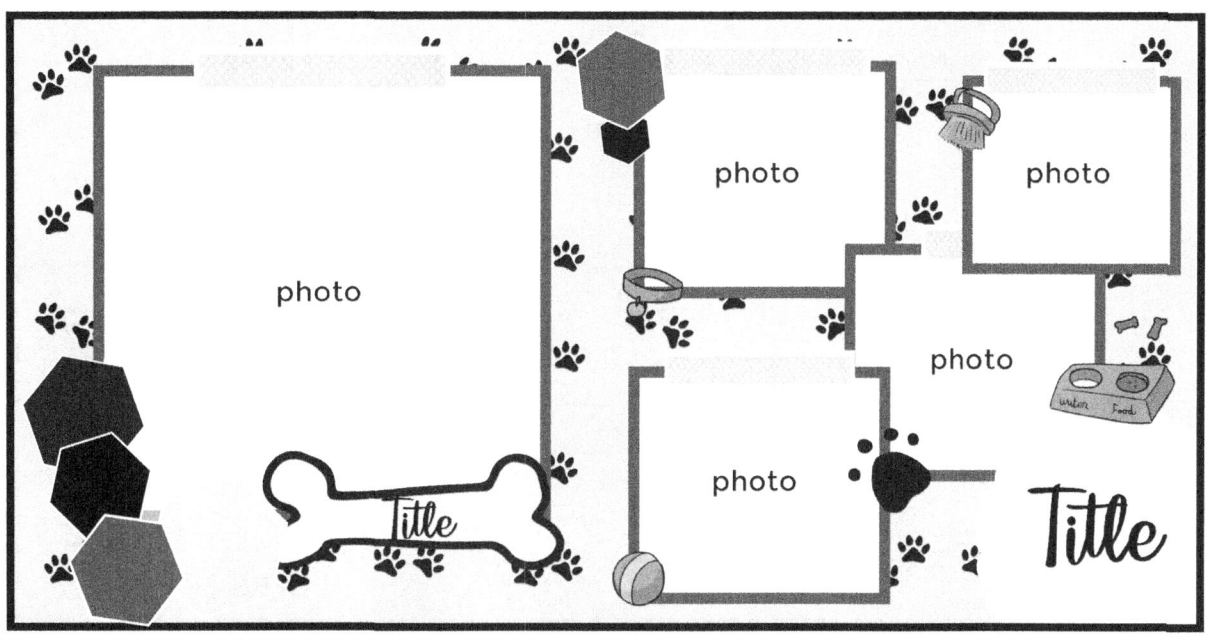

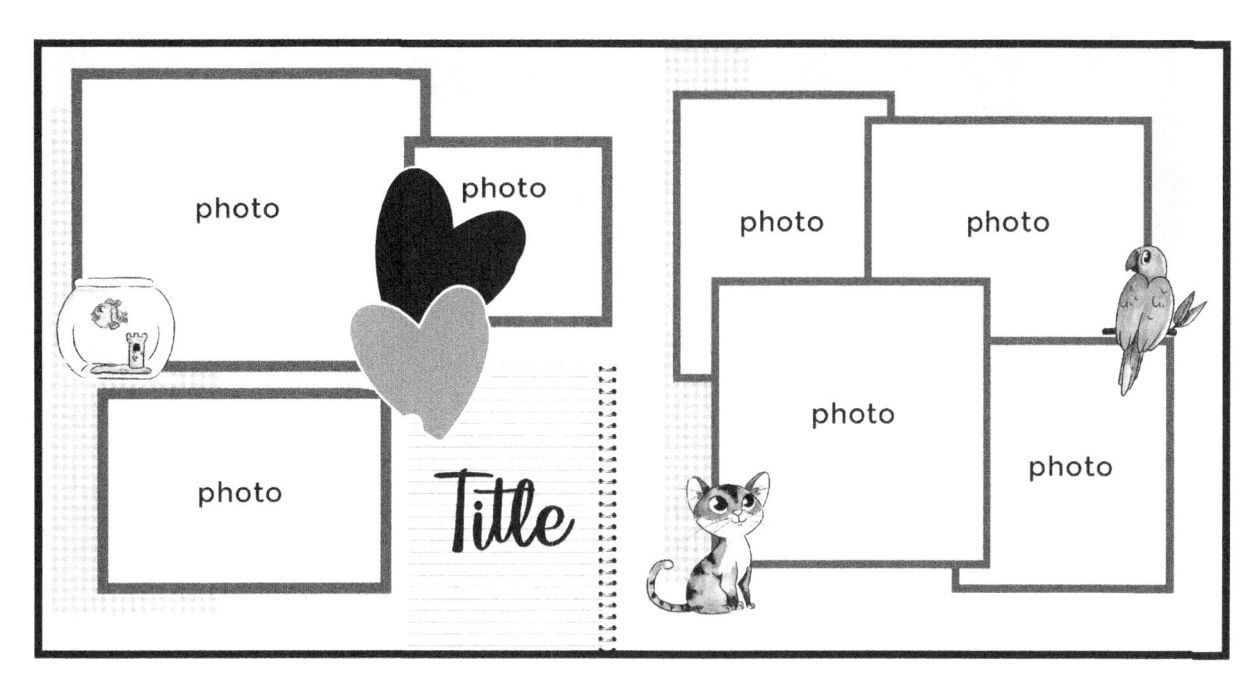

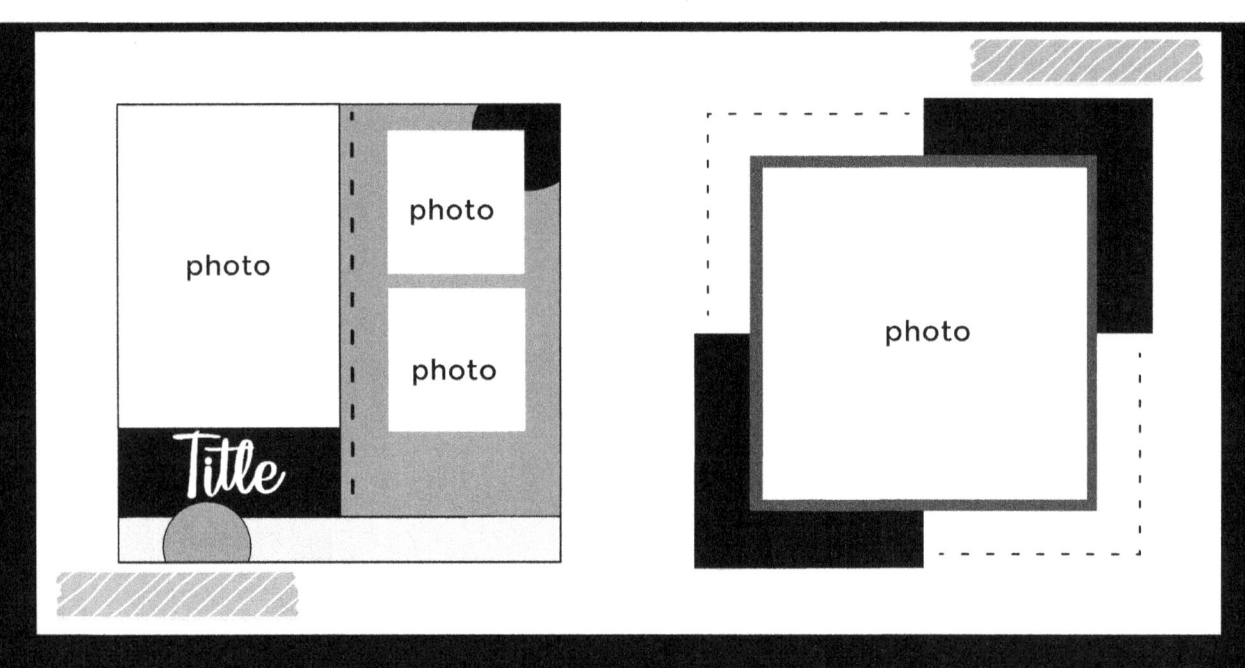

photo photo photo photo

Title

photo

photo photo photo photo photo

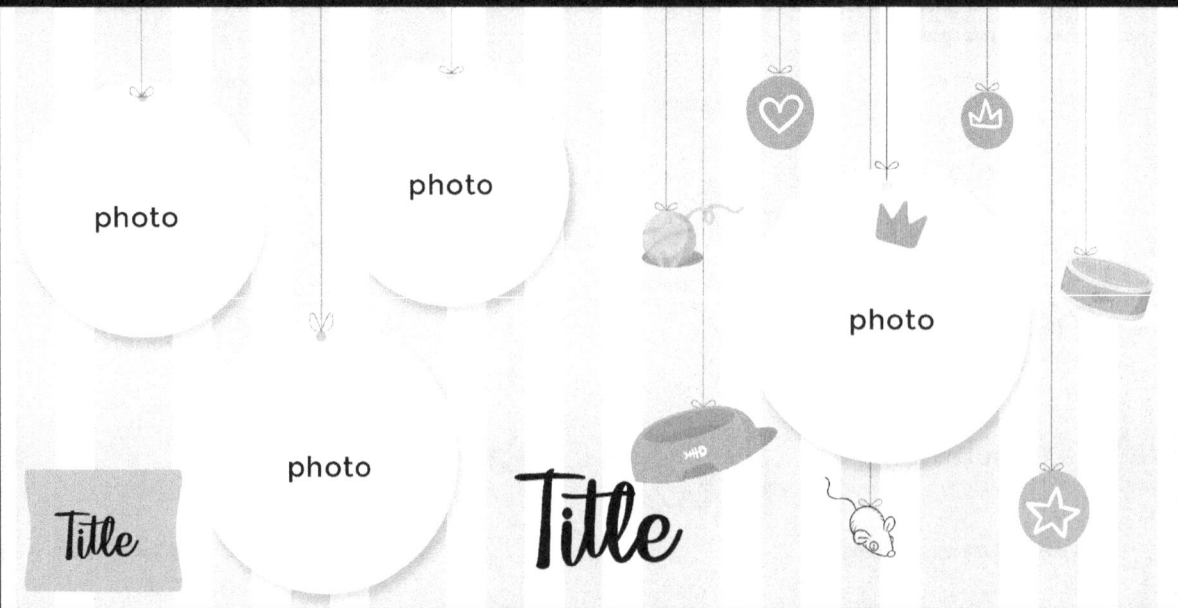

Title

photo photo photo photo

Title   *Title*

144

Title
photo
photo
photo
nf mrm
Title

Title
photo
photo
photo
photo
photo
photo
photo
Title

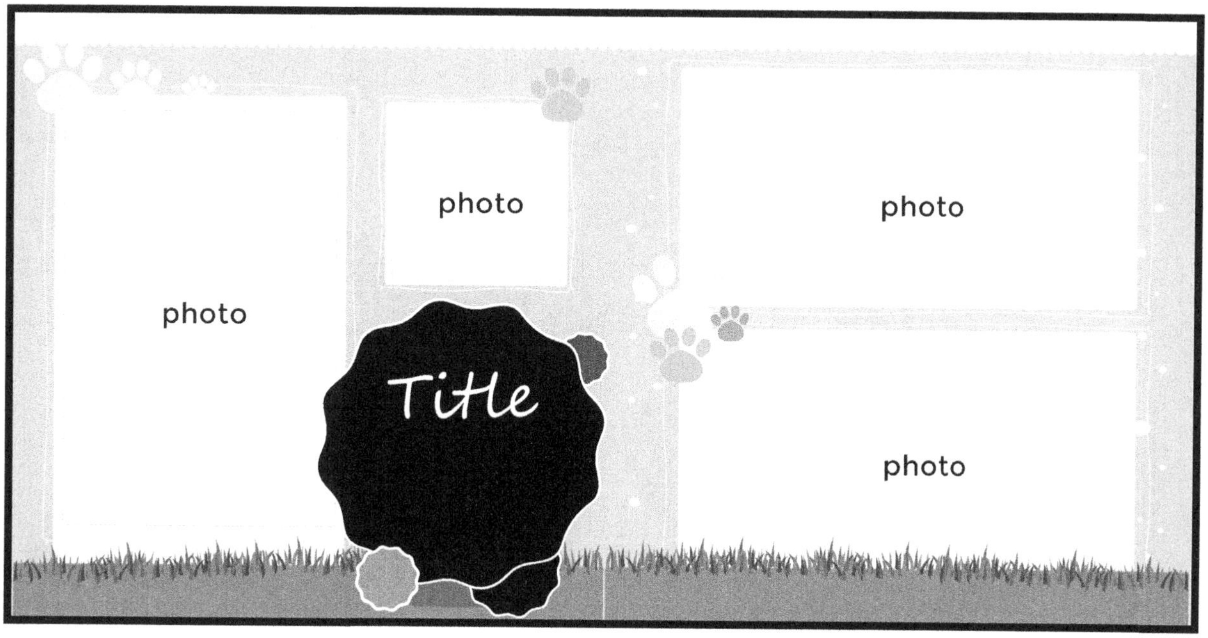
photo
photo
photo
Title
photo

146

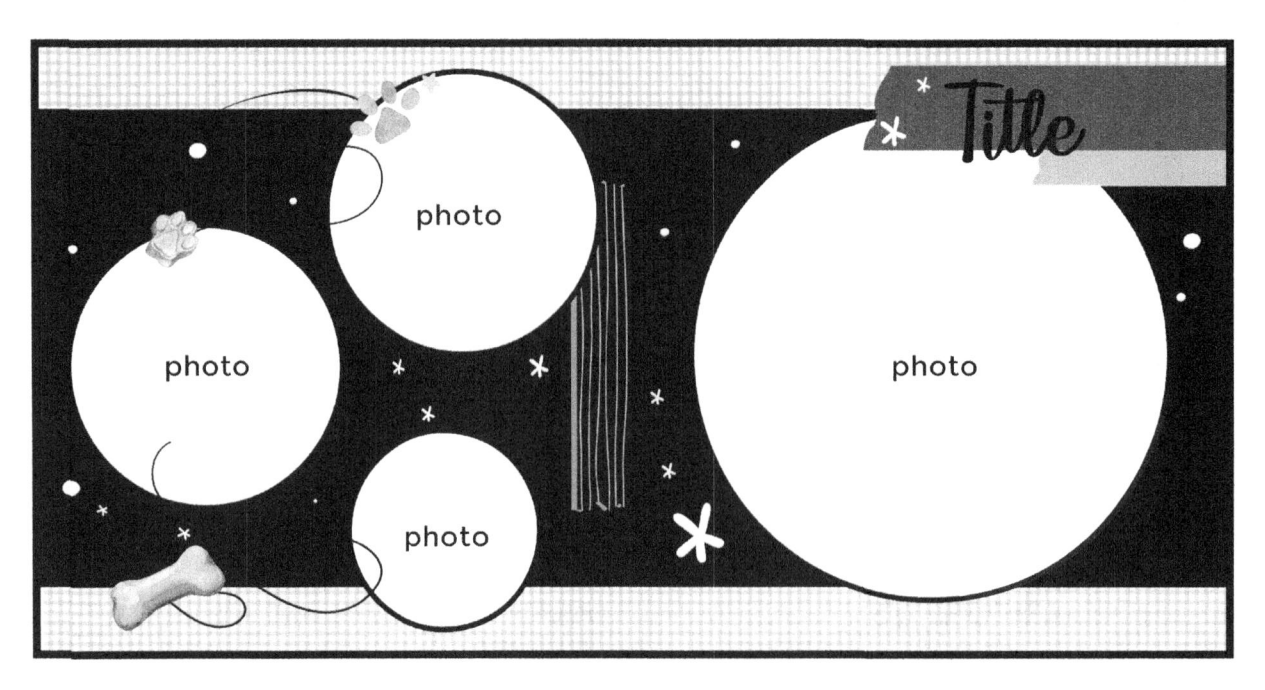

147

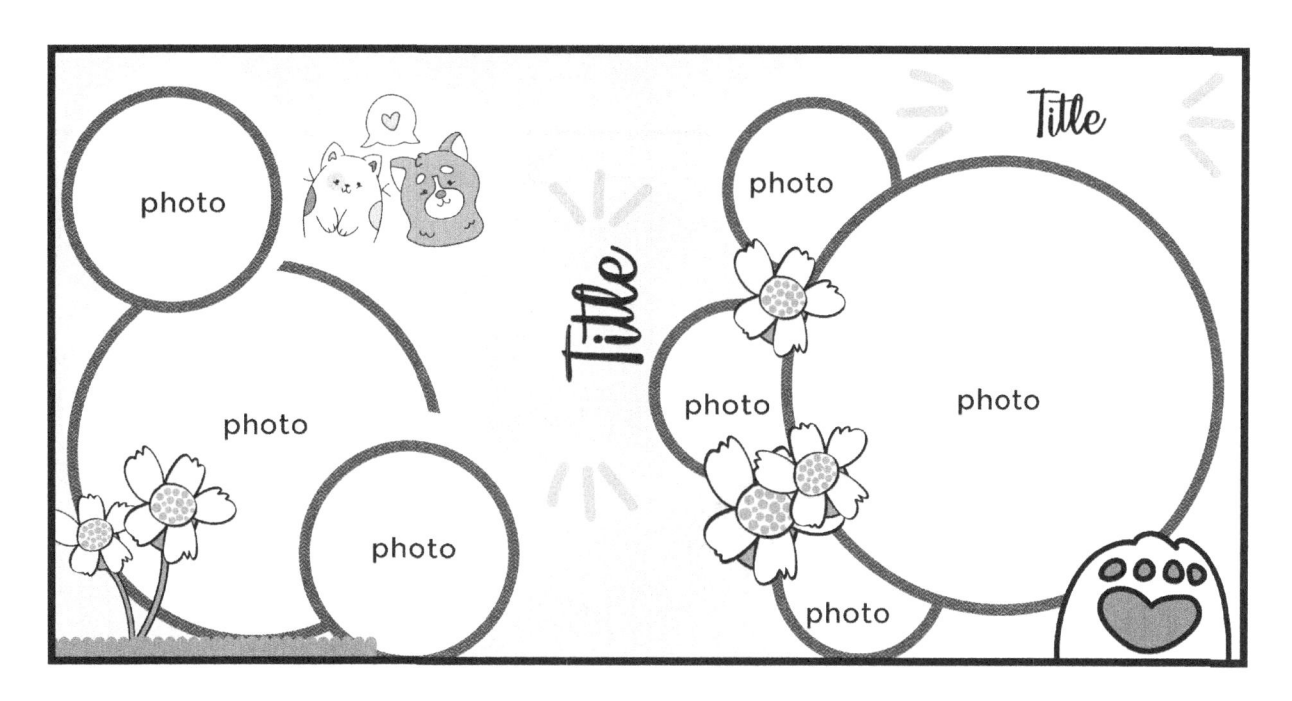

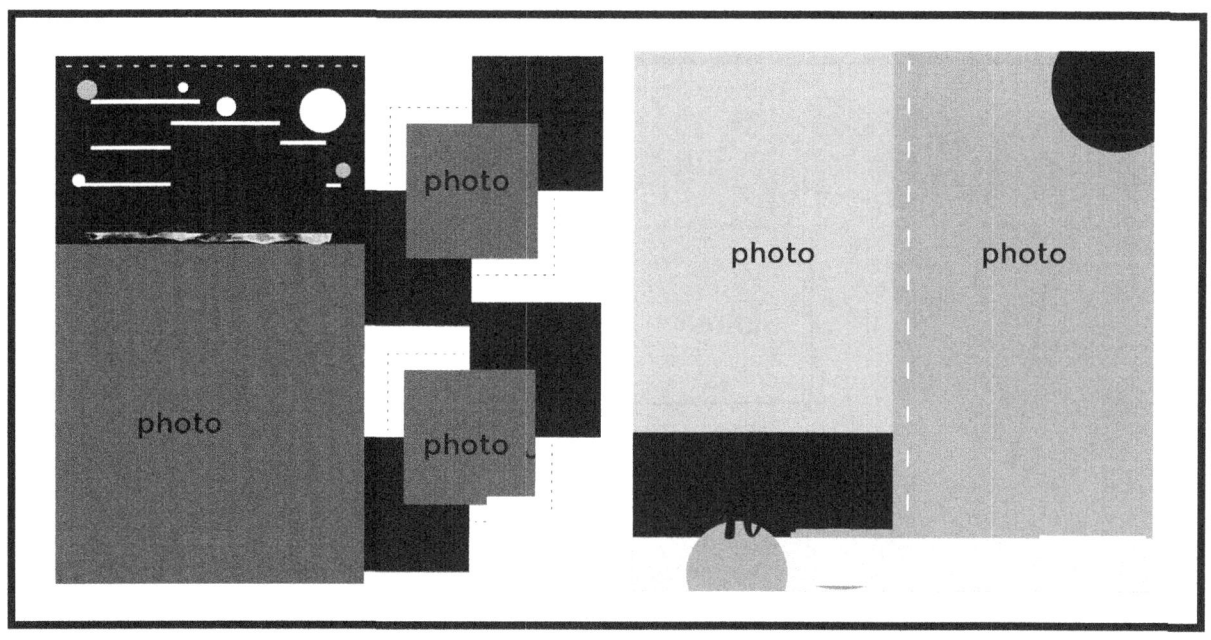

Romantic

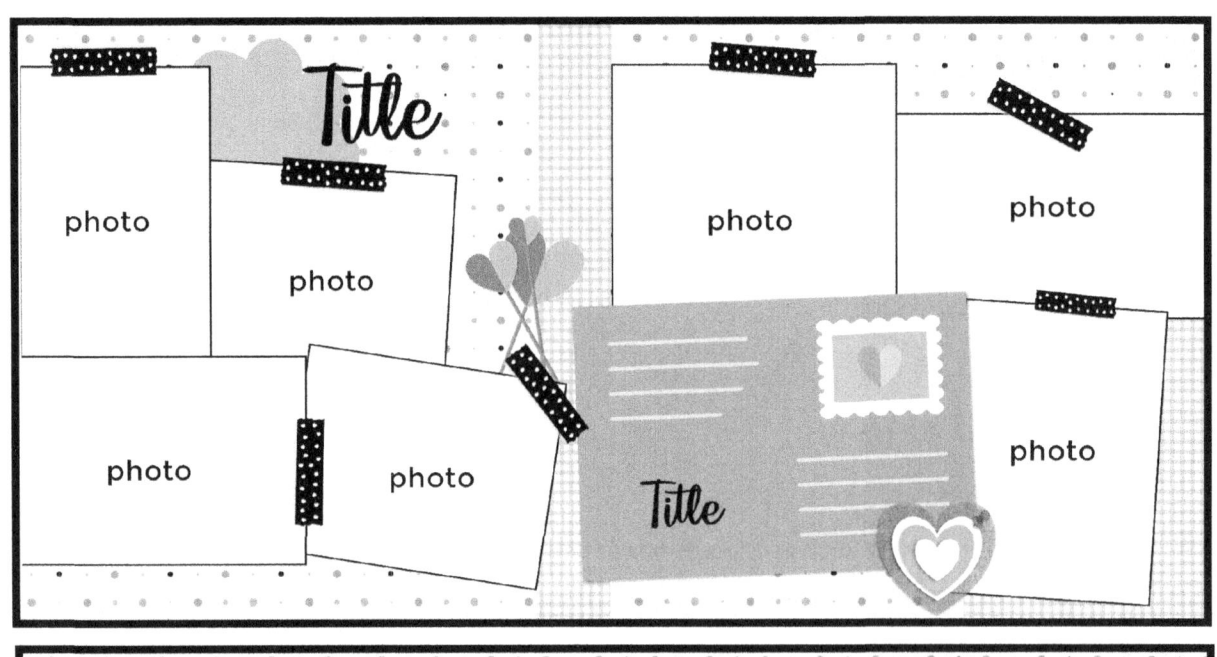

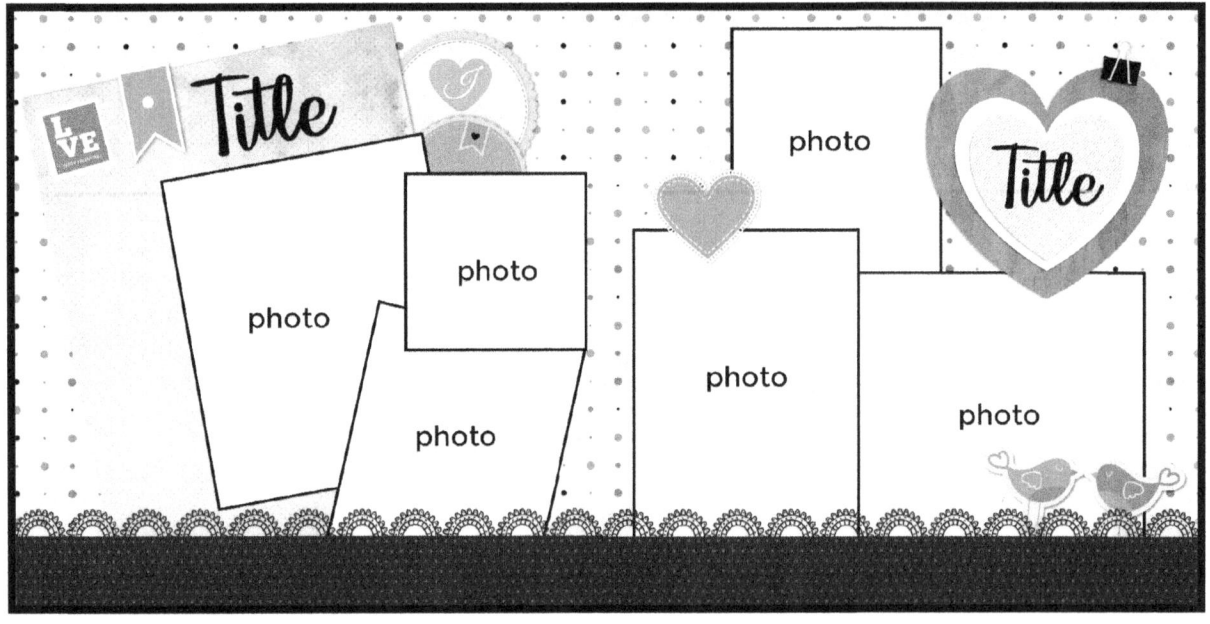

149

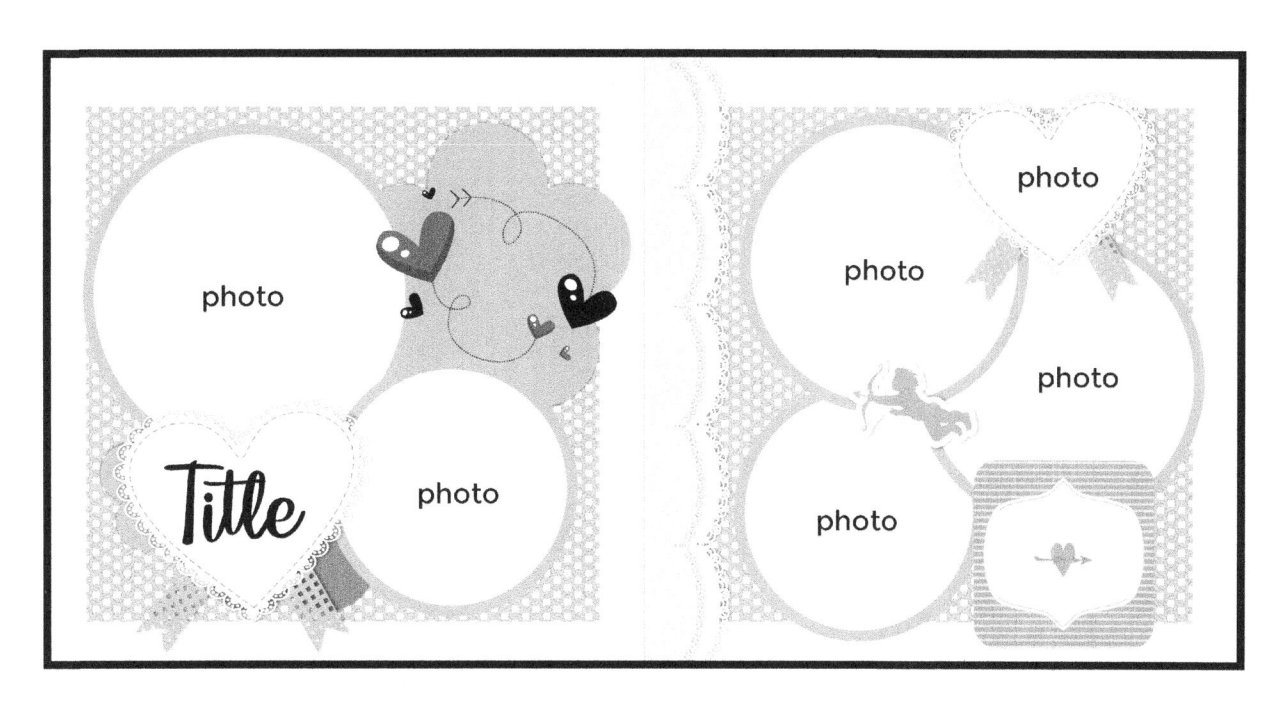

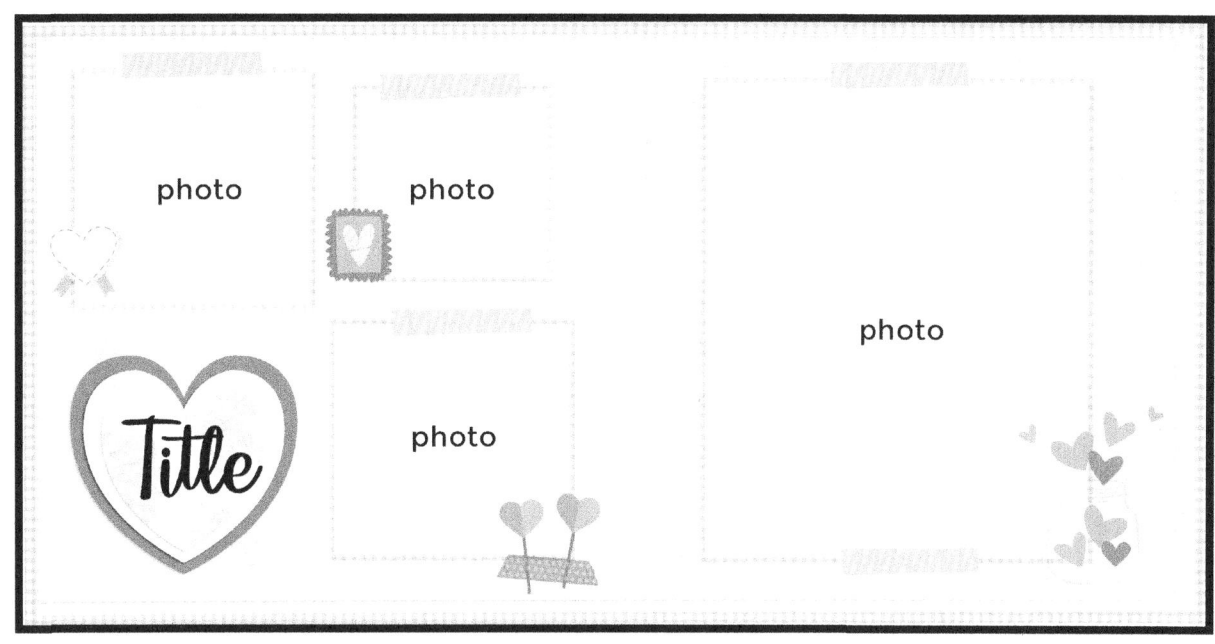

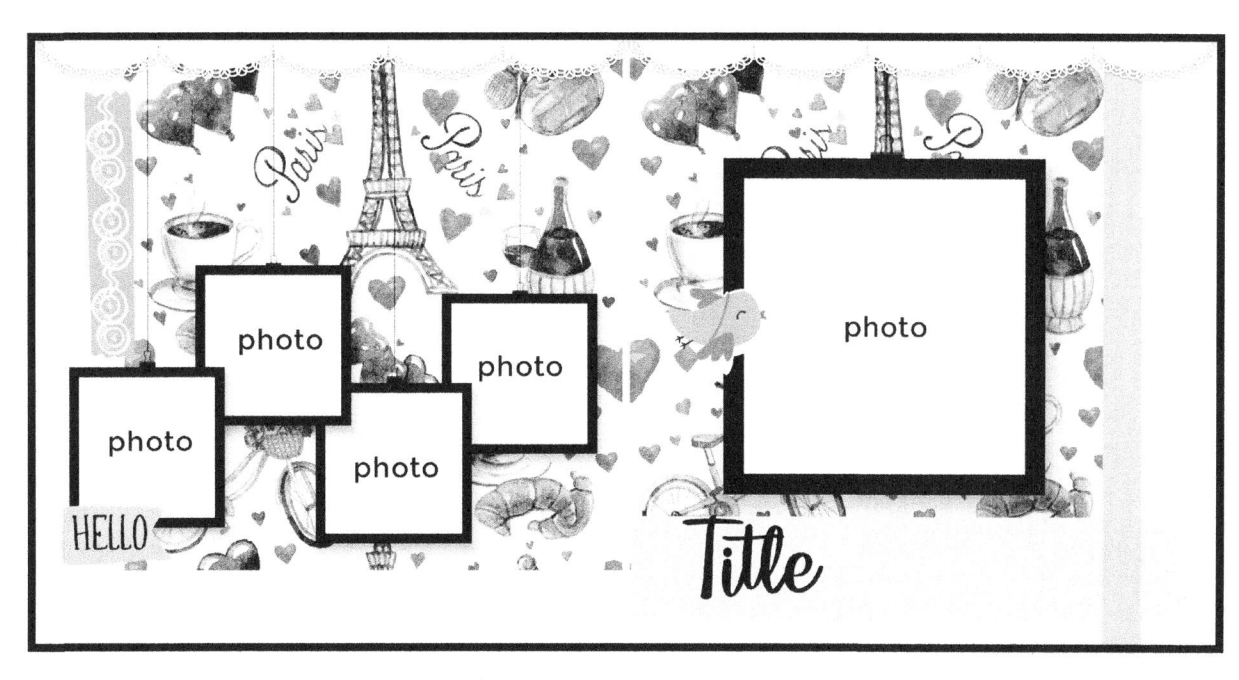

150

151

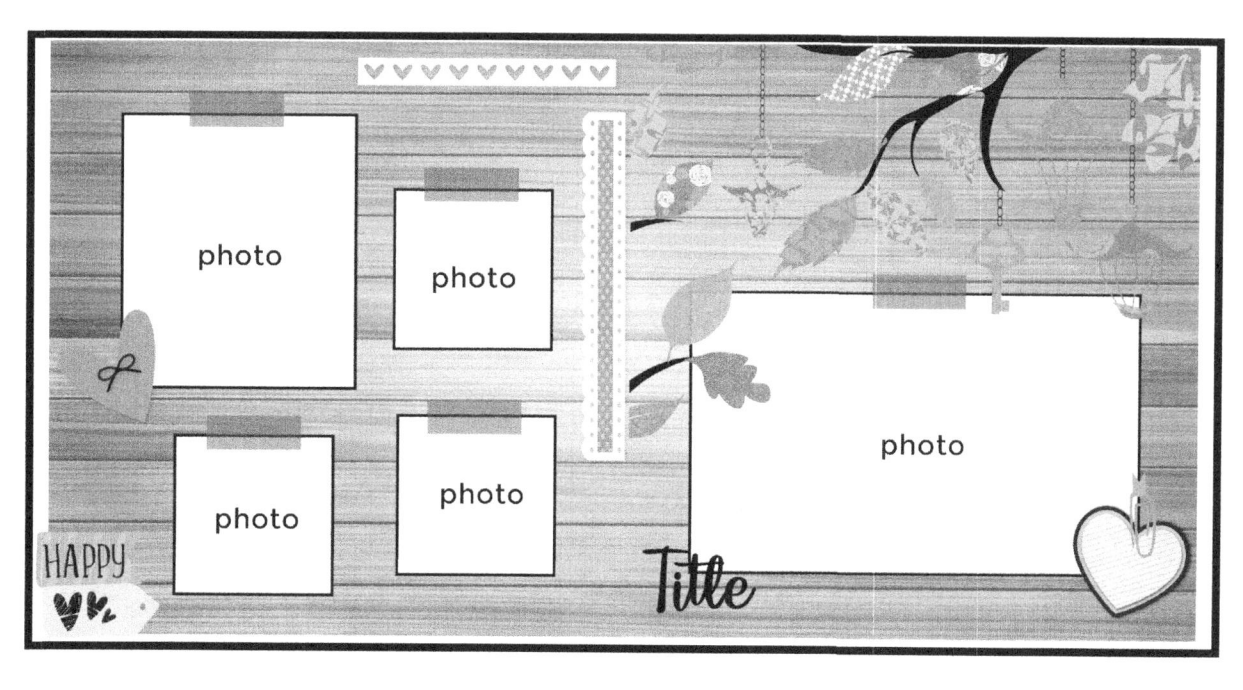

152

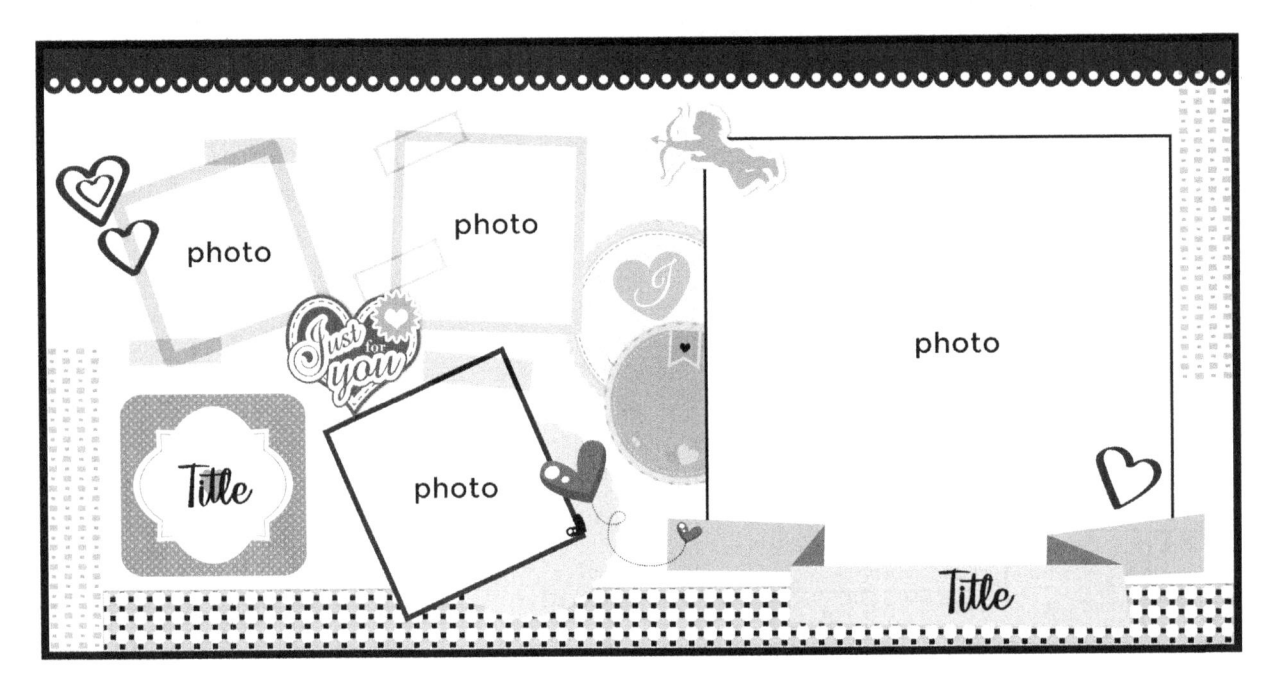

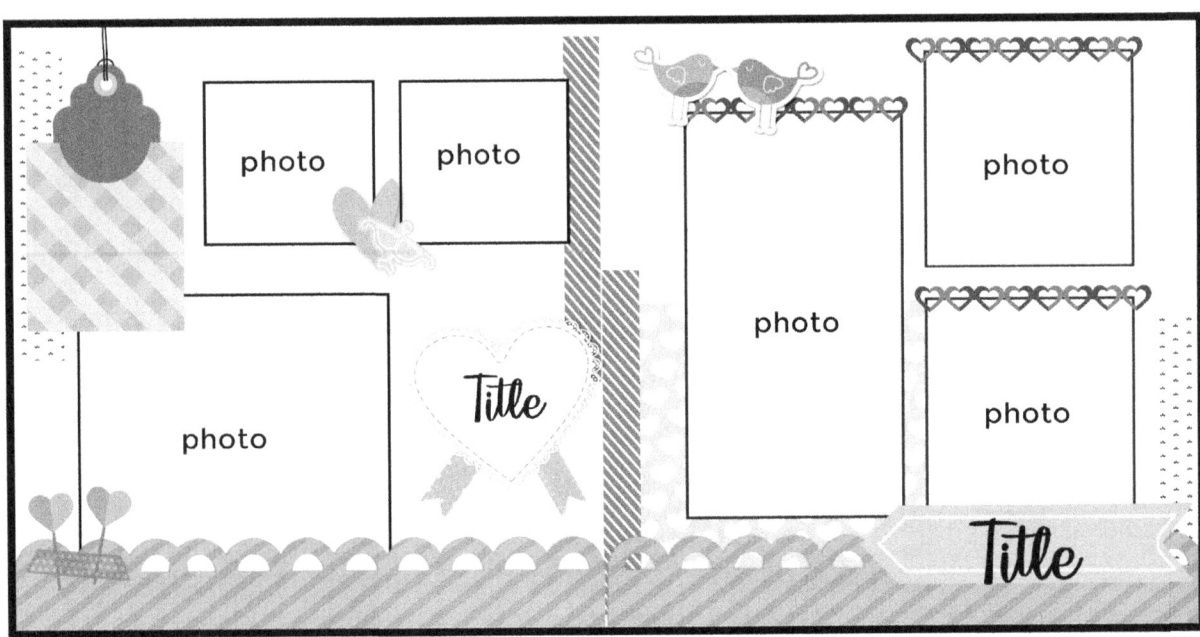

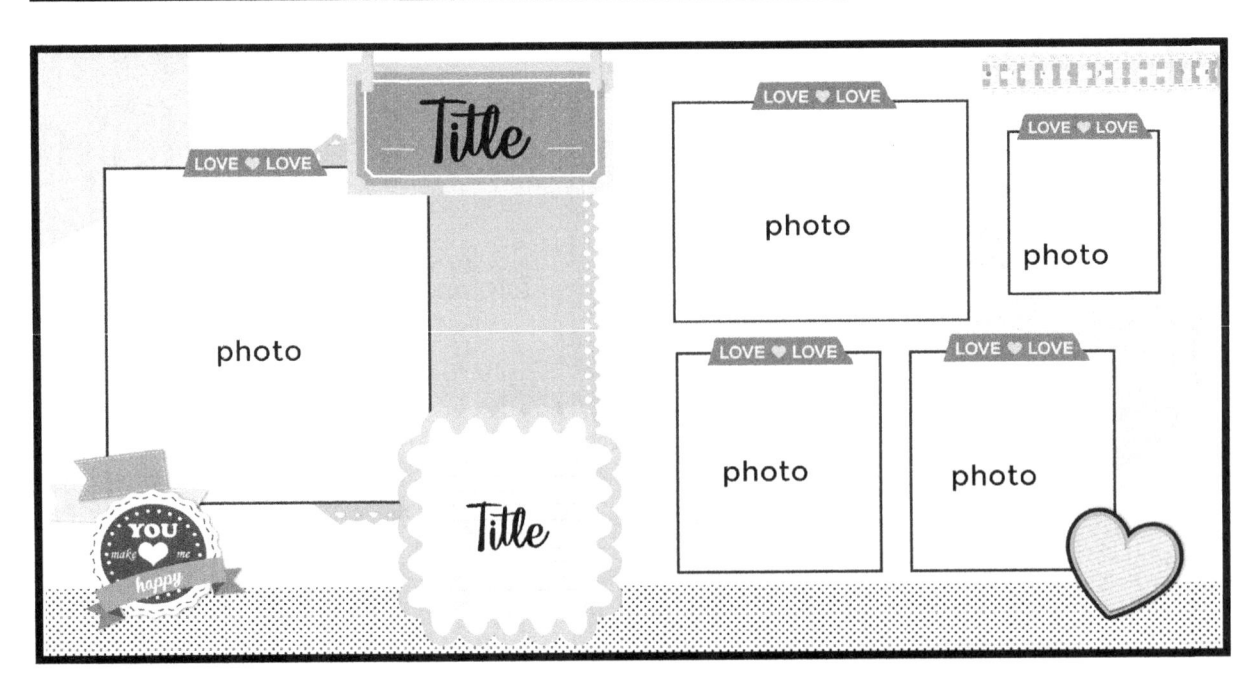

153

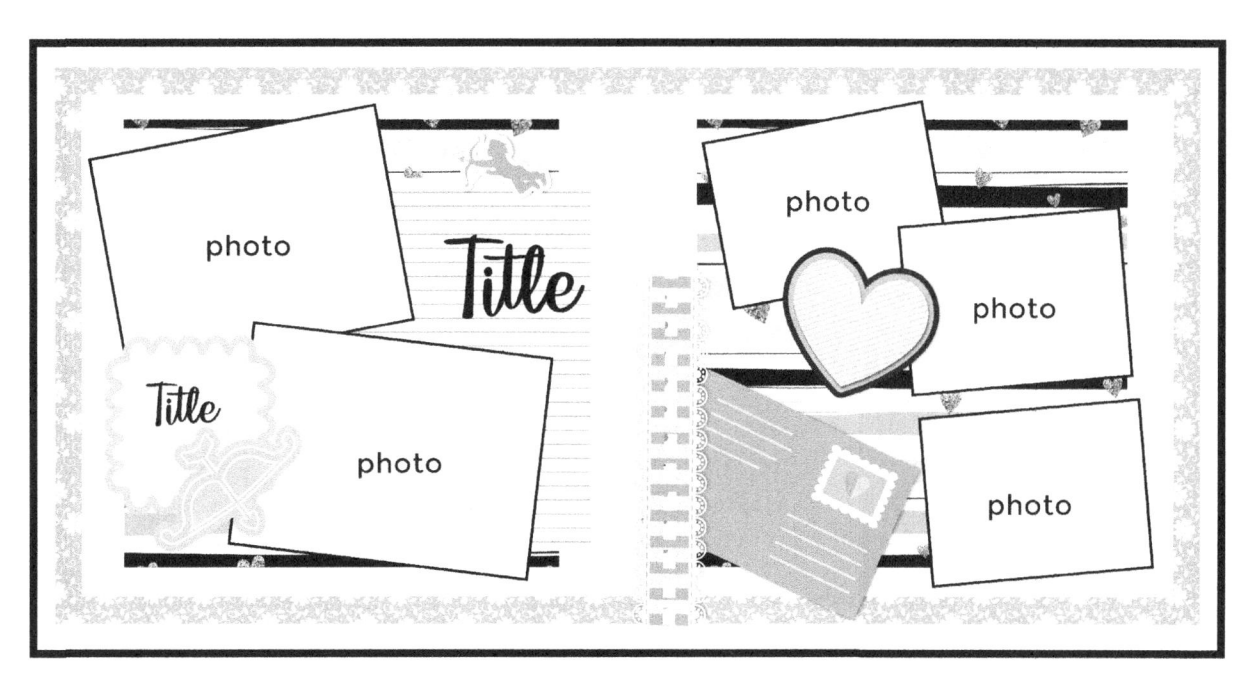

154

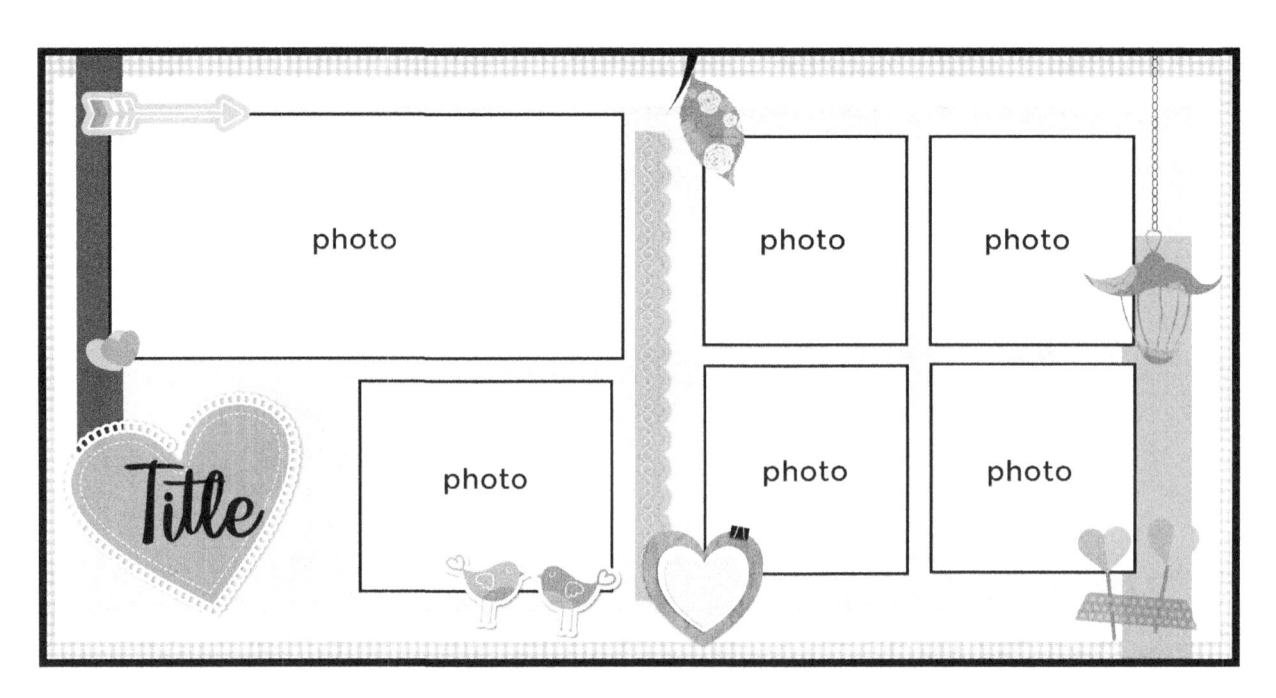

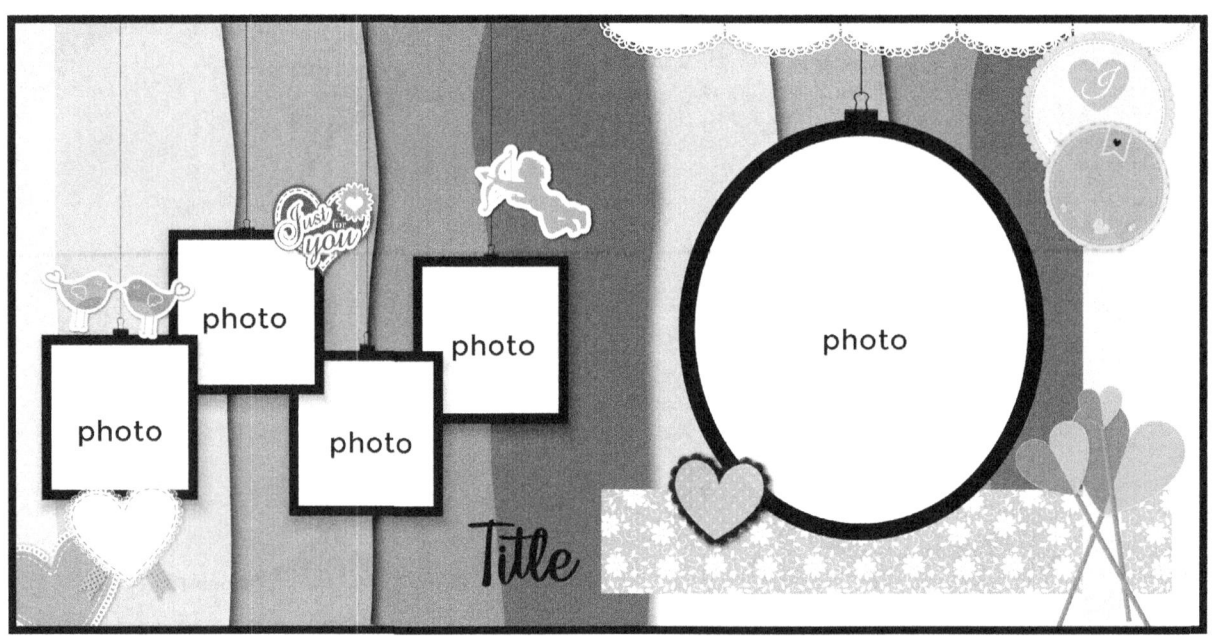

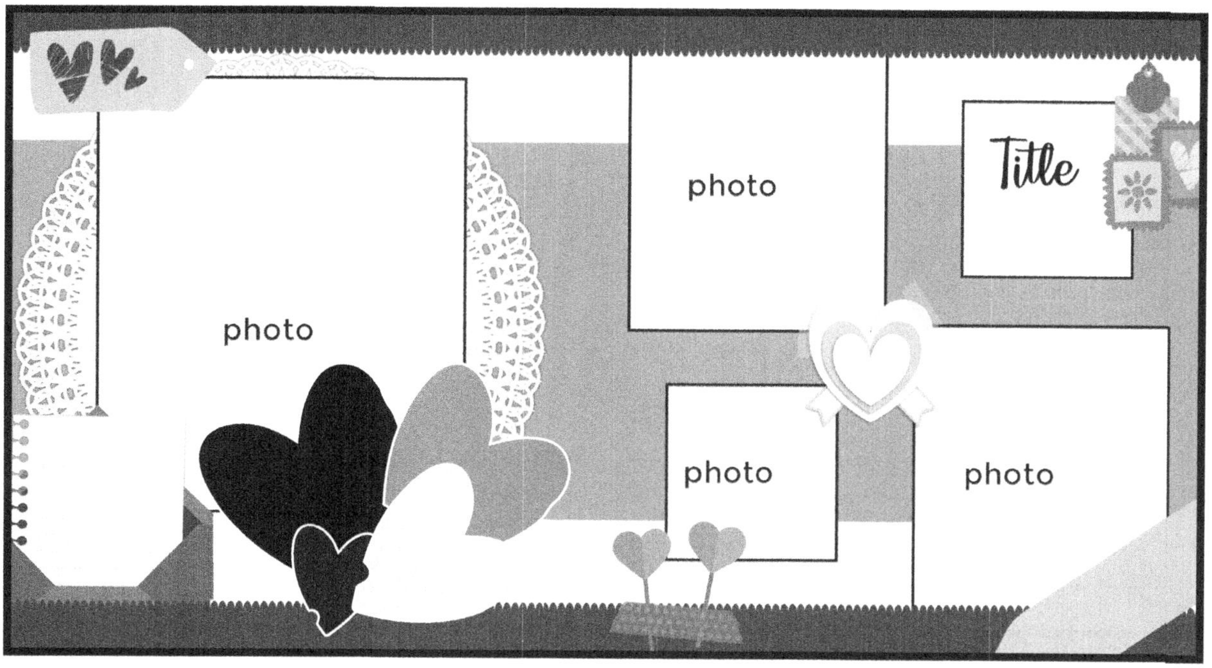
photo
photo
Title
photo
photo

Just for you
photo
Title
photo
Title
photo
photo

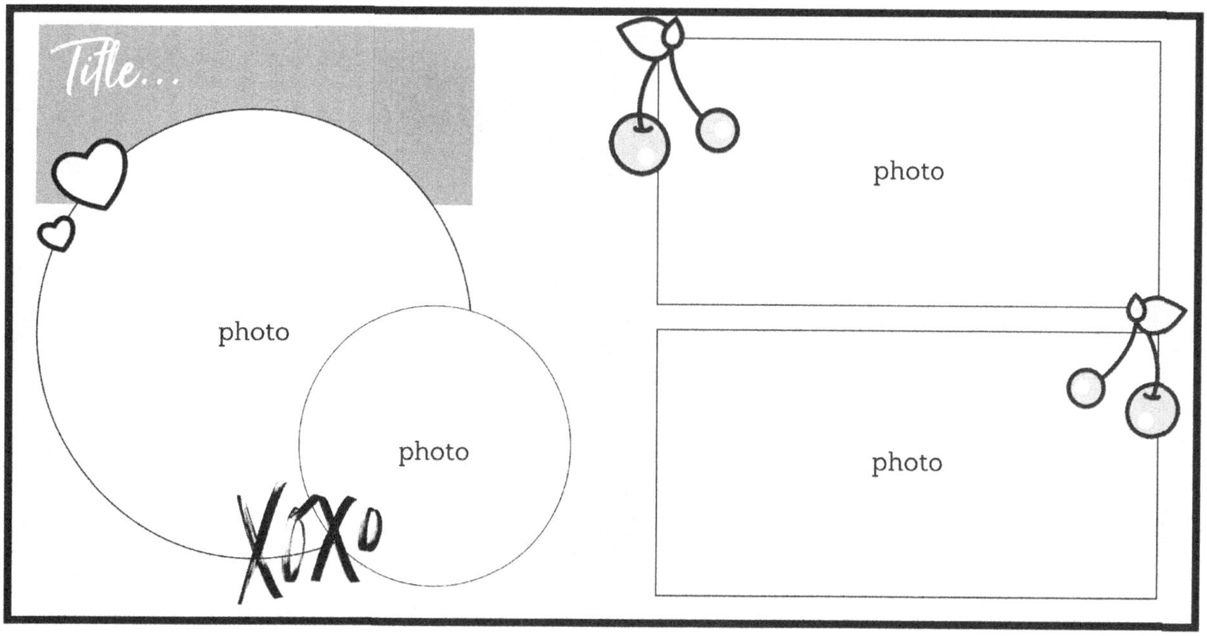
Title...
photo
photo
XOXO
photo
photo

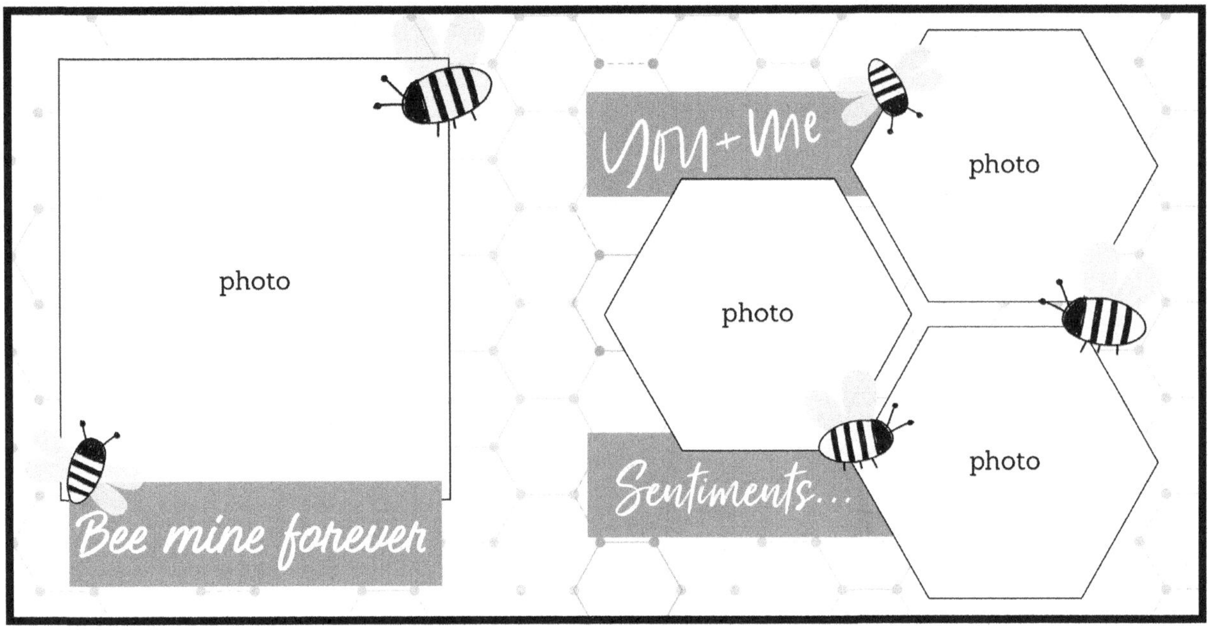
photo
Bee mine forever
You+Me
photo
photo
photo
Sentiments...

photo
Title
YOU & ME
photo
photo
Title

photo
Title
Title
photo
photo

157

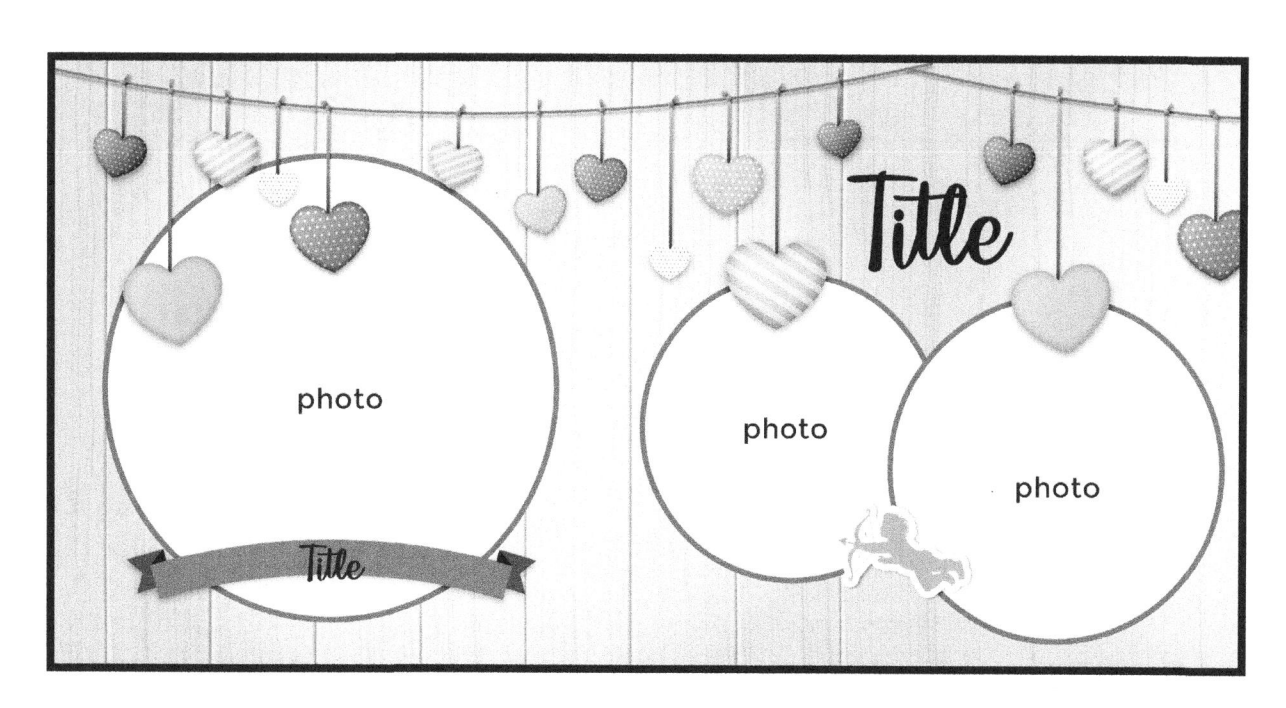

Title

photo

Title

photo

photo

Title

photo

Title

photo

photo

photo

photo

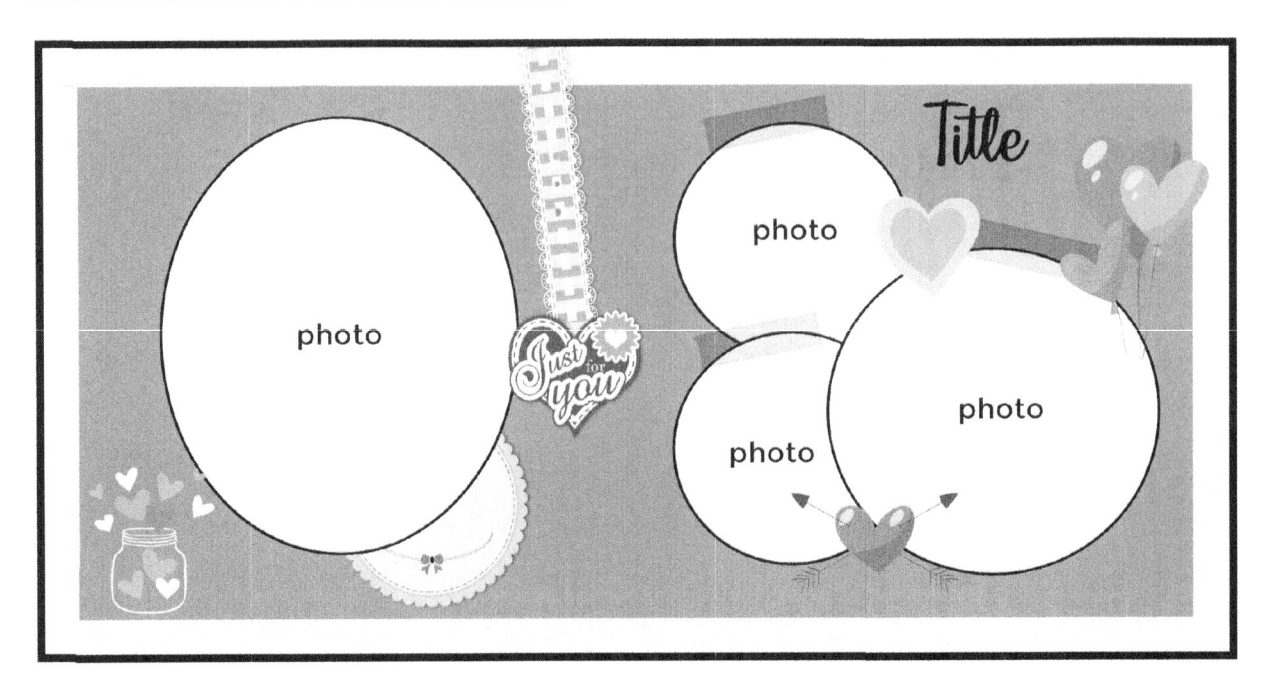

Title

photo

photo

photo

photo

158

159

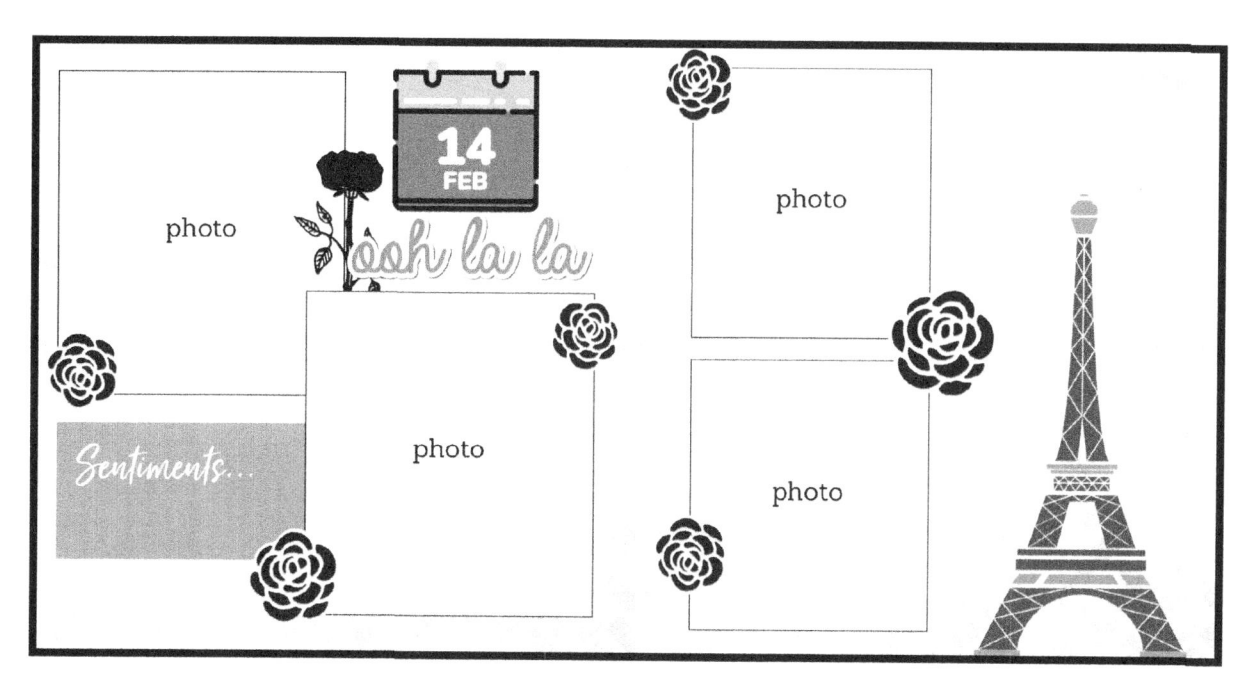

Vacation

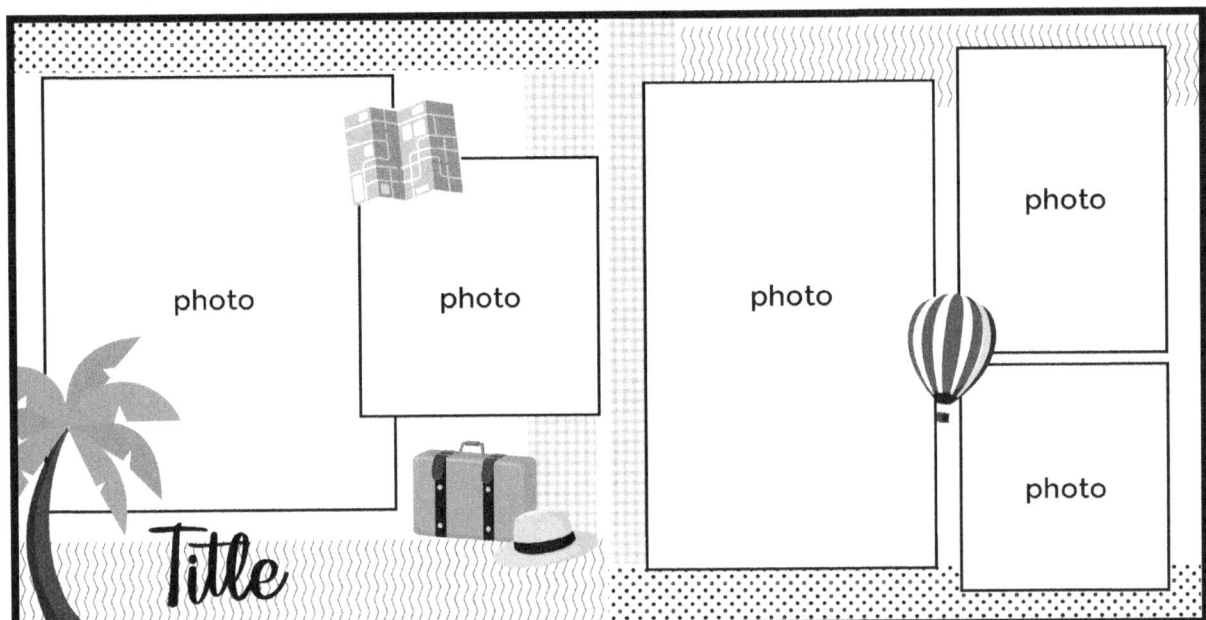

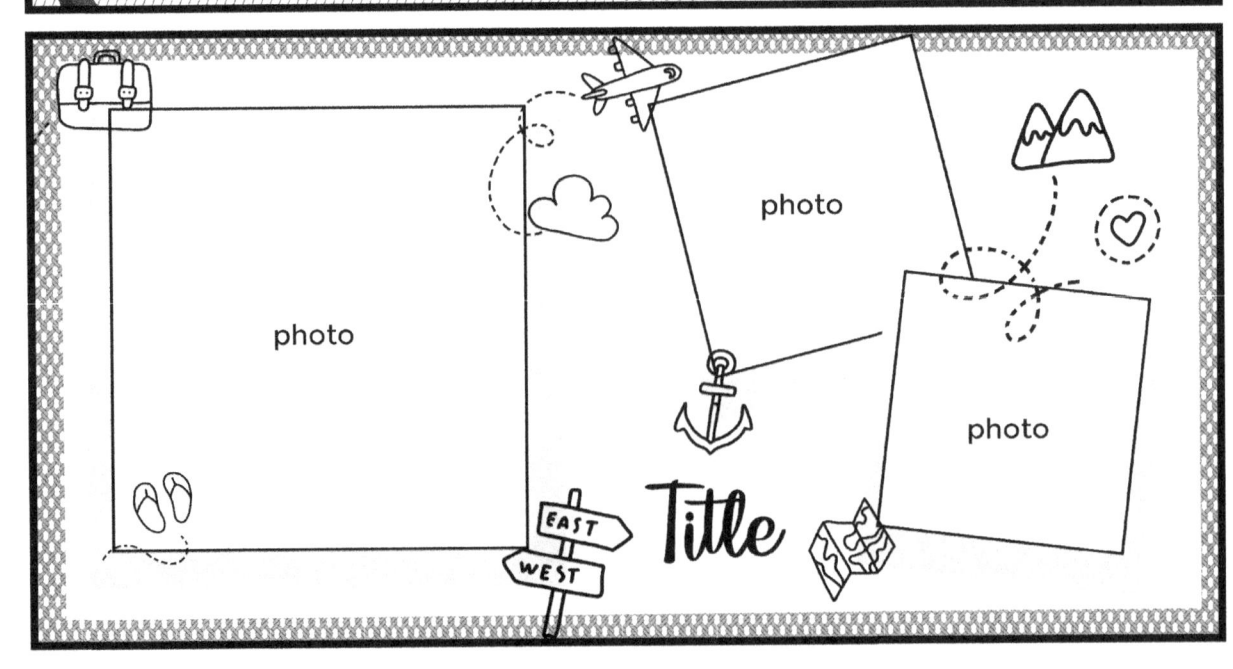

Vacation Time!

First trip to...

Title

Title

160

161

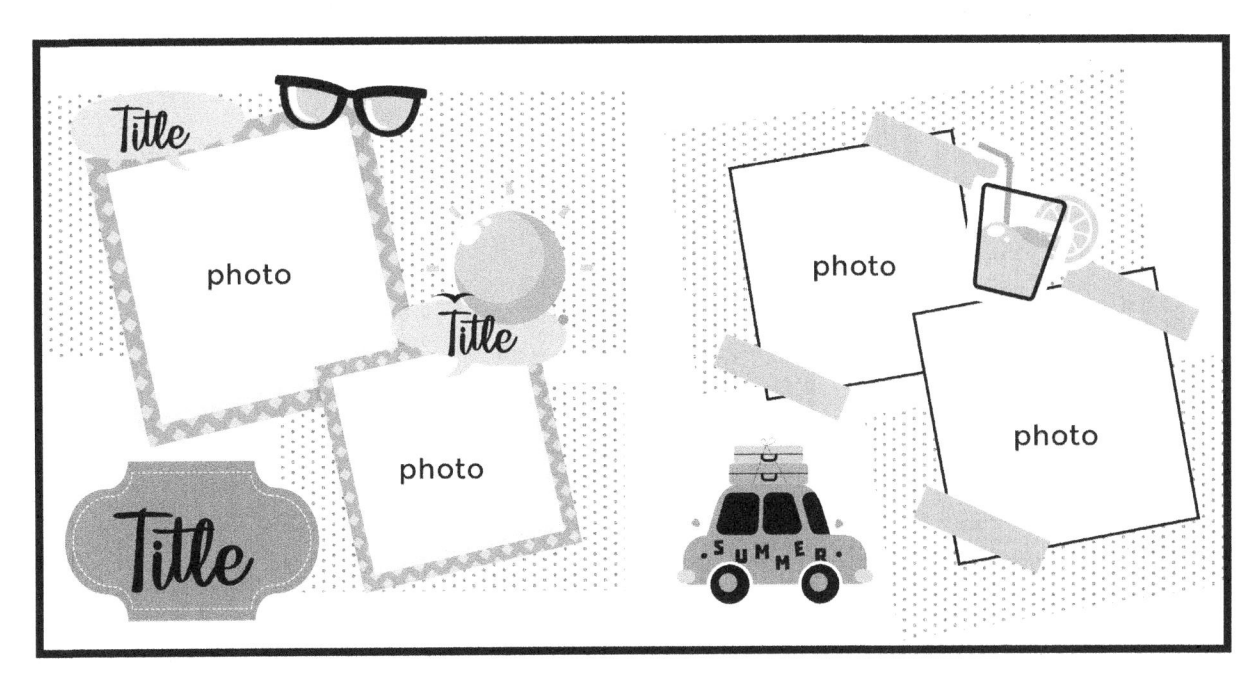

162

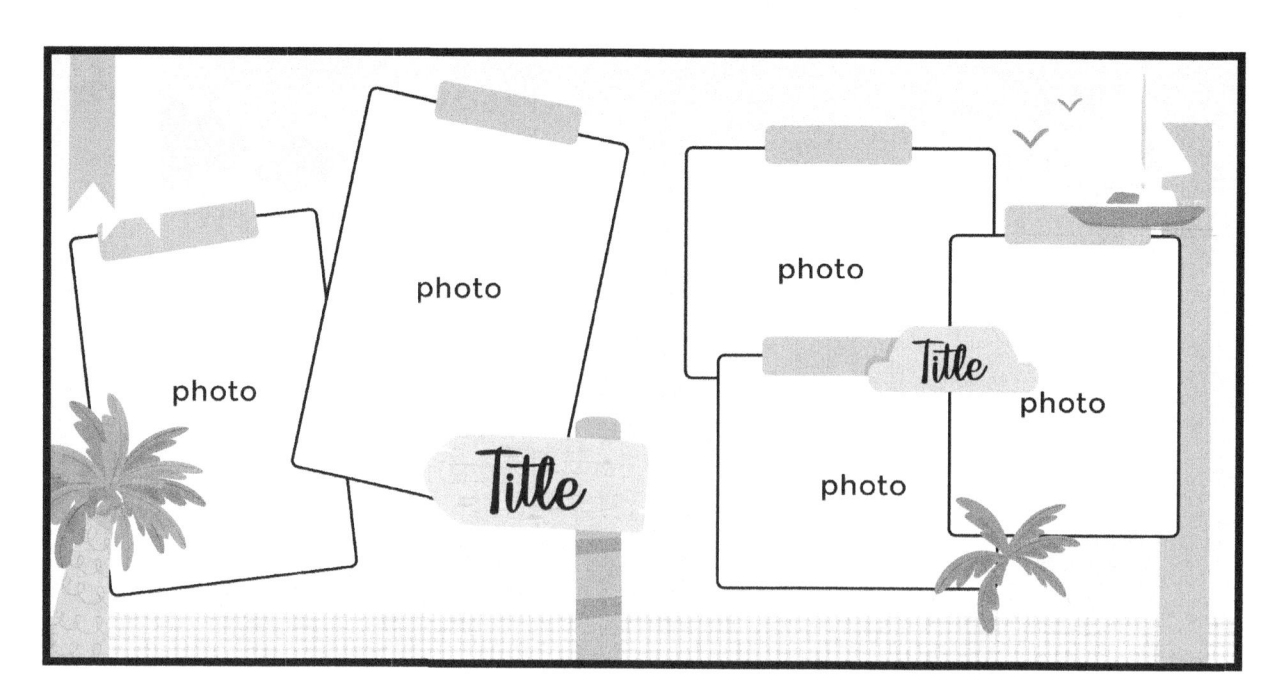

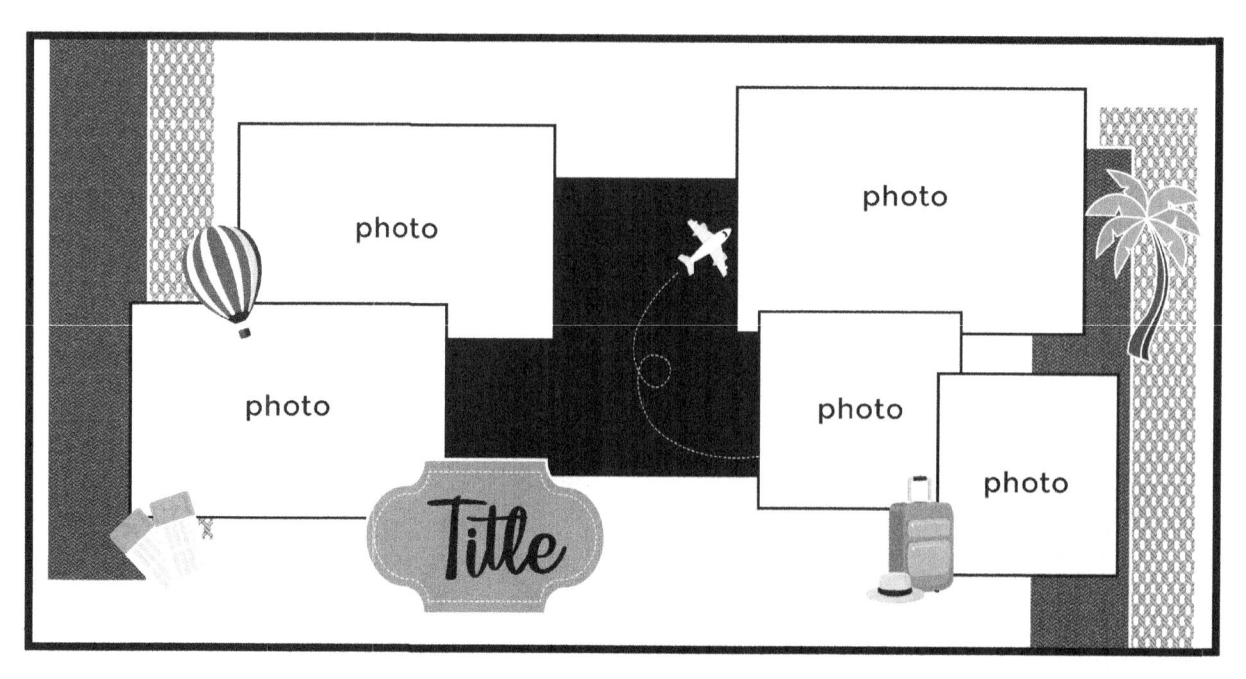

163

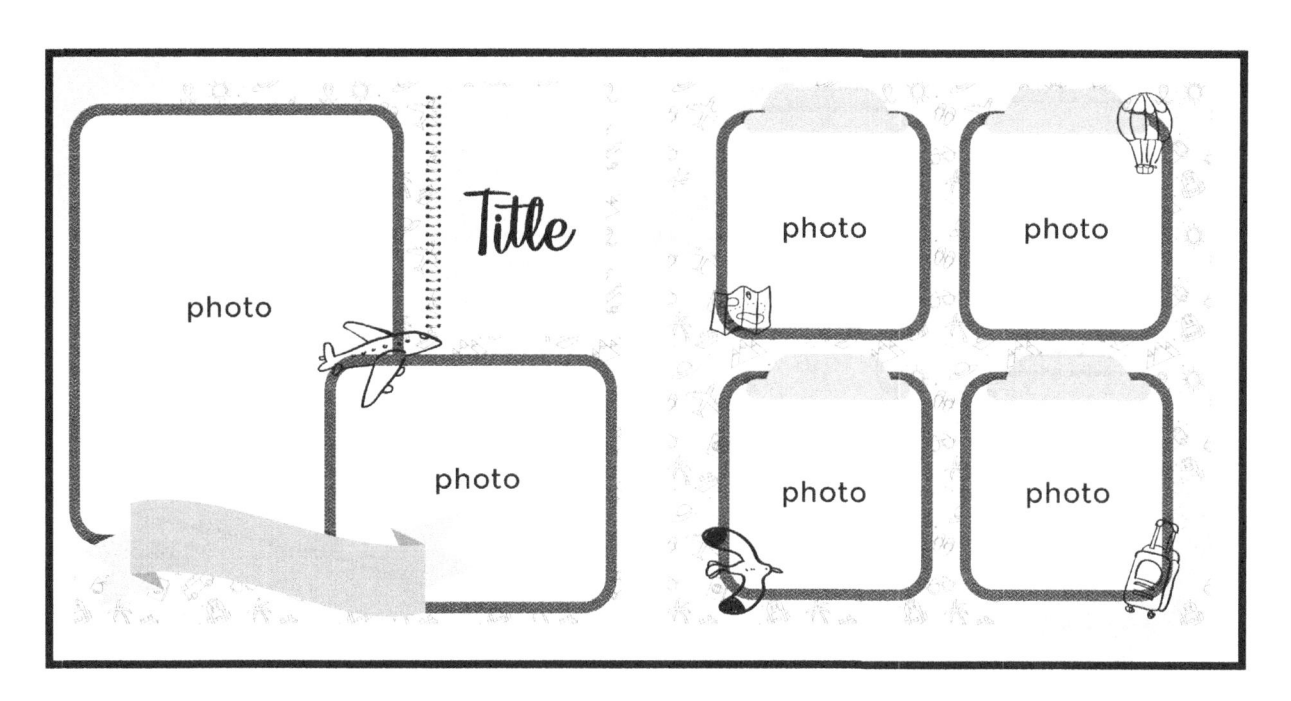

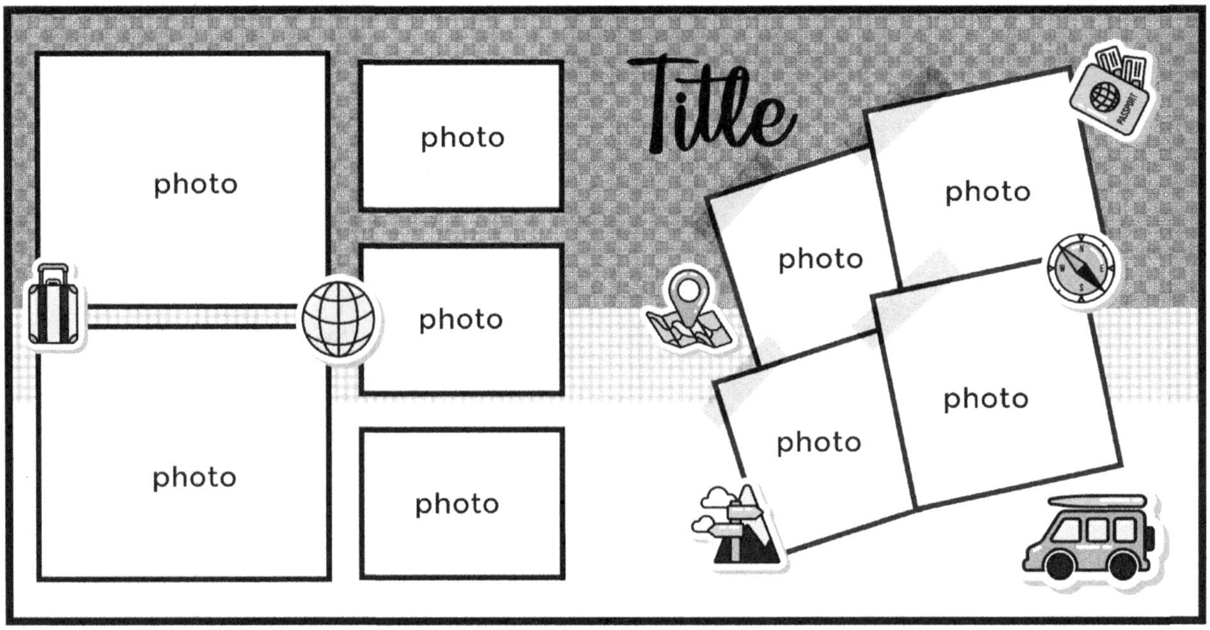

Title
photo
photo
photo
photo
photo
photo
photo
photo
photo

Title
photo
Title
photo
photo
photo

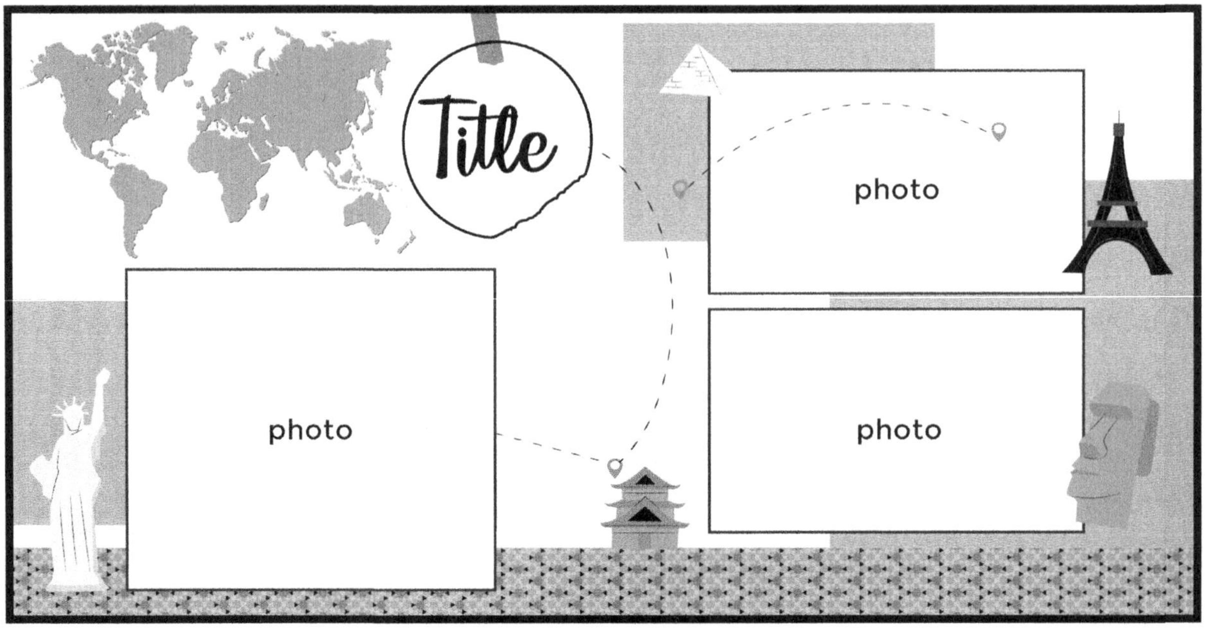

Title
photo
photo
photo

165

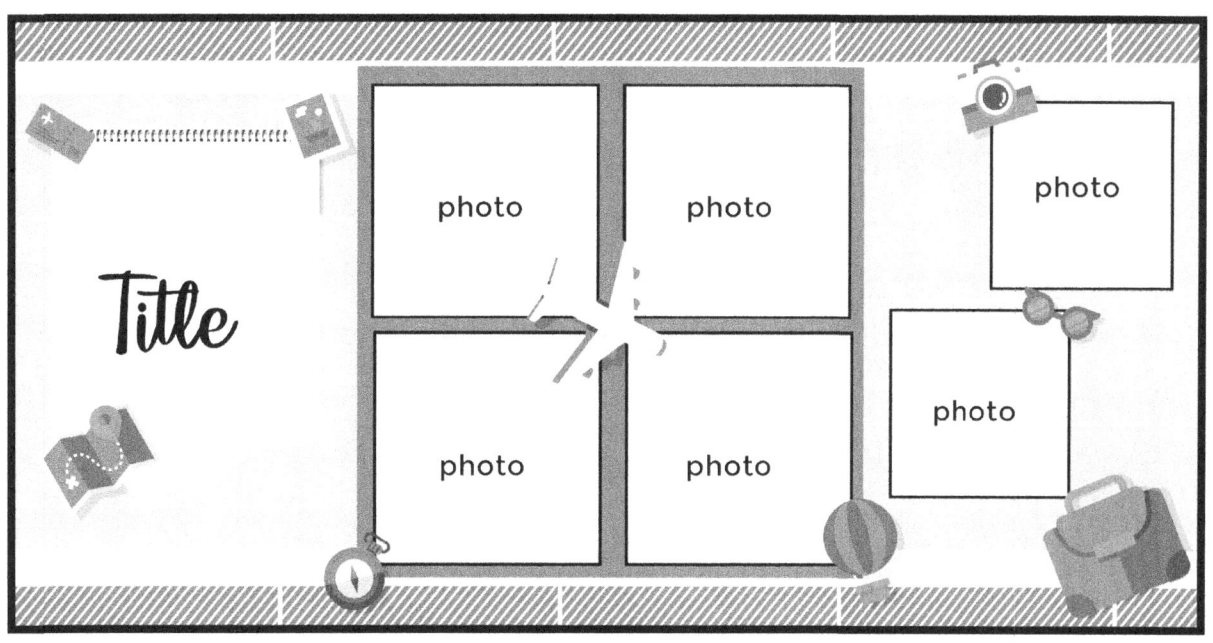

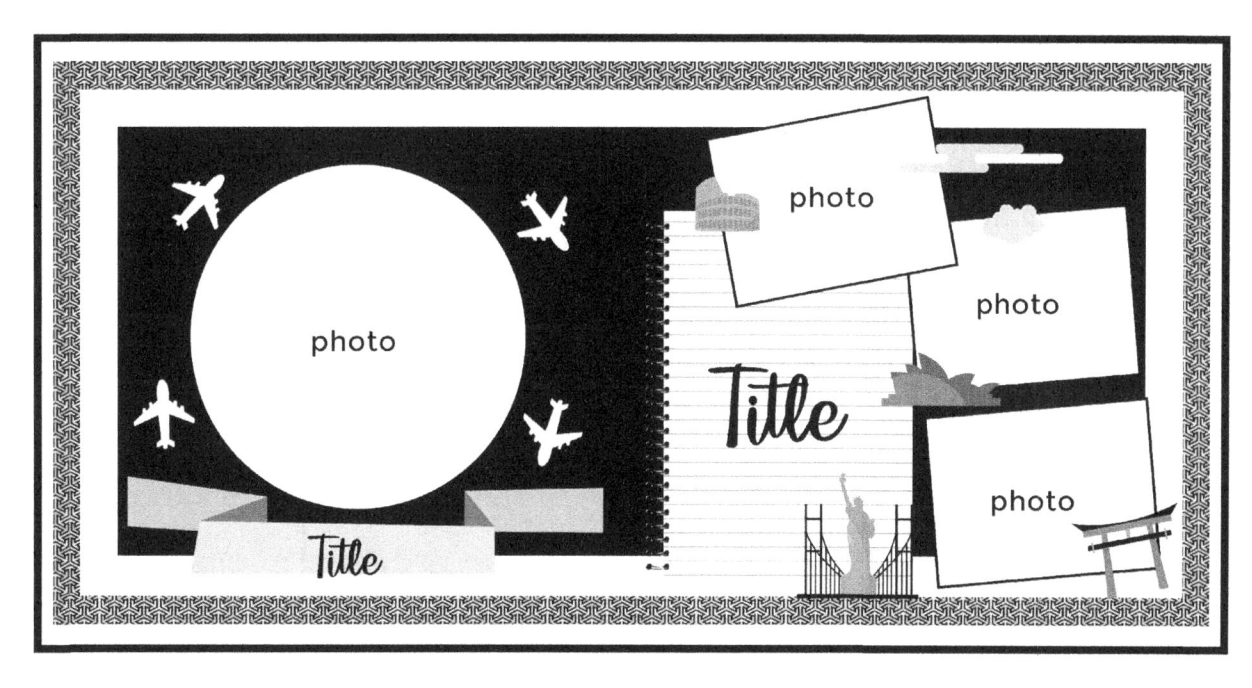

166

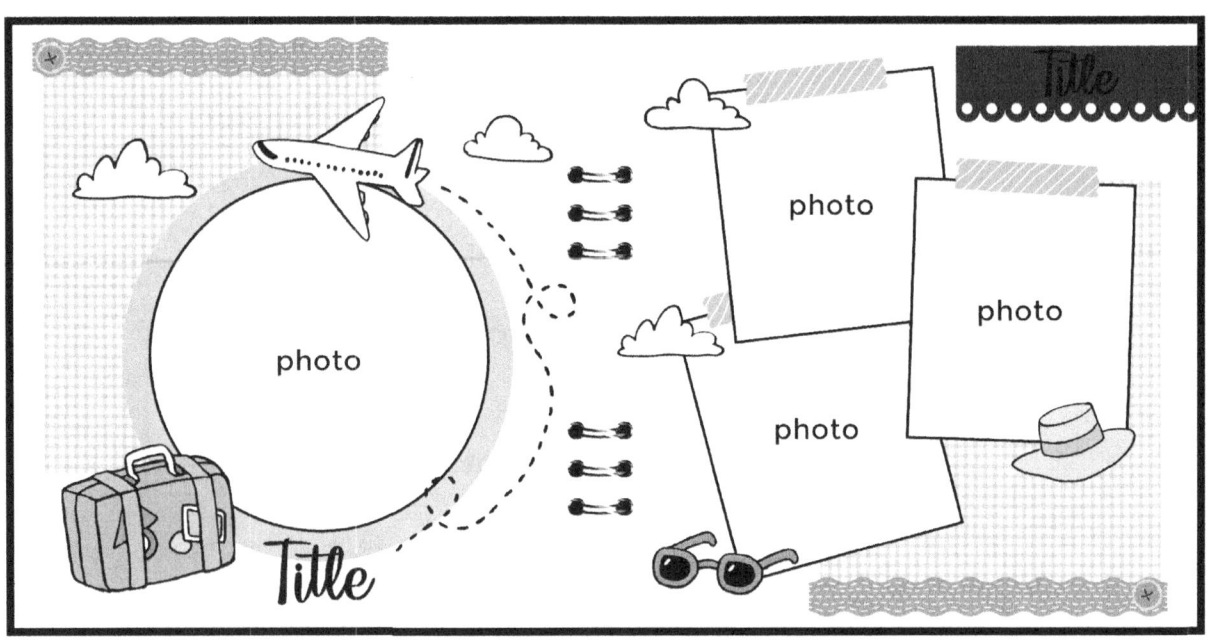

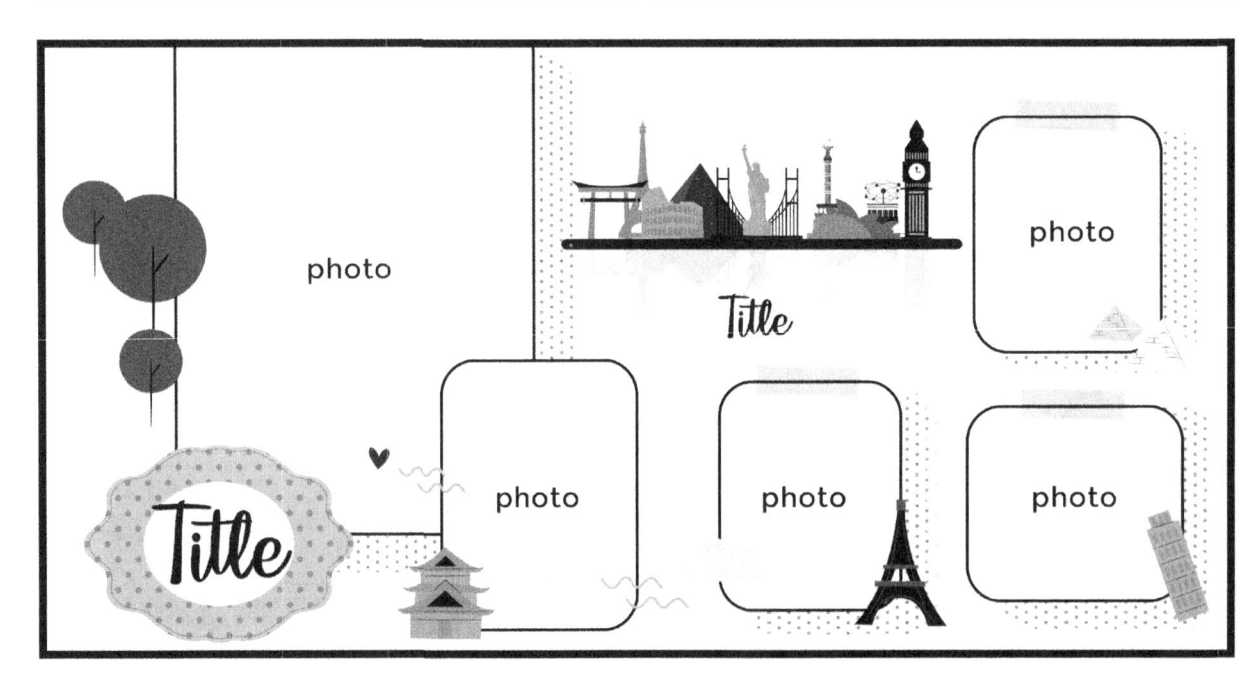

167

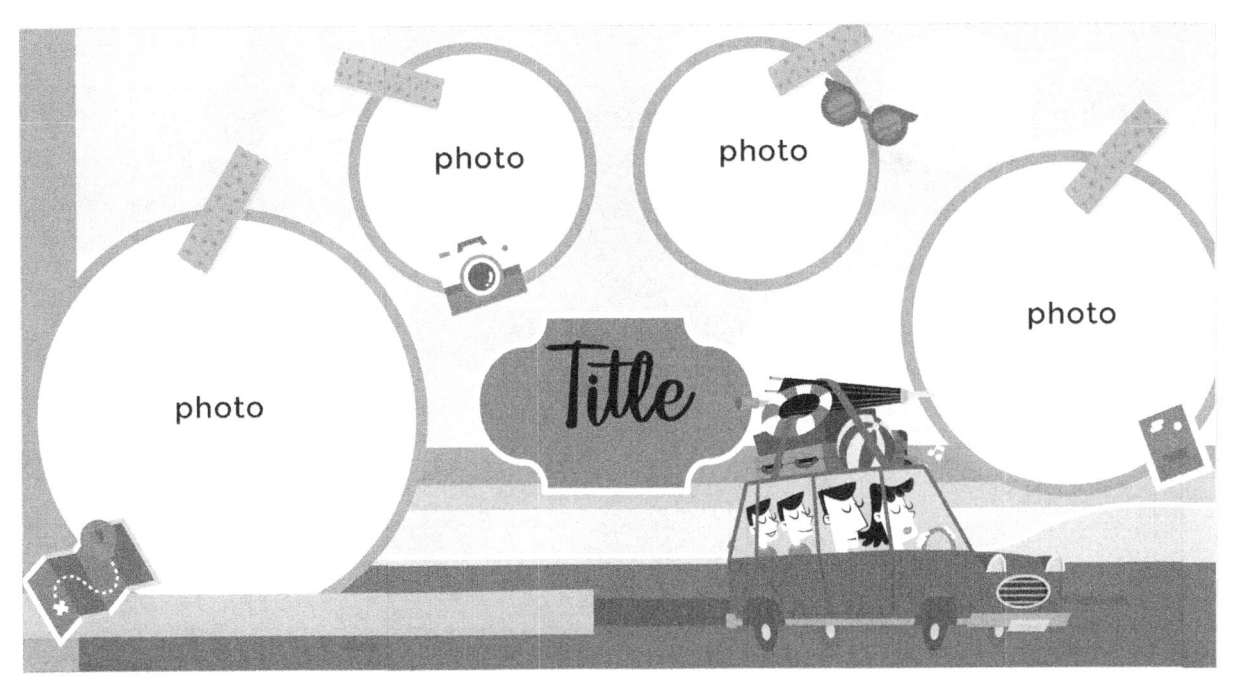

168

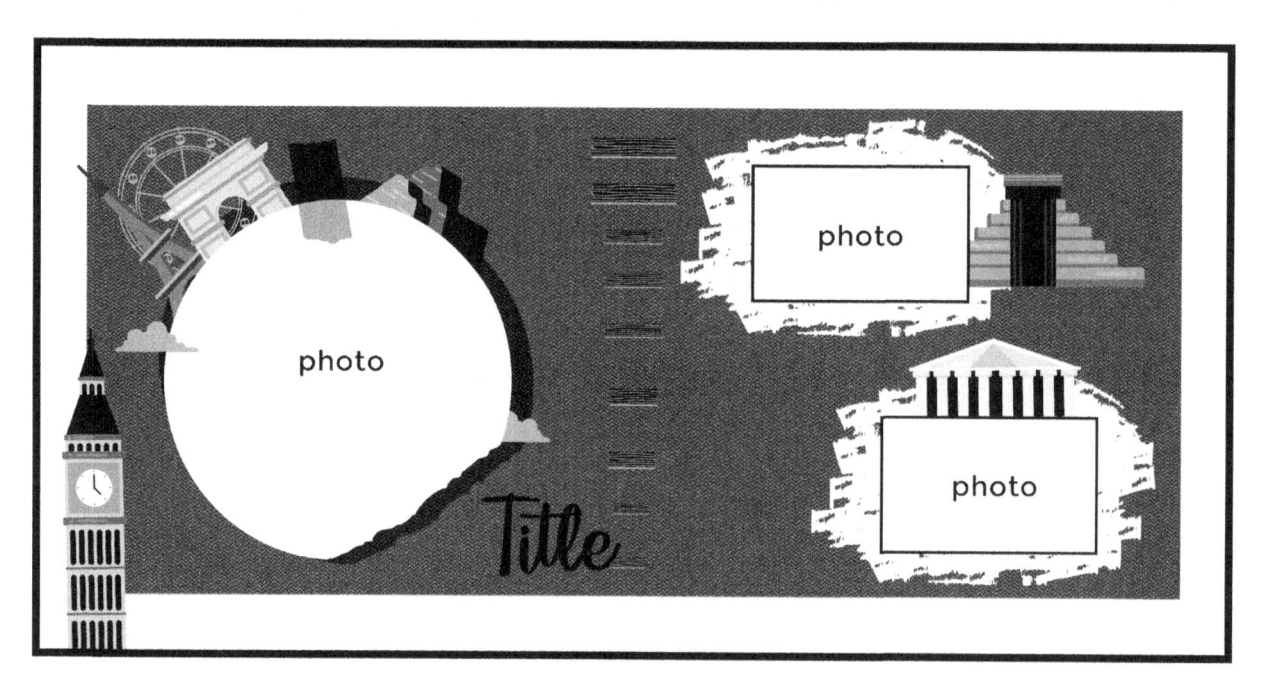

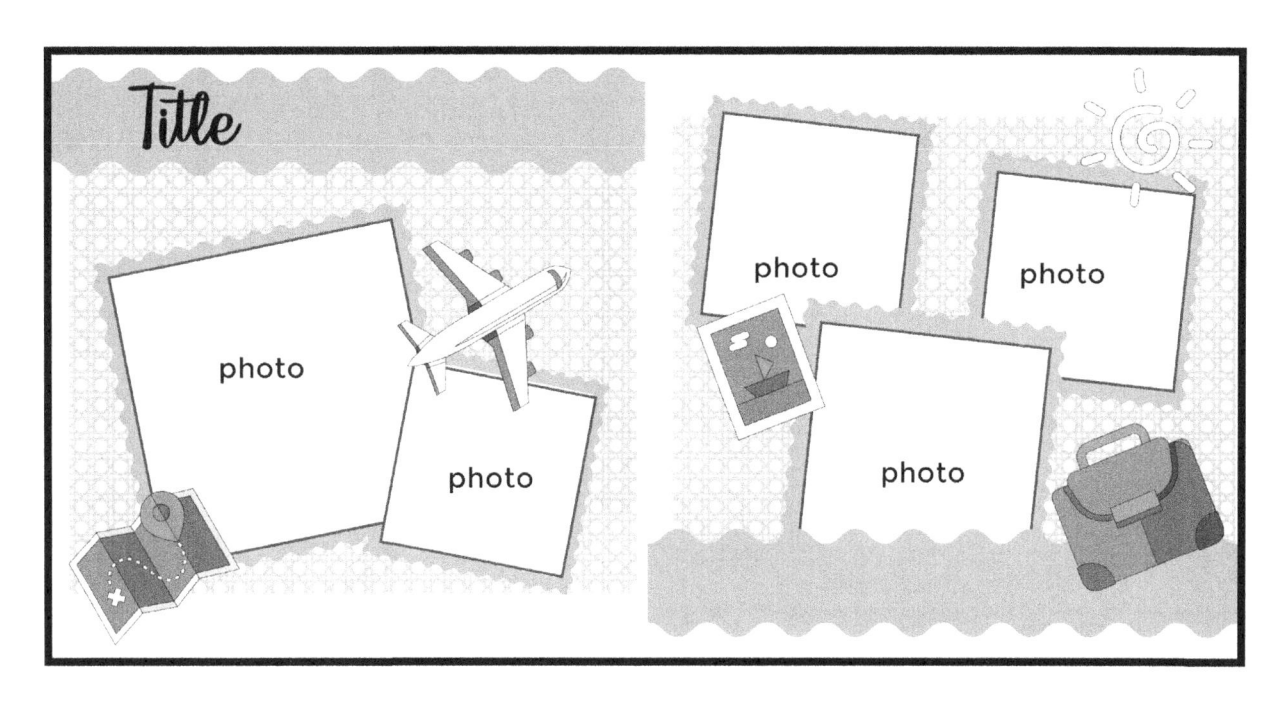

Title

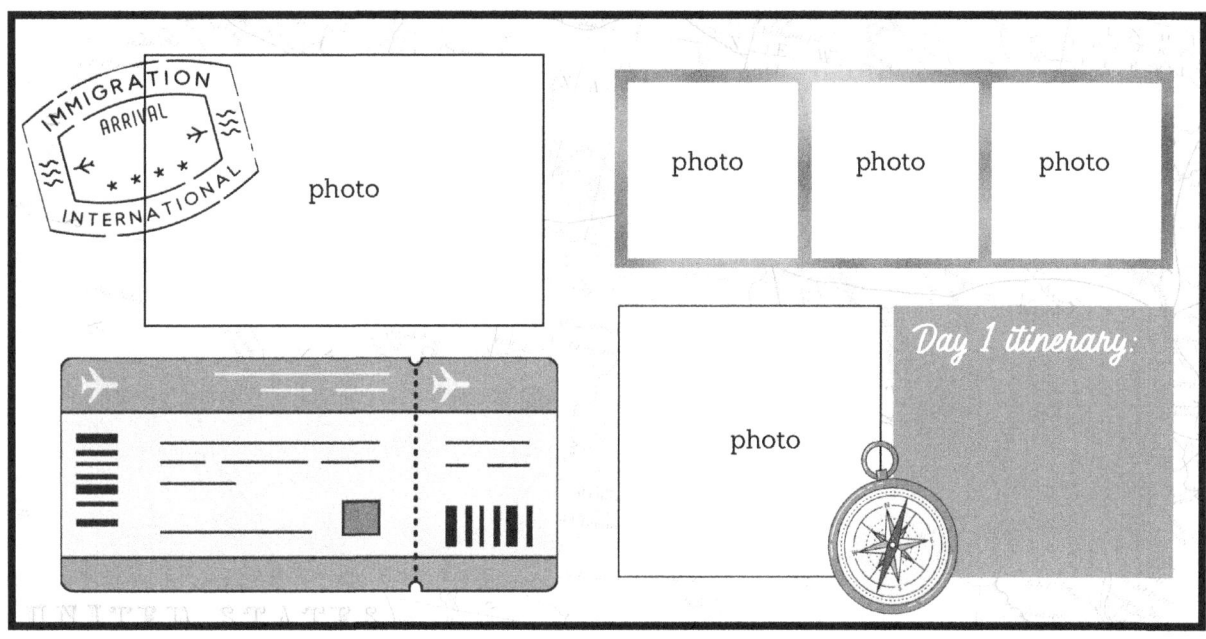

photo
photo

photo
photo
photo

Day 1 itinerary:

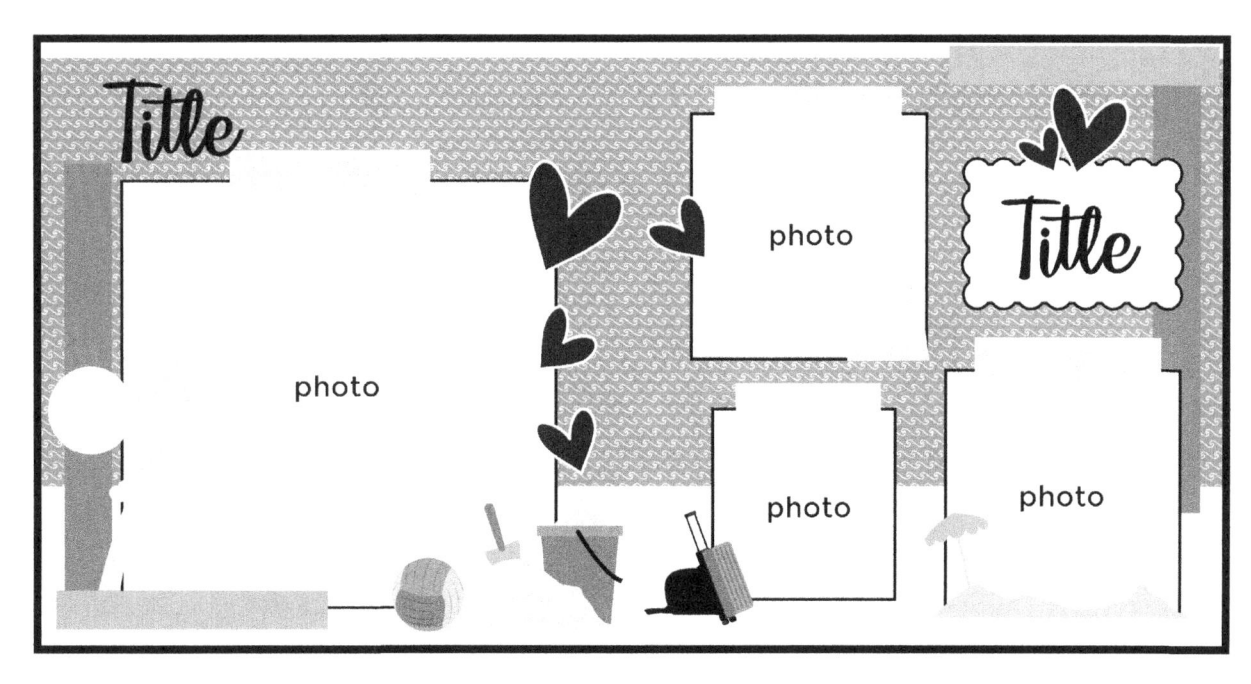

photo
photo
photo
photo

Title

photo
photo
photo
photo

Title

169

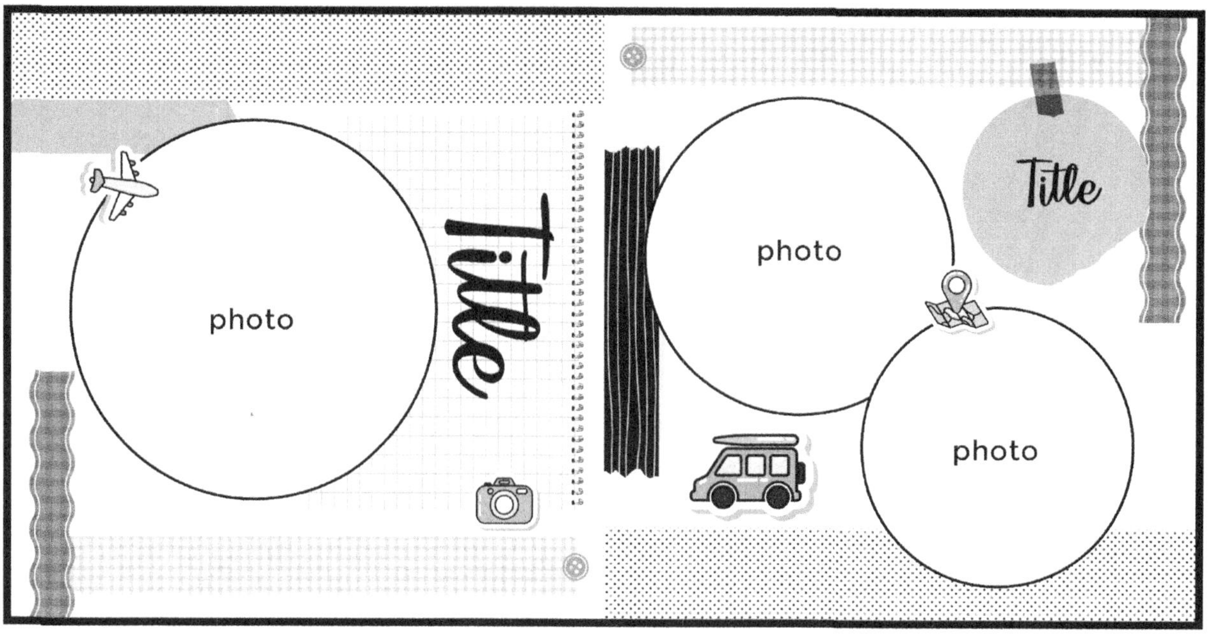
Title
photo
photo
Title
photo

Title
photo
photo

photo
photo
photo
photo
Title

Title

Title

ENJOY VACATION

Sentiments...

171

Wedding

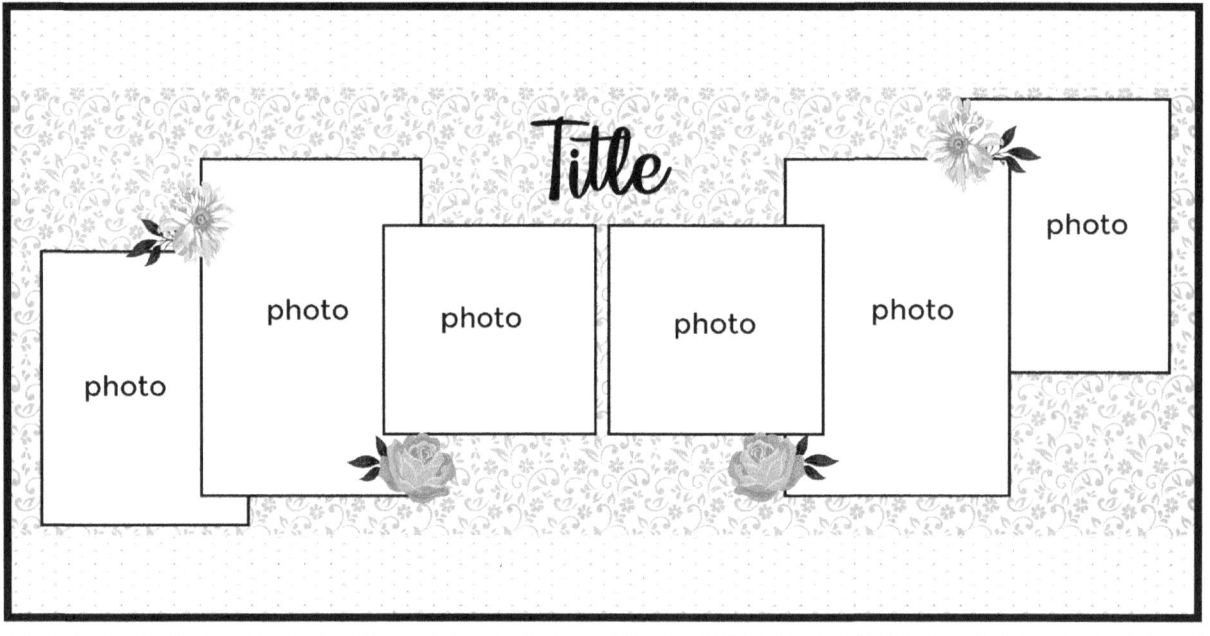

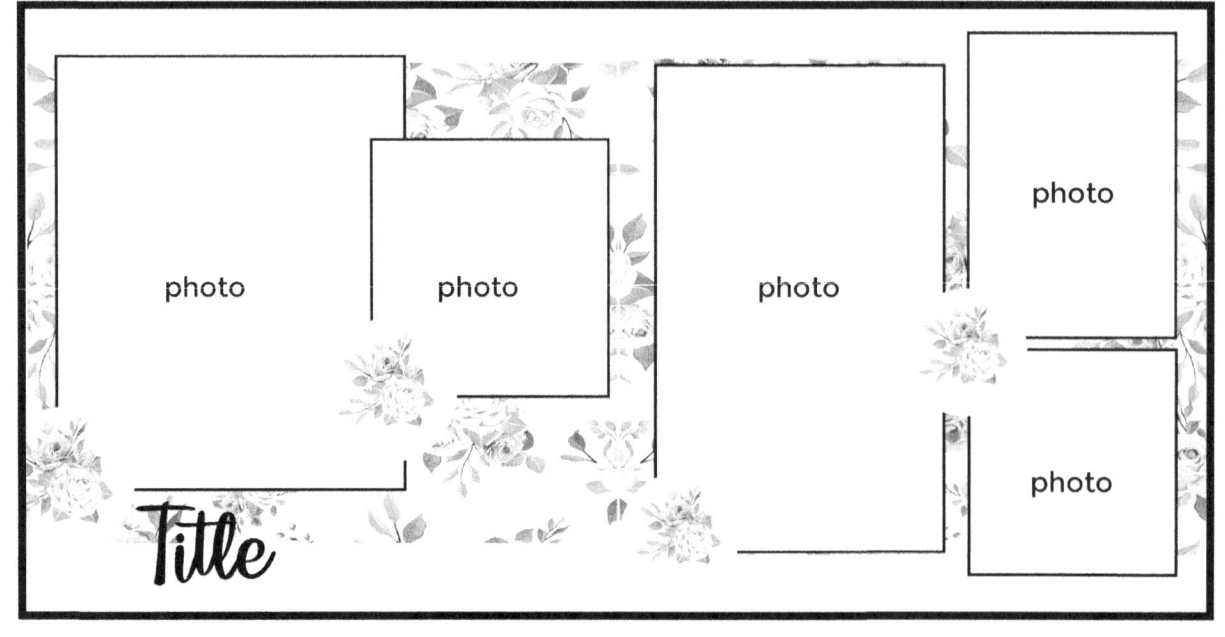

173

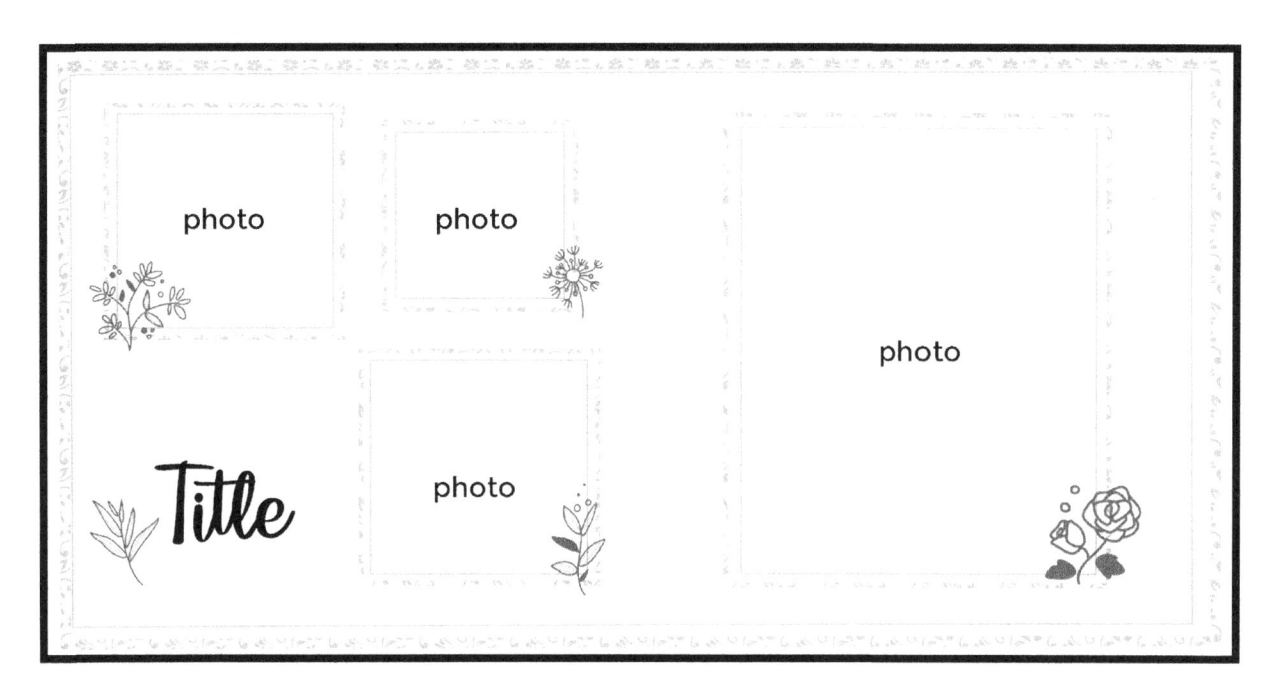

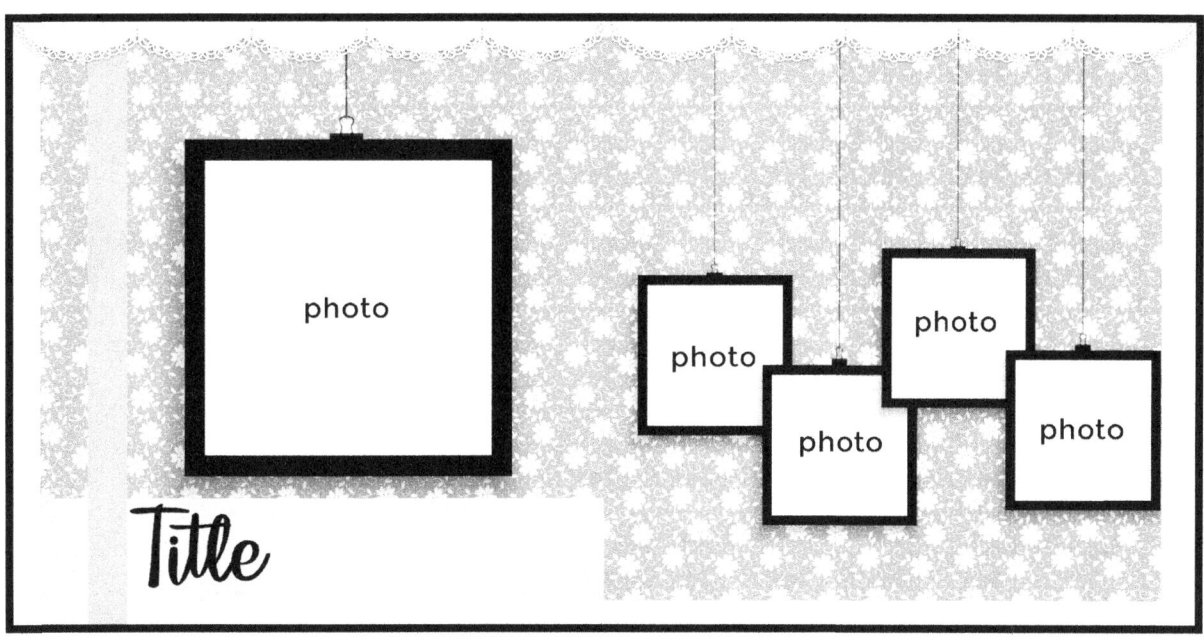

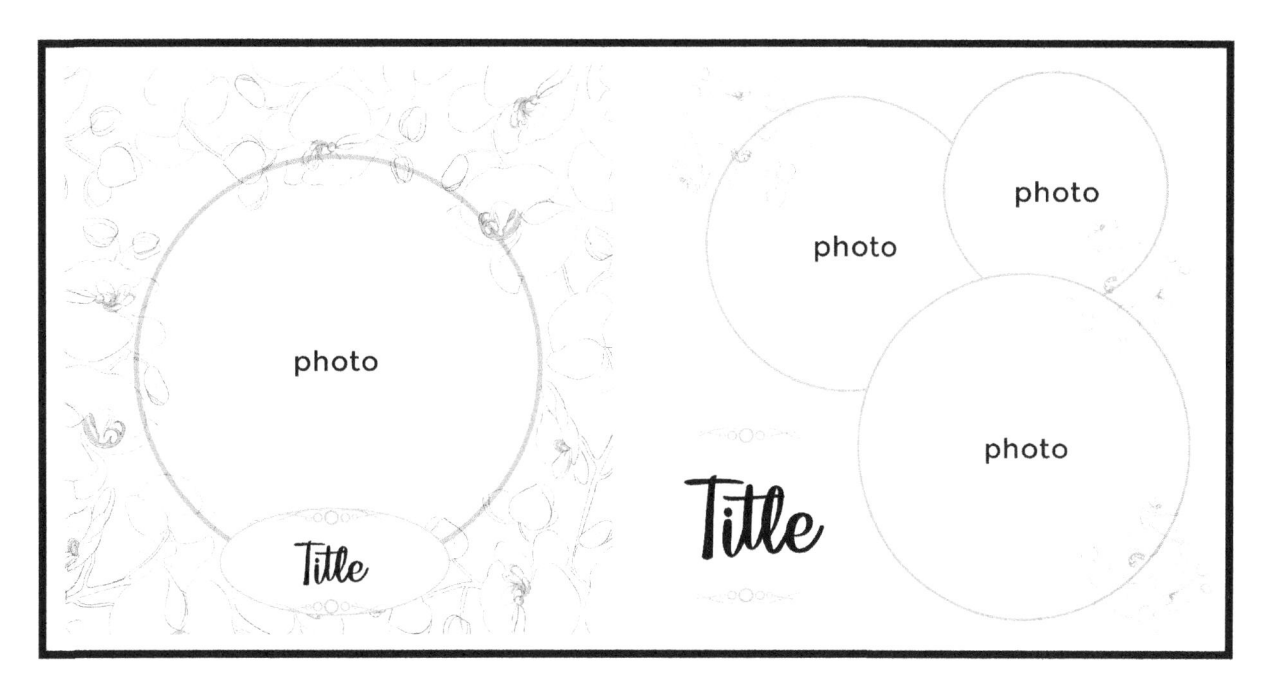

174

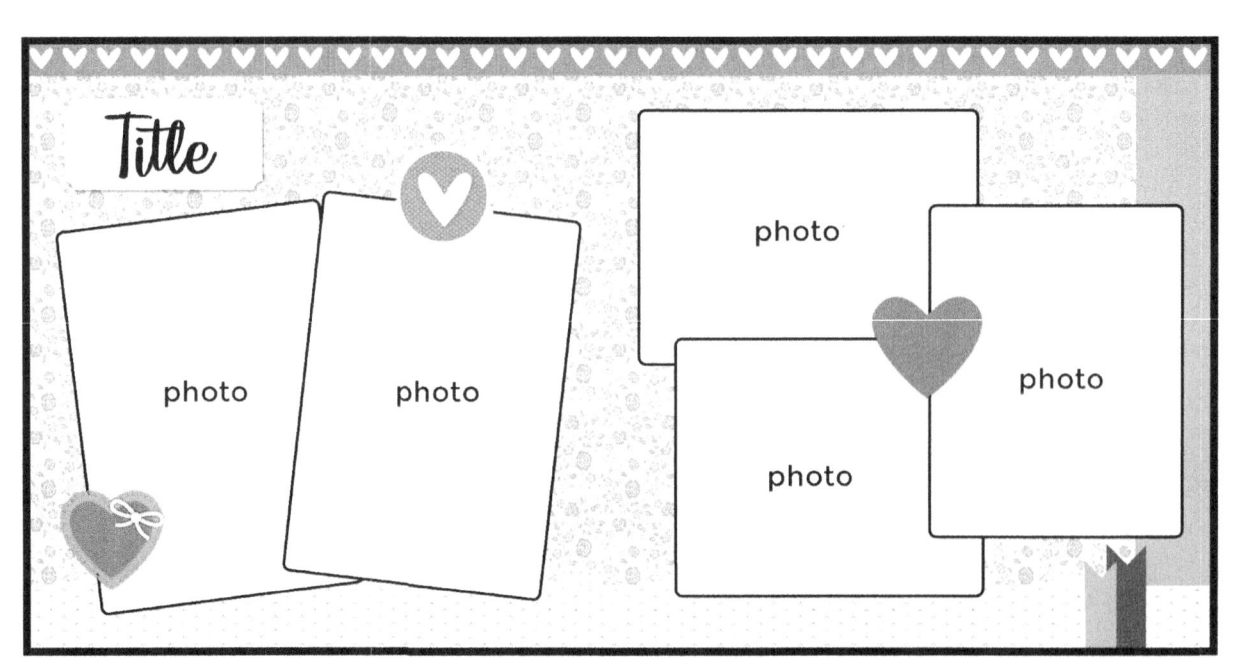

Title

photo

photo

photo

photo

Title

photo

photo

FOREVER LOVE

photo

photo

Sentiments...

photo

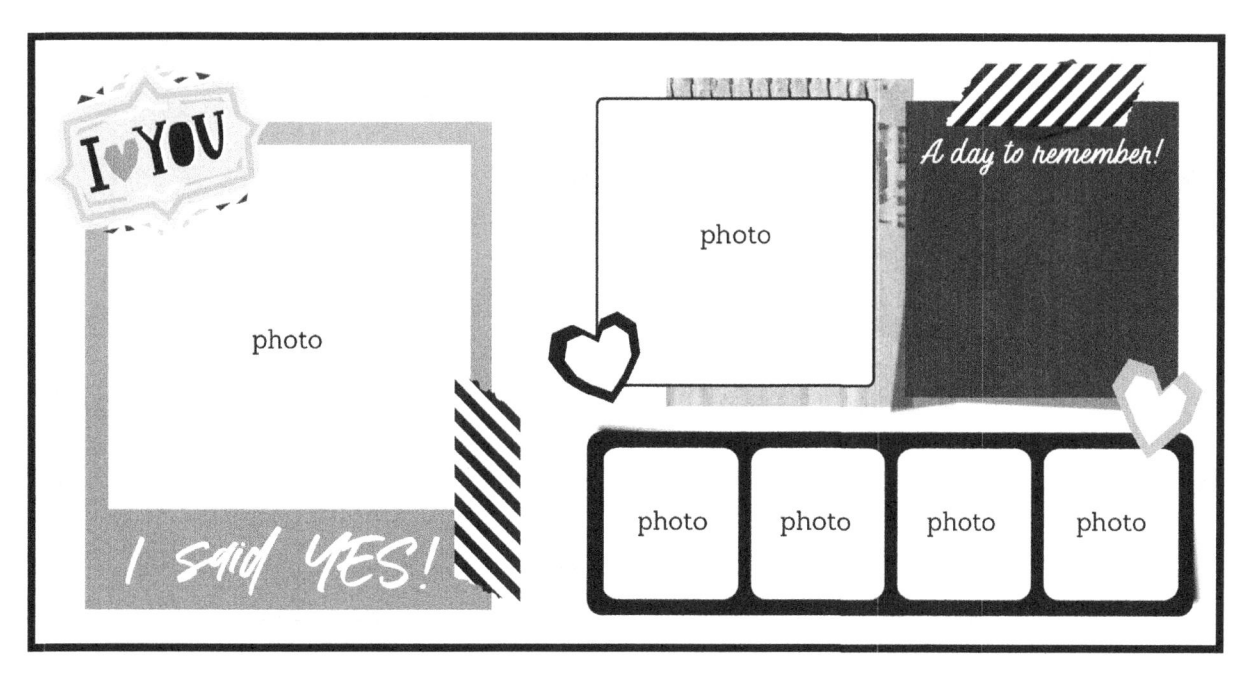

I ♥ YOU

photo

photo

A day to remember!

photo

photo

photo

photo

I said YES!

175

176

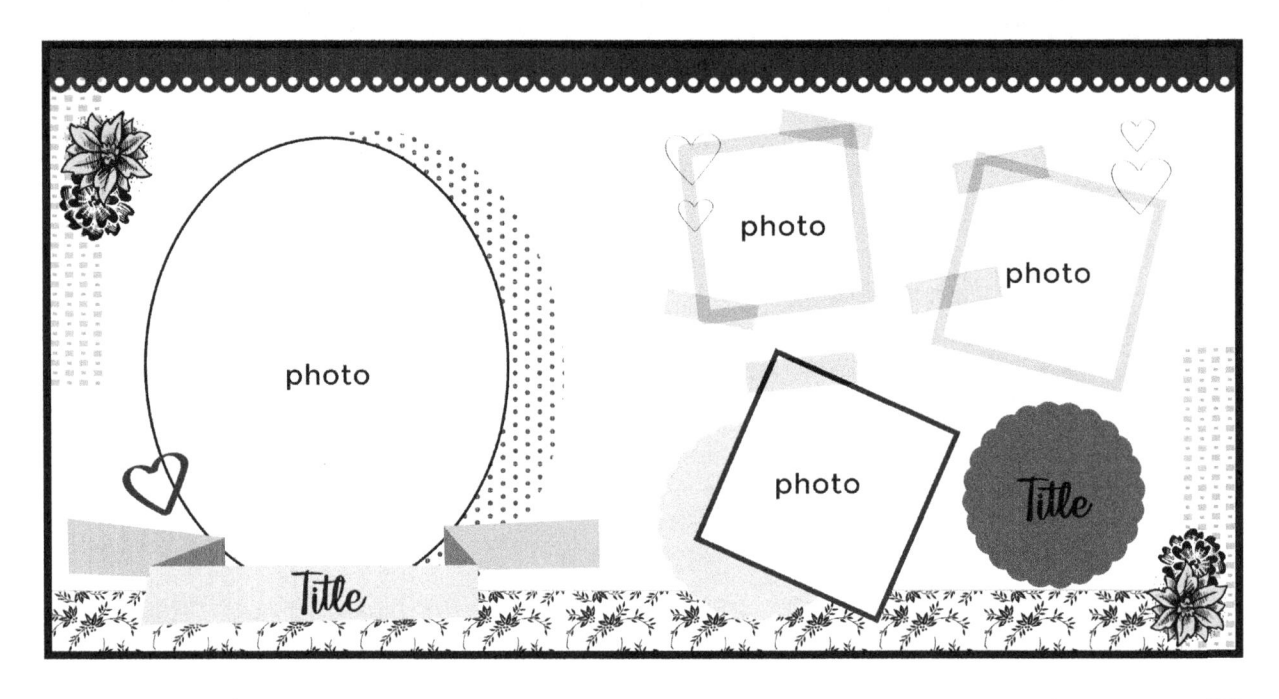

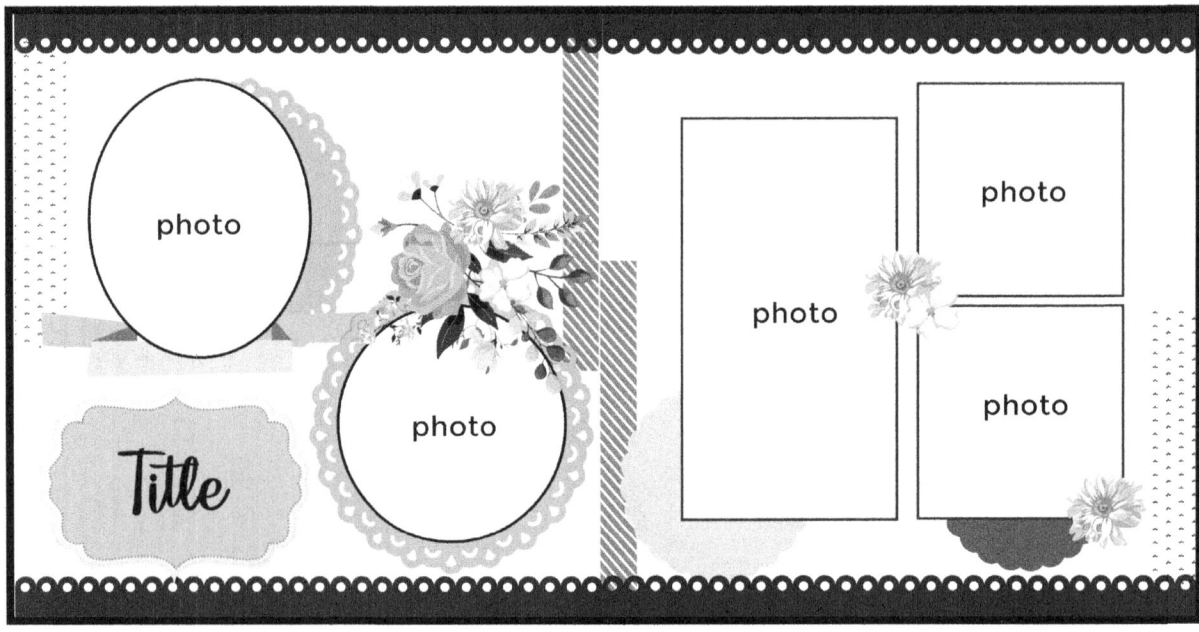

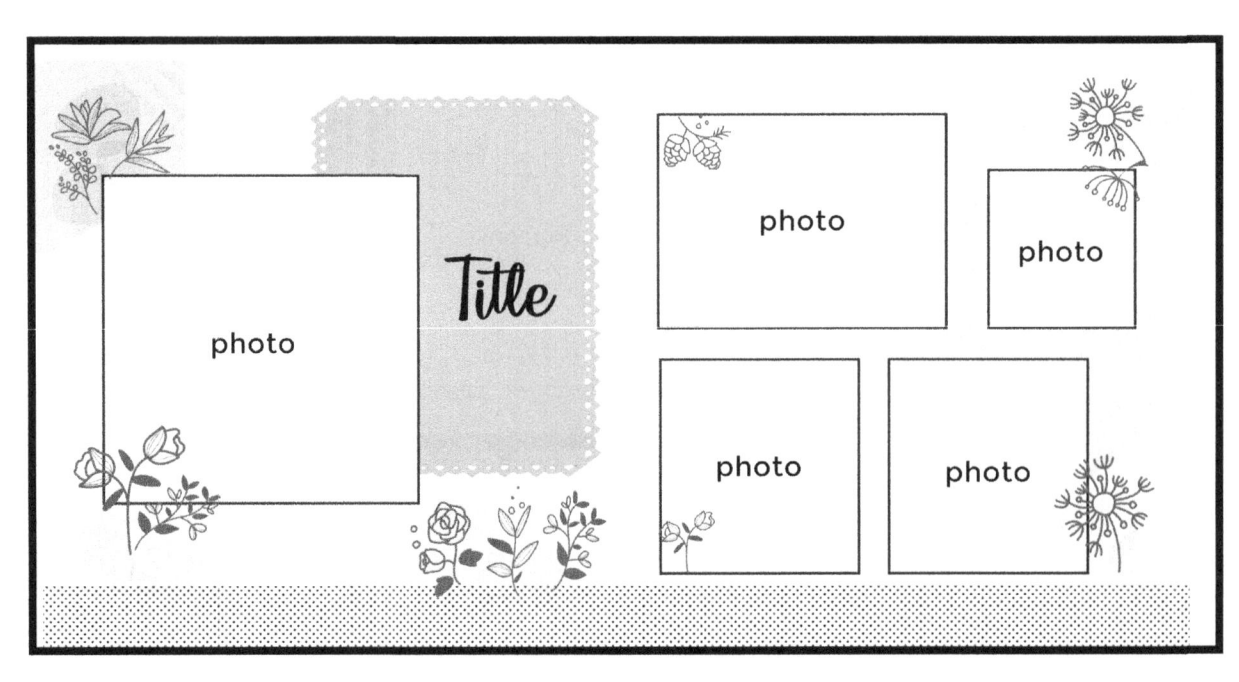

177

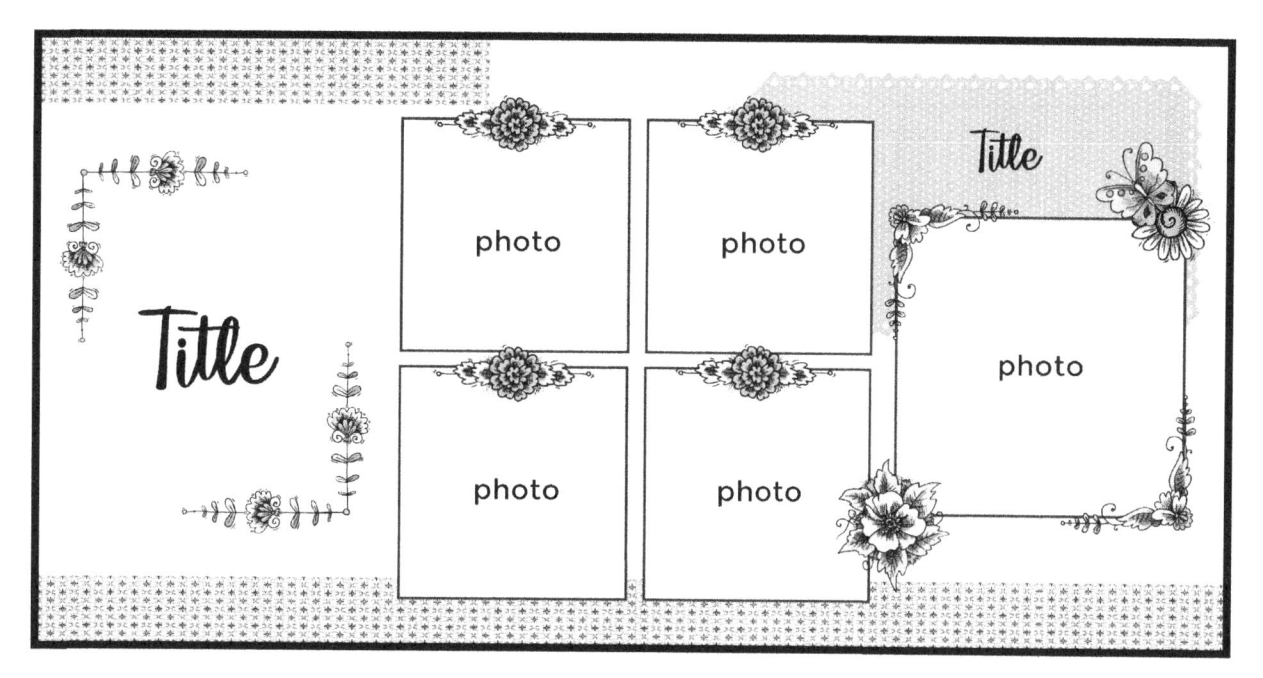

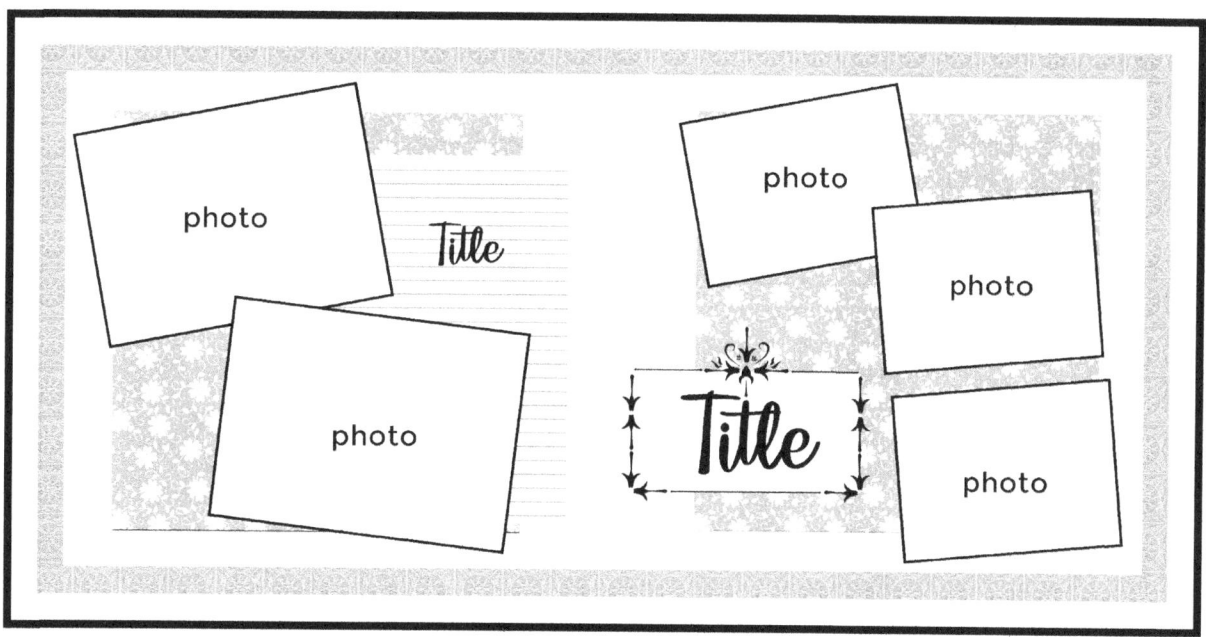

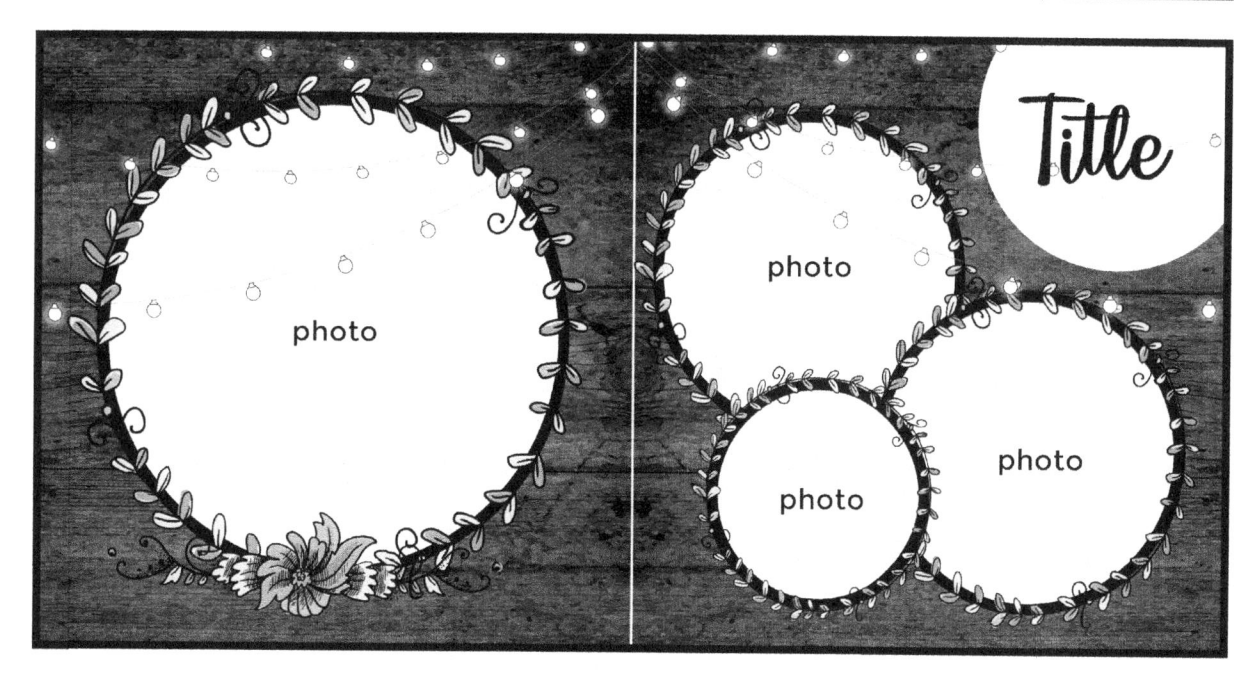

178

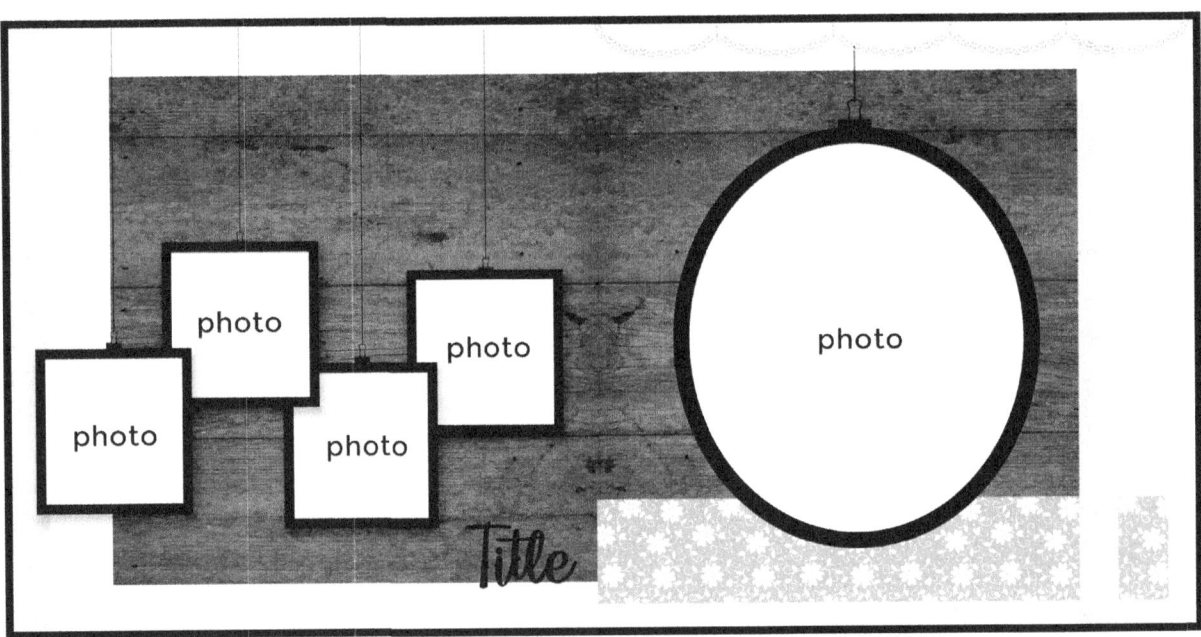

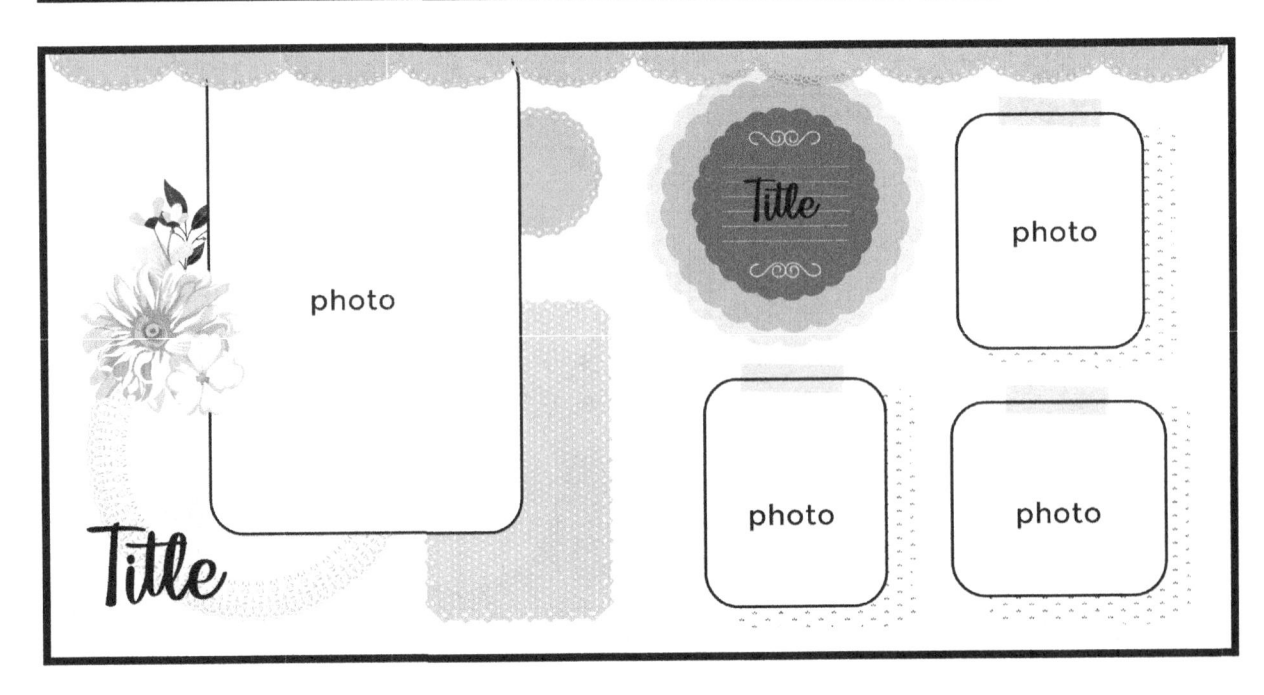

179

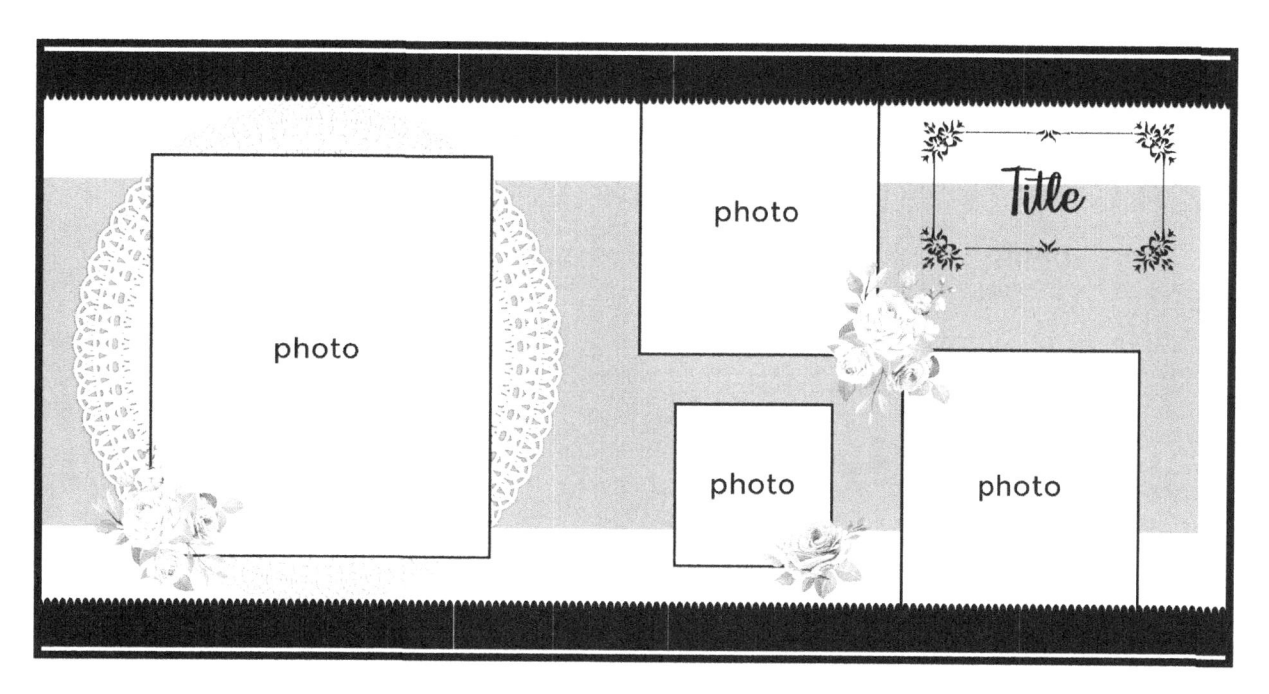

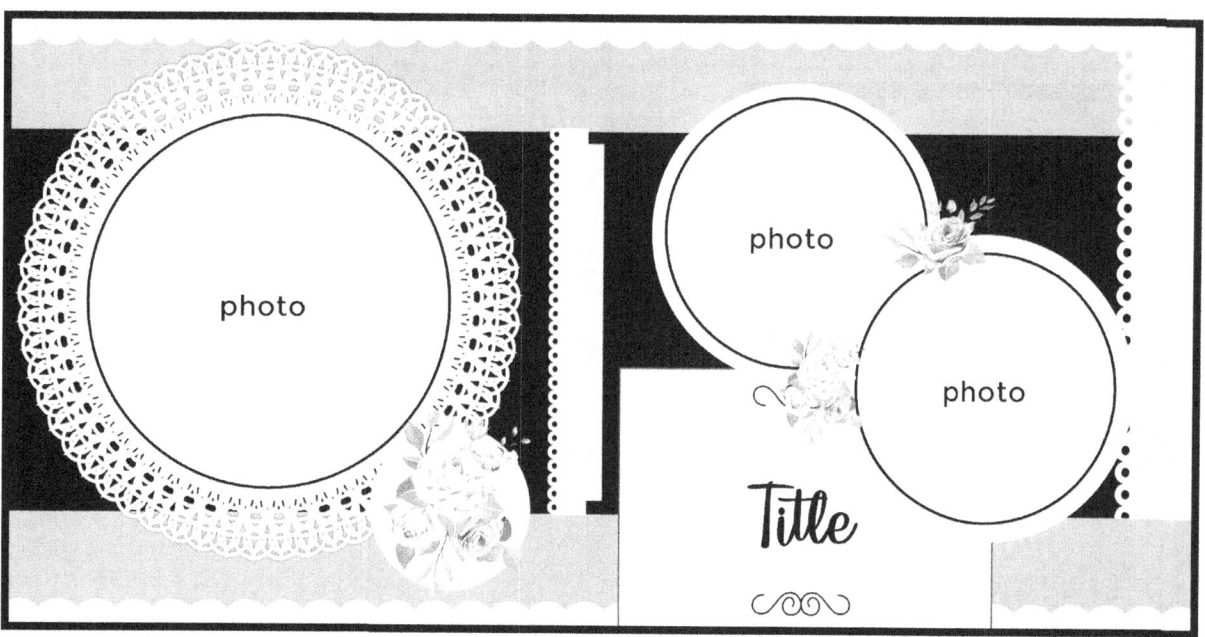

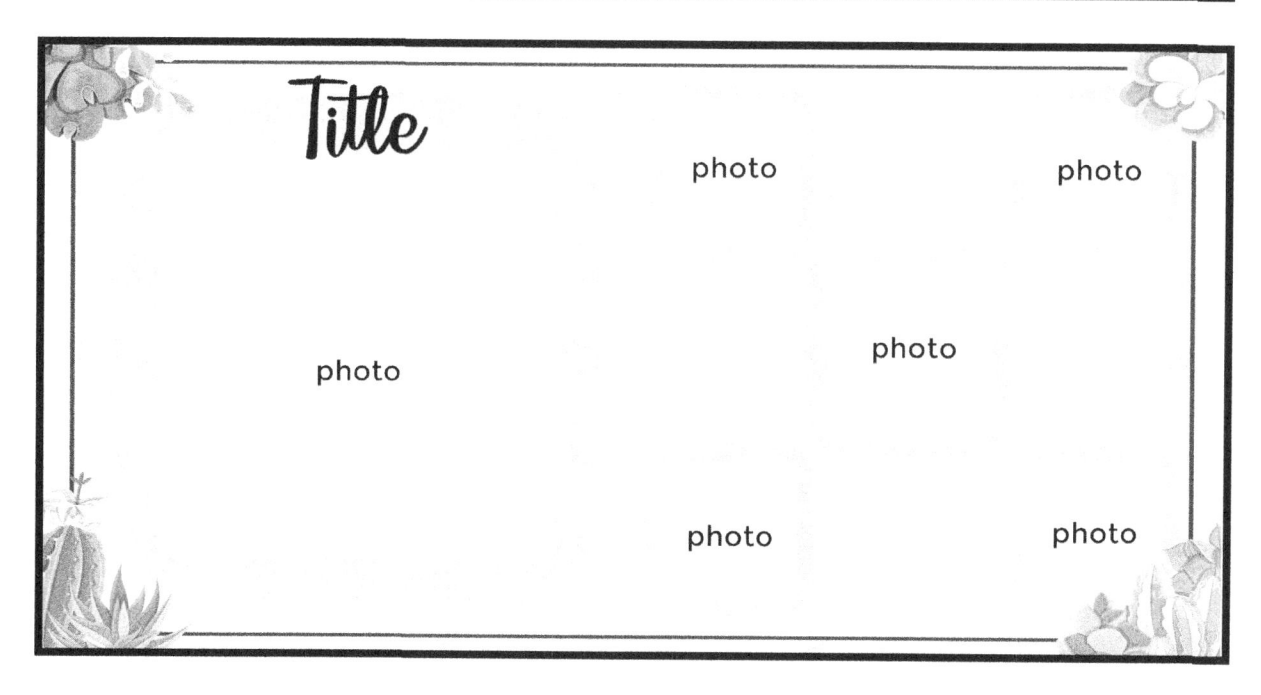

180

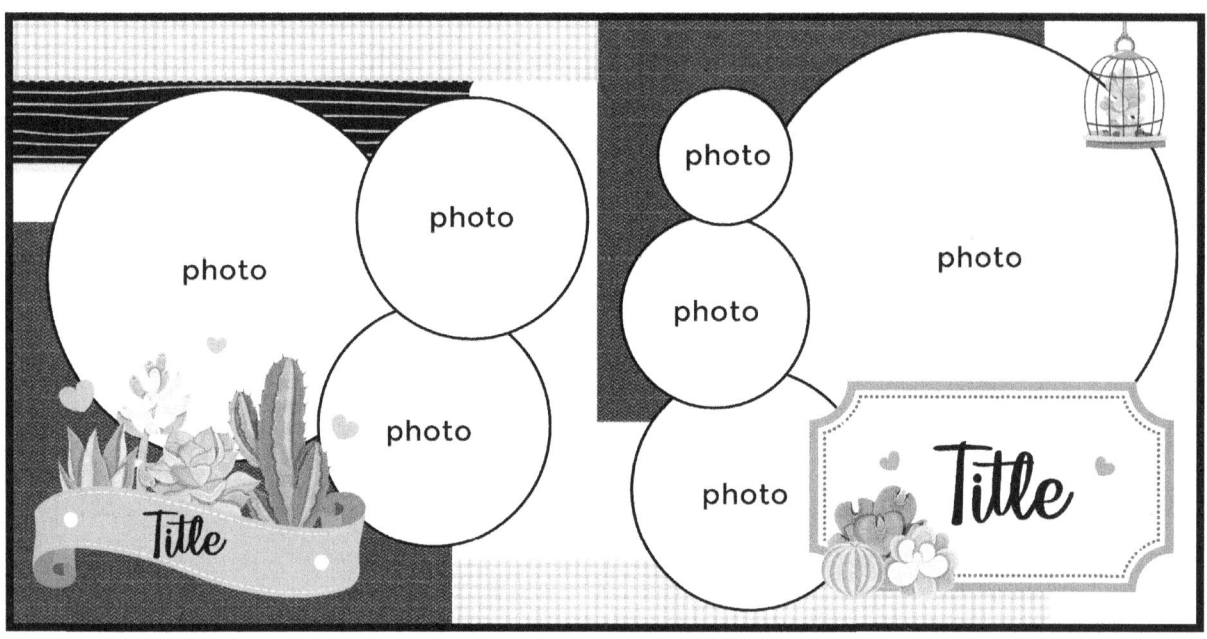

181

182

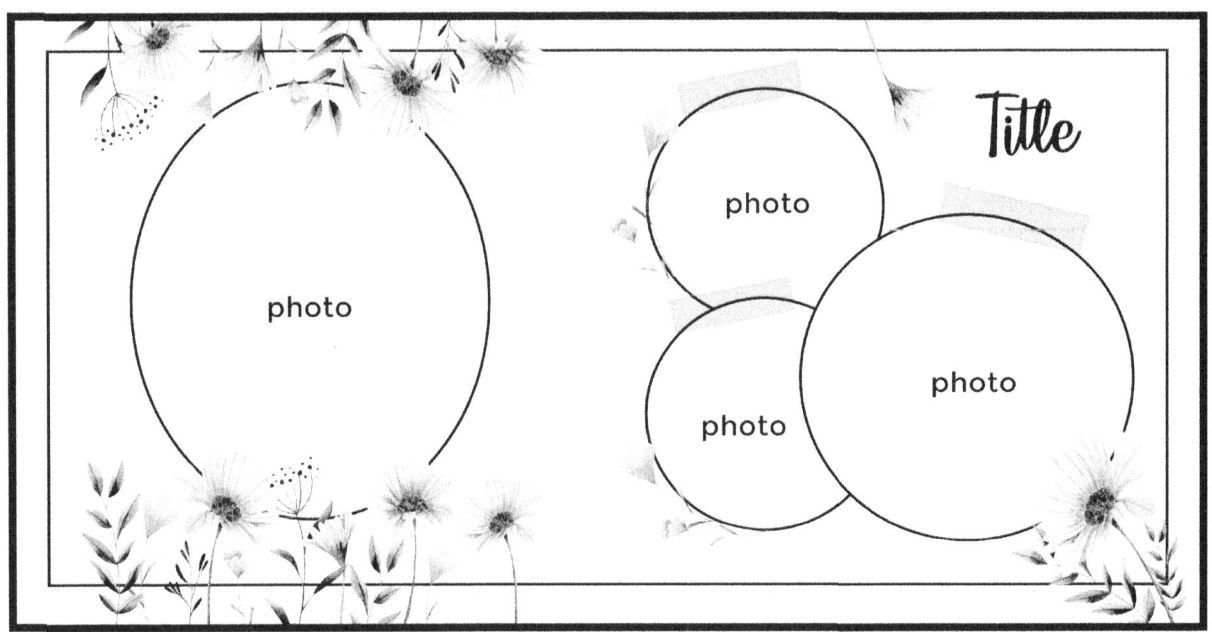

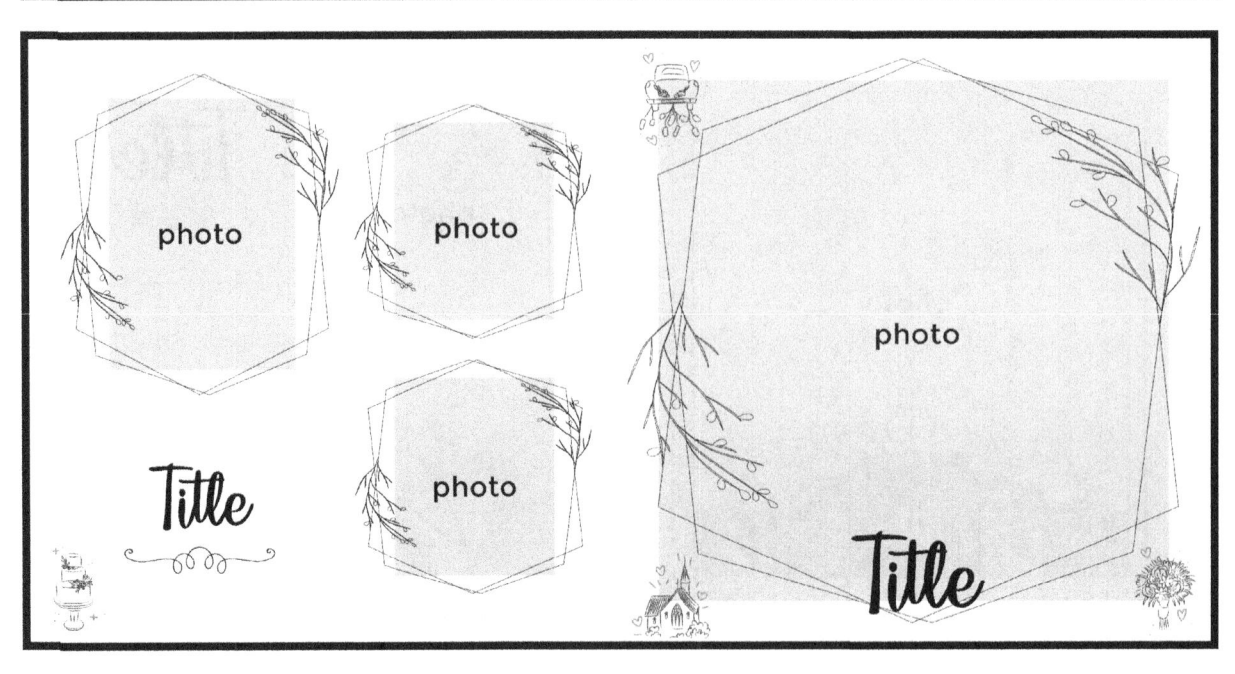

photo

photo

photo

Title

Made in the USA
Middletown, DE
14 February 2023